STORIES FROM JONESTOWN

STORIES FROM JONESTOWN

Leigh Fondakowski

University of Minnesota Press
Minneapolis
London

Published by the University of Minnesota Press
111 Third Avenue South, Suite 290
Minneapolis, MN 55401-2520
http://www.upress.umn.edu

Library of Congress Cataloging-in-Publication Data
Fondakowski, Leigh.
Stories from Jonestown / Leigh Fondakowski.
Includes index.
ISBN 978-0-8166-7808-2 (hbk. : alk. paper)
ISBN 978-0-8166-7809-9 (pbk. : alk. paper)
1. Peoples Temple. 2. Jones, Jim, 1931–1978. 3. Cults—California—History—
20th century. 4. Cults—Guyana—History—20th century. I. Title.
BP605.P46F66 2012
988.103'2—dc23 2012034548

Printed in the United States of America on acid-free paper

The University of Minnesota is an equal-opportunity educator and employer.

UMP BmB 2023

Created from interviews with the survivors
of the 1978 Jonestown tragedy

*This book is dedicated to all of the survivors
and to the memory of Barbara Moore and David Shular.*

Contents

···

Two Days in November   xi
Lost Voices   xvii
List of Interviews Included in Stories from Jonestown   xxi

Part I. Collect All the Tapes, All the Writing, All the History

Nobody Was Paying Attention	3
I Was His Son	8
My Button Was Fear	16
Jonestown Vortex	22
A Godly Life	31
A Man of His Word	41
The Air They Breathed	47
Eternally Grateful	55

Part II. Until We Meet Again

Take the City Today	63
Too Black	74
Homicide Is Suicide	80
We All Participated	86
Sole Survivor	101
Hundreds of Kids	105
This Is Big	118

Waylaid   121
Stigmata   127
The Dream   138

Part III. To Whom Much Is Given

Sixty-seven Cents   143
Nefarious   151
We Were Rising   159
The Basis of a Book   171
Beyond Truth   178
It's No Mystery   180

Part IV. The Promised Land

What a Place for Them   187
Exodus   193
That's Jonestown   204
Perfect Religion   235
Trapped   244
Second Chance   252

Part V. Those Who Got Away

The Known Dead   259
My Children Are There   265
Conspiracist   278
Target Practice   284
Undetermined   290
Something to Gain   296
Legacy   300
I Won't Say Anniversary   305
A Bittersweet Gift   310
After   314

The 918 Deaths of November 18, 1978   323
Acknowledgments 333
Index 335

Two Days in November

....

ON NOVEMBER 17, 1978, the residents of the agricultural project known as Jonestown put on a concert for U.S. Congressman Leo J. Ryan (D–CA). The Jonestown band, the Jonestown Express, performed a set of songs on a makeshift stage above which hung the hand-lettered sign, "Those who do not remember the past are condemned to repeat it."

Jonestown was a self-sustaining agricultural community, a small city carved out of virgin jungle by members of Peoples Temple, an interracial and intergenerational group whose vision was to create a utopia in the jungle, free of economic and social injustice, where all races and ages of people could live and work together.

Congressman Ryan had come to Jonestown to investigate claims made by relatives in his San Mateo County district that their family members were being held in Jonestown against their will. His entourage included print and television media as well as some of the relatives themselves. Ryan had met with these family members, who had organized into a group and entreated him to make the trip. He had also read affidavits from former Peoples Temple members making serious allegations about conditions in Jonestown, including the prevalence of guns, torture, and so-called White Night suicide rituals. Given what he knew of the Temple's good works on behalf of the poor and disenfranchised, these allegations seemed extraordinary. He had to go see for himself.

Jim Jones, the leader of Peoples Temple, had not wanted Congressman Ryan to come into Jonestown. In the months leading up to Ryan's visit, he ranted over the loudspeakers positioned throughout the 1,200-acre complex for hours on end, well into the night, disrupting the sleep of the entire community. These were tirades about the evils perpetrated by the United States, the injustices done to the poor, to the working class, to black people. The rhetoric was increasingly volatile, pointing to violence and isolation as the only means to avert the far-reaching hand of the U.S. government: "They want to destroy us. They want to take our seniors. They want to take our children, they want to take us down."

On this November night, however, the people in Jonestown played music and entertained Ryan in the open-air pavilion with a tin corrugated roof that served as the central gathering place for the community. There was a bass player, a lead guitarist, a drummer, and backup and lead singers who took turns covering rhythm and blues hits from the 1970s.

NBC cameraman Bob Brown filmed the entire event that night. People of all races and ages dressed up for the occasion in colorful shirts and slacks and sat side by side on wooden picnic tables. The older children and teenagers gathered in front with the band. They teased each other, smiling for the TV cameras. The younger kids and babies sat on the laps of seniors. People mingled and danced.

Jim Jones was there. So were his wife, Marceline Jones, and several of his top-level aides. There were men and women in the audience who had been followers of Jones since the early days of his Christian ministry in Indianapolis. There were people in the crowd who had not been in Jonestown but a day, and there were longtime residents who were fatigued, sleep-deprived, and even drugged. There were some who wanted to leave Jonestown, standing right next to others who were happier than they had ever been in their lives. Now representatives of the Concerned Relatives (as the oppositional group of families had come to be known) and members of the press were also sitting among them. The tension in the pavilion was thick, but the music was soulful and eased the heavy feelings that hung in the hot evening air of the South American jungle.

Absent from the pavilion that night were three sons of Jim Jones: Stephan, a biological son; and Jim Jr. and Tim, two of his adopted children. The three were among a group of young men who were in Guyana's capital of Georgetown competing in a basketball tournament against the Guyanese national team.

One of the first songs the band played that night was a cover of George Benson's "The Greatest Love of All." When the song reached the familiar and climactic lines "If I fail, if I succeed, at least I live as I believe. No matter what they take from me, they can't take away my dignity," the audience stopped the band cold with two to three minutes of uninterrupted applause and shouts from the crowd both exuberant and defiant. "It was the people of Jonestown talking," one survivor would later say.

When there was a break in the music, Ryan got up to speak. He took the stage and with microphone in hand thanked the crowd for their hospitality:

"This is a congressional inquiry, and I think that all of you know I am here to find out more about your life here in Jonestown. But I can tell you right now that from the few conversations I've had with a couple of folks here already this evening that whatever the comments are, there are some people here who believe that this is the best thing that's ever happened to them in their whole life."

After Ryan made this statement, the crowd erupted again, whistling, screaming, stomping, and applauding. Rendered speechless by their outburst, he searched for what to say, trying to muster a pithy response. "Too bad you all can't vote in San Mateo County," he awkwardly said. "By proxy!" Jack Beam, one of Temple's oldest members, yelled something from the crowd. Ryan smiled.

The tension, at least for now, had lifted, and the music started up again.

What the media knew but had not yet reported was that Vernon Gosney, a Temple member who had arrived in Jonestown just a few weeks before Ryan's visit, had passed a note that night to NBC reporter Don Harris. It said, "Help us get out of Jonestown. Signed, Monica Bagby and Vernon Gosney." Vern didn't know who the congressman was, so he had passed a note to the person he thought was the congressman. Full of fear, and trying to be discreet, Vern dropped the note. A child standing nearby saw the exchange and began to shout, "He passed him a note! He passed him a note!" The drama had begun.

The next day, on the morning of November 18, the media went on a tour of the community and interviewed many of its members. At about 1:30 in the afternoon, Congressman Ryan's aide Jackie Speier was walking the slated wooden paths lined with plants and flowers in Jonestown when Edith Parks quietly yet urgently approached her. "I am being held prisoner and I want to leave," she said. It was the first open admission by a Temple member that some people were in fact being held against their will.

Speier scrambled to find Ryan, keeping Edith Parks close by her side. Meanwhile, NBC's Don Harris had arranged to do a sit-down interview with Jim Jones, the only on-camera interview Jones granted that day. Harris pressed Jones hard on the issue of whether or not people were free to leave. Jones answered, "Anyone who wants to can get out of here. They come and go all the time." Harris pressed him further: "One thing to be explored, and that's this question of—well, for us, the thing of fear. This is a good example: last night someone came and passed me this note." Harris pulled Vern Gosney's note from his pocket and read it out loud. Jones, in his signature aviator sunglasses and with his speech slow and measured, answered, "People play games, friend, they lie, they lie. What can I do about liars? This is a man who's going to leave his son here."

As the news spread that members were leaving with the congressman, people from all over the community started gravitating toward the pavilion. Tension was building, and a few more people decided that they wanted to leave. Ryan then realized there were too many defectors to fit on the plane. Plans had to be made for a second plane to fly from Georgetown, the capital of Guyana. Families were torn apart and deep loyalties were broken, as two dozen or so people expressed their desire to leave that afternoon with the congressman. The arrangements for a second plane complete, Ryan gathered his party to leave on the Temple truck for the airstrip. Before they could do so, there was an attempted—but thwarted—knife attack on Congressman Ryan by a member of the Peoples Temple. Dazed from the attack, Ryan hurriedly joined the others on the truck. "You are leaving people here who do not want to stay," Vern Gosney shouted as they made their way out of Jonestown.

When they arrived at the tiny airfield in Port Kaituma—for visitors, the only way in and out of Jonestown other than by boat—the congressman's group got out of the truck, unloaded their bags, and prepared to board the two planes: a twin-engine Otter and a Cessna. As the entourage and defectors stood waiting, a tractor-trailer full of young men from Jonestown with guns pulled onto the airstrip. Quickly, the men jumped off and began shooting the members of Ryan's group.

Congressman Leo Ryan was killed instantly, as were three newsmen and defector Patty Parks. Ryan's aide Jackie Speier, Concerned Relative

Anthony Katsaris, and Vern Gosney were severely injured. Several more sustained less severe wounds and were left for dead as the truck returned to Jonestown.

"We got the congressman," the men announced when they arrived back at the community. "We got them all."

Still in Georgetown with the basketball team, Stephan Jones received a call the night before from his father ordering him to come back to Jonestown: "We want you guys back here," he said.

"We're not coming back," Stephan answered.

"You are disobeying a direct order," Jones countered.

"Thank you for sharing, but we're not coming back." The conversation ended. It was a decision Stephan would regret for most of his adult life.

Back in Jonestown, on the afternoon of November 18, a simple announcement was made over the PA system calmly telling everyone, "Report to the pavilion, please report to the pavilion."

Several hours later, hundreds of Temple members would be lying dead on the very spot where, the night before, they were alive with hope and song and music.

Lost Voices

MOST BOOKS ABOUT JONESTOWN end on November 18. While still covering the rise and fall of the movement called Peoples Temple, this one begins on that fateful day because it is the story of survivors: the hundreds left behind to piece together their own history and re-create their lives in the aftermath of Jonestown.

November 18, 1978, was a tragic day in human history. The world watched in horror as the reports came through on the nightly news: 918 people, most of them Americans, lay dead in the South American jungle. Of the 918, one was a U.S. congressman—the only member of Congress to be killed in the line of duty—three were journalists, and 914 were residents of the agricultural project known as Jonestown.

First reports were of a shooting at the Port Kaituma airstrip. Then came the news about the bodies back in Jonestown. Aerial photos showed shocking images of piles of bodies lying facedown, decomposing in the humid jungle air. As the media pieced together the bizarre details of what happened that day, they reported a "mass suicide," death induced by ingesting a drink containing a mixture of cyanide and other sedatives, the taste masked by grape flavoring. Though the term *mass suicide* would ultimately prove to be an extreme simplification, the nation was stunned.

More than eighty members of Peoples Temple who were living in Guyana survived that day in 1978, and thousands of members and former members living in San Francisco and Los Angeles also survived. For them, and for everyone else who still remembers that day, simply hearing the word *Jonestown* can evoke vivid images of the tragedy that unfolded there.

In 2002, I received a call from David Dower, the artistic director at Z Space Studio, a theater development center in San Francisco. I had just completed three years of work with Tectonic Theater Project on *The Laramie Project,* a play and HBO film based on interviews with the people of Laramie, Wyoming, in the aftermath of the brutal beating and death of gay University of Wyoming student Matthew Shepard. I was one of a team of theater artists who traveled to Laramie within weeks of Matthew's murder to talk to the people of the town.

David had long believed that a play about Peoples Temple could "open a lens on the way we viewed Jonestown." When he saw our production of *The Laramie Project* at Berkeley Repertory Theatre, he had a hunch that we could use the same techniques to tell the story of Jonestown and Peoples Temple.

I participated in a conference call David organized with a handful of survivors and former Temple members in the Bay Area. They were disillusioned by a proliferation of documentaries, books, and films about Peoples Temple that focused primarily on its leader, Jim Jones, and the deaths in Jonestown. The survivors were portrayed as mindless victims—cultists, if you will—with Jones as mastermind and perpetrator. They wondered in that phone call if the conversation about Peoples Temple could ever get beyond "they drank the Kool-Aid," the catch phrase now associated with the deaths and a shorthand reference to blind adherence to a leader or policy.

Peoples Temple was a political movement and part of the larger history of the civil and social rights movements of the 1960s, particularly in the San Francisco Bay Area. The Temple had a long, rich history, which began in Indiana in 1955, moved west to California a decade later, and emigrated en masse in 1977 to fulfill their dreams of the Promised Land in Guyana, their utopian endeavor known as Jonestown. Progressive figures from across the country and around the world supported and stood in solidarity with the idealistic group and Jim Jones. Yet most of what people remember about Jonestown or Peoples Temple is limited to one day—November 18, 1978—and one set of graphic images of dead bodies lying facedown in the jungle. Why was this so? Why was the rest of this history not told?

Furthermore, why can't history hold on to what has been discovered since that day, for example, that many people in Jonestown did not actually die at their own hand. Both murder and suicide took place that day in 1978—the cyanide mixture was injected as well as ingested—and the decision to die was not made by Jim Jones alone.

I gathered a group of collaborators—theater artists like myself—to work with me on this project. Greg Pierotti was my main collaborator, along with Stephen Wangh and Margo Hall. Together, we began the three-and-a-half-year process of collecting more than a hundred interviews with these survivors, many of them recounting their stories for the first time. We also interviewed members of the press, politicians, and community leaders in the Bay Area as well as families who lost their children, sisters and brothers, cousins, and parents in Jonestown, and we spent countless hours in the archive at the California Historical Society in San Francisco, where what remains of Peoples Temple—boxes of internal documents, letters, clippings, and photographs—are now stored.

From more than three hundred hours of tape-recorded interview material and excerpts from hundreds of pages of archival material, we created the play *The People's Temple,* which premiered at Berkeley Repertory Theatre in Berkeley, California, in 2005—in the community where many of the survivors and their families still reside.

There is still no resolution to this story, no closure for many of the survivors. And the children of Jonestown survivors now have their own stories to tell. We came to care very much about the people at the center of this story, both the living and the dead, and the many and irreparable ways their lives were altered by these events. Peoples Temple failed. But the story does not end there. The lives of the people who built the movement, and how they have survived, still bear examining.

The members of Peoples Temple represented many races, classes, and ages of society. They were professional people and blue-collar workers, both religious and nonreligious. They were politically progressive and committed to social change—possibly even social revolution—to right the injustices of racism and the inequalities of capitalism. They were committed to one another. How they built their dream of an egalitarian society is both an inspiration and a cautionary tale.

After the play opened in Berkeley, what remained of our research, the hundreds of hours of tapes and interviews (only a small portion of which were used in the play), was stored away in cartons. I hoped that eventually I would publish them, as I wanted more of the material to live in the world. This book is an extension of the life of the play, another way to reach an audience beyond the final blackout in the theater.

This book is created from extensive interviews with the survivors, edited and distilled, as well as the observations of the writer. The volume also includes archival documents—including letters, biographies, transcripts of audiotapes, and newspaper clippings—all housed at the California Historical Society in San Francisco. The primary source, however, is the interviews, the largest collection to date on this subject.

I invite the reader to experience these conversations as we did, to feel as if you too are being taken into the speakers' confidence, and are hearing the many contradictory stories, the acceptance, the defensiveness, the accountability, the regret, the anguish, and the pain that will never go away. I invite you to draw your own conclusions and, I hope, to identify with the survivors along the way.

Traveling across the landscape of America, we found these lost voices. Shrouded in secrecy for decades, the survivors and their families are part of the fabric of American society: they are ordinary citizens, our neighbors, coworkers, and friends, though we might never know about their association with Jonestown. They are disparate voices now, separated, when once they were united and spoke with clarity and singleness of purpose.

Perhaps with time and distance, these survivors will once again reclaim the thing many valued most: *community*. For only they can truly know what it means to survive a tragedy of this magnitude. These are the stories of the survivors. It is a privilege to tell them.

List of Interviews

INCLUDED IN *STORIES FROM JONESTOWN*

Survivors of Jonestown and Former Members of Peoples Temple

Juanita Bogue	Claire Janaro	David Shular
Michael Briggs	Grace Stoen Jones	Janet Shular
Tim Carter	Jim Jones Jr.	Liz Forman Schwartz
Jean Clancey	Stephan Jones	Neva Sly
Tim Clancey	Laura Johnston Kohl	Nell Smart
Danny Curtin	Garry Lambrev	Eugene Smith
Hue Fortson	Debby Layton	Hyacinth Thrash
Vernon Gosney	Shanette Oliver	Mike Touchette

Families

Rod Hicks
Reverend John and Barbara Moore
Rebecca Moore and Fielding "Mac" McGehee
Patricia Ryan

Investigators, Journalists, and Scholars

Melody Ermachild Chavis, member, Larry Layton defense team
John R. Hall, scholar, University of California–Davis
Jack Palladino, member, Larry Layton defense team
Tony Tamburello, court-appointed lead attorney, Larry Layton
    defense team

Margaret Singer, author and cult expert

Julie Smith, author and former reporter for the *San Francisco Chronicle*

Phil Tracy, former reporter for *New West* magazine

Politicians and Community Leaders

Mervyn Dymally, lieutenant governor under Jerry Brown in 1976

Donneter Lane, head of the Council of San Francisco Churches

Reggie Pettus, local business owner in the Fillmore district of
San Francisco

Reverend Arnold Townsend, San Francisco community organizer

PART I

COLLECT ALL THE TAPES, ALL THE WRITING, ALL THE HISTORY

Nobody Was Paying Attention

THE PROJECT BEGINS. It is the twenty-third anniversary of the Jonestown tragedy. I fly in from New York. The memorial service at Evergreen Cemetery in Oakland is scheduled to begin at 11 A.M. Men in dark suits unload a tent and white wooden chairs from a small Ryder truck parked on the side of the road. The groundskeeper, a red bandana in his back pocket and a blue one wrapped around his head, appears over the back of the hill, pushing a lawnmower, preparing the grounds for the ceremony. It is a windy day, the air is crisp and the sun strong—the kind of Bay Area weather that runs hot and cold simultaneously. The early morning air at Evergreen is saturated with the smell of cut grass and gasoline as the groundskeeper maintains an even rhythm appearing and disappearing behind the hill.

Toward the back of the cemetery, on the southeast corner of the grounds, a single massive grave holds the unidentified and unclaimed bodies of Jonestown—420 bodies. A simple grave marker distinguishes the spot. Every year on November 18, a small group gathers on this hill to honor the dead.

Margo Hall meets me at the cemetery. Margo is a member of our creative team to research, conduct interviews, and create a stage play about Peoples Temple and Jonestown. As our Bay Area contact and collaborator on the project, Margo lives in Oakland but grew up just outside Detroit, a city from which several Peoples Temple members hailed. She is African American and passionate about documenting the black survivors in this process, a piece of the story not often told.

3

The white outdoor-event tent at Evergreen is set up by 10 A.M. with enough folding chairs to accommodate about thirty people. People start to gather. It's a rare occasion: many survivors will be together in one place, at one time.

Presiding over the service this November morning is the Reverend Jynona Norwood, an African American minister in her forties. Norwood is the niece of Fred Lewis, an elderly man in a royal blue suit who sits in the front row. Fred Lewis lost twenty-seven relatives in Jonestown, the largest loss of any single family. Reverend Norwood has been presiding over this memorial every year since 1978. Her plans to create a larger monument on the site in 2001 have not yet materialized.

The service begins in song. Fred Jackson steps forward. He is about seventy years of age, dressed in black from head to toe: black pants, shirt, shoes, and sport coat, with thick black hair coolly slicked back on the sides. His long gray sideburns and a graying moustache are the only contrast to the picture.

He pulls a cassette tape from his jacket pocket and drops it into a large karaoke-style boom box sitting on a folding table up in front. He takes the attached microphone, starts the tape, then sings along with the instrumental music for a song called "We Must Never Forget." Jackson did not lose family or anyone close to him in Jonestown, but the event touched him so deeply that he has not only written a song but has come to this memorial service every year for the past fifteen years to sing it.

The lyrics include a passionate and repetitive refrain: "We must remember, we will remember, we must never forget. . . ." Jackson taps his foot keeping time.

The wind blowing through the tent's canopy makes it difficult to hear the music, but Jackson's soulfulness shines through and sets the tone for the service. He can really sing, and his lyrics shoot straight from the heart. This group is still mourning its dead.

Reverend Norwood next introduces the guest speaker: Margaret Singer, an acclaimed cult expert. Singer is a controversial figure in the survivor community, as she was heavily involved in the "deprogramming" of Temple members before and after Jonestown. She is nearing eighty but seems strong and in good health. She speaks slowly and emphatically.

This is Margaret Singer:

"I've watched hours of Jim Jones on film. And he knew what he was doing. Jim Jones was just one more huckster. He had been tricking people even as a little kid.

"Even as a young boy, Jones was what we call a character-disordered boy, meaning: a psychopath, a guy who has no conscience about tricking people out of their money and property, and no conscience about lying.

"How was it that this guy that people thought was just one more minister had gotten all their money, their cars, their jewelry, their books, everything? What was it that he did? These little old black grandmothers, and a few white grandmothers, that were on Social Security and retirement checks, they turned their checks over to him. He existed off of those little old ladies.

"I've probably talked with maybe three hundred–plus former Peoples Temple members, and they all seemed quite real, and they all described to me the same kind of guy that they could hardly believe in retrospect how they had been so trusting of what turned out to be a real shark."

She looks out over the assembled crowd.

"All cults are basically confidence schemes. A person gets your confidence and then once they get your confidence, the trickery starts beginning. I have dealt with people that have been in five thousand different cults. I go over to the library at the university and read, read, read because I'm very interested in persuasion down through history. It's been done the same way. And nobody was paying attention—in Berkeley, Oakland, San Francisco. Nobody was paying attention."

Singer's talk is singularly focused on the cult angle of the story. The racial issues she moves past with only a mention of "old black grandmothers" who were taken advantage of by Jim Jones. I look at Margo. The crowd shifts in their seats as Singer returns to the front row.

The podium is now open for anyone in attendance to share "words of testimony." Reverend Norwood begins with a special invitation to survivors to come forward first.

There is still lingering tension as Laura Johnston Kohl walks up to the podium. She chooses her words carefully but makes it perfectly clear that she does not agree with Singer's assessment that she had been brainwashed or been a member of a cult. With tears streaming down her face she concludes, "This was the best time of my life. And these people were my family."

Reporter Tim Reiterman, who was part of Congressman Leo Ryan's entourage in Jonestown, steps up to the podium next. "This story never leaves you," he confides. "It stays with you for a lifetime."

Grace Stoen Jones, whose son John Victor Stoen—John-John—is buried here with the other bodies, a boy whose paternity and custody were the foundation of the greatest controversy in the Temple, says, "I was a defector. And so I've always felt like an outsider. But today, we stand together."

Patricia Ryan, daughter of the murdered congressman, is last to speak. Even though Congressman Ryan described his trip to Guyana as a fact-finding mission, the Temple considered him a threat. But now, having lived through her father's death, Patricia is inextricably linked to this community. The tragedy of Jonestown has cast a wide net.

"I am proud of my father for what he did," Patricia shares with the group. "He was a man of his word."

The crowd is racially mixed, but all the people who have spoken have been white. We soon discover that most of the black faces in the crowd are not—as we first think—survivors. They are members of Norwood's church in Los Angeles who have traveled here to support her.

≈ ≈ ≈

There is a man sitting cross-legged on the lawn just outside of the tent. He is within earshot of what is going on inside, yet he keeps himself apart. I inquire about him: he is Stephan Jones, the only biological member of the "rainbow family" of Jim and Marceline Jones. Someone I hope we will be able to interview.

After the sharing, Reverend Norwood takes center stage again. She stands at the podium, microphone in hand. I bow my head, anticipating a final prayer. Instead of closing with a prayer, Reverend Norwood points to me in the crowd and says, "And you there? Would you like to introduce yourself, tell us why you are here?"

My anonymity abruptly shattered, I manage to stammer, "My name is Leigh Fondakowski. I'm an artist . . . a playwright. I'm here because

I want to write a play about what happened, a play about the people of Jonestown." The tent falls silent.

My collaborator Margo has her head down—way down—hoping she is not called out next, but Norwood encourages her to speak. "I'm working with Leigh," Margo says. She then explains her personal connection to the story. "My father is a musician and he knew the Hicks family well," Margo explains to the crowd. "I grew up with Marthea and Shirley Hicks in Detroit." Her personal connection seems to soften the feeling that we are intruders at this event.

Reverend Norwood speaks. "Welcome. You are welcome here," she declares. "We are glad that you are here."

I Was His Son

MARCH 15, 2002
OAKLAND, CALIFORNIA

STEPHAN JONES DRIVES UP in an old white Volvo station wagon with his pit bull pup Kali and a cardboard box full of old photos and photo albums. Dressed in a cotton shirt and running pants, Stephan looks like he just took Kali for a nice long walk in Tilden Park to clear his head before we talk.

We have arranged to conduct a series of interviews for two weeks in March—mostly with people we met at the memorial service back in November, but a few names we have found online—and to visit the archive in San Francisco.

My longtime collaborator Greg Pierotti flies in from New York. Greg and I have been working together since 1998, as part of a team of theater artists who went to Laramie, Wyoming, to conduct interviews with the people of the town in the aftermath of the brutal beating and death of gay University of Wyoming student Matthew Shepard. That yearlong interview process culminated in the creation of *The Laramie Project*, the stage play and subsequent HBO film. Since we had worked as an interview team throughout the *Laramie* process, Greg was an obvious choice to be my main collaborator on this project. We thought our experience with *Laramie* had prepared us well to lead the rest of the team and to investigate Peoples Temple and Jonestown.

Greg and I meet Stephan in an apartment we borrowed for the week in the Lake Merritt area of Oakland.

Stephan removes a manila folder from the cardboard box and holds it by the corners. I can read the label: *The Other Side of Jim Jones*.

"My dad claimed to be God," Stephan says frankly and evenly, "but you probably know that, right? I've kind of drilled down into that, and I've come to the realization that in his universe he was, he was God."

Stephan is a man of quiet intensity. Lean and athletic, he is about 6'4", with striking features, a masculine jawline, and deep-set eyes. In all of our encounters I see a look in his eyes, a curiosity tempered with deep sadness, a sorrow as seemingly vital to his being as his lungs or heart.

This is Stephan Jones:

"I had a very loving mother and a loving father. Dad wasn't around much. And his life was pretty full up with his life, you know, with him. And in many respects so was Mom's life, filled up with him."

He takes a breath.

"My Dad was a raging addict. And I don't just mean chemicals. I mean, he was an addict personality. He was into power, sex, food, drugs, whatever he needed to fill that hole, he was *using*. But most of all he was addicted to adulation. And Mom, well, Mom was trying to manage and fix that. She loved him, and she was hooked on him. To use a modern-day term, she was codependent."

After another pause, he adds more to himself than to us, "Oh boy, I don't want to go too deeply into that."

He opens the folder on the table. It is filled with snapshots of Jim Jones. Out of the thousands of photos of his father, Stephan has chosen about twenty candids: *The Other Side of Jim Jones*. The pictures look and smell like the past: old borders, faded colors, sticky residue on the surface.

He spreads them out on the table in front of us. His gaze alternates between the snapshots and us.

He picks up the first one, a picture of his father hugging an elderly African American woman.

"This isn't even one of the better ones," he admits. "But imagine what that hug meant to black people coming into the Temple. My dad was always ready to hug and plant a kiss on an elderly black woman. He empathized with them, with their pain. I remember a time, sitting in a meeting, and this woman was literally screaming in pain over the miscarriages she had had working in the fields as a sharecropper in Mississippi. She was recounting miscarriage after miscarriage, and Dad kept encouraging her: 'Go on, let it out.' Her blood-curdling screams filled the whole room. Dad was sitting up on stage, tears streaming down his face, and he said, 'How can we live in a society that could do this to you?' People were nodding along and crying."

Stephan picks up another photo. "He loved animals," he laughs. Then another. "This one really captures his warmth, his heart." And a third, Jim Jones relaxed and smiling at a podium: "This really captures his playfulness." Stephan points to something outside of the camera's frame. "He's ribbing somebody here over on the side." As he flips through the stack, he comes across one of his father wearing aviator sunglasses, the iconic image of Jim Jones most people remember. He shakes his head. "Those sunglasses, I tell you," he remarks and quickly moves on. "It's nice to see pictures of him without those sunglasses." He turns over a few more shots and then confides, "My father was a pretty sick man—very sick at the end. Pretty sick from pretty early on. But he also had a real beauty about him, for lack of a better way of putting it. I've never used that word in relationship to him, but I think it probably says it best. So even when he was pulling the wool over on people, he was tapping into something that was real."

He looks down at the photos again as if searching for proof of what he is about to say. "He could light you up. He could light me up. I could be sitting there *hating his guts,* and he could light me up. My father could preach up a storm. And what he was talking about was integration, social change. Sometimes he would even hint at revolution. 'We're all brothers! We shall overcome!'" Stephan's voice rises, echoing his father's. "'We've got to turn the tables, we've got to balance things out, we have got to get it right!' And then along with that, the congregation is mostly black, and we're singing spirituals: the place is booming, stomping, rocking, vibrating when we were singing. And he's the guy up on the stage, he's the white guy up on the stage, and he is the *man.* He would come down off that stage and reach his hand out and his arms and just hug and kiss elderly women and pick children up in his arms—that's one of those times that he definitely tapped into something that was real. He was a politician kissing babies," Stephan concedes. "But I know my Dad, and he loved bridging that gap. He loved reaching out to somebody and saying, 'You know what, you're okay by me, you have a home here.' That meant something to him. I know it did."

He pauses again.

"You don't know me," he says directly, "so you don't know my relationship with my father. I have no desire to paint a good picture of my dad. It's just been fairly recently in my life that I've come to forgive him. And no one hated him more when he was alive. No one. Nor after he died, but I've been outside Peoples Temple now as long as I was inside, and I'm looking for a rounded view, an honest view, a balanced view, a broad enough view of who my father was and how he showed up for people.

"A lot of people were harmed," he continues, "were taken advantage of, were fooled, were abused in many ways—and even murdered—by the definition of the word. But I believe we all had some responsibility in varying degrees. I refuse to believe that everyone was wholesale bamboozled by this one evil man, and I include myself in that."

He picks up each snapshot again, carefully, one by one, studying them as if they were as new to him as they were to us. "I went through thousands of pictures of my father, and I picked out these because they're as close to candid as you'll ever find a photo of him. He always had a camera going, he had camera radar, you know, but these are the images you don't see—anywhere—of a man, a handsome man with a charming smile, a playfulness about him. But towards the end, which is mostly what you see of my dad, his heart was long gone.

"My dad was a worn-out man. Mostly he was worn out by the constant vigil he kept over his own delusion. But here—." Stephan gestures to the photos. "Dad had a great sense of humor, which turned sort of dark and sinister toward the end, but he had a really great eye and he loved to laugh. He genuinely loved people. He had people hooked. People either were hooked on him or hooked by him. And most of what you see, you know, out in the world, is just the craziness, the sunglasses, and the loud darkness about him. Why would anybody follow that guy? Why would anybody sign up for that for a second?"

His eyes return to the photos on the table.

"I've kept these pictures. I was going through some photos for a 20/20 special for one of the anniversaries a few years back, and I happened on these photos. I put them aside, and I put on some music I really love and went through them one by one, and I had just the sweetest cry. Because for all these years, all I could remember of my dad was what I hated, and that's a sick place to be. It was just tearing me up. I absolutely had to forgive him and, you know, ultimately, myself, but he had to come first. Many would argue that I needed to come first, but I hated him so much, that there was no way I could get to me without going through him first. And I really, really got to look at how much I'm like him."

Another pause.

"I want to tell you a story." His eyes finally lighten. "I remember my father taking me outside and pointing up to the sky, and he would pick a star or a planet, and he would say that that was the planet that he and I were from." He stops to laugh at the memory. "I remember going as a kid, 'I don't think so,' but also thinking, 'Wow, cool,' you know? And wanting enough to believe that—to believe it. Okay, there's a really strong voice right here saying, 'There's no goddamn way me and dad are the only people, or the only whatever, from that planet.' But there was an even stronger voice that said, 'Yeah, I like the way that sounds.' And that 'I like the way that sounds' had no problem drowning out the voice that said, 'Uh-uh, no way.'"

His next laugh is at himself.

"I'm special. Not only was I part of something that everybody knows about, I have a special place in that: I was his son. I've never said that before, but it's true. Apparently, I'll take fame any way I can get it." He laughs again.

"You've got to find a way to humanize him. Otherwise people just won't get it. We don't want to identify with somebody who does horrible things. I should know. I've got his evil genes." He smiles.

He looks down at the photos, silent for a moment, before continuing. "I want you guys to know that I don't have any secrets around this anymore. I'm clear that when I go into something like this, I cannot decide what I can tell about myself and what I can't. It has to be a commitment to honesty."

He carefully places the collection of snapshots back in the folder, then puts the folder back into the box. "I'd be happy to leave these with you. Keep them in this order and put on your favorite piece of music, and please go through these before you do your thing."

Before wrapping up our first interview, he takes a last long look at us. "I really do miss those people. And I've often referred to them as the people I didn't know that I loved. And then to lose them, just like that . . ." He snaps his fingers. "They're gone.

"You can't imagine the guilt I feel about the decisions I made—if I'd made others I might have saved lives, might have changed events, if only I'd done this, if only I'd known.

"We never believed Dad would go through with that, you know, and like looking back, that's pretty delusional. But you just have to know the whole story. You just have to know my father."

With that, he walks out.

Greg and I look down at the folder on the table: *The Other Side of Jim Jones*. Our process has begun. "You take them," I say to Greg. Our aim is to create a play about survivors, and yet Stephan's directive is clear. If our intent is to humanize the people, we can't exclude Jim Jones from that equation.

≈ ≈ ≈

Jim Jones founded Peoples Temple in the Pentecostal tradition in 1955 in Indianapolis, where it grew to a membership of more than three hundred. At first independent, the church became affiliated with the Disciples of Christ in 1960, and five years later, when he was was thirty-three years old, Jim was ordained as a Disciples of Christ minister.

Jim met a young nurse-in-training named Marceline Baldwin in the late 1940s. They fell in love and were married in June 1949. Stephan had shown us a photo of his parents as a young couple, sitting side by side in lawn chairs. Marceline is in a print polyester dress, hair pulled up tall in back with short bangs in front; sitting next to her, Jim sports an orange shirt and is smiling broadly.

Jim and Marceline were the first white couple in the state of Indiana to adopt an African American child. Jones was also instrumental in integrating the Methodist Hospital in Indianapolis.

It was July 1965 when Jim and Marceline moved their family along with more than one hundred Peoples Temple members from Indiana to Ukiah in northern California. After holding services in a number of facilities around Mendocino County, Peoples Temple built a brand new church in Redwood Valley. The building had offices and classrooms and a swimming pool that was used both for recreation and baptisms.

They also created a shelter for animals, organic vegetable gardens, and a community kitchen. Jim worked as a local schoolteacher. Jack Beam described the community: "There were a hundred people, ten families in all, and forty-five cats and dogs!"

Stephan Jones remembers the cross-country trip from Indiana to California. What he remembers most are the motels and waiting on the pass on Highway 20, watching the cars go by, knowing that a caravan of families from Indiana would soon come over the rise. "We played a game. Each person took a turn, and if they came on our turn, we won. It was exciting. It had been weeks since I'd seen Dad."

Over its twenty-three-year history Peoples Temple recorded hundreds of hours of audiotapes, including oral histories—or remembrances—of its members. In one of these recordings, Jack Beam recalled the early days of the church in Indiana:

> I was with Jim in the beginning when things first got started. You see, word had got out all around Indianapolis. Jim's "gift" began to operate. Well, the Laurel Street Tabernacle got wind of him and said, "Let's bring him in, let him do his act. We'll see if we dig it." I'm stating it coldly, but you get the point. All Jim did is heal about three people that Sunday, and I mean, the word went out like wildfire, and the next Sunday afternoon, you couldn't even get in the place. It was packed out and people out in the parkin' lot, lookin' in the doors.
>
> Well, about the third time that Jim had come there, some black people had come and they'd been crammed way back on the back row—and some didn't even get in. So Jim told his wife Marceline, he said, "By God, I want them right up on the platform with me." And, by God, Marceline brought them right up there. Well, shit, after the service we had a board meeting, they told Jim, or we did 'cause I was on the board—we told him, "Don't be bringing the niggers on the front. I'll tell you what we'll do. We'll build a church for the niggers, and you can minister to them, and then you can come and minister to the white people." I was still a racist back then. Lotta people had this problem: they wanted the healings, but they were tore up on the race issue.
>
> Now, Laurel Street Tabernacle wasn't no goddamn shabby house on the hill. This was a brand new church, and everything in it was brand new, and Jim was gonna be the pastor! He said to us, "The most segregated

institution in the United States is the church at eleven o'clock on Sunday morning, and I'll have no part of that," and he walked out of that goddamn thing. I said, "There's a guy with balls, man, he's walking out." My wife said, "I like them, they're a nice young couple," and I said, "I do, too," and we went with him. He was preaching scorching sermons—Jim could outpreach anyone at that time and it would electrify people—"Out of one blood, God made all nations to rule on the face of the earth," the whole racial thing from a biblical standpoint. Boom. Boom. Boom. What he wanted to say, but they was religious people, "You want the fuckin' healing? Well, stick your money up your fuckin' ass, if you don't love these black people." He'd have to coin it in all loving biblical words. But they could not question the healings 'cause they were real.

My Button Was Fear

....

THE NEXT PERSON ON OUR INTERVIEW LIST is almost as iconic as Stephan. Ex–Temple member and Jonestown defector Debby Layton is the author of *Seductive Poison,* the most well-known Jonestown memoir of its period. Greg and I meet Debby at a coffee shop on College Avenue in the Rockridge section of Oakland. It's a neighborhood of ethnic restaurants and quaint cafés, a friendly enclave for commuters to the city of San Francisco.

Debby arrives at Peaberry's Coffee ready to talk shop, letting us know she wants to be a paid consultant on the project. Greg explains to her that we are just getting started, but that the way we work, we interview people and all of the material becomes fodder and text for the play. No one person "consults." Every interviewee has an equal voice. "Besides," he explains, "we have no idea what story we are going to tell, whose voices will be included and whose will not."

"Okay," she says skeptically.

As we talk, Debby tells us that she wrote her memoir so that her daughter could read in her mother's own words what happened—the mistakes that she made, the context and circumstances she found herself in, her relationship with Jim Jones—rather than picking up the story from other sources. In the book she notes that she felt compelled to tell her daughter because her own mother had lied to her for years both about her grandmother's suicide and about her Jewish heritage, and she felt it was time to stop the lies. By writing and publishing *Seductive Poison,* she staked her claim as an authority on Peoples Temple—and over the years the media listened.

Debby also happens to be the sister of Larry Layton, the only Temple member convicted of charges stemming from the murder of the congressman. On the last day in Jonestown, Larry posed as a defector, recruited by Jones to initiate an attack on the congressman.

Larry had a gun. He didn't kill anyone, although he wounded two defectors (Vern Gosney and Monica Bagby) before a third defector (Dale Parks) wrestled the gun away. He was arrested, tried, and acquitted by the Guyanese court for attempted murder. The U.S. government still needed to bring an indictment in such a high-profile case, and Larry was the only one they had. So upon Larry's acquittal in Guyana, U.S. marshals took him into custody and escorted him back to the United States. Leo J. Ryan was the first congressman in U.S. history to be killed in the line of duty.

It took two trials, but in 1986, Larry Layton was convicted of conspiracy to kill a congressman. His first trial ended in a hung jury, but in his second, the government finally got a conviction. He spent more than two decades in prison. A petition for presidential pardon was literally on Bill Clinton's desk when he left office in January 2001, but it was not granted. At a parole hearing in September 2001, just one week after 9/11, Vern Gosney, one of the defectors Larry wounded in the incident, flew to California at his own expense to testify on Larry's behalf.

Larry was finally released on parole in April 2002, about a month after our meeting with Debby at the coffee shop.

Lisa Layton, who was Debby and Larry's mother, died in Jonestown, but not on the last day. One of seven Jonestown residents to die of natural causes, she succumbed to cancer less than a month before the mass deaths and five months after Debby herself escaped from the Guyana jungle with only her passport and a few possessions.

Debby decides she is not willing to be interviewed for the project, but she keeps her consulting offer on the table should we change our minds. She asks about our upcoming interviews. We explain that we are going to meet Grace Stoen Jones the next day. She looks at us from across the table and then places her hand firmly on Greg's arm, cautioning, "Whatever you do, do *not* ask Grace about John-John."

The following morning, we drive about twenty minutes northeast of Oakland to the town of Concord. We park our rental car in front of the white ranch house of Grace and Walter "Smitty" Jones and gather up our backpacks and tape recorders. "What should we do about John-John?" I ask Greg as we head toward the front door. We agree to play it by ear.

Grace greets us warmly at the door and we go inside. She shows us to her dining room table, which opens out from her kitchen, and asks if this is a good spot for the interview. She offers us water or apple juice. The family dog sleeps comfortably nearby.

We are not the first. Grace has done countless interviews about Jonestown.

The people who first went public with their accounts of Peoples Temple after the mass deaths were often ex–Temple members, particularly those who were part of the group known as Concerned Relatives, and their point of view dominated the media in the early days and for many years after. Among them, Grace had been outspoken. She was a central figure in the story: she was the mother of John Victor Stoen, John-John, the boy whom Jim Jones claimed to have fathered, and who became a symbol, a focal point in the fight between relatives back at home and Temple members abroad.

This is Grace Stoen Jones:

"In a way I feel guilty, because I didn't want to join the church. And I didn't go into the church to be altruistic. I followed Tim Stoen because I was in love with him. I was nineteen years old. It was in October of 1969. I had met Tim at a Peace Day march. I had never been to a Peace Day march in my life," she laughs, "but a friend had invited me and so I went. Tim approached me and asked what was going on. He was a lawyer, an assistant district attorney, and he told us he was going to run for Senate. Then he asked me if I wanted to have a Coke. We started to date. One time he said, 'I want you to meet this man, Jim Jones.' So I went. I wasn't even thinking. I went and it was okay, but it wasn't for me. My thing was: 'This is great. This is beautiful. Not for me,'" she qualifies. "But it's great . . .'"

Grace has a gentle voice, and her manner is warm yet reserved.

"I loved the children. I loved the integration. I loved being in the country. I thought it was all beautiful—but I just didn't feel it was for me."

≈ ≈ ≈

Tim Stoen had met Jim Jones in Ukiah in 1965. Tim was starting a legal aid service, and he needed to clean and renovate a building. Someone said to him, "Well, if it's for poor or minority people, Jim Jones and his church will help you." So Tim called Peoples Temple and they said yes, and when he showed up to the site, there were thirty Peoples Temple members already there with their own mops and brooms and buckets. Tim discovered Jim Jones cleaning the toilets and was impressed with his humility. "How can I ever repay you?" Tim asked. Jim replied, "Well, if any members of our church need legal advice, can they call you?" Tim said they could.

Tim eventually asked Grace to marry him. Grace remembers, "Jim Jones said to Tim, 'I could really use a lawyer in my church.' Tim said, 'I'll give you one year of my life.' He turned to me and asked, 'Is that all right with you?' I said, 'Hey, I can do anything for one year.'" Grace laughs, then admits, "It took me six years before I had the courage to leave."

She pauses.

"I feel like I am in a catch-22 because if you talked to Stephan," Grace continues, "we all saw it so differently, you know? Stephan has gotten real into his dad. I don't want to hurt his feelings. He can say whatever he wants. But what I have to say, I saw it from a different perspective. What I went through and what I felt. I have to say, I know I was brainwashed when I left."

She pauses again. This time she softens.

She wants to clarify that there were aspects of the Temple that were meaningful to her. Above all, the music seems to capture what she appreciated the most.

"There's an album, you know," she explains. "Peoples Temple produced an album: recordings of the choir. It might even be at the California Historical Society, but I have a copy," she says with a smile. "We had a children's choir in the church. The children would get up and sing first, and then the regular choir. I'll tell you some of the songs. 'He Ain't Heavy, He's My Brother,' 'Blowin' in the Wind.' 'How many roads must a man walk down—,'" she briefly sings. "When I hear them on the radio to this day, it just stops you in your tracks. They were so beautiful." Suddenly, her reserve gives way to tears.

"And then, people would get up and testify about Jim Jones and how he saved them. This would go on for two, three hours. After everybody's all pumped up, Jim would come in. He started wearing a robe. At first he wore a suit and tie when he preached, but then he started wearing a royal blue robe, and sometimes it was black. People would be just freaking out," she gestures her arms for emphasis, "going crazy dancing and everything. It's like a car that's been on a trip—warmed up—it's not gonna react the same way as if you had just turned on the engine. Jim would start talking. He'd read the newspaper and rant and rave about things that were in the paper. He would talk about the Bible and rant and rave about that. He hated the Bible. He thought the Bible was racist. He'd always talk about using it—the sheets—as toilet paper. He would throw it on the ground and stomp on the Bible. I once heard someone say, 'Wow, this man doesn't fear the Word of God.' It was wild."

Grace explains the hierarchy in the church for us. "There was a little group that consisted of eight to ten people at any given time. Those were his most trusted, the most dedicated people. Next, there was the Planning Commission, our governing body. It was prestigious to be on the Planning Commission.

"I was probably the person confronted the most in Planning Commission meetings. I was brought up in front of the group a lot because Jim could never really break my will. You know other women just—I mean they worshipped the ground that Jim walked on. But I never did."

"Why did you stay?" Greg asks.

"I stayed because my son John Victor—John-John—was in the church. Then they took John from me. They took all the kids and rearranged them everywhere. We were in a meeting, and my son was having trouble being potty-trained, and my husband, Tim, brought this up in the meeting. He said, 'I think John should be moved out of our house.' What say did I have? So when we went home that night, I said to him, 'I hope there's reincarnation. I hope you come back as a woman and have a child. And I hope that child gets taken away from you just so you will know what it feels like to have your child taken away from you in front of all these people and have no say.' No, I never was a believer," she adds with finality. "Many people saw it from a different perspective. But I stayed out of fear. My button was fear."

At the end of the interview, we understood Debby's warning not to ask Grace about John-John. We don't press her about her relationship with Jim Jones or her son's paternity. We put those questions aside for now, especially since our first interview with her feels like the very beginning of a continuing conversation.

Jonestown Vortex

MARCH 10, 2002
SAN DIEGO, CALIFORNIA

THE TIMING IS GOOD for our next interview. We are to meet Rebecca Moore and her husband, Fielding "Mac" McGehee, in San Diego. Mac and Becky have been studying Jonestown longer than anybody. We hope that they can shed some light, offer some direction, and connect us with other possible interviewees.

Rebecca is a tenured professor of religious studies at San Diego State University, and Mac is an editor and writer. He prepares dinner for us, a dish he calls "Pasta Pierotti" in our honor. Rebecca tells us to call her Becky, and we all laugh awkwardly when she jokes about the sparkling cider she is serving: "It's not poisoned, I promise."

Becky lost her two sisters, Carolyn and Annie, in Jonestown. Both held leadership positions in the Temple, and Carolyn had a son with Jim Jones. Becky has written five books on Jonestown to date, scholarly works that open Peoples Temple and Jonestown to consideration beyond the media hype about cults and Kool-Aid. One of these books is a collection of family correspondence. Another is called *A Sympathetic History of Jonestown*, the writing of which prompted Becky and her husband to seek access to thousands of pages of classified government material. Because a U.S. congressman died in Jonestown, what remained of Peoples Temple—hundreds of letters and documents—was collected and catalogued by the FBI and initially withheld from public scrutiny.

Becky and Mac have spent ten years filing scores of Freedom of Information Act requests and a lawsuit to gain access to all of the FBI material. In a small room next to their kitchen sit five file cabinets full of the thousands of documents they received as a result of those requests.

Then there are the tapes, seven hundred audiotapes, including meetings, services, sermons, and conversations recorded by Jim Jones and Peoples Temple over the course of its history. The federal government used excerpts of these recordings in building their case against Larry Layton. Though the government eventually convicted him, the transcriptions it made of perhaps a dozen tapes represented a small piece of the material Jim Jones and Peoples Temple left behind. The FBI summarized all of the tapes, but poorly, since most of them had nothing to do with the Layton case. Mac has been transcribing these tapes for years—his count in 2002 when we meet him is seventy-five tapes out of the seven hundred. He makes written transcripts of these tapes available online to researchers and to the public.

Mac and Becky founded, and funded through their own resources, the Jonestown Institute as a means to share this material and information, to reshape the legacy of Peoples Temple, and to keep the survivors of Jonestown connected. They created and maintain a Web site, *Alternative Considerations of Jonestown*. Each year, the institute publishes *the jonestown report,* which includes information on projects related to Peoples Temple and Jonestown, as well as news and writings from survivors themselves.

Mac is in the process of creating a database project to name all of the people who died in Jonestown. The State Department's list of the Jonestown dead in 1978 had only six hundred names on it, which meant it was missing more than three hundred names. Mac describes his project as beginning with the question, "Who were all the other people?" And his answer, "Well, most of them were kids."

In the aftermath of Jonestown, he explains, the State Department was not going to put a name to a body unless it had a definite identification. If a person remained unnamed, it was because he/she either did not have a passport or because their body was decomposed beyond recognition. Through exhaustive research, Mac has identified two hundred of the three hundred unnamed dead. He tells us the night of our interview, "Even just last week, I found five people—children—and all are under six years old. I feel like, 'I've given names to five kids who didn't have names before.'" He considers naming everyone who died to be his most important work.

After dinner, the four of us retire to the living room for our interview. I look around. I see a photo of Becky's father, the Reverend John Moore, from his years as the minister at Glide Memorial Church, a United Methodist church in San Francisco that has been a home for countercultural ideas and progressive politics since the 1960s. Another photo depicts all three of John and Barbara Moore's girls, Becky and her two sisters, dressed in their Sunday best, their social activism well rooted in the Christian church.

We set up our handheld tape recorder on the living room table. Greg pulls out his notebook.

"We have to warn you about the Jonestown vortex," Becky begins.

"*Vortex*?" Greg asks.

"Whoever gets into contact with us is sucked into this," she continues. "It's the Jonestown Vortex. You guys will be sucked in, too."

Mac looks us straight in the eye and echoes, "Our lives were changed a lot, but this story also changed everything else that happened in our lives. The fact is, we wouldn't be here if it hadn't been for Jonestown," he reflects. "But where else would we be? And what else would we be doing?"

This is Becky Moore:

"We thought that we were done with Jonestown in 1988. We gave all of our materials to the California Historical Society. But it's kind of like trying to escape your destiny, like Oedipus, right? You can't. Come 1998, ten years later, it was clear that this is who I am, and I don't see an end to it. It's not really what I chose for my life, or Mac chose for his life—definitely not—but it's a responsibility.

"I think about the Oklahoma City bombing," Becky reflects, "and the World Trade Center, the attack on the Twin Towers. Those are events where there was a great loss of life, and the public response was sympathy to the victims. But with Jonestown, the public response was distancing or outrage, even blame. It was anything but sympathetic. I'm still angry about that. Everything from media accounts to the government first deciding that they would bury the bodies in Guyana and then 'Oh, okay, the Guyana government doesn't want them there, it's an American problem,' so moving them to Dover, Delaware, three thousand miles across the country, away from the majority of relatives who might have demanded some answers. The only reason the bodies were buried was because the San Francisco Council of Churches got the money together to pay for the cost of the transport, the cost of the burial at the local cemetery, and found a cemetery." She finally takes a breath.

"So I just think, how different the reaction is. People are allowed to grieve or admit some connection to those disasters, whereas in Jonestown it was very shameful."

I bring up the memorial service and the polar points of view expressed about cults.

"I have difficulty at the memorial services because it's so anticult, and it's so focused on Jim Jones rather than on the people who died, that really the meaning for me is lost," Becky says.

"Was this a cult?" I ask.

"Pretty early on, at least within a few years, I really rejected the brainwashing explanation," she tells us. "There's pretty clear evidence that my sisters were involved in planning some sort of mass death. I have a letter from my younger sister Annie describing killing people. Somebody had to order the poison, somebody had to mix the poison, somebody had to administer it, and it wasn't Jim Jones. People had agency, and I would say they had free will. I think the brainwashing explanation is much more dehumanizing than to say, 'You know these were good people who did a terrible thing—an evil thing.' Brainwashing lets them off the hook morally. But it also takes away their humanity. Then they are just robots, as if it was just a matter of mind control. To me, it is much more meaningful and humanizing to say: they made choices and they made bad choices."

Becky's older sister Carolyn had a more political outlook on Peoples Temple than her younger sister Annie, who held a more religious view. "This is the only place I've seen true Christianity practiced," Annie wrote in a letter. "But," Becky reflects, "they both very strongly felt that the church was meaningful. That's why it is so baffling to explain what happened. What did happen? Did parents willingly murder their children and then kill themselves? Did people resist? Were they forced to take the poison? There's evidence both ways. There's evidence that people had rehearsed suicide—mentally practiced dying to prove their loyalty to Jim

Jones and the cause. So, if you practice this ritual, what happens when it's the real thing? How voluntary is that?" she asks.

Becky explains that she and Mac have moved from calling what happened in Jonestown "suicide" to calling it "murder/suicide."

"The children certainly didn't have a choice in the matter, and senior citizens were injected as they slept. So they didn't have a choice," Becky acknowledges. "And yet you talk to some survivors, and they say, 'Well, I wish I had been in Jonestown rather than in Georgetown or in the States. I wish I had been there that day. If I had been there, I would have taken the poison.' So it's really this great mystery, and there will never be closure because there are so many questions that are still unanswered."

Becky clarifies that she uses the term *survivor* to mean anyone who was a member of Peoples Temple on November 18, 1978. Hundreds of active members were not in Jonestown when the murder/suicides occurred. They were conducting business in the capital of Guyana or were still back in the States in San Francisco and Los Angeles.

According to Becky, the initial impetus for making all the Freedom of Information requests was to prove that her sisters did not commit suicide. She calls it "a quest for truth and justice and the American way." But the more information she and her family received—that the people of Jonestown had practiced and rehearsed suicide on several occasions and discussed killing themselves numerous other times—the more letters she saw from her sisters talking about planning, the more she realized that her sisters were not victims after all. "There's a distinction between the leadership group and the rank and file," Becky points out, "and the leadership were the fanatics."

She explains that in the first days after November 18, the news had only reported four hundred dead bodies in Jonestown, although her family knew there were close to a thousand people living there at the time. She remembers her mother saying, "I think of Annie leading a group of children out into the jungle escaping." She had to tell her mother, "Mom, Carolyn and Annie were the fanatics. I don't think they're alive."

She gestures to the photo of her father, the Reverend John Moore. "You should talk to my parents," she suggests. "They will talk to you. They are living in Sacramento now. My dad is eighty-two years old and my mother seventy-eight. They are in good health."

"If I were ever to write a memoir about Becky's dad," Mac adds, "I would call it *Seconds from Tears*. That's how close it is for anybody who went through it."

Mac closes the interview by saying, "We can give you a list. Our contacts. Everything we know about where people are, who we think might be persuaded to talk. We'll help you in any way that we can. Most likely, no one will want to talk to you," he admits. "But it's important that they *do* talk to you."

When the tape recorder is turned off, I ask Becky if Peoples Temple was a political movement, a black movement, or a church. She answers, "All of the above." She then reflects that this story will always consist of both fact and hypothesis, because there are parts of this story that died along with the people who died in Jonestown. There are pieces here that history will never tell.

We assure Mac and Becky—and ourselves—that we will keep searching, keep making connections. We will keep interviewing until we can feel the breadth and scope of the story and discern how best to tell it. With that, we hug Mac and Becky good-bye. They are allies now and, quite unexpectedly, fast friends as well.

≈ ≈ ≈

Like Mac and Becky, Jonestown survivor Laura Johnston Kohl lives in the San Diego area. I had heard Laura speak at the Evergreen Cemetery memorial, a counterpoint to Margaret Singer's anticult speech. Laura is part of the Jonestown speaker's bureau, a group facilitated by the Jonestown Institute to educate the public about Jonestown, and is more open than most about her involvement in Peoples Temple. She loved the people in the Temple, both those who died and those still living. They are family to her.

Laura is one of the survivors to acknowledge that if she had been in Jonestown on the last day she would have died with the group. I watched an interview with Laura on Anderson Cooper's CNN news show in November 2003, on the twenty-fifth anniversary, during which he continually pressed her as to whether she would have "taken the Kool-Aid." Try as she might to change the subject, Laura could not steer him off this question, eventually relenting with a "Yes—."

Her "Yes" was actually a "Yes—but" as she attempted to contextualize her position, but Anderson Cooper cut her off before she could explain.

"Taking the Kool-Aid" was not as simple as it seemed. There were deep loyalties in this community. Many people had been members of the group for decades. There were many decisions and events—political, social, emotional, and psychological—that led to what happened that final day in Jonestown. Would Laura have watched her entire extended family die in Jonestown and then chosen to continue to live? Her answer is "No." Anderson Cooper's question was impossible to answer in a two-minute segment.

Laura survived because she was working in the Temple offices in the capital city of Georgetown when the murder/suicides took place. There were about fifty Temple members at any one time who worked in the capital, acquiring food and supplies and bringing them through customs, welcoming new members from America, and getting them registered for visas and signed up for health insurance. They also maintained relations with the American embassy and Guyanese government.

Mac had described his father-in-law as always being "seconds from tears." So is Laura. Even when sharing fond memories of her time in Peoples Temple, she holds a crumpled wad of toilet paper—a stand-in for tissues—to wipe the tears from her face and delivers a wad to Greg who has become emotional, too. "This is high class," she jokes as she unwinds the paper from the roll. "I've been emotional in anticipation of this," she adds, more seriously. "I'm an emotional person. I'm not a really good poker player. That's just part of my personality."

This is Laura Johnston Kohl:

"The reason that I joined the Temple was because of all the feelings with it. *All* our feelings were met. Sometimes we were sad, and sometimes we were happy, and sometimes we were politicized—but we were never bored—*ever*. So that's why I went, and that's why I stayed. I mean, that's why I stayed." She wipes a steady stream of tears from her eyes. "But in a way, I'm the odd man out because I have different feelings. Grace lost her son. So my perspective is really different, and unfortunately, a lot of the people who felt like I did—they perished. The people who are the most vocal are the ones who survived, and so it would seem 95 percent of the people were afraid or angry. It may be that 95 percent of the survivors felt that way, but the people who were in Jonestown, who had not been coerced, who felt with all their heart that that's where they wanted to be and that's what they wanted to do—." She breaks down, unable to speak. When she recovers, she continues her thought.

"And so, even though I'm a minority in some groups, I'm not necessarily a minority of all the people who were involved in the Temple over the years. Some people were fearful. I didn't feel that. I went to Guyana in 1974. I loved Guyana. Seeing the sunset, sunrise in the tropical rainforest, it has to be heaven. I don't even believe in heaven, but I was there when I was in Jonestown."

She pauses to add a note of personal caution. "You're going to talk to a lot of people, and most of them are on the side that they had such tremendous losses or they weren't involved and knew secondhand, that if you talk to a whole lot of them you're gonna think, 'Well, maybe that's the way it was: maybe it was a cult.' But it's just because there aren't people to interview who would give you the other point of view—because they perished."

≈ ≈ ≈

After our interview with Laura, we study Mac's survivor list. We had met a few at the memorial service and Mac's list accounted for a few dozen more.

When we start calling people on the list, very few want to talk. Most survivors had rebuilt their lives under a veil of secrecy and shame. They had been burned so many times by the media. There was no reason to believe we would be any different.

There are also fewer black voices on the survivor list, illustrating—as Mac and Becky suggested—one of the gaps in the history of this story. The movement had a predominantly black membership, and the majority of people who died in Jonestown were black. Compounding the problem, our collaborator Margo Hall reports from the contacts she has made that those who did survive are also more reticent to talk. There is a stigma within the black community related to Jonestown, that black people were duped by a white man. She is uncovering their fears over representation: how will their stories be told?

Greg takes Mac's list and continues the cold-calling. He calls one survivor and asks to speak to her by the name she had while in the Temple. "Who is this?" the woman asks sternly, her voice almost frozen with fear.

Before Greg can tell her who he is or why he is calling, she says, "I haven't been called that name in twenty years. Please don't call here again, I beg you." And she hangs up.

The shock people felt when we cold-called them to ask for an interview was never going to work. We had hoped that Mac and Becky would shed some light and offer some direction, and indeed they did. But they also forced us to look more squarely at the commitment that we have made as a group.

A Godly Life

MARCH 12, 2002
NORTHERN CALIFORNIA

WE TRAVEL BACK TO NORTHERN CALIFORNIA to meet Garry Lambrev, an ex–Temple member who works as a public library branch manager in East Oakland. He is on Mac's list of contacts, but unlike so many others, Garry is willing—even eager—to talk. Garry is pensive with a permanently furrowed brow and a dimpled smile. A deliberate thinker, he takes the interview process seriously, willing to analyze every thread, examine every angle.

"Speaking of drama . . ." He laughs. As a poet and writer, he had spent many years writing plays and directing theater inside the Temple. He promises to track down some of the old scripts for us. Given what we see in his Oakland home—an archive of a life full of books and papers— it seems likely that he has them somewhere. His large two-story house feels as much like a storehouse for history as a place to sleep and eat.

When he was younger, Garry wanted to be a historian, to study twentieth-century Eastern European intellectual history, specifically Russian history. With a master's degree from Stanford University and a Woodrow Wilson fellowship to pursue a doctorate, he dropped out and moved to Ukiah, California, where one March evening in 1966 he met Jim Jones.

Openly gay, partnered for twenty-four years to Yani Herdes, Garry is familiar with our work on *The Laramie Project*. He knows about Matthew Shepard, has seen the play on the Berkeley Repertory stage, and wants to help. His desire is for the true story of the people in Peoples Temple to be told.

Greg and I sit at Garry's dining room table for the interview, a long, dark oak antique covered with a lace tablecloth. Garry grips the sides of his dining room chair as he speaks.

He first describes how he spent most of his time in college organizing as part of the student antiwar movement. He was arrested at the Oakland Naval Supply Depot, "me in my herringbone suit and tie," after going over the fences during one of the first protests against the Vietnam War. Though a good and curious student, he felt imprisoned by academia at a time when the world outside was exploding with antiwar protests as well as the sexual and gay liberation movements of the 1960s.

"It was 1966. I dropped out of Stanford with a thud," he emphasizes, then qualifies, "a soft thud."

By his own account, Garry holds a few unique positions in the history of Peoples Temple. He was the first person on the West Coast to join, the only academic, and—at the time—the only gay man in the group. He had met Jim Jones in Ukiah, about six months after the church moved there from Indiana.

This is Garry Lambrev:

"Ukiah, California, in February 1966 was sort of a typical Main Street redneck, not-much-of-anything Middle American California town. I took an entry-level job as a welfare worker for the Mendocino County Welfare Department. I made this sort of deal with the devil in my own mind: that if there is any sign of radical progressive—much less revolutionary—political activity in this new environment, you will immediately go right to it." He claps his hands for emphasis. "You will not shirk your duty. I didn't expect to be taken up on it. I thought this was a safe bet." He laughs. "There was nothing going on." He laughs again.

"The sign came almost immediately," he announces. "Nine o'clock one Wednesday morning, beautiful sunny day, middle of March. I was asked by my supervisor to go to the county courthouse to verify a couple of birth certificates. So I put them into my briefcase and started to walk the two blocks to the county courthouse. But as I came out of the Welfare Department, I heard and then saw this jalopy just banging its way down the street past me. It was something out of the circus, the quintessential rattletrap. My eyes followed it, and I saw the bumper sticker on the back of the car: 'Bill Drath for Congress.' I knew that Drath was the Quaker from Marin County running for the Democratic nomination in the first congressional district, which then stretched from Marin County to the Oregon border. I thought, 'Wow, somebody around here is interested in this?' Fifteen, twenty minutes later, as I cross the street on Courthouse Square, I notice that one of the cars that's stopped is the same old rattletrap. 'Oh my God,' kitty-corner from where I'm standing is the John Birch Society smoke shop, with the old men sitting on a bench in front, chewing on their cigars. I did something that I rarely do. I thought, 'What the hell,' and I just ran around the car, and there was this *huge* woman—I mean, she had arms that just went from here," he stretches out his arms, "to here, with a huge face and huge boobs. She was simply enormous. I said, 'Excuse me, I see your bumper sticker. Do you have any information about what is going on politically in this town?'"

Garry pauses, takes a breath.

"Her name was Patty Cartmell. She told me that she and her extended family, people who were not blood related, who were white and black, had just recently fled from the Midwest—from Indiana specifically—to the Ukiah Valley area. Their pastor, Jim Jones, the human rights commissioner for the city of Indianapolis, had become a scapegoat for the local right-wingers when he stood up for economic justice and the rights of African Americans.

"I knew something of the politics of Indianapolis," Garry explains, "so I had no reason at the time to be critical. I had just met a wonderful person who shared a life that seemed in some ways to embody my own hopes. She told me about the group. Many of them were still without jobs, and most of them had very meager, poorly paid employment. These were not professionals for the most part. And she invited me to her home that Friday night to meet her husband, her son, and her daughter, and although she didn't say it at the time, also some key friends of the big guy. I really didn't have any conscious idea of what I was walking into."

Garry takes another breath.

"So, that Friday, I arrived at Patty's home on a side street in downtown Ukiah. She opened the door and introduced me to two of her friends whom she had invited over—or as they put it—'had just dropped by.' One of them, Joe Phillips, became a very dear friend to me over many years and was the first significant person after my arrival to leave the Temple. Joe Phillips was Jim Jones's right-hand man. Joe was a miner's son in his early forties, then one of the older people in the group. He was there, I guess, to look me over.

"They asked me about my life, and they told me about their community. Joe mentioned that he'd come to a large meeting in Ohio that Jim had spoken to in his midtwenties, that he'd come there with his wife and his kids. One of his kids was just a few years old and had a major congenital heart problem that was threatening his life. He told me that Jim had basically created a miracle and saved his child's life, causing this congenital heart problem to disappear. His son, now fourteen or fifteen, was perfectly free of it and perfectly healthy, a vibrant young man. And I could see for myself he was very proud of him.

"At a certain point in the evening, I was told that there was a party out toward Redwood Valley where their pastor, Jim Jones, lived."

Garry pauses.

"I was extremely shy and felt incredibly awkward, but I went with them. I remember arriving at this shack, basically a two-room home, and maybe forty or fifty people were gathered around a wood stove in the middle of the room. The room was lit by the stove and some kerosene lamps, so there were as many shadows as there were lights. The adults were sort of clinging to the sides, and the young people were dancing to soul and rock 'n' roll." He smiles. "I mean, the rhythm was pounding. Aretha Franklin, a lot of black soul, the Supremes, Marvin Gaye. And feeling self-conscious and not wanting to dance, I just sort of faded into the wall. Where I faded into the wall, on my left was a man who seemed to be somewhere in his midthirties, approximately my height, considerably sturdier than I am, somewhat swarthier. And we got into a conversation very easily that went from the most mundane to the most esoteric and most profound, and then hopped, skipped, and jumped throughout the universes in the most extraordinary conversation I had ever had with another human being or ever since had with another human being. Finally, I sort of broke through and said, 'Excuse me, I didn't get your name. I'm Garry.' He said, 'Oh, I'm Jim.' And I said, 'Oh, you're Jim Jones?' He said, 'Yeah, I'm really glad to meet you.' And it was a sort of genius that I saw repeated many, many times over the years, in which Jim knew precisely how to approach any new person in terms of their own world, their own reality, even in terms of their own language. There were certainly lots of people who didn't want to be reached, who were put off by him. But I wasn't one of them. Although he didn't put any sort of pressure on me to come further into the group, I knew I had to. The door had been opened to me, and I went right to it."

Garry smiles at the memory of himself.

"Ordinarily on Sundays there were two services," he continues, "both of which took place in the schoolhouse of Christ Church of the Golden Rule, just below the pass close to Willits, beautiful, pristine woodland mountain valley, with deer and cows roaming in the same fields. When I came to my first meeting there I thought I had arrived in paradise."

He pauses.

"We had two meetings a day, and sometimes a meal between them. The first meeting would begin at 11:00 and would last generally to about 3:00 in the afternoon nonstop, and Jim was *the* pulpit: the living, walking, acting pulpit. And I remember at the time thinking, the time goes much too fast, and at the end I always wished there was still more. We spent our entire Sundays together."

≈ ≈ ≈

Of the seventy tapes that Mac McGehee had transcribed and made available on the Jonestown Institute Web site, many contain the sermons Jim Jones preached. Steve Wangh, the fourth member of our creative team, took on the task of studying these sermons, analyzing them, and making the connections between the stories our interviewees were telling us about Jim Jones and his actual words. This is an excerpt from one of those sermons:

> Jesus was just a teacher of mine. When they came to take him away, he didn't even know why they were coming to take him away. He said, "Well, for what good work do you take me away?" "For no good work," they said. "But because, you being a man, make yourself God," in the tenth chapter of John. And He said, "It is written, all of you are gods." So Jesus is God, I am God. You are God. He said, I'm no different than you. Everybody's a God.

≈ ≈ ≈

We ask Garry if the members of Peoples Temple really accepted Jim Jones as God. This was a challenging concept for an outsider to this story. Did religious people—black or white—really believe this man was God?

Garry pauses.

"When he said that he was God, I didn't disbelieve him for a minute," Garry tells us. "Jim Jones was the first person who proposed something that seemed workable. To create, as a cell unit, a revolution, a democratic revolution, an extended family, an all-American family in which all the races and social classes are represented. You got it!" He claps his hands again for emphasis. "He was right on. He was as American as apple pie. I felt that I had found it. I mean, we've got God with us, who needs a doctor? Who needs a lawyer? You've got God. But he got one thing badly wrong, right at the beginning. I knew it."

Garry folds his hands on the table in front of him. He gazes downward.

"Giving up responsibility is a fatal error for a human being to make, whatever the circumstances," he reflects. "To give over the definition of reality to somebody else, I think for me, abrogated my own dignity. I was aware of a certain loss of dignity, but I could never find words for it, because I could never quite afford to be conscious of it." He pauses again.

"I never actually thought that until right now. But there was a part of me from very early on that felt a loss of dignity. It's a very subtle but very essential something that we each have. I felt robbed of it, but I could not put my finger on it." Garry struggles to explain. "Because here was the source. Here was the mouthpiece, here were the hands, here were the legs, and I was here to learn, to follow orders."

≈ ≈ ≈

When Garry met Patty Cartmell on Main Street in Ukiah in 1966, the Temple had been in California only six months. The group did not reach out to people in San Francisco until after the death of Martin Luther King Jr. two years later. Garry describes that in the spring of 1968 there was a pivotal moment in the expansion of the Temple in Ukiah, when Jim "had prophesied" that Dr. King would be assassinated, only a few weeks before it actually happened. According to Garry, Jim told the group that the "secret government" would no longer tolerate King after he expanded his concerns from race relations to war and peace by voicing strong opposition to the war in Vietnam.

"So when Martin was gunned down," Garry recounts, "it was like a power came over the Temple. Here was a man who could see the future. And what he saw was desperate and grim."

Garry acknowledges that Jones "dealt with it brilliantly." He responded to an open invitation in the *San Francisco Chronicle* from Macedonia Baptist Church on Sutter Street, the largest Baptist church in the city, which had invited people to attend a memorial celebration of Dr. King's life. Jones brought every last one of the Peoples Temple members living in Ukiah down to Macedonia Baptist, helping to pack the church with white faces. "He actually brought the entire Temple—all hundred of us—down as a body," Garry explains.

"Jim took advantage of the situation to invite everybody in San Francisco—including the pastor and his wife—to come up to Ukiah to the county fairgrounds for a big bash," he laughs. "This was the first time that large numbers of black people had ever come to Ukiah. It was the beginning of the move really of lots of people into the church, and up to Redwood Valley and Ukiah."

Many accepted Jones's invitation and came to "The Valley," as Ukiah came to be called. "'The Valley' as in the Promised Land," Garry sighs, "and the Promised Land was then transferred from Redwood Valley, north of Ukiah, to Guyana."

Garry paints two versions of Jim Jones. The one he met in the early years, 1966–1968, as a member of an intimate extended family. And the one the world would come to know after November 1978. "Jim's life was very much on display," Garry explains. "Jim Jones didn't just serve as the husband of Marceline and the father of a group of children—most of whom were adopted. He was the pastor of a seven-day-a-week active community, who also worked a full-time job as teacher of a sixth grade class twenty-five miles across the coastal range in Boonville down in Anderson Valley. I was the welfare worker for the area, and I knew the families, I served the families of many of the kids who were in Jim's classes. They didn't know I was part of Peoples Temple, but I heard their stories about Jim Jones, this incredible man who would stand up for his students, who wouldn't let them get trampled by the system. I can remember a woman crying, telling me about what he had done for her daughter. He taught evening school at Ukiah High, Government and

American History, two courses that were open wide to the community. You didn't have to be enrolled to come, you just came, and they were extraordinary interactive courses. I didn't see where the man had a moment of privacy. I mean, whatever one thought of his ideology, at that point at least, I couldn't question his motives. He was living what to me was a godly life."

Garry leaves us with a final thought.

"But it's very disempowering to have a myth in which all power remains—even in retrospect—in the hand and the head of Jim Jones. Those of us who have survived, we know that the power of Peoples Temple was a power of the people, who we were together in the time we spent together. That power was extraordinary. Never in my life before or since—never—have I been in such immediate contact and interaction with people of all races, particularly African Americans. It's been the only glimpse I've had in this lifetime of a real, functional, multiracial society. In that respect, at least, Jim Jones was quite successful."

≈ ≈ ≈

Garry encourages us to contact his close friend Liz Forman Schwartz who is living in Southern California, near Los Angeles. Liz was part of this wave of people who came up from San Francisco to "The Valley." Greg explains that he has been on the phone with Liz already a number of times, but she is wary and has asked for time to think it over. "Maybe you could call her?" we ask. He did, and Liz agrees to talk.

Liz and Garry have always been close, always protective of each other. When Garry left the Temple in 1976—before the group moved en masse to Jonestown—he left in the night with Liz, who had seen enough behind closed doors to realize it was time to go.

On the drive down to Los Angeles, Greg is on the phone with Liz when she tells us she wants to have a lawyer present for the interview. Frustrated, but resigned, Greg tells her, "We're just going to turn the car around, Liz. We do not want to cause you this much stress." We turn the car around and head back north to San Francisco. Within a short time, Liz calls back and beckons, "Please come." So we turn the car around again once more and head south again.

This is Liz Forman Schwartz:

"Some friends of mine in San Francisco, I forget how they heard about it, but they said, 'Liz, you have to hear this. There is a man who has an interracial community in the countryside—grape country—he's a socialist, he's also some kind of psychic and healer, we're not sure, you know, whatever.' What else did they say? That was enough! That was a lot! And so we decided that we had to check this out.

"So I walk into the Redwood Valley church, and there's a two-hundred-voice interracial choir. And of course I'm a great nature lover, and here it is beautiful, the vineyards and everything, and they're singing, 'What the world needs now is love sweet love'—you remember that song? I'm just like, 'This is it! Believe this!' This is everything that I've ever wanted.

"And then Jim starts to speak. He had to have known. He was so Marxist that day, you cannot believe it. I mean, here I am, this red-diaper-thirty-one-year-old baby, and he starts in, and I cannot believe what he's saying. And I'm seeing white Anglo-Saxon Protestants from the Midwest totally integrated with black people. I was the second Jew, by the way, that ever came there. Sharon Amos was assigned to me because they felt: get over to that woman now because she's Jewish and we need more Jews here! I tell you guys, nothing has ever compared to it before or since.

"He knew how to teach his people how to make you feel welcome. I mean, what didn't they have that I had always wanted? *Community.*"

≈ ≈ ≈

Garry calls us after our interview to say that there are things he left out when we spoke. Or, rather, he clarifies, questions we did not ask him that he feels should have been asked. "I think there are reasons to seriously question, or perhaps challenge, the official government media view of what happened at Jonestown—what really happened," he stresses.

"A crazy man went off with a thousand people from the United States—poor, uneducated people, mostly black—and had them drink poison? I don't know that there's anything explicitly false about that, but at best it's only part of the picture."

"What are you referring to, Garry?" I ask.

"Jim would become unduly paranoid. I didn't know how to evaluate that, and I still don't know how to evaluate that. I was appointed to an ad hoc committee to serve as advisors to him in the fall of 1967. The first thing that Jim had us do was check the floor, the walls, the furniture for hidden microphones, because he was afraid that the schoolhouse had been bugged, and it was not safe. I was very dubious at the time. I thought, 'Who would bug this place?' He gathered us together and shared that we were, as a group, increasingly under suspicion by the government, and the corporate elite that ran the government. He was afraid that we were not going to be able to develop, in terms of our vision, inside the United States. And we needed to begin plans—contingency plans—for going elsewhere. And we began planning for a possible move to the Soviet Union.

"This strand was never completely lost, even after Jim had moved the entire Temple to Guyana. He engaged a number of people to teach everyone at Jonestown Russian as part of an open plan to take the entire Jonestown population to the Soviet Union. He continued to explore that option, perhaps in desperation toward the end."

Garry pauses.

"As you continue talking to people, you might find that there is more to the story here than meets the eye."

"What do you mean 'meets the eye,' Garry?"

"You said you were going to speak to Patricia Ryan. When you do talk to her, ask her about the Hughes-Ryan Amendment. That was legislation sponsored by her father, Congressman Leo Ryan. Ask Patricia about her father's opposition to the secretiveness of the CIA."

After another pause, Garry sighs. In a tone that is both sincere and urgent, he says, "This story is big. There are hundreds of documents related to Peoples Temple and the government investigation into what happened at Jonestown—at least ten boxes—that remain classified. So clearly," Garry concludes, "there is still more that we don't know. I may spend the rest of my life trying to understand what really happened."

A Man of His Word

MARCH 14, 2002
SACRAMENTO, CALIFORNIA

WITH GARRY'S TALK of political intrigue fresh in our minds, we drive north to Sacramento to meet Patricia Ryan, Congressman Ryan's daughter. I had introduced myself to Patricia at the memorial service at Evergreen Cemetery back in November, and she had agreed to talk. She invited us to her Sacramento home. When we arrive, she greets us at the door with a firm handshake. "Please, come in, and call me Pat."

Her father was fifty-three years old when he was shot and killed on the tiny Port Kaituma airstrip six miles from Jonestown. He was a member of the U.S. House of Representatives from the eleventh district in California, and a member of the International Relations subcommittee. He had gone to Jonestown to investigate claims from relatives of Peoples Temple members that their family members were being held in the jungle community against their will. Some of the people in Jonestown were his constituents. He had invited other members of Congress to go with him, and several had agreed, but by early November all of them had backed out. According to Pat, her father did not want to go either. "He was tired, he was sick with a cold, but he made a promise, and he was a man of his word."

Ryan was an English teacher before he was a legislator, a Jesuit-educated scholar with a master's degree in Elizabethan drama.

Pat tells a bit of the family history, memories of her father's life in politics, a life in the public eye. "I'm obviously biased, but I've been around politics my entire life and I'm still doing it, and I've never known anybody like him," she says proudly.

She begins her father's story by showing us a mug shot. She then explains that when the California state legislature was considering a change to the indeterminate sentence laws, her father—then a state senator—thought that he ought to know firsthand what these legislators were talking about when they changed it. After much persuading, he convinced the director of the state corrections office to let him spend a week as a prisoner in a maximum security cell in Folsom Prison.

Moreover, he wanted to be incarcerated without anybody knowing about it, and with no special treatment. That meant he would be strip-searched, have his hair cut, have a mug shot taken, and be put in maximum security for seven days. Eventually he got his way.

Ryan developed relationships with some of the prisoners, including convicted murderers, got to know them, talked to them. Pat recalls going to visit him during family visit time at the prison. "He wanted to be a regular prisoner," she tells us.

When he got out, she says, her father did not talk to anyone in the family for three days. "It was a traumatic experience for him, being in there." She also told us he wrote a play based on his experience.

On another occasion her father went to Newfoundland to protest the hunting of baby seals. An environmentalist in the early days of Greenpeace, he appears in a photo lying down on the snow, face to face with a seal pup. Pat still has a poster-sized version of this picture on the wall of her office. "He literally threw his body in between the hunter and the seal and said, 'You're not going to kill this thing,'" Pat laughs.

The CV of her father's life in politics, as Pat tells it, includes his most public battles, all of which received a lot of media attention: the Folsom Prison lockup, the seal pup hunt, and Jonestown.

≈　≈　≈

Leo Ryan's involvement with Peoples Temple came about through his acquaintance with Sam Houston. They had met years earlier in Washington, D.C., when they shared a hotel room as chaperones for a group of high school students in the marching band that performed during the inauguration of John F. Kennedy. Sam Houston's son Bob—a member of Peoples Temple—had been killed by a train the day after he decided to leave the Temple, and Sam believed it was not an accident. Sam called his friend Leo Ryan, now Congressman Leo Ryan, and said, "My son's mysteriously dead. My grandchildren are in Guyana and their mother is here in the United States. Something really strange is going on inside this Peoples Temple."

Two of the former Temple members we had already interviewed, Debby Layton and Grace Stoen Jones, also went to Washington to talk with Leo Ryan about what was happening in Jonestown. Ryan assured the two women as well as the other members of Concerned Relatives that he would try to get the government to investigate what was going on in South America. If that failed, he told them, he would personally go down there himself and check it out.

He did. Absent any support from his congressional colleagues, he took an entourage of reporters, including a film crew from NBC. Banking on the assumption that he would be safer with the press cameras rolling, he believed no one would harm a U.S. congressman with *NBC Nightly News* watching. The press felt more secure knowing that they had a member of Congress with them. It was a good news story, after all—two sides strongly pitted against each other—members of Concerned Relatives, some of whom went on the trip with Ryan to Guyana, and the people of Jonestown: families versus families. There were allegations of guns, torture, and suicide drills.

By the time Leo Ryan left for Jonestown, stories about Jim Jones and Peoples Temple were all over the local papers in the Bay Area. Pat remembers reading some of them. She recalls saying good-bye to her father before he left for Guyana. "People don't really believe this when I tell them, but I remember him walking out the door, and I knew I wouldn't see him again until he came back from Guyana, and I said to him, 'Dad, don't let anybody shoot you or anything.' He gave me a hug and said, 'Oh, don't worry about it, I'll be fine.'" That was the last time Pat Ryan would see her father.

This is Patricia Ryan:
"I was in the car with the radio on when I heard that my father had been shot. We didn't know at that point if he was dead. I just started shaking. My legs started shaking. It was hard to drive. You don't know how you're going to react to something like that, but I just thought, 'I

can't take anymore. I can't.' I flipped the radio off. I drove over to my mother's house. I waited for her and my sister to come home, and when they walked in, I had to tell them. My brother was alone when I got there, watching it on TV. We were up all night, waiting to find out whether my father was dead or alive. I had the radio on all night.

"We found out at five o'clock in the morning on the radio. I know the government knew before that time that he was dead, and why they didn't tell us, I don't know. We were all in shock, walking around like zombies. The phone was ringing off the hook, and the press was knocking on our door. We knew about my father's death, but we didn't know about his aide Jackie Speier, so we were worried about her. We didn't know at that time about the murder/suicides. We just knew about what happened on the airstrip. We were watching TV like everybody to find out what was going on."

She pauses.

"The funeral was four or five days later. We were scared. We were told that there were hit squads out there, and that we were in danger of somebody coming and finishing off the family. There were lots of rumors going around, so we were afraid for ourselves. Hundreds, thousands of people came to the funeral. But I remember there were police snipers on the houses all around the church, prepared for anything to happen. I remember Mayor George Moscone from San Francisco coming into the church. He had sent us a letter of condolence. I didn't know at the time that he was a big supporter of Jim Jones. I remember them taking my father's casket off the plane with this flag draped. There are pictures of that. Pretty, pretty difficult."

"One of our interviewees mentioned that there could have been more to this story, even suggesting a possible cover-up or conspiracy," I prompt.

"My grandmother was really pushing for an investigation," Pat answers evenly. "There was a hearing. They heard a lot of testimony from State Department officials and people like that. There was supposed to be a follow-up hearing because the Foreign Affairs committee promised to have another hearing, but the morning of the hearing they canceled it. They said it was because of litigation that was pending, and they didn't think it was appropriate to hold an investigation while litigation was pending against the government. Basically, I think Congress white-washed it. I think there was a lot of damaging evidence: the State Department's knowledge, the documents that they had that they didn't give my father before he went to Jonestown, the fact that there were probably CIA operatives down in Guyana who knew a lot more about what was going on there than they let on."

Leo Ryan was the coauthor of the 1974 Hughes-Ryan Amendment, requiring congressional oversight of the Central Intelligence Agency—a law designed to prevent the CIA from conducting covert missions without congressional knowledge. This was the legislation Garry Lambrev mentioned when we spoke.

If the CIA did know what was going on in Jonestown and did not inform Congressman Ryan, they would have been in breach of the very law Ryan himself put in place.

Pat pauses and then admits, "It was so hard dealing with the fact that he was not there anymore. He was a huge influence on our lives." She begins to cry. "And everybody knew about what happened. We heard about it every day for years. So to me, it was trying to have a normal life and deal with the loss, and I didn't want to keep digging it up. I don't think in the end there was a full-blown conspiracy or anything like that against my father, but I do think the Congress at the time made this story go away very expediently, before we had all the answers."

≈ ≈ ≈

I remember Pat speaking at the memorial service back in November, while Stephan Jones sat outside the tent, two survivors linked by the actions of their fathers. "What is it like to go to the services," I ask, "and see Stephan?"

"It was probably the second or third memorial service that I had gone to," she recalls. "And this is probably twelve, thirteen, or fourteen years after, but still emotionally you go to those things, and I'd see people who were former members. I'd seen pictures of Stephan Jones—this tall, thin, intense-looking guy, you know. At one of these memorials I knew who he was, and so I went up the hill and went over to him, and I stuck my hand out and I said, 'Hi, are you Stephan Jones? I'm Pat Ryan.' I sort of took him aback. And he apologized. He apologized to me for what his father did to my father. I said, 'It's not your fault, you didn't do it, your father did it.'"

Pat then confides, "In the big picture, though, at least I can be proud of my father. It's a lot harder for Stephan, because he has to live with the knowledge of what his father did."

The Air They Breathed

MARCH 14, 2002
SACRAMENTO, CALIFORNIA

A SHORT DRIVE from Pat's Sacramento home, we find Reverend John Moore and his wife, Barbara. Their daughter Becky, whom we interviewed a few days earlier with her husband, Mac, has arranged for us to meet her parents, now living in a newly constructed assisted living complex, a gated community designed to feel like a small town or neighborhood.

Greg and I arrive at their cozy apartment, and Barbara greets us enthusiastically. The contents of their life and home seem oversized for this condo-style two-bedroom unit, yet the apartment has a feeling of warmth to it, with family pictures proudly crowding every flat surface. They seem genuinely happy to see us.

John and Barbara have been married fifty-seven years. They have raised three daughters. They are close to Becky, who lives in San Diego. The other two, Carolyn and Annie—and a grandson—died in Jonestown.

Jonestown is not an easy subject for John and Barbara to talk about, even twenty years later. Their oldest daughter, Carolyn Moore Layton, was Jim Jones's mistress and one of his closest confidantes and advisers. Jim was the father of their grandson, Kimo, who died in Jonestown, apparently at his mother's hand, a fact that John considered the hardest thing he learned after Jonestown.

Though no longer actively ministering, John seems to "preside" over the interview as one could imagine he once presided over his congregation. He is not a preacher in any fire-and-brimstone sense; rather, he is a guide, a contemplative Christian, gentle in voice and manner. He looks for the lessons of Jesus in everything that occurs, searching for the humanity in *everything* God places in our lives.

Barbara offers us coffee. She has prepared a coffee cake for us, still baking in the oven when we arrive, and gives us a quick tour of her new home. She seems thrilled to find herself less isolated than in their previous community, with people her own age across and down the hall, regular company at meal times in the dining room. She shows us a picture that Annie had painted when she was a teenager. John follows along and Barbara leads the way, pointing out the mementos of their lifetime together, first through the living area, a peek into the bathroom, then the kitchen. Greg clicks on the tape recorder. "Well, what do I say when I want to get those things out of the oven?" Barbara asks, self-conscious. Greg puts her at ease, "You can just lean over to the tape and say, 'I'm going to get the things out of the oven now!'" which Barbara appreciates. "Oh, people will say, are you roasting bodies or things?" she jokes. Her humor is similar to her daughter Becky's. Barbara and Greg share a good laugh.

We sit down on their sofa and they sit across from us in separate chairs. They finish each other's sentences, defer to each other constantly, Barbara doting on her husband, and John, careful and affectionate with his wife.

This is John and Barbara Moore:

"Well, the last interview we had, which was with TV cameras, was, I thought, disastrous, absolutely disastrous," Barbara says. "John was great and I was just right off the wall." She gestures as if to erase the event from her memory.

"We're not sensational enough for the TV people," John adds.

"No, no," Barbara agrees.

"They want you to be angry or, you know . . ."

"Or weep," Barbara completes his thought. "They like weeping very much."

"Not too rational, not too cerebral," John explains. He turns to her and gently encourages her to begin, "Go ahead, Mom, just start the conversation."

"Well, our relationship with our daughters was very good," Barbara begins. "We were never angry and they were adjusted, and not into the drug scene or anything of that sort. We had a very good relationship. We didn't want them to be affiliated with Peoples Temple, but even after they went to Guyana, they called us long distance every couple of weeks and wrote regularly." A look of confusion registers on her face—she can't seem to remember where the letters from her daughters are. "Mmm, the letters—did they save them?" she asks.

John reassures her. "They are published, the letters," he whispers, jarring her memory.

"Oh. Oh," Barbara says, relieved.

John picks up the thread. "I think I would also say it was a fun home. The girls were healthy girls. Carolyn was oldest, by six years. Becky is our middle daughter. We lost a couple of children along the way, a stillborn, a newborn death." He looks at his wife, who nods. "Carolyn was very much into the youth group in the church," he continues. "She was concerned with social justice issues."

His face lightens when he speaks of his youngest daughter. "Annie was the comic in the family, whimsical. Her sisters had grown up and left home, but Annie was going to take care of her mother." He turns to his wife, and they smile knowingly. "When I say she was whimsical, you know, one Sunday at church she was playing the guitar, and she disguised 'Ninety-Nine Bottles of Beer on the Wall' in the postlude." He laughs.

"Worked out just beautifully. Nobody knew the difference," Barbara adds.

She suddenly gets up and begins walking around the apartment while her husband continues to talk. "Becky and Annie played at Carolyn's wedding. Becky the flute and Annie the guitar." Barbara calls out from the next room. "Classical music," she adds proudly.

When she returns she hands Greg a ceramic figure—a guitar player that Annie had made in high school. Greg holds it for a minute, then places it on the coffee table in front of us. It was more than just a trinket from childhood. Annie was an artist.

Barbara again wanders off, this time to check on the coffee cake. Again Greg assures her, "We've got hours of tape."

"We moved to San Francisco and I became pastor of Glide Church in 1962 in the fall," John continues.

"You know, he's a clergyman," Barbara interjects, calling from the kitchen. "A Reverend Doctor. Reverend Doctor Moore. Good ole John," she says affectionately.

"I think that there was a oneness about our life in the church and our life in the home," John stresses.

"The churches that John served, they were always liberal and pretty hang loose, and they had a good time. Our kids had a good time, and we did, too." Barbara says, returning with the coffee and cake.

"I was much involved in the gay liberation struggle in 1965 in the sermons I preached," John continues. "The girls went on marches against the Vietnam War. So that's kind of the air they breathed."

"But it took a long, long time for me at least to figure out why they were so intrigued with Peoples Temple," Barbara admits, "because Jim Jones gave me a big pain in the neck. But, as I look back now, I have the feeling there was the social worker instinct with both of them. They were going to help."

"Both Carolyn and Annie," John adds.

"Both Carolyn and Annie, although Carolyn—"

She looks at John. "Shall I mention that she—fell—"

"Sure," John affirms.

"Fell for Jim," Barbara explains.

"Sure," John repeats.

≈ ≈ ≈

Their daughter Carolyn had been married to Larry Layton for less than a year when they moved to Ukiah. Finishing his senior year of college, he was a conscientious objector and he was looking for alternate service placement. A town just outside of Ukiah offered some prospects in a nearby state hospital. Carolyn applied for teaching positions. It was 1968.

Carolyn was doing her practice teaching when Martin Luther King Jr. was killed. The kids at her middle school cheered when they heard the news, which—John told us—"just knocked her off her feet." Carolyn and Larry had heard from some young people in the community about a church with a great preacher named Jim Jones that was integrated and was really doing things. So they decided to try Peoples Temple.

"We didn't hear from Carolyn for a while," John recalls, "a number of months, so we just decided to go over," a three-hour drive from their home in Davis. "When we arrived, Carolyn told us that she and Larry were separated and they were getting a divorce. Carolyn said she fell for somebody—a pastor—and she wanted the pastor to come over and talk with us. That was Jim Jones." John sighs.

"What went through my mind," he recounts, "I thought, 'Oh my God, here's another Sinclair Lewis character, the preacher, you know, hypocritical preacher. What's his name, Barbara?'" John waves his hands in the hope of jarring his memory. "What was his name?" he asks again.

"That's what happens with age," Barbara smiles.

"Okay," John sighs.

"Elmer Gantry," Barbara recalls.

"That's right. Elmer Gantry, the evangelist preacher who was charismatic and had a few women on the side, and all the rest. And Annie thought the same thing, 'How could she do that? That's so stupid.'

"That's what made it so surprising," he continues, "when Annie finished high school, it was 1972, and Carolyn invited her up to Ukiah. After one weekend, Annie came home and said, 'I've decided to join Peoples Temple.' And I thought, 'Oh, God, isn't one daughter enough?'"

≈ ≈ ≈

Carolyn and Annie would visit their parents, but never on the holidays. Holidays were reserved for their Peoples Temple family. Then Carolyn called one day to say that she was pregnant with Jim's child and wanted to move back in with them for a while. There was a back bedroom in the house—they had moved to Berkeley by then—and Jim Jones was a frequent visitor. Stephan Jones later told us about his father taking him along on one of his visits to Carolyn. He listened to them flirting and laughing behind a bedroom door and was overwhelmed by a sickening feeling that he was betraying his mother by virtue of even being there, even though, as a kid, he had no choice.

John and Barbara accepted their daughter's decision and welcomed Jim into their home as often as he stopped by. That was when they began to see the "two sides of Jim Jones," both the paranoid and the good. "We often had dinner together," John recalls, "and we let Carolyn and Jim Jones know that we thought they were paranoid. There was always somebody that was out to get them. They did have their enemies. It wasn't all paranoia. That was a part of the problem. But they had secrets, and people with secrets are always vulnerable to being paranoid. We also let

Carolyn—and Annie—know we didn't like the adulation of Jim Jones. We thought that was sick," John adds firmly.

≈ ≈ ≈

Peoples Temple had two residences in Ukiah for seniors, and one residence for developmentally disabled citizens. They were a group that practiced integration and worked on every social issue that the Moore family had been involved in. Peoples Temple was "way out on the forefront," John says, then acknowledges that Jim Jones "was out on the forefront, too," but with one caveat: "I always felt that Jim Jones thought he was the first one to care about social justice issues. By which I mean, compared with the Berrigans, Daniel and Philip, and Dorothy Day and the Catholic Worker movement, that whole Catholic tradition in the history of social justice, works of mercy, a sense that we're a part of a long line that's thousands of years, hundreds of years before us. Jim didn't have that sense of history," John reflects.

"No, he thought he was the beginning, I guess," Barbara adds.

"He didn't have those roots," John finishes.

The couple recalls a time that they went to one of the plays in San Francisco that Peoples Temple produced, Lorraine Hansberry's *A Raisin in the Sun*. They had seen the play onstage before so they knew how Peoples Temple had rewritten part of it. The crucial line in the original—John's description—comes when the daughter decides, "There is no God." The mother replies to her daughter, "In this house there is God." In the Peoples Temple rewrite of the script, though, the mother echoes the daughter's line: "There is no God."

"Which was interesting," Barbara says, raising her brows.

"Yeah, it really took the guts out of the play," John snaps. "Jim Jones was talking to women, black people like the mother in that play, and Barbara and I always felt that they liked Jim, they liked where they were living, they liked everything else, but in their hearts they were saying, 'There still is God.' God is still here."

"He didn't wipe God out for a lot of the people," Barbara adds.

John struggles to explain the underlying theological logic of the Temple leader. "Jim Jones said, 'I'm the only God you'll know.' He's quoted as having said to people, 'As much of a God as you'll know.' But in a real sense he functioned in the life of the people as God functions in the life of others. People trusted him. Their basic trust was in Jones, their loyalty was with Jim Jones. From my perspective, that's the role of God. That's the way people relate to God."

"He took care of them," Barbara expands. "My religious belief is that all these people are looking for Jesus. Well, Jesus for a lot of people is three meals a day and a roof over their head and a *job*. Jim Jones was providing that."

"We were just observers," John admits, "but there were some good things in Redwood Valley."

"Believe it or not," Barbara adds, "these were college graduates— twenty-six people or so from the Burlingame area, which is upper middle class, which always shocks people when you tell them. They served lunch everyday at this church. They ran a retirement home, a literacy program. They had a swimming pool. I also want to make clear too, they had a good time. A lot of them were having a *good* time. They were having the time of their lives!"

The Moores have donated all of their family correspondence to the California Historical Society. They also published many of those letters. When we look at the letters, we discover an incredible portrait of a family in general, but especially of a young woman, Annie Moore, whose language conveys a sense of her youth and enthusiasm, her vulnerability. Annie first came to Peoples Temple in 1972 full of optimism and hope, ready to do service in the kind of community she thought embodied the work and words of Jesus Christ. With Temple support, she went to school and became a registered nurse. This is an excerpt from a letter written by Annie Moore to her sister:

Dear Becky,

Well, I have finally made up my mind for good I think and am not going to stay permanently with you. . . . The reason is because (and you'll probably groan) I'm going to maybe live with Carolyn in one of her church dorms. I visited her and her church a week or so ago and I am convinced that it is a good place to be. . . . Her church or Jim Jones has and knows more secrets about the world than any other group or person. Also their church is socialist in the real sense (the kind of society Jesus was talking about). . . . So that's my decision. I am also convinced about Jim Jones' power and his "words of wisdom" when I saw him pull incurable cancers out of peoples' throats. I've never heard of any faith healer who could do that. . . . Mom and Dad are really bugged by my decision because they think that Carolyn's church is a real weirdo church . . . but I'm glad I will be involved with Peoples Temple. You probably think that I am brainwashed and stuff, but I think I am a sensible person and no one can tell me what to do. . . . Now you know what I have decided. . . . I hope you won't be angry with me for not coming to stay and I hope that you won't think that I don't love you. Maybe you'll be relieved. . . . I hope you will still like me. Love, Annie

Eternally Grateful

MARCH 19, 2002
SAN RAFAEL, CALIFORNIA

THE NEXT TIME WE MEET STEPHAN JONES, it's on his turf. He lives in a wooded area of Marin County, just over the Golden Gate Bridge in San Rafael, in a small cabin-like house with fading green siding and a steep series of two-foot-wide staircases leading up to its perch at the top of a forested hill. There have to be at least ten staircases in all, linked together by a series of square decks. When I first get out of the car and look up, the house appears to be floating.

Walking up the many levels of stairs feels like walking a labyrinth, a long meditative climb with a plateau after each level that turns on a tiny angle toward the direction of the house.

Greg and I sit with Stephan at his kitchen table, where a back window offers a lush view of trees, birds, and sky. Stephan has written extensively on his experiences in the Temple. Like many writers, he has a "day job" to support his family. Somewhat private about what he does for a living, he quickly dispatches the calls coming in on his cell phone, but from what we can gather, he sells commercial office furniture.

Stephan wants to talk again about photographs, about history. He talks about two distinct sets of pictures. The ones of his family, the personal photos that he has kept and shared with us, and the hundreds upon hundreds of others he has donated to the California Historical Society for preservation. "I wanted to make the photos available," Stephan explains. "I know I wasn't going to keep them as well as the historical society would."

He has been going to the California Historical Society on a regular basis, working with the photo collections.

"I've been trying to document who's in these photos. Where I think they are, what I think they're doing, whatever information I can fit on the back of the photo," Stephan tells us. "It started out as a responsibility to identify the photos, but I don't know, it's been good for me to see those people and remember them."

Stephan has decided not to identify anyone who is still living.

"I don't know why," he admits. "I guess I felt like I needed to respect their privacy. But those who have passed away, even if I couldn't remember the name, I would do whatever research I had to, because it was a lot to remember. I tried to just set it aside, to wait for it to come to me. First couple of times I beat myself up pretty good when I didn't remember a name."

Stephan uses yellow Post-it notes to stick to the back of each photo as he jots down places and names.

I had seen the volumes of photos at the archive—there were literally thousands—and I wonder if it is even possible for him to make his way through them even if he spends the entire rest of his life doing nothing else.

"There are quite a few photos," he acknowledges. "Most of them are of Dad, binders and binders full. Out of the thousands, you might find ten candids."

Stephan pauses as his thoughts find their way into words.

"I say I've forgiven myself for a lot of things that I haven't forgiven myself for. I feel like I failed a lot of people and I hurt a lot of people. And I feel anger—and I don't want to feel angry—but I get so angry when I hear people talk about, 'Yes, but we were wonderful,' and I realize they're just wanting to balance out the image of the crazy cultists piled up in the jungle. But that's just not what I want to do.

"I didn't experience the Temple as a healthy place," he explains. "I was just talking to my partner about it. I have anxieties now. Where does that come from? I lived in terror the first nineteen years of my life. We faced annihilation on a daily basis, but then my father would always swoop in and rescue us, you know, 'It's all okay.' Then you're eternally grateful to him. But you forget, 'Wait a minute, you're the one who created the terror, you're the one who created the danger and now you're—.'" He sighs. "'But we're grateful to you for saving us from it.' That happens all the time in abusive families. *Eternally grateful*," he repeats.

"Never saw Dad. No love, no appreciation, no anything, and then he would come in and just love you up, and it could all melt away, because my dad's here. I think that he did that to a lot of people. And I don't think it was just scheming to control people. He was just a kid in a candy store—and we were his candy."

≈ ≈ ≈

Stephan had already shown us one photo of his parents as a young couple. Now we ask him about another we had seen at the archive: a black-and-white headshot of the two of them, Marceline looking off to one side, Jim behind her, slightly out of focus, grinning boyishly. Stephan knows it immediately. "That's an old photo of Dad and Mom," he says with the smile of a proud son, "when they were just courting, dating. He's seventeen, she's maybe twenty-one. I got it from my aunt, my mother's sister. I wrote a short piece about my parents and called it 'Fire and Water' because he was fiery and she was cool. That's how they look in that photo."

He pauses to look at the picture in his mind's eye.

"It was good for me to see them like that: to see my father, such a boy. He just couldn't believe how good he had it to have this woman. My mother is just beautiful and sure and strong."

The thought of this photo prompts him to go deeper into his own past.

"My early childhood I remember being really wonderful. I had a lot of time where I could just go out and be in nature. My imagination just ran free. I remember being a little boy, and every year the creek behind our house would dry up, and the fish of course would die. So I had to stop that. So every year before the creek dried up, I would go around catching as many fish as I can, putting them in buckets and walking them down to the river, which is probably a mile away, and letting them go. But of course then people noticed that I did that and they thought, 'How wonderful,' right? And in an instant, it went from me wanting to save the fish to me wanting to please these people. I think it's probably a great analogy for my father. I'm sure that he rolled up his sleeves and charged in and really wanted to do some good stuff early on, and folks said, 'Wow, aren't you great?'"

A deer suddenly appears outside the kitchen window. I look up and see it first. Stephan turns around. "It's one of the things I love about living here," he laughs. "That's a young buck. One time we had a deer and a cat lying together back to back, a house cat."

He pauses to retrieve his train of thought. "I'm trying to do this justice, you know. I've been to the shadows. I'll be happy to share some stories with you about my own monstrosity, the things I did in Jonestown that I'd give my life now to change. You pump a little bit of alcohol into me back then in one of my enraged moments and I can see myself being taken over by that demon rage. It has its own life. At least that's my experience of it."

≈ ≈ ≈

The interview is winding down. Stephan has to go work. "Who have you guys been talking to?" he asks as we pack up our things. Greg and I rattle off the list of interviewees. "This is where I was going with the question," he stresses. "Are you able to talk to any black folks?"

"They've been pretty hesitant," I explain. "Even some of the black women that our project commissioner David Dower introduced us to and who were initially going to talk, they've decided not to talk to us, at least for now."

"Really?" Stephan seems genuinely surprised. "Why did they change their minds?"

"I don't know. At the very least, though, we're going to sit down and talk with them to find out."

"We can't write the play without those voices," Greg admits.

Stephan agrees. He says he will do everything he can to help us.

≈ ≈ ≈

"It's painful for people to talk about," Stephan reflects, "but on the other side is the healing. Part of how I found healing is by telling my story, listening to other people tell theirs. It's the art of storytelling. I don't have to tell you, the best theater lies in identification."

We are going deeper with Stephan. He is going deeper with us. As we descend, the stairway to Stephan's house feels like a labyrinth, much like the story of Peoples Temple. Our talk with Stephan is a fitting way to end this first round of interviews.

PART II

UNTIL WE MEET AGAIN

Take the City Today

A MONTH LATER, I drive from the Bay Area down to Los Angeles, a lonely six-hour stint on Interstate 5, a stretch of road that members of Peoples Temple knew quite well. As the Temple grew, it expanded its ministry from the Redwood Valley area in Ukiah (where many members had begun to live communally) to San Francisco and Los Angeles. Temple members would travel by bus to the cities for weekend services. Neva Sly was the first one to tell us about those bus trips. She was one of the regular bus drivers. "I don't know how many stories you've heard about those buses," she tells us in her smoker's voice and attendant cough. "We had thirteen Greyhound buses going up and down the highway. Every week. I mean, it's a big deal. People would get off work on Friday, and the buses would leave at six, and we would drive into San Francisco, have a meeting in San Francisco, get back on the buses anywhere from one to three in the morning, and we'd drive all night to LA."

The bus drivers would communicate by radio from bus to bus. It was a whole operation that eventually expanded to a cross-country ministry.

On the three-hundred-mile stretch of I-5, I think about Neva and the caravan of Peoples Temple buses. I wonder what I-5 looked like twenty-five years ago. It has a few rest stops and gas stations—probably more than back then—but it's still an incredibly boring drive.

I remember Neva's description of the landscape: "Nothing. Nothing." And she's right. "Every time we went down, our eyes," she laughs, as she holds her eyes open with her index fingers and thumbs, "oh, God, it was

63

horrid. Here we are going down, and I turn the PA on, and just for or- neriness, I said, 'Look what God hath put asunder.' Another driver came back with, 'Ah, but Neva, look what man hath plowed under.' This went on for a half-hour, us making rhymes back and forth. Unbeknownst to us, all the PAs were on. Jim was up in the front bus just busting out laughing. We were really good at this. The only thing was afterward Jim said he wished he had tape-recorded it. I wish he had, too, because it was so funny. It was so good. You know, just off the top of our heads. We had a lot of really great experiences on the buses. We really did. Until Jones got into his drugs and everything went awry. He wanted everything from cocaine, heroin. I think speed was the other one."

Neva was the also first to tell us that the most coveted spots on those bus rides were either the metal racks above the seats or—better—the cargo bins underneath where the luggage would usually go. Those were the two places on the long rides where people could lie down, and the only time they could get eight straight hours of sleep. They would use a wire to prop open the door of the luggage bin to keep from suffocating. But they weren't worried at the time about their safety, because they be- lieved that Jim Jones—Father, as he was known—would protect them.

Arriving in East LA, I pull over and call Hue Fortson to let him know that I am on my way. Hue is the first African American survivor who will go on the record for our project. Hue—now Pastor Hue— and I meet up just after a service at his storefront Christian church is letting out.

The room is set up with rows of what look like hotel banquet chairs, ten chairs on each side, with an aisle down the center. There is a simple wooden podium from which to preach and a cross of Jesus mounted on a freshly painted wall behind the pulpit. Pastor Hue is wearing a black suit and white priest collar. We shake hands and he pats me on the back warmly, then invites me to sit down on one of the brown chairs in the front row. He sits to the side of me, a few chairs over to my left. The tape recorder is on a chair between us. "A lady at my job gave me a check for $1,000 to buy these chairs," he tells me proudly. "She had never even been to any of our prayer meetings, but on our lunch hour at work I prayed with her. And she said, 'You need to buy some good chairs—with cushions.'" Hue laughs.

He points out his kids playing on the side with some other children and introduces me to his wife, Linda, as she passes by. This is a ministry the two of them have built from the ground up. They first started ministering in their living room a few years back and recently rented this storefront.

"God is the forefront here," he underscores. His wife walks by again and Hue tells her he'll call her on her cell phone when he's through with our interview. She looks me over, nods, and gathers up the kids to leave. This is his second wife; Hue remarried after losing both his wife and his three-year-old son in Jonestown.

This is Hue Fortson:

"I had a rude awakening years ago. Matter of fact, it was right after Peoples Temple, after I came back from Guyana." He crosses his legs and holds his knee with both hands. "The brokenness that I came out of helps me to see other people more as God would see them, and as a Christian, that's what I like to do. I don't even wear a cross. I know the *meaning* of the cross. It was a sacrifice that the Lord made for us, an atonement that He made for us, the final atonement, to be exact." He points to the cross up on the pulpit. "We try to teach people that. Not only that, I can share life with other folks who are about to get out of here because they don't feel anybody loves them, or they don't feel that they belong.

"When Jesus got down off the cross, He rose again. In other words, He kept goin'. And so that's what we need to do."

There are several folks still milling about and chatting inside the small room. Hue rises from his chair and ushers them to the door. He closes the double doors to the street behind them and turns the lock.

"It's nice that people like to stay longer," I say.

"I know," he answers with a smile. "When you gotta kick them out, you know you're doing something right."

Hue was a member of the Episcopal Church before and after Jonestown, but there is no indication of any formal affiliation in his storefront church.

"What first drew you to the Peoples Temple, Hue?" I ask.

"Well, at this time Jim Jones was coming down to the Embassy Auditorium in downtown LA. Ninth and Horan. And my mom had heard about this man Jim Jones—Peoples Temple—and she said, 'You oughta check it out because they have all races all working together.' So I went down there to show her that this can't all be true, there's a hole in there and I'm gonna find it." He laughs. "But when I went there, they did have an interracial choir, they were singing contemporary upbeat songs that you could relate to, and when they had people to come out to share words of testimonies, they'd have a black, then they'd have a white. Now, most of the churches I came from were all black. So all you saw was all black.

"But then the clincher was when Jones his-self came out. He didn't come out in the traditional dress like a preacher would, you know, a robe or that kind of thing. No. He came out in a velour shirt, a *stripy* velour shirt, black pants, black shoes, and these sunglasses. And boy, 'this bro's cool,' you know." He laughs loudly. "That's the first thing that caught my eye, okay?" He nods his head and smiles.

"And this was his favorite statement: 'We as poor black and white people need to work together.' He would have articles from the news—the *Free Press,* the *San Francisco Chronicle,* the *LA Times, Jet* magazine, *Time* magazine. He would use a piece of the Bible and then he would glean all the negative articles to make a whole sermon around how bad things were—about how the blacks were treated, and how we as people need to come together—'cause the people united would never be defeated. Simple stuff. But you begin to think, because it makes sense what he's saying. This was even before Angela Davis came to the forefront and Huey Newton and all those guys. That was later down the line. So it captivated me. And it would take somebody that really had a spirit of discernment that could see through him. I didn't at that time," Hue says.

When I ask Hue to tell me about the services, his eyes widen with memories of that time, and his gestures follow his descriptions.

"His pulpit was made like a horseshoe up there, and he would constantly drink. Cranberry juice was his favorite, cranberry, Dr. Pepper, sometime orange, sometime apple, and always water, but constantly drinking. He had you believing that, okay, you didn't have Martin Luther King anymore, but here you got this guy who sounds like he's on fire. You heard the expression 'a silver-tongued orator'? Jones had a way of *talking,* and he'd take his voice and go *up* and go *down* and bring it back *around* and show you! He went through all these antics to actually jumping off the pulpit, running, all kinds of stuff. You would get excited, and people rally behind it because what he was saying sounded good, sounded like something we could, like we could go take the city today! And you'd be ready to do it!

"So we joined up," he continues. "I think I may have been twenty-three, somewhere in that neighborhood. A little while after that they bought a big brick building over on El Dorado and Booth. You got these grandiose ideas, 'Oh cool, we're in a brand new building, we're starting to work, and I can get busy.' That's when I really began to jump in with both feet. Even though I was fearful," he clarifies, "even though I was doubtful of some of the things that I heard, and even some of the things that I saw him do from the pulpit, I was afraid to question. Then I got to the point that I was afraid to actually walk away from it, too."

This seems to be emerging as a theme, so I ask him to talk about some of those things that he overlooked.

"Well, one of the things was Jones began this massive campaign against the Bible. I wasn't that much of a Bible scholar myself, so I'm listening to him, but in retrospect I realize what it was. It was deception to pull you away from any kind of support you would have with the Bible.

"Mind you, Jones's favorite statement was that old Flip Wilson line, 'What you see is what you get.' It's where he took it that was the deception. If you see me as a father, I'll be your father. You see me as a friend, I'll be your friend. You see me as God? I'll be your God. But who knows what God's like," he confides, "especially if you don't know the Word for yourself." He shakes his head.

"His thing used to be, 'I'm a God that shaves twice with a razor, I've got jet black hair, and I ride on the back of the bus. I don't buy expensive cars and waste the people's money, I ride on the bus with my people.' Now, it's true, he did ride on the buses, but when he got to the cities—say LA or even San Francisco—and he needed transportation, a car was made available, even if they had to rent one. And it wouldn't be a Volkswagen, okay? It would be a nice car, okay? Now, as far as his hair being black, it comes out that he used to dye his hair in order to keep it that jet black. There were times when he would say, 'A lot of you don't really know who I am.' Boy, that was true. If anybody should have gotten the Academy Award, he should have.

"I think at one time, maybe in the earlier days, he may have been very sincere. But I think that by the time I got there, something had happened that made him bitter. He wanted this power, and he gained

Take the City Today 67

it because a lot of the elected officials gravitated toward him. Even the late mayor of Los Angeles, Tom Bradley, he came to the Temple. Mervyn Dymally, who's still around in politics. He came over to Jonestown."

"I've heard about him," I interject.

"Yeah, he used to be lieutenant governor. He went over to Jonestown a couple times."

≈ ≈ ≈

I later meet with Mervyn Dymally at his office in San Francisco City Hall. Dymally is the only politician in the Bay Area who will talk to us about Peoples Temple. As lieutenant governor in the late '70s under then-Governor Jerry Brown, Dymally was the only Trinidadian to reach such a high office in California. He visited Peoples Temple during its years in California and accompanied Jim Jones on a trip to Guyana in late 1976.

Dymally sits behind a large formal desk with his nameplate centered precisely in front. Our meeting is cordial but formal.

This is Mervyn Dymally:

"Well, in the first place, it is not easy to discuss this subject, which is laced with much controversy. Most people have a very subjective view and they don't look at it from a historical perspective. It seems to me whatever you may think about Jim Jones, whatever the circumstances were, there's a history here, and that history has to be told."

He places both hands on his desk and leans forward in his chair.

"I first became aware of Jim Jones during the case of the Fresno Four," he explains. "In this case in Los Angeles—the guy's name was Bill Farr—these editors were held in contempt for publishing some grand jury transcripts. Jones sponsored a dinner on their behalf and invited Governor Jerry Brown, Mayor George Moscone, Willie Brown. It was a Who's Who in San Francisco politics. There I met him for the first time.

"Jones had a very pragmatic approach to politics," he notes. "It is said that the difference between defeat and victory for George Moscone was Jim Jones's operation. If you look at the results of that first mayoral election, it was very, very close. Closer than anyone anticipated. Jones was appointed to the Housing Commission after Moscone's election. He was, at the time, well thought of, highly respected in the political end of things."

≈ ≈ ≈

Back in the storefront church, Pastor Hue is getting drowsy. But he has a few more stories he wants to tell. He recounts a time that one of the Temple members borrowed his car to run an errand for Father. When Hue next used the car, he opened the glove compartment and found a stack of 3×5 cards with little notes on them: "Name, address, telephone number, color of bed spread, color of walls," etc. On his way to return the stack of cards to the woman who had borrowed his car, he ran into Jim Jones.

"Is there something wrong?" Jones asked. Hue showed him the 3×5 cards. And Jones said, "Oh my God, did anybody see these?" "No, nobody but me," Hue replied. Jones said, "Oh man, this is vitally important. I'll make sure they get it, and I'll make sure that does not happen again." Then he added, "You're a pillar in this church. You're one of the few young black men that I can trust."

Hue laughs when retelling this story. "Not knowing that I was setting my own self up," he sighs. "So after that, I get this call that Jones wanted to appoint me to become a PC member. Planning Commission. It was supposed to be the high echelon, the governing body of the church. Little did I know that those cards ushered me into this position for two reasons. One, he thought I was trustworthy, and two, he wanted to keep his eye on me, okay?"

According to Hue, the 3×5 cards were documented little notes collected by Jones's inner circle, "missions" they were called. These members, predominantly women, would drive to the houses of the congregants when they weren't home and peek into the windows or look at the mail in the mailbox, writing down little pieces of information. Jones was able to convince many of the congregants that he was clairvoyant by citing details like the color of their walls or bedspread, items on their kitchen table, or a letter they had received in the mail that week.

Pastor Hue is really sleepy now—his eyes are getting heavy—but he wants to finish. "They say hindsight is better than foresight," he reflects, "but, man, sometimes it makes you wonder how you can be so vulnerable. But I'm a firm believer—and I know this may sound crazy—that I had needed to go through that, so that I could come to where I am now. Now I know who I am, and what God has purposed in my life, in spite of everything else that has happened. Even though I lost my first wife and my three-year-old son down there in Jonestown, it made me a better man in more ways than one. Not only to my wife and my children now, but the community, people's lives. Not just black people, but all people, because my heart is tender for them. Especially those who are trying to find their way . . ." His eyes close and he drifts off to a gentle sleep at this final thought. I'm not quite sure if I should wake him or let him rest. Suddenly his eyes pop open and he says, "You want a soda? There's a store right here."

Hue had visited Jonestown early in the fall of 1978 but was sent back to the United States to work in the Temple on Geary Street in San Francisco. That's where he was—in the Temple's radio room—on November 18, 1978, when the radio operator received the message from Jonestown on short wave radio, "Let's do the White Night." That message meant the group was dying and that the members in San Francisco should follow suit, as they had all pledged to do. Not a single one in San Francisco did.

On the drive back to the Bay Area, I think about Hue ministering to the broken people in his storefront church. And I think about Jones, preaching up a storm, attracting huge crowds to his Temple in LA.

In the early 1970s, the Peoples Temple choir recorded an album of gospel songs and rhythm-and-blues tunes. Marceline Jones performs on the record, and there's a children's choir led by Don Beck. There are voices of people who later defected from the Temple, of people who survived November 18, and of people who didn't. Neva Sly was the first survivor we met who had an actual recording, and she had played a number of her favorite songs for us. As I drive, the lyrics to one of the more upbeat songs on the Temple album came to mind:

Something got a hold of me,
Oh yes it did, I said, something got a hold of me.
I went to a meeting last night, but my heart wasn't right,
Something got a hold of me.

≈ ≈ ≈

My collaborator Steve Wangh e-mails me a file full of the sermons of Jim Jones. He has edited down the lengthy sermons into excerpts starting from the early days in Indiana and created a timeline of sermons from Ukiah to San Francisco to Los Angeles. I search the file for a sermon from the time that Hue had described and find this excerpt:

All right now, you brace yourself. I've prophesied the date, the hour, the minute, and the year, they're gonna put people in this country in concentration camps. They're gonna put them in gas ovens, just like they did the Jews. You say, "We're not having any concentration camps." The jails are filled with nothing but poor. As Senator Edward Brooke said—the black senator from Massachusetts—he said, we already have concentration camps. He said the prisons of the United States are filled with 80 percent black, poor white, Chicano, but most of them are black. He said, that's already a concentration camp. [Pause.] You say, "Well, they're there because they committed crime." Oh, is that so? [Pause.] They were hungry, and they wanted some food. [Pause.] Fifty percent of the black youth today have no jobs. Fifty percent of the Indians have no jobs. Unemployment's rising rapidly. The prime interest is 9.7 percent today. You know what it was in the Crash of 1929? Ten. [Pause.] This country has always had to have a war, or a depression. I tell you, we're in danger tonight, from a corporate dictatorship. We're in danger from a great fascist state, and if the church doesn't build a utopian society, if it doesn't build an egalitarian society, we're going to be in trouble. [Pause.] Watergate? Did Vice President Spiro Agnew go to jail? Nah. Did President Richard Nixon go to jail? Never, never. But if a black takes a piece of bread, he'll go to jail.

Another excerpt from around that same time:

These ghettoes rotting around you, old rotten buildings, fallen down around themselves. They'll never do anything about these ghettoes. Never.

≈ ≈ ≈

In the California Historical Society, there are bus flyers from this period, too. The ministry of Peoples Temple, once exclusively on the West Coast, exploded, developing into cross-country crusades. "Miracle ministry of Christ through Pastor Jim W. Jones," reads one of the flyers. "Pastor Jim and eleven Greyhound-type buses full of Temple crusaders are traveling the country bringing a message of hope to those who are seeking refuge." An image of Jones in profile, smiling and handsome, appears with the text: "Jim Jones helps everybody that comes to him. Jim Jones has never turned an older person away, he gives them a home, whether they have money or not. Jim Jones has never turned a little animal away even."

There are more flyers offering holy water, prayer cloths—tokens in exchange for donations. These would simply be 1970s kitsch if it weren't for what happened in Jonestown.

I remember survivor Laura Johnston Kohl pointing out that on these bus crusades, "Jim's message was to reach blacks. So we'd take a map of each city, and we'd have hundreds of thousands of leaflets, and we'd leaflet the whole black community."

She explained that Temple members would travel on "advance crews" not only to pass out the flyers in black neighborhoods but also to look for free spaces for the whole congregation to stay overnight.

"Lot of people were religious in the Temple," Laura added, "but I don't think Jim was ever religious. I don't think he believed in God or anything. I don't think that held the least bit of interest for him, except to use it. The authentic Jim was a political animal who knew how to read the system and get the most out of it. He said, 'You know what? The money is in the churches.'"

Some of the cities Peoples Temple targeted were Houston, Shreveport, Atlanta, Philadelphia, Chicago, Detroit, and the city of his beginning, Indianapolis—all cities with significant black populations.

Neva Sly had described an incident that occurred in the South on one of these cross-country bus trips. The buses would often stop in parks and public places to picnic and let the kids play outside. "You've heard about Gulfport, Mississippi?" she asks, but we haven't.

"Oh, my dears, where have you been?" We all shake our heads, ours in ignorance, hers in good-humored derision.

"When we went back east and we got to Gulfport, Mississippi," she explains, "we stopped the buses for dinner. It's getting on evening time, so all of our kids and everybody are out there. As we're getting the tables set up for dinner, all of a sudden I hear gunshots. *What the hell was that?* I yelled at my husband, Don, and I said, 'Look!' Back in the trees you could see these white hoods. It was Klan. Our kids are out here, you know, these African American teenage boys out there were our security guards, getting the people back on the buses. 'Never mind,' I say, 'get your asses on the bus. They're after you, not us! We're the white ones, honey, get on the bus!' Don and I both are just shoving these kids toward the bus. 'Go, go.'

"You know," she then adds, her voice calmer in reflection, "when you're in a place like that, where they have such a profound line of black and white, and you don't normally think that way, it's hard to shift gears. It really is. Sure enough, here are all these damned guys coming out of the woodwork with their hoods on, their guns, you know. Never been so scared in my life.

"But I'll never go back there," she promises. "Gulfport, Mississippi. We got on that bus and headed back to California. Much to my chagrin, I hear they still have a lot of that going on."

Along with the bus flyers at the archive, there are several editions of *The Family Good News,* a newsletter published by the Temple. In one edition, there is a poem under the heading, "HAVE A HAPPY DAY From your Grandma Bates":

Begin the day with friendliness.
Keep friendly all day long;
Keep in your soul a friendly thought.
In your heart a friendly song.
Have in your mind a word of cheer
For all who come your way;
And they will greet you, too, in turn
And wish you a happy day!

Underneath the poem is written, "Thank you, Grandma. And we hope more of the family will send in original songs, poems, stories and thoughts for the GOOD NEWS."

Grandma Bates—Christine Ella Mae Bates—died in Jonestown.

Too Black

MAY 24, 2002
OAKLAND, CALIFORNIA

VERNON GOSNEY IS A JONESTOWN SURVIVOR, although seriously wounded in the attack on the congressman and his entourage at the airstrip at Port Kaituma. He was twenty-five at the time and had been in and out of the Temple since he was nineteen. Vern features prominently in the story of the last two days in Jonestown. He was the one who passed a note on the day of the congressional visit: "Help us get out of Jonestown. Signed, Monica Bagby and Vernon Gosney."

It was this note to the congressman—the one NBC reporter Don Harris later thrust into Jones's hand during the final interview—that was one in a series of cascading events that led to the deaths in Jonestown.

Vern e-mails to let us know that he will be visiting the Bay Area in May; he lives in Hawaii but travels often to visit his family in northern California. My collaborator Margo Hall and I set up a time to meet with him. Vern is a small man with a thick moustache and thinning brown hair. He works for law enforcement now. He wears a thick silver necklace and rings on both hands. Vern is openly gay; because I am too, I expect to feel some kind of a kinship, but instead Vern feels distant, reserved.

He wants to know who we've been talking to for the project. I had recently met with Stephan again, so I mention to Vern what a great interview it was—just making conversation. "I guess when you're in a cult, you don't really know people," Vern responds coldly.

"What do you mean?" I ask.

"You just know the face they're showing, or the role they're playing, their false personalities. Maybe on the twenty-fifth anniversary, I can come to the memorial. Maybe I can meet him," Vern says.

"You never met Stephan?" I am surprised.

"I did," Vern replies. "I'm just saying that—well, my experience of him when we were in the Temple was that he was a very angry, very hostile person. Very hateful."

"He talks a lot about that. He has many regrets about who he was then," I explain.

"Yeah?" Vern replies skeptically. "It would be interesting to meet him again now."

≈ ≈ ≈

Vern's note to the congressman was the first admission, though a secret one, that some of the people in Jonestown wanted to leave. Temple members gave up their passports once they were in Jonestown, making it impossible for them to get out on their own. How did Vern get to the point of wanting so desperately to leave? We ask him to start at the beginning.

This is Vern Gosney:

"I was living in Seattle with Cheryl, and a friend of ours told us about this healer Jim Jones. About three days later, there was a flyer on our car announcing that he was in town. So we went. Jim Jones talked about socialism. He talked about equality, and there was a lot of music and there was dancing. I hadn't had any exposure to Pentecostal, you know, *the experience.* I was raised as a WASP, and everything is very conservative and serious, like, 'Bringing in the sheaves, bringing in the sheaves.' And these people are dancing and shouting!" he cries. "It was just so wonderful. Many were healed and people were coming out of wheelchairs! I remember especially this very large old woman, she had been healed in the wheelchair, and the next day she's just carrying this casserole for a potluck. She's walking down the street, humming to herself, singing, just blissed out to the max. There was music and people getting raised from the dead. It was pretty good." The recollection makes him smile.

"The Temple painted itself as a place where things like color or sexual orientation didn't matter," he continues more seriously, then adds, "That was a place where I was very naive."

"What do you mean?" I ask.

"I was an actively gay person in my teens," Vern explains. "I used to come to San Francisco, and my only experience was with men. When I met Cheryl, she was a totally different person from anyone I had ever met. I grew up with an alcoholic mother who pissed on herself, you know, it was really very degrading. But with Cheryl, here's this woman who's a survivor from Harlem, who's strong, dignified, who's the warrior goddess. I mean, when you walked down the street with Cheryl, no one would fuck with you—no one man or woman—nobody. She was that strong. And I fell in love with her. I was not necessarily oriented towards all the women in the world. I was in love with Cheryl.

"I was nineteen when I married Cheryl," he tells us. "My family disowned me because I married a black woman. My mother didn't speak to me at all. My father met her and said, 'Your children are going to look like gorillas.' He was a horrible racist.

"We couldn't rent an apartment at that time because no one would rent to an interracial couple, so we wanted to be part of the community in Redwood Valley. It was, in a way, a Utopia, it was free of racism, no rich people, no poor people, and everyone had the same. We didn't know when we joined that there were rules. No drugs, no alcohol, no smoking, no sex. We were casual drug users at that time, and drinkers and stuff. We were celibate for a few months, then finally we had sex. And it was like, 'Oh, oh, oh God!'" He laughs. "I think we left soon after that." He laughs again. "That was something I could not maintain.

"And then Cheryl got pregnant. Mark—our son Mark—was born. Cheryl had a cesarean section and the doctor gave her too much anesthesia. She was a warrior, she was a robust person, and so I guess he gave her anesthesia according to her weight. She never woke up from the anesthesia. She was given too much. She had a cardiac arrest. And by the time she was revived, her brain was gone. She was only twenty-one years old.

"So I had this $2 million lawsuit against the hospital for medical malpractice. And I had the trial. One of the things the doctor said in the trial was that she was too black—they couldn't tell that she had lost oxygen because she was too black. And the doctor, he was acquitted, by a jury of twelve people. The first thing I did afterward was I called Peoples Temple. I said, 'This is what's happened.' What I was told was, 'This is what happens when you leave the Temple. You have to return right away.' So I did. And I thought, 'Everything that Jim Jones said about the United States is true.'"

≈ ≈ ≈

Cheryl didn't die right away, Vern says, but remained in a coma on life support. The sadness in his voice as he talks about this is as profound as anything we've heard so far.

"After this happened to Cheryl, I went back to the Temple, but I got strung out on heroin. I quit my job and moved to Redwood Valley. The drug treatment program in Peoples Temple—they had a lot of drug addicts there—was if you get caught, we'll beat the shit out of you with a rubber hose. That was their drug treatment program. Which, of course, is not effective."

"We've heard about addicts being cured in Peoples Temple," I say.

"They did not," Vern counters, "because I *used* with the other addicts in the Temple. I mean, I'm sure some people, yes, they did get clean, and they found useful, productive lives there. But that was not my experience with the people that I knew. There was a whole subculture of drug users."

"In Peoples Temple?" I am shocked.

"Yes," Vern confirms. "One of my best friends, her husband was a heroin dealer in Los Angeles, so she's the one who told me the great secret about heroin is that you don't shoot it, you snort it, and it's not addictive," he laughs. "It was the days when cocaine wasn't addictive either, because cocaine wasn't addictive in the beginning."

Vern is clean now and living a productive life. He has some distance from his addiction, which seems to allow him the freedom to laugh at this part of his past.

"This whole subculture of people using within the Temple, it's part of what probably saved my life," Vern continues. "Having one foot in and one foot out of the Temple. I lived communally, my time was basically taken up with long meetings, handing out the newspapers, writing letters, or caring for children. But I also had a job, so I still had my contact with the outside world. Some people didn't have jobs. So I would sometimes sneak off after work and either go drink, go to the discos, go to the bathhouses, which I would get in trouble for when they found out."

"Sounds like you were leading a double life."

"I got called on the carpet because I went to orgies and had group sex. They thought it was so horrible and disgusting and animalistic."

Vern is very cynical about Peoples Temple but can become reflective very suddenly, as he does now.

"When I look back on it, I had always been searching for a family. That was underneath everything. I wanted a family because, by the time I left home, all my brothers and sisters were either living in foster homes or juvenile home, or with other relatives. So I didn't have a cohesive loving family. Peoples Temple was everything that I wanted, as far as family goes. The people there were very beautiful. They were not weak people. They were strong, strong people. They believed in this cause, and they wanted to create this new world."

"But what about the punishment—?" I ask.

"I was an addict when I was in the Temple," Vern begins. "If I got caught smoking, as punishment I'd have to raise $200 by the following week. Caught drinking? Raise $200. Have sex with an outsider? $200. I always had to raise money. I would go to the Tenderloin in San Francisco and the prostitutes would give me money. 'Oh, here's $200, honey.' The prostitutes felt sorry for me."

He sighs.

"I think Peoples Temple put up with more stuff from me than they would have because I had a child. Edith Cordell, who was one of the oldest members of the church from back in the Indiana days, was taking care of my son, Mark, at the time. There was no legal paperwork granting custody to her or to the Temple, but she was basically raising him. The leadership didn't want to hurt Edith. They put up with me because they wanted the child."

"We heard about how they took all the children and gave them to different parents," Margo says.

"Yes, that's what they did," Vern replies. "I wasn't exactly the model parent at the time. But I had this $2 million lawsuit. Peoples Temple wanted the money."

I ask Vern how he ended up in Jonestown, considering how disillusioned he was with the Temple.

He pauses.

"After I lost Cheryl, I was completely strung out on drugs. I have this little child, and I'm thinking he's going to be raised in this racist country. I don't know where else to go." After a long pause, he ends with: "There was hope that I was going to have a better life for me and my son."

Homicide Is Suicide

JUNE 5, 2002
BERKELEY, CALIFORNIA

A FEW WEEKS LATER, my colleague Steve Wangh flies in from New York to help with interviews. Steve is the oldest member of our collaborative team, closer to the age of most of the survivors. I had worked with him as a writer on *The Laramie Project*, but I wanted him to be with us on the ground during the interview phase for this project.

It's late spring when Steve and I meet Melody Ermachild Chavis, a private investigator who was a member of the legal defense team for Larry Layton. (The others on the legal team were defense lawyers Tony Tamburello and Marianne Bachers, and investigator Jack Palladino; we met with all of them.) One of Melody's duties was to conduct interviews with survivors when they first returned to the United States early in 1979.

Melody has a quick mind and boundless energy for her cases. She is still in touch with Juanita Bogue, a former Peoples Temple member who, like Vern Gosney, left with the congressman on November 18 with her family, a decision that rocked the Jonestown community. The Bogue family had been one of the most devoted families in the Temple.

We arrive early, around 8:30 A.M. Melody is a death penalty investigator now. Her job is to reconstruct—through exhaustive interviews and medical, social work, and foster care records—the personal histories of defendants to present during the sentencing phases of jury trials. Guilt is not the issue. Most of the defendants she works with are guilty. Her job is to humanize them, and by presenting the mitigating circumstances that led to their crimes, prevent them from being sentenced to death. "I assemble the information into their whole life story from beginning to end," she explains.

Melody speaks about the next generation—the children of survivors. Her belief is that the real legacy of Jonestown is continuing violence. One of the defendants she is currently working with is Juanita Bogue's son Chad in a high-profile case. Melody is in the middle of preparing for his trial.

This is Melody Ermachild Chavis:
"Juanita's son is so young. Chad had just turned eighteen when he allegedly killed an Oakland police officer, and now we're preparing madly for his trial, which will begin in September. He's been in Antioch prison almost three years awaiting trial. The crime occurred in January 1999. It takes forever to go to trial."

Both Steve and I are stunned to hear the news about Chad.

"People get so startled when I say in my caseload alone I worked with three children of Jonestown families who killed people, who were facing the death penalty," Melody recounts. "One of them, Tracy Cain, is on death row. There was Michael Briggs. I worked up his whole trial, wrote his life story, and then he was offered a life-without-parole deal, which we took. The third is Chad. It's amazing," she says. "But at the same time, after twenty-two years of working on this job, and really looking deeply at the roots of violence in this country, you know, going back in the generations of the families of my clients, it doesn't surprise me. I'm working on a theory about the roots of violence that I'm sure is true, which is about passing down trauma from generation to generation.

"Chad was nine or ten years old at the tenth anniversary of Jonestown," she continues, "when he saw a movie on television about the tragedy, with no preparation. Everybody gathered around and watched that movie. When it was over they told him, 'That's what happened to us. We were there.' None of the kids had any special therapy or any therapy, period, for this healing. Part of what happens is a feeling of shame, feeling doomed like, 'What's wrong with us?' 'Why would your parents do such a thing?' 'Or your grandparents?' 'Why would they kill themselves?' 'Why would they associate with something so horrifying as the death of 918 people?'"

She sighs. "It wasn't ever explained to them. Chad's been very curious about it. I've given him books to read in jail. It's still very hard to understand. We can't understand this very easily. I spent a decade of my life trying to understand this. To literally comprehend it.

"But the violence is not mysterious," she says. "To me, that is not mysterious. There are material conditions that breed violence. It can be cured, but people have to stop and look at it and then start to heal. People are still living out all that brutality. Unless it gets healed in some way, reconciled, acknowledged. First of all, acknowledged. The Jonestown people carry it. It's a shadow over their lives, and these Jonestown children, they were raised by people who were deeply traumatized."

Melody was "a stringer" when she was hired on in the Jonestown case. She had just become an investigator during the winter of 1979. She had been a kindergarten teacher before that and then went to paralegal school. Describing herself as "a leftist, feminist, socialist at the time," she adds, "I still am coming from a social-change perspective." She got an offer to work with investigator Jack Palladino and his partner, Sandra, so she quit her job and joined their team. By 1981, she was immersed in the Peoples Temple case and went to Guyana with Jack and defense lawyer Tony Tamburello.

At that time, she says, her agenda was to save Larry Layton. Her team had to prove that he had not known of the plan to kill Leo Ryan. They also had to document what was common knowledge within the Temple: that Jim Jones had a need-to-know style of leadership where everyone was divided up and didn't know the entire plan. "That was very true of Larry Layton," Melody explains, "and losing the case was just a tragedy, the best example of a true scapegoat. When you look at the indictment, it has about twenty something people on it. And they're all dead, every single one of them, except for him. So the conspiracy all landed on him because he lived."

Many survivors don't remember talking to Melody, but she remembers what it was like interviewing them in 1979. "There was a continuum of them being 'deprogrammed.' That was the word for coming out of a cult, if you could deprogram yourself or get yourself out of it. In '81, there were still people who thought that Jim Jones was telling them what to do, could read their minds, couldn't possibly be dead, must be living. They were still loyal to him. And then on the other end were the people who realized it was something terrible, but they were also suffering from such horrible guilt, they could hardly live. And grief—I've interviewed people whose children all died but they lived, just by where they happened to be. Some people had gone to Georgetown to buy things or to go to doctors' appointments, some were on the basketball team, some were on the staff that rotated between Georgetown and Jonestown.

"There were these different groups of survivors," Melody explains. "The people here in the Bay Area, the radio orders came through for them to die, and they didn't. Thank God they didn't kill themselves. When we interviewed them all again in '85, they had changed, moved along. I was very happy that a lot of them had gotten better. But some just didn't make it. Juanita hasn't done well at all. There's a class system to it. The people with more resources obviously got treatment, got help."

Melody has a theory we haven't heard before. She believes that what happened in Jonestown was a methamphetamine crime. "I've investigated so many since then," she explains. "Meth makes you kill people, and Jones was on meth. I have a photo I took of a drawer," she struggles to remember the exact detail, "or a box, I found in his cabin, and it's just filled with syringes. They were shooting meth. He and his sex partners and other leaders.

"Well, everybody was his sex partner," she clarifies. "As a little boy, poor Michael Briggs was raped by Jim Jones. Everyone had sex with Jim Jones. That's a meth thing. My meth clients all do that. I recently talked with a meth expert in LA, and he's writing a book about serial killers and serial rapists and meth. That drug can make you rape your own children."

"I thought that methamphetamine was a more recent drug," I say.

"It's popular now," Melody replies. "But Jim Jones got on to that, figured it out. Jonestown is one of the first of those big crimes. That's an important piece, which I didn't get at the time. That's how you can talk all night long, rant and rave on and on, talk for eight hours, nine hours."

≈ ≈ ≈

Melody has dug out her old files and file boxes and put them in the back of her car. "One of the things I have is some of the Flavor Aid packets. I just went and picked them up when I was in Jonestown and put them in a plastic bag. I went to my storage, and I saw that the mice hadn't eaten them or anything. It's not Kool-Aid, it's Flavor Aid, just so you know. What in the world could anyone do with them?" Melody asks with a wry lilt in her voice. "I'm not gonna sell them on eBay or something. I want to give them to you. I found my slides, too. I'm a gold mine for you guys."

Melody has arranged for us to meet Juanita Bogue. "Juanita grew up in the Temple. Her parents joined in Ukiah. That's why her family's departure from Jonestown was so significant," Melody explains. "When Congressman Ryan was leaving that day, and *her* family said, 'We want to go with you,' all of a sudden it was the final straw, because once someone so influential left, I think Jim Jones had to realize this could be the beginning of the end.

"And they did go. They tried to gather everyone up. They got onto the truck. One sister was left behind. Marilee refused to get on the truck, and she died that day in Jonestown. Juanita was maybe twenty years old."

Juanita was pregnant with her son Chad when she left with the congressman, though she didn't know it at the time. "Chad was conceived in Jonestown," Melody informs us. "His date of birth does jive with that. Except Juanita doesn't know who his father is." Chad is mixed race and Juanita is white, Melody explains, so his father is likely black. She suspects he could be among those who survived.

"I think that Chad and different young men I've met and gotten to know," Melody reflects, "reach a place where they just truly are despairing. They really don't see any possibility of help whatsoever. It takes a lot of factors for them to commit an act like Chad—to allegedly kill this cop—it takes a gun, it takes a car, it takes the other boys to be there, but the underlying thing is that total, total hopelessness. So homicide, in some ways, is suicide. It's always so close to suicide. My clients have all lived through it to have their trial, but so many die while committing the crime."

Melody suggests that she sit in on our conversation with Juanita, then adds, "I'll just be quiet, but I'll be there with you, if that's okay." Then she contradicts herself.

"I might say something because she's not a good reporter. She has a very long, longstanding case of post-traumatic stress disorder from all this. I've interviewed her a number of times now about her son, and sometimes she's just making it up as she's going along. She's so much in delusions or denial, she tries to tell me, 'Oh, my boys got really good grades.' They got all Fs and Ds. 'They were on the honor roll.' She's kind of trying to make it better than it was sometimes."

Melody notices the time. "I told Juanita we would come at about 11:30. We better get going now."

We All Participated

JUNE 5, 2002
OAKLAND, CALIFORNIA

MELODY DRIVES a late-model Toyota station wagon. We pile into her car and head to Juanita's place, passing block upon block of treeless streets, dilapidated buildings, and abandoned cars. Steve and I are both quiet in the car. "This is Ground Zero in Oakland," Melody says, puncturing the silence. "Tons of crack around, and meth, AK-47s, the whole nine yards."

As we approach Juanita's building, Melody tells us that Juanita is agoraphobic and as a result doesn't get out much. She is intermittently clean and sober, and Melody is not sure in what condition she will be on that spectrum today. And then a final warning, that Juanita is emotionally frail, that we shouldn't push her. She sometimes goes in and out of an almost trance-like state when talking about Jonestown.

We have to wrap around to an alley in front of the building to find the stairs. The two-story building looks like a motel from the 1970s, covered in thick coats of light-brown paint, uneven in the spots where it covers up graffiti. As we climb the concrete stairs to the second floor, residents hanging out on the stairwells look us over.

We arrive on the second floor and walk down a breezeway to Juanita's apartment. We pass the front picture windows of several side-by-side units; there are no curtains or shades, so we can see right in. The places are all fit with screen doors, and most of the apartments have their front doors open with only the screens between them and us. The main door to Juanita's place is open, too, and we can see her through the screen sitting in a recliner facing the door. She sees us and gets up to let us in.

She offers us some soda and we accept. I sit in a well-worn green leather recliner. Steve sits on a brown love seat. The carpet is wall-to-wall shag, and the walls are paneled in brown, too. There is a TV set in front of the picture window. We hear a pounding bass coming from the apartment downstairs.

Juanita sits in her recliner with a TV tray to one side with an ashtray, remote control, a glass of pop, and a pack of cigarettes on top. We pull out our tape recorders.

Melody jumps in. "Is that okay with you?" she asks.

"I figured they was gonna do something. I was just hoping that it wasn't videotape," Juanita replies.

"No, no videotape, just audiotape," I assure her.

"Then I'd have to put makeup on," she laughs. "Anybody know how to do that?" Steve and I look at each other confused. "Just joking with you." She looks a little tired but seems in good spirits.

"I'm gonna see Chad tomorrow," Melody says.

"That's what I wanted to know. Could you take a letter? Will they let you take a letter down there?"

Juanita pulls out a child's crayon drawing on a sheet of white 11×7 paper.

"Oh, is that Boo Bear's?" Melody asks.

"Boo Bear's drawing," Juanita nods.

Melody turns to Steve and me to explain. "Chad has a little teeny brother, his nickname is Boo Bear. He's like a year and something. How old is he now?"

"Six," Juanita corrects.

The telephone rings and Juanita picks up. It is an old, beige rotary line with a long cord. She talks a minute, explains to whomever is calling that she is busy at the moment. She hangs up, then says to us, "My neighbor wants to bum a cigarette."

In the meantime, Melody is strategizing about how to get the letter and drawing in to Chad. "You know, I think I could slip this in with my legal papers," she suggests.

"They don't let you take stuff like that in?" I ask surprised.

"They won't," Melody sighs. "But he'd be so happy to get it."

≈ ≈ ≈

When Juanita is ready to begin, I turn to her and say, "I don't know how much you remember from growing up in Redwood Valley in the Temple, but any memories you have or anything you could talk about would be great."

"I thought I was gonna get to answer questions," she says awkwardly, "easy questions."

"Easy questions, yeah," I assure her. "Just tell us what you remember."

This is Juanita Bogue:

"My parents were living in Redwood Valley. Jim Jones used to be a night school teacher, and my parents went to the night school where he taught at. I think that's how he got a lot of recruits, was through the night school. At the time that my parents joined, I was living with my grandparents, so when I came back one summer, it was like bizarre. I was about ten or eleven maybe. Still in elementary school, I remember that much. Making us stay up all night, going to these church services day and night. Why would your parents do this? I was just set in the middle of it and expected not to ask any questions.

"And when you did ask 'Why?' they would get very upset," she continues, warming to the subject. "You're not allowed to ask 'Why.' You didn't really have family groups once you joined the Temple. They would give my parents new kids, and they would give us to another family. To break down the family unit, right? But what possessed them to just go along with everything so blindly is what I couldn't understand."

I ask her about the services next, if she remembers any details.

"Yeah," she yells. "What Jones really reminded me of?" She leans over and whispers into the tape recorder, "I think this is off the record." She smiles. "I always thought he was alcoholic or something, because boy, once he got up there, he'd just ramble on endlessly till two or three o'clock in the morning. He wouldn't stop. Whatever it was that pissed him off or ticked him off, he reminded me more of an alcoholic. Like if a man gets mad and he's drinking, he'll make the whole family stay up all night and listen to him yell and yell and never stop! That's more or less what he reminded me of."

"Did you have any friends that you could say this to?" Steve asks.

"No," she gestures dismissively. "They beat the living daylights out of you." She laughs. "You don't say stuff like that. You only talk about the things they want you to talk about. You're supposed to spend that time praising Father."

Father was the term Temple members used when referring to Jim Jones.

"Did you think of leaving?" Steve asks.

As if answering the most obvious question in the world, "Everybody thought about leaving!" she exclaims. "But there is no way to leave. There's no way out. You saw what happened to us in the end when we tried to leave." She laughs again, this time with more irony in her voice.

"There was no leaving," she stresses. "My little brother, Tommy, was one of them who did try to escape. He had to walk around with a chain and ball around his leg for, God, I don't know how long. Every place he went, he had to drag a big-ass ball—it was like about the size of a bowling ball—chained to his ankle."

"Where was that? Was that in Jonestown?" Melody asks.

"That was in Jonestown," Juanita answers.

"And he was one of the ones they buried in a box under the ground," Melody interjects.

"Yeah, that's right," Juanita confirms. "Part of their discipline. They would bury them in the ground and then make animal noises to scare 'em to death. I don't know why Jones did that to people. I can't tell you."

Juanita estimates that she was about sixteen when she went with her family to Jonestown. She then becomes more certain when she remembers: "I was just old enough to get my driver's license," she says. "I had just got my driver's license."

"Do you know why your family decided to go?" I ask.

Juanita takes a breath, then a sip of soda. "They had a movie, like a video movie made?" she recounts with an upward inflection. "And everybody that was there was all happy and everything, and they're having a party and everything, right? Then when you get there, you find out it's not really like that." She sighs. "You want to know what they did to us when we first got there?" she asks.

We tell her we want every detail.

"Okay," she starts in. "You get off the boat, you ride a trailer into Jonestown, right? You have all your worldly belongings packed into cases. When you get off, they give you a slip of paper that says your new dorm number, and they say they'll bring your clothes later. Then that night you go to a meeting and find out all your worldly possessions have been taken care of for you. You got the clothes on your back. Unless you were his kids or his kids' girlfriends," she jabs. "They could have their clothes, but the rest of us, everything was taken. A lot of people got very upset, but after wherever they took 'em to, and they came back, they were no longer upset. In fact, they were happy to do it. That was just it." It's Juanita's second reference to the more severe discipline in Jonestown.

"You had to give up all your jewelry, if you were wearing any jewelry at the time," she continues. "Everybody had to take their jewelry off and give it to 'em because after we got there, we found out we're all starving to death, and Jones needed more money, more money, more money. Who knows what we needed all this money for, but he needed more of it. Nothing was ever enough. That's why we worked all the time. He would sell the stuff upriver, plantains, vegetables, bananas, all that stuff, making bread. He would take it to like an open market and sell everything. That's what we had to work so hard for."

"What was it like, your average day in Jonestown?" I ask.

"It was like five o'clock, they'd get you up in the morning. You work for twelve hours. You come and you take showers. You eat and you stay in a service all night till two, three o'clock in the morning. You wake up at five o'clock again and you start over. If you worked out in the field, you would take like a butter sandwich or something. You couldn't walk in for lunch and then walk back again, because it was too far—like three miles—so you'd take sandwiches."

"Were you a field worker?" I ask.

"I worked at the piggery, shoveled pig shit," she says bluntly. "I cleaned cages all day. And I'd feed the pigs. We ate rice and gravy. They would take the pigskins and fry it and make a gravy, and that would be gravy over your rice. I don't ever recall having a plate with meat on it, and I was there for a couple of years."

"Did you know people who were actually happy, who liked living down there?" Steve asks.

"No. No," she says quickly, emphatically.

Remembering the words of Laura Johnston Kohl, who said the people who were happy had perished, I ask, "Do you think maybe some of the people who died had a better experience?"

"No," Juanita says with conviction.

"It wasn't possible?" I ask.

Juanita looks me squarely in the eye and says, "Everybody who got off that truck the first day when they came in, and looked and saw the lie he had told, they realized what he had done. Now he had full control. If you tried to say anything or do anything, a whole crowd of people—ten, twenty people—just jump up and they'd start beating the living daylights out of you, taking turns, your own kids, your own parents, anybody. Anytime you said anything against him, they'd run and tell Father, and then there'd be an instant meeting and start beating you up. Anything you said about him, a whole mob would just bum-rush you. It would just be over stupid stuff. Anything. Like we grew a lot of fruits, right? If you were walking by an orange tree, you had been working out in this field all day, and you pick an orange and you eat it, that'd get the living daylights beat out of you and you'd be on the chain gang for a couple of weeks.

"I know," she says forcefully. "Because I was one of those people that got bum-rushed a lot.

"See, I didn't have that instant fear of Jones that most people had," she continues. "I don't know why either. If he would have asked me about it, I would have told him how I felt about him, which is why he didn't particularly care for me. That's why I got to work on all the crews miles out of town with no food, no water, nothing. He just really did not like me."

"When they were doing the beatings," Melody asks, "would they justify it in terms of their ideology, 'How dare you take an orange, it's for the children, it's for the poor people, something like that?'"

"If Father didn't say you could have an orange, then you don't get an orange. If you take it upon yourself to pick you an orange anyway, that's not a good idea."

"But back in the States before you went, it was, 'We're going to create a new society,' right?" Melody asks.

"Yeah," Juanita says.

"Did any of that ever make sense to you? Any of that social message?" I ask.

"He said the reason why we had to go to Jonestown was because we was sick and tired of dealing with racism and classism. He had this long speech that we was all going so that we could have a better way of life. We were supposed to be going there to do missionary work, like set up a church and help the poor or whatever like that."

"Did you ever believe any of that or think you were part of something important?" I ask.

"Oh yeah, we all believed it," she nods. "We were all assigned jobs here in the States before we went. Father talked to each one of us personally and told us our mission in life."

"And what was yours?" I ask.

"Field worker," Juanita answers as bluntly as before.

"When you were back in the States, though," I clarify, "before Jonestown?"

Juanita struggles to remember. "Probably like a nurse or something. You'd either be a schoolteacher or you'd be a nurse," she says.

Steve leads her to the last two days in Jonestown. "So at the end, when you escaped, had you been waiting for this moment?" he asks.

"No," Juanita replies. She breaks down their plan for us. "Richard Clarke and Jerry Parks, those two and me worked at the piggery. Richard and Jerry, they plotted every day. Jerry was so obsessed, I was like, 'Why don't you just walk out, right?' So that's how the plan got started. The plan was to escape through the jungle. One person would be in charge of getting the food together, and one person cut the trail. Richard's the one that cut the trail. Then the next thing you know, it ended up being too many people to escape with. Everybody wanted to leave. Every day the group got bigger and bigger."

She pauses, then explains: "See, somehow Jones got wind of our plan just about the same time as the congressman was coming. That's when he really flipped out. I never did see the trail, but they say they used it. It ended up being about thirteen people?" she ends with a question.

We ask her what she recalls about the last day.

"That morning the congressman was there, stuff fell apart. That's when my father decided to take our whole family out with the congressman.

"They rounded us all up and took us up front," Juanita remembers. "Do you know like in the newspaper picture, where you see us all standing there at the end with Jim Jones? That's what he's telling us right then. And what he's gonna do to us: 'I told you nobody leaves here unless you leave in a pine box.'

"They dragged me up front with all my belongings and told me, 'Get out with the congressman,' and told me they was gonna kill the congressman and kill me, too."

"I don't know if you feel like talking about your sister Marilee who died there," Melody says gently. "You think she felt differently about it?"

"She felt completely different about it," Juanita explains. "Jones tried to throw her out too with the rest of us, and she screamed and begged and would not leave. She believed he really was God or whoever he professed to be. She was a few years younger than me, though. She just really did believe."

"You remember her screaming to stay?" Steve asks.

"She was telling Jones to kill us," she yells. "She would kill us for him, if he wanted her to.

"When we got on the truck to leave," Juanita continues, "Joe Wilson jumped on the back and told us what was gonna happen: 'When we get you out here, we're gonna kill you.' And we tried to tell the congressman that, but he wouldn't believe it. He said, no, he could handle this. Well, you were wrong. We tried to tell him all the way up to where they started shooting at the airstrip. And that's when everybody just took off running. They just shot up the airplanes, everything, innocent bystanders, everybody was shot up."

Steve takes a deep breath. "So, why are you alive?" he asks.

"I don't know," she answers. "I think I was actually sitting in the seat next to Patty Parks, the one that got her head blown off, and so we all really did look like we were dead. Everybody was just covered with—it was horrible. It was horrible. They left us all for dead. We certainly all looked dead."

"So, you just laid there?" Steve asks.

"Yeah," Juanita replies.

I start to ask a question but Juanita cuts me off. "I was surprised he didn't come back to get me, though, because man, they was mad. I think Jones was more scared of all the stuff that he had done. He was the one that was really afraid they was gonna come in there and get him, but he had so brainwashed us that we believed that they was gonna kill us, too."

"Had you made it to one of the planes?" I ask.

"Actually, we were just walking over there," she clarifies. "We were like in a small group, trying to stay by the tall grass and everything, because we kept trying to tell them what was about to happen. But they just told us to get on the plane. They called our names from a list, and I was one of the first ones to get on. People that was in a line still getting on, people on the staircase, all got shot up."

"So Ryan really didn't believe what you were saying?" I ask.

"I think the man was more in shock," Juanita laughs. "He'd gotten in way over his head, you know, 'Try to stay calm and keep your cool,' and everything? He just tried to give off the impression that he still had a grip on it, or control of it, but he should have known," she says soberly. "He didn't have a prayer."

"Did you have any idea at that time what had happened back in Jonestown?" Steve asks.

"Yeah," Juanita answers. "We had practiced it a million times. We knew he was doing it this time."

"How did you know?" I ask.

"He'd already shot us all up!" she shouts.

"So you knew that that would trigger the poison?" Melody asks.

I stop Juanita on this point. "I've heard people say they went through those drills, but they never really thought it was ever going to happen. How did you feel?" I ask.

"I figured he really was gonna do it," Juanita replies, "and one of these times it was gonna be the time. You don't have somebody sit there for hours and hours sharpening cutlasses, teaching us all how to practice cutting our heads off and all this. It's too bizarre. It was just way too bizarre. You knew sooner or later he was gonna snap." She pauses. "I thought there was dead bodies buried all over the place in Jonestown. People he'd killed that he got mad at. You either worked the day shift or you worked the night shift. They kept rotating everything so you couldn't keep up with anything. We were turning into zombies. We were starving to death. Everybody was just so sickly, losing so much weight, eaten up with all kinds of rashes and everything. You more or less started doing just whatever you were told."

"Didn't really think for yourself after a certain point?" I prompt.

"No," Juanita answers. "He would do this ritual thing every night where he would like read a newspaper or something and then make you memorize it and then give everybody tests. And if you couldn't pass the test, then it was back to the work crew, the chain gang. I don't know how anybody could retain anything because of the way he kept it up, but that was a part of his brainwashing thing to make you crazy."

"What did you think when you'd found out what had happened in Jonestown?" Steve asks.

Juanita seems resigned, almost depressed at this question. "I don't think you really had a will to survive anymore," she acknowledges. "The real reason we really left was to get even with Jones because we knew it'd piss him off. We didn't think we were gonna live. We had no idea that we were gonna live at all; we did it just to piss him off."

"You didn't know when you escaped that you were already pregnant? Is that right?" Steve asks.

She nods. "I didn't know until I was about five or six months pregnant. I couldn't figure out why I couldn't stop throwing up, and the doctor . . ." Her voice trails off and Melody finishes the thought.

"I remember you told me you were just so totally traumatized you couldn't notice what was happening even to your own body after that."

"I think the doctor's the one that suggested to me, 'Are you pregnant?'" Juanita explains. "It never even dawned on me."

"Did you have a place to stay when you came back?" I ask.

"My father's relatives had sent for us," she recounts. "They had sent us plane tickets to come home. We stayed with them when we first came back for about two or three years after Jonestown."

"What did you do after you came back?" Steve asks.

"I was in San Francisco. Just started my life over again. I tried to put Jonestown behind me, have my kid, you know. Got this good-paying job working for the Teamsters. It was fine till the government tried to subpoena us to make us go back to Guyana. They go in and tell my boss that I was part of Jonestown, that they want to take me back to South America to testify. I come into work that day, there was nobody in the whole office. The whole office is empty, with a note on my screen: 'Your services are no longer needed.' My job has been terminated. I was fired. Just like that. When I called my boss to ask him why, he told me, 'Please don't call again.' See, I was from Jonestown, 'Those people are crazy,' he said. 'It might not be a safe environment for the rest of the employees.'"

"But you'd already had the kid then?" Steve asks.

"Yeah, I already had Boo by then. He was about a year old."

"Boo is your son Chad?" I ask.

"Yeah, that's right," she says.

"And Boo Bear is your six-year-old?"

"Yeah, I guess I confused you with that. Boo and Boo Bear."

"I have it straight now," I say. "Go on."

"I had gone to school to be a keypunch operator. Control Data Institute. I had graduated that course, got me a good-paying job, got me my first apartment. I lost it all just like that! Start over again."

"Some people we've talked to say having a kid helped them relate to new life," Steve continues. "How was it for you?"

"That's what really changed my life," Juanita agrees. "Because I was pregnant, I had to change my life. I had something to live for now, I had somebody to care for and some reason for being. I just didn't let it play over and over in my mind what had happened or be depressed, because I had to build a life. I think that's what let me pass away from it more than other people." She pauses.

"I still mourn them, terribly," she confides. "And it does keep a certain part of me depressed still, but at the same time, I had to move on. I needed to get a job. I needed to find a place for us to live. I don't know. Maybe having my son did help. He was such a cute kid, too."

She pauses again.

"A lot of people lost their kids there," she explains. "They were still alive but their children were dead. It would be hard to have another child after you just let all your kids get killed. I came out pregnant. I didn't lose my child there. If I hadn't already been pregnant, I probably wouldn't have had any kids. You get this feeling of being a failure after that happened to you, after the brainwashing is done, you think, 'How did I let that happen to me?' You lose a lot of your self-esteem."

"But it wasn't your fault," Steve says. "Your parents joined."

"Well," Juanita sighs, "a lot of people blamed me: 'Why didn't you grab my children, why didn't you do this, why didn't you do that?' I was just a kid, why didn't *you* do it?! But it's easier to blame somebody else. Quite naturally, hindsight is better than foresight, or however it's said. I felt like a failure when I came back. You think you could have done something different."

After a long silence, Juanita continues. "Years later, I had like a breakdown, I guess you would call it. My memory started coming back. That's when I realized what had really happened. But at the time, I couldn't remember."

"How have you talked to your children about Jonestown?" I ask.

"Oprah Winfrey did a show on it once," she explains, "and that's how my kids found out. I never talked to them about it. Like now, my six-year-old doesn't know, but sooner or later something will come up where he'll be old enough to understand, and then he'll know. I don't think DJ knows either, my ten-year-old. I just think the two older boys know."

"So you have four kids altogether?"

"Yeah, four sons." Juanita smiles.

"You remember how Chad first found out?" Steve asks.

"Probably when I had my breakdown," she replies. "I think he was about eight years old."

"Because you were just in so much pain at that time?" I ask.

"I don't remember at all what happened," Juanita admits. "I have no idea. Alls I know is I just started screaming and banging my head on the walls, and I could not stop. I just couldn't stop."

"Before then, everything had seemed to be getting put back together?" I ask.

She shakes her head. "I had blocked it out of my mind completely. I just went on with my life. I never associated with anybody from Jonestown or even with my parents. I just went my own way and I just kept going. But for some reason, one day it just all came flooding back."

"What happened when it all came flooding back?"

"They put me on these pills," she recounts. "I lasted on them for probably one or two doses. It slowed me down a whole lot, and I ended up flushing the pills down the toilet. Once I got my grip back, I was okay. I would just work on blocking it out again.

"Happened to me a little while ago, too, when that stuff first happened with Boo and his trial. I had to get back on some pills again."

Juanita brings up the subject of her son Chad's murder trial. There are some pictures on the walls of the living room. She stands up and goes to them.

"I got a picture of all the boys," she says as she points to each one of her sons. "Those are old pictures. That's too long ago. They don't look like that anymore."

"Chad has grown up in that jail," Melody explains. "He looks like a man now."

Juanita points to a group photo, a portrait taken in a studio. The background is of palm trees. "That's my four kids," she smiles. "We told everybody we went to the Bahamas."

"We're gonna show this one in court," Melody adds. "He is very, very sweet to his brothers, such a nice big brother."

"He is," Juanita agrees. "He was." She notices that she's using both the present and the past tense and opts for the present. "He is a good kid," she says.

"You guys care if I smoke a cigarette? I'll stand over here by the door."

"What happened to Chad?" I ask.

"Melody probably knows better than I do," she admits. "I don't know at all. It's more than I can handle. I think I'm a strong person. I know I pray to God every now and then, and I always pull myself back together. But it's not easy. When we went to court, the cops took up the whole courtroom so none of us could come in, and then they tried to throw us out."

"They had a big police presence at every hearing," Melody explains. "They have the widow. And they've already named an overpass on the freeway for the officer. By all accounts, he was a really nice officer."

"I still don't believe Boo did it," Juanita growls.

"What's it gonna be like for you when this trial comes up and Jonestown is brought into the trial?" I ask.

"They're gonna bring that into it?!" Juanita says, surprised.

"It'll be a limited part of it," Melody tries to soothe her. "It's a significant fact about Chad's life that both you and the man who you thought was his father were survivors of it in different ways. So we'll talk about that a little bit, what that's like, how hard it is, and some of the effects on you."

Juanita finishes her cigarette and turns to Melody. "I was wondering, do you think it really did affect my kids?"

Melody pauses to think about her answer.

"I think the fact that it was hard for you, Juanita, that once in a while the horror of it would come over you, at times it was hard for you to cope. There was a certain amount of instability because of it. I think it's very wise of you to think about how to tell DJ and Boo Bear, because once they realize, they need to understand it as best they can.

"But I think we also have to acknowledge," Melody continues, "nobody can say Chad's in the trouble he's in because of Jim Jones. That's just too simple. There were a lot of other effects on him, growing up in the neighborhood out there, getting in with the kids, you know, the police brutality."

"I try so hard to teach them that no matter what anybody tells you, you figure it out on your own," Juanita tells her friend. "You've got to dig deeper, always dig deeper, and make sure that you know what somebody is telling you is a good idea. I'm wondering if in a way, I put that in 'em too much. All my kids are really strong willed. It's not easy to break 'em down."

Juanita sits very still for a long time, but she has one more thing to say. "Everybody in Jonestown was really nice, sweet people. They were really beautiful people, and they don't know how they ended up in that. I went through a big head trip about it because loving everybody so much, right? To see how we were so badly abused. You didn't even realize you were being abused while it was happening to you—or I should say— while we all participated in it. Because we all did. I took turns going up there and beating people up, too. People took turns beating me up. It wasn't anything personal. And a lot of that is hard to live with, but you got to just accept it.

"We all participated in it," she repeats, "every last one of us. That's why none of us are any more guilty than anybody else. We're all equally just as guilty. We could easily have been standing there, as been standing here. I think that's the one reason why it's so hard to hate anybody, no matter what side you're on."

Juanita has told us many things that we've never heard before, and we tell her so.

"I figured all the stories would be basically about the same."

≈ ≈ ≈

Steve and I are back in the car with our piles of documents along with the Flavor Aid packets. "It's not even Kool-Aid," I say. "No, but this is interesting," Steve says as he holds up the plastic bag with the packets.

The Flavor Aid packets are purple with a cartoon-looking graphic on the front of a boy and a girl smiling as they enjoy their drink. I begin a catalog in my mind of all the archival material we have been handed so far by the interviewees—the photos of Jim Jones from Stephan, files from Melody's storage unit, the Moore family letters, the packets of Flavor Aid—and we haven't even scratched the surface of what remains of the history of Peoples Temple. Melody has also preserved a collection of clothing buttons in a coffee can. These were the buttons that popped off the clothes of the people who died in Jonestown as their bodies bloated in the jungle sun.

My mind flashes on an image of Juanita standing by her screen door smoking a cigarette. She was sober the day we spoke and incredibly lucid. *Where is her healing?* I say to Steve. *Where is her second chance?*

Sole Survivor

....

CORCORAN STATE PRISON
CORCORAN, CALIFORNIA

MELODY IS DETERMINED for us to meet Michael Briggs, who is among the children of Jonestown serving life in prison. Michael's foster mother died in Jonestown, along with his biological siblings—Tony Linton and Donna Briggs—who were fostered together.

"He was just kind of left behind," Melody says. "He's serving life without parole. He was sexually abused by Jim Jones and kicked out of the Temple. I think he would probably talk to you. I haven't seen him for many years. I don't know how many years, maybe five. I have thirty-four former clients on death row, and many more than that in prison, so I don't write to them all. Sometimes I hear from some of them."

She lays the groundwork for us by visiting Michael and telling him about our project. He agrees to put us on his visitors' list. My collaborator Margo Hall exchanges letters with him to work out the details, a process that takes several months. Eventually, our visitors' status is approved. Margo and I make the scenic-barren drive south to Corcoran State Prison, a complex of more than twenty institutional buildings, including a hospital and a factory, with three different levels of prison security—from minimum to maximum—for upwards of five thousand inmates.

We follow all of the directions for visiting the prison—we have our plastic baggie full of quarters to buy Cokes or toiletries for Michael from the vending machines, all our paperwork in order—but we don't know one of the tips to have a chance of actually getting inside. People line up as early as 5 A.M. to get on the daily visitors' list. When we get to Corcoran

Prison, the parking lot is packed, and the visiting line is out the door. We wait for several hours but along with many other families are eventually turned away.

Michael is disappointed when he hears that we came down and did not get in to see him. We try again a second time—getting there significantly earlier—with the same result. We decide corresponding might be better. I send him some questions, and he sends me an eleven-page, handwritten letter on yellow legal paper. He writes in print with big bubble letters, and a small open circle above every lowercase *i*. This is from the letter as Michael wrote it to me:

I hope this letter finds you well in health and in spirit.

Thank you for your consideration in allowing me to participate in your project. The memories are still painful. Yes, even after twenty some odd years. I don't think I will ever be able to put it behind me. Even though the hate has diminished. I am still haunted by the pain, even still I awake some mornings, feeling like a stranger not only to my surroundings, but myself as well, as if I am the sole survivor of a world devoid of life. Where your own voice seems so loud due to the silence of those lost, you cease to speak.

Forgive my ramblings, and bear with me through my bad penmanship and sarcasm.

My first encounter with the Temple was in 1970, when Jim Jones was introduced at the church my foster family attended (Mount Zion Baptist Church). It was on a Saturday, and after the service, those of the Mt. Zion community housed for the night those of the Temple. The following day the Rev. Jones put on a grand performance of his healing powers, using the knowledge gained from those who had been sheltered the night before. He knew the names of family and friends, pets, and objects within the homes. I remember him calling the names of Georgia Lacy, my then–foster mother. Oh, but the highlight of his display was the regurgitation of cancer by some unknown individual in the congregation. It's funny in a way, looking back on this, because the smell of rotting chicken innards is enough to bring tears to your eyes. At the least, to turn away, yet after the service all I could hear was, "I seen it with my own eyes." You know I once thought that Jones turned bad through drugs. Not true. Looking back, his intent was to deceive all along!

I was nine years old I think, my foster mother became very active within a year. Selling the home in San Francisco and separating with her husband within two years to be closer to the Temple. In 1975 I was removed from the Temple, and returned to San Francisco to be placed in a group home. This order was given by Jones himself due to my disruptive behavior, and curiosity towards everything outside Temple events. In 1977 after my release from Napa State Hospital I returned to the foster home and the Temple. The foster home was the only home I had ever known. And my brother Tony and sister Donna still resided with Mrs. Lacy.

With the Temple, there was a lot of traveling. The long hours on a hot bus, state to state, meeting after meeting. Yes, meetings are what I remember most. In Redwood Valley, the number of meetings began to increase to seven days a week, and last from about 4:00 pm to 4:00 am. Every night. It seemed as if he'd never shut up. He took control over every aspect of one's life.

I lived in a foster home the majority of my life. I was lucky to have been placed with my younger brother and sister. However, I did spend time with the Bogue family while in Redwood Valley. A time I remember fondly with my best friend, riding bikes, and spending summers at the lake. I love the openness of rural living.

Mainly I remember the loss of my brother and sister. But on another note, I was going through puberty, so I remember my friend Tina, and Lawanda, and the games boys and girls play.

As for Jim and Marceline Jones, they were looked upon as royalty, but upon my return in 1977 that love that was shown them before, now seemed automated. Fear and paranoia seemed to have infested the youth, at least the youth that was not a part of the Jim Jr. and Stephan Jones circuit. The congregation appeared tired, beaten down, confused, suspicious of one another, yet the smiles remained firmly painted on their faces.

I left the Temple the second and final time in 1977, just months after returning. This came about when Chris Lewis threatened me with violence for refusing to pass out Temple pamphlets. He came into my bedroom. After a brief scuffle I realized I had to leave. I didn't want to leave my brother and sister, we had become very close, it seems closer than ever. Yet I had to leave. I lived in the streets for a few weeks and then landed one afternoon on my grandmother's doorstep, and lived with her for several years.

I had some friends at the Temple, not a lot. But good ones. I don't think I was capable of love then, but if I were to have loved someone, I would say Thomas Bogue. He was like a brother. I was so happy he survived Jonestown.

I survived the best I could with the limited knowledge I had. Mrs. Lacy never prepared me for adulthood like her adopted son Phillip Lacy. After all, I was just a foster child, a pay-check!

My grandmother did the best she could with the grandson who had been damaged by years of sexual and psychological abuse. It pained her to see what had become of me. Yet she never wavered. I could always count on her. Though I know I broke her heart again and again. I once remember my grandmother striking a Temple sentry, and six or seven other Temple sentries blocking the entrance after her demands to see her grandchildren were refused due to Mrs. Lacy denying her home visitation. She had the heart of a lion, in such a small frame.

I learned of the events on November 18th on *ABC News,* when my grandmother called me into her room to help her check the list of the names streaming down the broadcast. I will never forget the look in her face, such a pretty lady at her age suddenly seemed old, and tired, void of color. Even her two poodles seemed near death as time stood still, as a name we both did not want to see appeared on the T.V. screen. You ask about what legacy if any they may have left.

For this question I am at a loss for words.

I will end this letter saying this. I believe in my heart that the majority of people in Jonestown deserved much better than to die in some jungle at the hands of a mad man!

This letter is for Tony Linton, and Donna Briggs. Until we meet again.
Sincerely,
Michael Briggs

Hundreds of Kids

....

THE INTERVIEWS WITH MELODY AND JUANITA and the letter from Michael have added a new dimension to the story: the next generation of Jonestown survivors. My next interview is with Phil Tracy, a former reporter involved in the story early on, who is familiar with the foster kids in the Temple.

In August 1977, fifteen months before the deaths in Jonestown, *New West* magazine published an exposé of Peoples Temple written by Phil Tracy and Marshall Kilduff. The cover story, "Inside Peoples Temple," included the tagline, "Jim Jones is one of the state's most politically potent leaders. But who is he? And what's going on behind his church's locked doors?" Within three months, there was a mass exodus of about seven hundred Peoples Temple members from Los Angeles, Ukiah, and San Francisco to Jonestown, Guyana, in the South American jungle. The article was not the only thing that precipitated the mass move to Jonestown. But in Phil's mind the two events were inextricably linked.

≈ ≈ ≈

I pick up Phil Tracy in a beige-colored Ford Escort I've borrowed. Dating from the early '90s, it has no power steering, no power brakes, no air conditioning, and only an AM radio. Phil doesn't care; he doesn't drive. As a true urbanite, when someone with a car is giving you a ride, you only care that it has wheels, not if it has power windows.

When I pull up at his apartment in San Francisco's Bernal Heights district, he is just coming out the side door, his rumpled shirt half-tucked into his worn khakis, carrying a bag of trash in one hand and an over-stuffed legal-sized envelope for me in the other. The envelope is so full its sides are splitting open, the tips of newspaper clippings sticking out. The only organizing principle of those clippings in that ratty envelope that I could see is simply that each and every one of them be kept together.

Phil walks down the stairs, secures the envelope more tightly under his arm, takes the lid off one of the cans, and jams the bag in. It is a simple act: putting out the garbage. Yet when I watch him doing it, it is like watching a man beat back a devil.

He jumps in the car before I have a chance to get out and properly greet him.

"Hi," he says.

"Hi," I reply. We shake hands awkwardly from our respective bucket seats. He looks through the passenger window back toward his apartment, a bizarre expression on his face. He and this borrowed car are a perfect fit, I decide.

Phil Tracy has been a reporter in the classic sense: a working-class, no-frills man of the people, with a little *All the President's Men* thrown in. He had described himself once as a "journalist from the time when journalism was an honorable profession," and I could see him very clearly as a poster child for "the way things used to be."

"Go straight, take a left at that light," Phil gestures anxiously. He wants to get us where we are going, but faster. "Go," he directs impatiently, "drive that way." I do my best. Unfortunately, it isn't easy to drive this car. It is hard to steer, hard to turn, and even harder to stop. His anxiety is contagious.

Phil and I head toward Third Street in Bernal Heights. He wants to go to a bar—"I need a drink," he says—but I didn't know of any, so I let him decide where we'd go. We park the car around the corner on Cortland. Phil checks the signs to make sure we don't get towed. We cross the street.

I am suddenly aware of what an odd pair Phil and I make. He is still clutching the overstuffed envelope. I am carrying a notebook and a Radio Shack handheld tape recorder in my backpack with a couple of ninety-minute tapes, a playwright twenty years Phil's junior, trying to act the journalist now looking for the story. I imagine he's taking us to a standard neighborhood bar: a quiet, dark, slightly depressed place, with no music, maybe a TV, where all the rest of the old guys like Phil hang out.

Instead, he takes us to a place called The Ramp. It is bustling with college-aged kids. When he opens the door, the noise from inside the bar spills onto the street as if it were liquid, alive.

"Maybe this will be too loud," Phil shouts.

"No, it should be okay," I shout back.

He ushers me through the door, then walks straight to the bar while I look around for a table. I spy a tall round one with two tall stools next to a pillar. I sit down, take my tape recorder out of my bag. Phil returns with a scotch and water for him and a Coke for me. "Is it okay if I tape this?" I ask.

The music is way too loud. Phil is practically yelling, but even so, his words are garbled. He seems out of breath, like he doesn't have big enough lungs to project over the music, even across this tiny table. I slide the tape recorder closer to him. I, too, lean in so that I can distinguish his voice from the rest. I press "record" and hope for the best.

"I can only tell you that part which I know, okay?" he answers evenly.

He takes a sip of his scotch and jumps right in.

This is Phil Tracy:

"I came to San Francisco in 1970 and moved into a commune. The commune was a political commune in the sense that the people involved had very strong political leanings and very strong political feminist leanings. I eventually got kicked out of that commune," he half-chuckles to himself, "because, well, I had a bad attitude, what can I tell ya?" He lets out a second muffled laugh. "I was not psychologically connected to the people there anyway, except the girlfriend that I had, but she *insisted* she was a lesbian, so that kind of diminished the emotional connection, if you know what I mean. But that's another story." He cracks up.

"My first job in San Francisco was as a column writer for the *National Catholic Reporter*. I was not a reporter at that point. I was not a Catholic, but nonetheless this is what I found myself doing," he says wryly.

"I was being paid $50 a week to do this column. Only because I lived in a commune in San Francisco could I have all my basic needs covered for $30, which gave me $20 to buy dope, which was a fairly large amount of money back then, and I could even get in some ice cream," he barks, then takes another sip of his scotch.

"There was an incredible amount of structure to San Francisco political beliefs at that time, which didn't exist in New York or Chicago. I used to participate in something called the Food Conspiracy—you know, we always used to dress these things up with good names—which was basically a food-buying program where the communes would go to this farmers' market on Alameda and buy quantities of food and then separate it to the individual communes. Now, I'm sure you're familiar with farmers' markets, they're a very common thing today, but in 1970 they were not common at all, and they bore no relationship to the farmers' markets that you have today, which are very boutique and serving individual people. Back then, for example, the minimum they sold in potatoes was a hundred pounds. So you had to have a hell of a lot of people in order to participate. We found a way, by joining these communes together. People would donate their Saturday until three o'clock, and some guy donated a store front that was an artist studio the other six days of the week, and that's how we put it all together."

He's downplaying it, but I can see the pride he still has for those bygone days.

"The same thing was true in terms of day care. I mean, there were a number of children that were produced out of these communes," he laughs, "and people had desires to go places, you know, like Grateful Dead concerts or things like that, and these desires were often very common. So people set up day care centers so that seven or eight people could look after fifteen or twenty kids, which freed forty people to go out and do these kinds of things. That was a very exciting concept to me," he explains.

He looks down at his glass. It is empty.

"I need another drink," he says.

"Okay," I say and put the tape recorder on pause. The next round is on me.

I get the drinks, return to the table.

"The commune stuff connects to Jim Jones," he assures me. "It connects to Jim Jones because when I started studying what Jones was doing, a lot of it was working! I mean, he was feeding six hundred, seven hundred, eight hundred people a night in shifts! And they had access to things that as individual families these poor people never would have had access to. They had whirlpools and sonograms. I'm talking about in the '70s, right? This was not ordinary equipment at that time. So I didn't come into this thing thinking Jones was a freak because he was a collectivist," he acknowledges. "In fact, I thought he was on to something. The collectivist part worked. I thought that worked," he repeats emphatically. "But, nonetheless, I came into it with great suspicion." He takes a hold of his glass and pulls it toward him.

"Economy of scale is an incredible thing," he continues. "What Jones was doing was he was using economy of scale to buttress his economics by connecting into the money that the State of California gave to foster care homes. Jones had a political connection, and he had a track record: they'd been doing this for years. I mean, the state was paying foster care an average of $5 a night for supper, and Jones was feeding them for fifty-five cents, and the difference went into Peoples Temple's coffers. He also had a bunch of old people who were on Social Security and who couldn't probably live very well as individuals because of the rent involved. But if he warehoused them in these homes that he had—where he slept twenty or thirty people, five or six people to a room just on a cot and told them they were doing it all for Jesus—well, he could make a lot of money that way. Social Security became a pretty big, potent part of his income."

He downs his scotch in one gulp. About thirty seconds pass.

"Look, I don't think Jones started out as a bad man," his voice drops to a lower register. "Jim Jones started out as a twenty-five-year-old Disciples of Christ preacher in Indianapolis, Indiana. Let me tell you, I was in Indianapolis, Indiana, in 1963 at a civil rights demonstration, and that was the goddamn South! We were heckled and had eggs thrown at us, the whole bit. And Jones set up an integrationist congregation, an extraordinarily brave act for which he was beaten up a couple of times.

"I don't know, it's beyond me to say where it went bad," he adds, then pauses as he rifles through the clippings in his folder. After a few moments, he pulls out an original copy of *Esquire* magazine from 1961.

"Look at this. Maybe this will clue you in."

He holds the magazine up for me to see and begins to read from the cover in a kind of mock singsong reporter's voice. "*Esquire*, the magazine for men. Read our style section, 'The well-appointed wardrobe of President John F. Kennedy.' Or our feature article '9 Places in the World to Hide' by Carolyn Bird." He pauses for emphasis. "Jones moves out to Ukiah based on an article about where to hide from nuclear war in *Esquire* magazine!?! This is not," he laughs, "what I would call the most rational approach to things. Not to mention that in all of northern California there can't be more than two or three different locations in which the temperature regularly hits a hundred degrees in the summertime than Ukiah, California. So, clearly, he didn't have *convenience* in mind."

Phil finishes and in a quick motion smacks the magazine down on the table for dramatic effect.

"I remember, I had an interview with Jones in San Francisco. First, I was given a tour—it was totally staged—and then I was shown into his office. It's a fairly elaborate office with twelve-foot ceilings and stuff like that, and all the blinds are down, which is okay, except the guy's wearing sunglasses, right? And furthermore it's sixty-five degrees. Well, excuse me, lady, but I'd been around a lot, and I'm more than conversant with what speed freaks think are ideal circumstances. And they don't connect with the rest of us. So I knew I had a wooden nickel here right off the bat.

"I just wanted to reassure him and then get the hell out of there. So I proceeded to sit there and assure him, 'I have no desire to exploit factions within the church,' which in point of fact, I did. It was a standard speech. I said, 'But I do have one question,' and he said, 'What's that?' I said, 'Why do you feel compelled to have all these bodyguards here?' Jones said, 'I know that you're not a threat to me, and it's in no way a reflection on you, it's just that they have to be here all the time because of the overall threat.' I said, 'Yeah, that's what I'm getting at? What's the overall threat?' He said, 'Oh, the Ku Klux Klan. The Klan is liable to strike at any time.'" Phil pauses again for emphasis. "In San Francisco!?!" he shouts. "It was totally absurd. The Temple was certainly malignant by the time I found it."

Phil drops his eyes to his empty glass.

"I don't know if you can answer this or not, Phil," I jump in. "But there are lot of people out there who want to explain this event like this: Jones was a cult mastermind, he brainwashed all these people, and he knew from the beginning what he was gonna do. When you met with those people, what did you see in them? How do you explain it?"

He picks up his glass, looks me in the eye.

"I'm a big fan of Xena. People who are a big fan of Xena understand the dark side. People who are a big fan of *Star Wars* understand the dark side, although they understand it somewhat differently from the Xena fans. I think all of us have a dark side, things we could let ourselves get into. Things we could let ourselves do. Sex is the least of it. Being a, you know, a *messiah* is far more appealing than any sex scene you can come up with. Or, even being the trusted assistant of a messiah," he explains.

It is odd how at home Phil looks in The Ramp. I watch his rough hands gently resting on the manila folder full of articles and clippings. I start a second tape.

"Okay, Phil, tell me how it happened. How did the *New West* article come to pass?"

He picks up the manila folder and starts rummaging through its contents again. He pulls out the original *New West* magazine, tangled as it is among the other clippings, and places it on the table between us.

"Marshall Kilduff covered Jim Jones as a *Chronicle* beat for the Housing Authority," Phil explains, "and Kilduff became impressed by the fact that Jones would show up with a bevy of bodyguards and a clique of a hundred people who applauded anytime he said anything. Kilduff did some research and discovered that there had been a couple of articles printed in the *Chronicle*, including one in which the author had been completely intimidated by the Peoples Temple staff. The things that she was writing were being made known to the Temple staff as she was writing them. They were confronting her as she was trying to do the research on her piece."

"Who was that reporter?" I ask.

"Julie Smith. She's a famous detective novelist now. Lives in New Orleans. She was a reporter for the *Chronicle* then. She was assigned to do a story on Jones but got completely stymied and in the end wrote a bouquet piece about the Temple, which she didn't believe for a second! Jones had just been appointed to the Housing Authority in San Francisco by the newly elected mayor, George Moscone. Per Jones's orders, Moscone had hundreds of people from the church at his disposal at a moment's notice, knocking on doors, packing rallies, papering the entire city with posters and flyers. It was zero-cost, total effectiveness. The position at the Housing Authority was Jones's payback." He pauses. Then backtracks.

"By that time, I had come from New York City. I was an investigative reporter, I had done a bunch of things in New York for the *Village Voice*, and so I said, 'Fine, I'll work with Kilduff.' And so we did. We got nowhere at first. I mean, the guy was traveling around with six black bodyguards, everywhere he went. We couldn't find anything out about him."

He reaches into the folder and pulls out some crumpled clippings.

"I was reading this shit today," Phil remarks. "This is really a funny story. The famous break-in at *New West* magazine. See, these people had started calling and writing letters to our advertisers saying we were planning to do a hit piece on Peoples Temple because they were integrationists and on the political left and that we were McCarthyites. You can imagine *New West* magazine, right? They had perfume ads and boutiques—so writing a political screed to somebody who's running a boutique on Union Street is about as hapless as you can get. I mean, the magazine readers would call the office and ask, 'Who's McCarthy?'" he laughs.

"So anyway, the Temple was beating us around. There's this guy, Bill Barnes. He was the guy that turned it for us. Barnes had a column. You'll have to find it," he points to the folder. "It's in here. He had a column in the Saturday *Examiner*. You know, *Saturday Examiner*, right?" He repeats, emphasizing the day this time. "Its readership is like, what, a hundred people? As I said, People at the Temple had run a campaign against us. They'd been calling me up, making threats, a lot of heavy breathing on the telephone, and all that kind of shit, and I walked into the office one morning, and I was looking at the window, and the window, it was jarred, you know. It looked broken. So I went and I looked at my files. Now, I don't know how you are about your files, but me about my files, you ask me how my files are set up, whether they'd been moved or not, I couldn't tell you in a million years! But I had a broken window, and my files looked moved! So I called the cops! Then I called a press conference. I figured if they're gonna fight me, I'm gonna fight them," Phil cries.

"The cops didn't believe it, and in fact they were right," he admits. "What had happened was Jon Carroll, one of my colleagues at the paper, had left his keys in Oakland one morning, and he'd climbed in the window himself. I assumed it was Peoples Temple."

When we met with Jon Carroll, he insists that he didn't break the window.

"Maybe he didn't break the window," Phil says, "but he had climbed in. There was a big boot print on the desk where he did.

"It didn't matter," he goes on. "This proved to be the final straw, and Bill Barnes wrote a column in the *Examiner* on Saturday saying, 'What the hell's going on with Peoples Temple?' Somehow that column got into the hands of all the ex–Temple members who'd been really incredibly intimidated. And they were afraid. They were genuinely afraid, and they were told that the press was in the pocket of Jones! But they started contacting us after Bill wrote his column. And it broke it wide open for us," he exclaims.

"I remember very clearly: we had a Saturday night meeting over in Berkeley with about seven or eight of these former Temple members. They started to tell us what was going on. I didn't want to hear it. I mean, Jones was fucking wives and arranging for the husbands to show up and see it. He was playing psychological games that you only hear about in pornography! He had taken people's houses, he had browbeaten them into selling their homes and giving all the money to the Temple. He had beaten this guy's daughter a hundred times with a paddle!?!" Phil sighs. "But it got me my best line of my life," he admits. "We were riding across the Bay Bridge, Kilduff and I, at the end of the night. He says to me, 'Do you believe 'em?' I said to him, 'What the fuck are you talking about? Will anybody believe us!?!'

"You know, this was such an incredible story, you couldn't believe it. As it was, we left half of it on the table. When you read the story we wrote, we never talked about the sex. We never talked about the drugs.

"That's how this thing got started, you know, were the drugs. This guy was, well, to put it sympathetically, he was a charismatic leader. The problem was that he came to believe that he had to have amphetamine in order to keep the hours he was doing because he was so important for the cause. And the difference between him and most amphetamine addicts is that he had access to hundreds of people, some of whom could write prescriptions. So that he had a steady supply. That's how he became the monster he became. Incredible, you know. He completely lost it. He was abetted by a group of really despicable aides who were not addicted to amphetamines but were addicted to power and to his vision, and they killed themselves. Terrible shit. Anyway, that's how it happened." Phil slams his hands down on the table as he finishes and abruptly starts putting the articles back into the manila envelope.

"So you had these seven or eight defectors in Berkeley, and they all just started telling you everything?" I ask, trying to keep the conversation going.

Phil looks back at me.

"Right," he answers.

He looks back down at his empty glass. He looks back up at me. Silence.

I am not sure what makes him continue, because I do not prompt him, but after a very long pause, he finally decides to start talking again.

"Slowly. It didn't all happen at once, although I mean the sex particularly didn't come out that night. The paddling came out that night. The intimidation of forcing people to give up their homes came out that night. The use of the system, the foster care for supporting the Temple practices came out that night." He pauses again.

"I don't know what else to tell ya, honestly." His voice begins to crack. "They had a number of kids, some of whom were juvenile delinquents and some of whom were simply kids who had the unfortunate circumstance to wind up with mothers who were junkies or fathers who were burglars, and they wound up in the foster care system. It's where I am personally culpable." He pauses.

"I made a couple of phone calls. I could have done a hell of a lot more. And I didn't. I was getting married. I was pursuing my own writing career. They were in Guyana, and I frankly didn't think that the State of California had any sway one way or another once they were gone. But there's no question about it, I let the foster care people slide, and the bastards never, ever addressed it. Never said one bloody word about it. And those foster kids, every one of them died. Every one of them died." He starts running his fingers through the manila envelope again, almost compulsively, but then he stops and sighs.

"It was a story of a lifetime and yet a failure of a lifetime, in a way, really," he says in a thick voice as his eyes well up with tears. "See, I sort of had this film in my head what was gonna happen with this story. I was gonna publish the piece, and the other journalists and other news outlets were gonna start asking the questions, and connecting the dots, and they were gonna find out I was right!"

He slams his fist down on the table again.

"And then they were gonna find out the stuff that I hadn't written!

About the sex and the drugs. But Jim pulled them out of San Francisco before that could happen," he explains.

"I didn't know how rich they were! Or that they could float seven hundred or eight hundred plane tickets at the drop of a hat, which they did. I mean, one day three weeks after we published the story, we went over there and they were gone. And then there was no getting them back."

"What did you think after November 18?" I say. "You talked about a film in your head . . ."

"Well, I felt pretty poor," he interrupts. "I don't know. I mean, you try and keep perspective, right? I mean, these sons of bitches came at me several ways, attempting to dissuade me from publishing this story, every way they knew how. And I beat 'em. I got it out! Marshall and I got it out. The people of this city had a right to know who this guy was and to arm themselves as a result, so that it wouldn't happen to them. I mean, what was I gonna do? Hurl myself in front of the airplane and say, 'No, don't take off!'

"But I'll tell you this," he is intense now, "in your life, you never want to get involved in a story in which you have a significant role in which hundreds of kids die, because you're never gonna feel good about it. And that's what happened. I didn't feel good about it all.

"Eventually, I stopped writing. I'd be a fool and a liar if I said that this wasn't part of it. I had an image of myself, and I could no longer square that image. I hadn't done everything that I could do. I hadn't done really much of anything except write the story." He glances down at the manila envelope, nods his head in its direction.

"I was reading a story on Reverend John Moore today. In the summer of '78, I was preparing a piece based on the conversation I had with a woman named Debby Layton, who had basically bolted from the Temple after she was already in Guyana for a period of time. She came back with stories about White Nights and what was going on, the kind of almost slave labor conditions that had taken place down there. I started writing a story about that.

"And then this Reverend Moore held a press conference in San Francisco. He had a couple of daughters down there."

"I met with Reverend Moore—John Moore—and his wife, Barbara," I say.

"Good for you," Phil replies. "Maybe he told you about his press conference. He extolled the marvelous egalitarian instincts that were being portrayed in Jonestown. How it was a paradise of freedom and hard work!

"Suddenly, I was in a jam. Either I could write the piece that put myself at tremendous risk for libel if I didn't put in what this other guy had said. If I did, then I was gonna wind up with one of these bullshit on-the-one-hand-on-the-other-hand kind of stories. I had no fucking interest in writing that. So in the end my editor said, 'Well, what could you do?' I said, 'The only thing I could do is go down to Guyana. And I ain't gonna do that.' He said, 'Why not?' I said, 'Because they'll kill me.' And I wasn't kidding. I was certain they would kill me.

"I don't know if I had known about Congressman Ryan and his crowd, whether I'd a gone along. Probably not, at that point I was trying to score screenplays, but it would've given me a thought."

He pauses.

"But when the news started coming through on that Saturday night, I felt like the world's worst failure. I had tried to do something to change these people's lives, and they'd all wound up dying. That's what you have. It never changed."

"Your feelings never changed, Phil?"

"No," he answers plainly. "I mean, I started writing again, I've done other things. I moved on. But I think if you have a sting like that and you're that close to it, I don't know. I suppose there are people who can separate themselves from the thing, but I couldn't."

Things are relatively quiet at the table after that. I ask a few more questions and he gives me short, nonexpansive answers, and soon the tape clicks off. The interview is over.

I put the tape recorder in my bag. The bar has cleared out significantly. We are quiet as we head back to the car. In our silence I feel that empty finality Phil had spoken of.

≈ ≈ ≈

Phil and Marshall's exposé in *New West* magazine was among the first hard-hitting negative articles written about Jim Jones in the Bay Area.

Prior to the publication of the *New West* article, Jones made sure only puff pieces—articles praising the church and its work—were ever written about Peoples Temple. His control of the press showed its first crack in 1972, when Lester Kinsolving—who was an Episcopal priest as well as the *Examiner* religion reporter—began to question the church in Ukiah.

Kinsolving had written an eight-part series of articles on Peoples Temple to run over the course of a week, from Sunday to Sunday. The first, titled "The Prophet Who Raises the Dead," expressed great skepticism of Jones's healing ministry and openly challenged him in the press. Only three articles ever made it to print, however, and according to Kinsolving, Jones was the one responsible for thwarting the rest of the series. Aside from the truncated Kinsolving series, there is not a single negative article about Jones or Peoples Temple between 1972 and 1976 that has ever turned up. Quite the contrary, Jones was praised at every turn, celebrated as a hero for blacks and the working poor. He was even named Humanitarian of the Year by one Los Angeles magazine. Jones called 1976 his "Year of Ascendancy." So when the *New West* article broke, it seemed to reveal a chink in his armor. Maybe he felt that his position in the power elite of San Francisco had diminished, and that the period of ascendancy had shifted to his opponents.

≈ ≈ ≈

Within weeks after the Jonestown tragedy, Marshall Kilduff wrote a book about Peoples Temple. He is now an editor at the *San Francisco Chronicle*. But not Phil. His writing career took a real hit. I drive him back to his apartment. He hands me the manila envelope. "Here," he says. "Keep this until you're done with the thing." I get out of the car, and we shake hands warmly, and he heads inside. In the rear view mirror I watch him walk up the stairs to his apartment. I pull the recorder out of my bag, rewind the tape slightly, and press "play." The music is loud, but I can hear every word. I label the tape, "Phil Tracy Interview: June 14, 2002" and put it in my bag.

This Is Big

....

FEBRUARY 1, 2004
NEW ORLEANS, LOUISIANA

AT PHIL'S ENCOURAGEMENT, I e-mail former reporter Julie Smith and speak to her on the phone. Phil was right: she is a famous detective novelist living in New Orleans now, but she has a more pointed view of what happened. "I found my reporter's notebooks, which I will send to you," she explains. I replay what Phil told me about her being stymied, but Julie is sensitive about the subject. She does not want to be portrayed as having been duped. She was a serious reporter at the time, and she wants me to know it. This was a story—an event—that still shakes her to think about, and she wants me to know that as well. "I figure by now you're about half-shrink—pretty unfazed by people's dramas," she tells me.

This is Julie Smith:

"I was sitting at my desk at the *Chronicle,* and the assignment editor says, 'Ms. Smith, we have a new Housing Commissioner, and it looks as if he can heal the sick, and possibly even raise the dead—would you be interested?' And I went, 'Wow. That's just my kind of thing. How very San Francisco.' I didn't know how I was going to write this, but I knew that I wanted to write about faith healing on the part of a city official."

Not knowing where this assignment would lead, she began to research. She soon found herself being spied on and intimidated by Temple staff, which many former Temple members confirmed were common practices in the Temple by then.

"So I make a phone call and say, 'Can I interview you?' Jones says, 'I want to get back to you.' And the next day, floods of letters began pouring into the newsroom, before I ever even got another phone call. And I said to Steve Gavin, the city editor, 'Something is funny.' And Gavin said, 'Well, let's just see what you get. Call around and see.'

"So I called Bob Mendelsohn. Supervisor Robert Mendelsohn. I said, 'What's the deal, Bob? Every time I make a move, ten people call the *Chronicle* and say how great Jones is. What's it all about? What's his significance to politics in the city?' And Bob says, 'Listen, Julie, Jones can mobilize five thousand people out on the streets for any cause—any candidate. If you're a politician, this is a powerful thing. And if he's against something, he can do something about that, too. Everybody loves Jones. This is a guy who gets things done.'"

Julie recounts what happened next. "Five minutes after I hung up— you know, no time at all elapses—Bob Mendelsohn calls me back and says, 'You know, Julie, maybe you shouldn't quote me on that.' So I asked him, 'Well, why not?' He says, 'I don't know, it may not be a good thing.' And that kind of thing had happened a lot. It was like everybody you called, somehow in ten minutes you were getting a call from the church about it.

"What happened was, I was heavy into indoor plants at the time—I had an awful lot of plants—and I'd be in mud up to my elbows, and the phone would ring, and it would be Jones. His timing was impeccable. I'm convinced they were spying on me. And he would say, 'Julie, I'm so worried, I'm afraid you're gonna say something terrible about us, and it's so important to our people, we do so much for them, and there could be a backlash for them.'"

"What would be the backlash? What did they mean?" I interject.

"Don't ask. It was just paranoia. I finally got to go to the church. But before the service they were showing me around, and I was taken to a tiny little room with no windows in it, and it was full of hanging plants. Well, why would you have a little room like that with plants and no windows? It didn't make sense. There was nothing in the room except a massage table. And all of sudden, all the people had all melted away, and I was in the tiny room with Jones by himself, and he said to me, 'You know, my wife has back trouble and I can't really have sex with her.' What is going on here!?!

"I don't know if he was so insane, he was trying to imagine that I would suddenly say, 'Whoa, Jim baby, come to me right now' or what! I got out of there. Nothing happened.

"There was minor faith healing in the service that day, and I wrote the story. And Gavin would turn it back to me and he would say, 'Well, can't we make this a little more objective?' 'What do you mean "a little more objective"?' I asked. Well, he sent it back to me six or seven times! And Jones was calling me every five minutes saying, 'Well, I've heard that you had to rewrite. I heard that it was a hatchet job.'"

Julie thought the final draft of her story was too soft, but it did conclude with two things that she felt were substantive, or, as she describes it, "two things in it that kept it from being a total poem to Jim Jones. A question: what is his importance to politics in this city? And some stuff about the faith healing." She sent the article to press, went home, and went to bed. She describes what happened next:

"Here's the kicker for me: when I woke up the following morning and saw that story—neither of those things was there. And I said, 'This is big!'"

To this day, Julie does not know who trimmed the quotes, though she scoured the paper afterward trying to find out. Somebody—either Gavin or someone higher up—just wasn't going to let it happen.

She adds a footnote a few months later by e-mail:

"We underestimated Jones. He didn't really think like an adult. I mean, he called the mayor's office at 2 A.M. Where was everybody's judgment? I think a lot of people just thought he was a well-intentioned bozo, but, for the record, I never for an instant thought he was well intentioned. Bozo, yes. But from the first moment, he scared the hell out of me. When Jones finally agreed to meet me—maybe I didn't tell you this part—he was sitting on a throne, surrounded by about ten of his followers. When he stood, the rest of them stood, as if at a prearranged signal. Swear to God, the hair on the back of my neck prickled, something that usually happens only when I see a spider. *That's* the point at which I thought, 'Something really wrong is going on here.' It was an amazing, scary thing to see."

That story didn't make it into her article either.

Waylaid

AUGUST 28, 2002
DETROIT, MICHIGAN

MY COLLABORATOR MARGO HALL calls with good news. Her childhood friend Rod Hicks is willing to be interviewed. Their families were
close, both fathers being well-known musicians in the Detroit area. The
Hicks family lost two of their own in Jonestown—Marthea and Shirley—
both musicians themselves.

Rod Hicks was their brother, nearing sixty, with a smooth, deep
voice, the epitome of cool. He is a bass player, a trombonist, and a poet.

I didn't meet Rod and only know him and his story through the interview Margo recorded with him. Yet so much of a person's story can be
found in their voice and in their words: their intonations and inflection,
their pauses. In Rod's case, I could hear it in the long drags he takes from
his cigarette and in the musicality of his speech. Margo's connection with
the Hicks family was the main reason she wanted to work on a play about
Jonestown. We are all keenly aware that she is the sole black collaborator
on the project, and none is more aware than Margo herself.

She is in Detroit for a visit so she is able to sit down with Rod. He and
his sisters were three in a church-going family of thirteen children. Like
Rod, Shirley Hicks had been a bass player, too. His older sister Marthea
was "full of talent." Rod speaks about both his sisters with tenderness and
a hint of mourning. He says of Marthea that "she was truly my hero, she
always was," and of Shirley that "she was almost my twin."

This is Rod Hicks:
"When Reverend Jones came to Detroit, he was speaking up at
Woodward. I was just a little guy. He came to my house and hung out

with Daddy, and then they all went to church that night. My father was truly impressed with the man. The next day he told me about how marvelous it was. He came back saying he's a powerful man, he healed some people. And my father was nobody's dummy." He pauses and laughs.

"He really admired the man. Jim Jones came in and sat down in his house and they talked. My daddy has been around all kinds of trickery people, all kinds of cats, cats pull rabbits out of the hat and all that. My old man is quite an intelligent man for his age, college guy at a time when black folks wasn't going to college. He was blessed to be able to do that and have some sense. I trusted and believed in my father. When he gave the man the okay, I'm figuring, 'It's cool.'"

· "Right," Margo says.

"It wasn't as much going to a different church, it was more like going to try something new. It was like an adventure, you know what I mean? An adventure. 'Okay, the cat is cool, y'all go ahead, be careful.' If they were going to run away with a rock-and-roll band or something, it would be a different thing," Rod laughs, "but to run off with the preacher, and the preacher's cool? You know how much love he had for his first-born daughter, and you know how a man is about his baby girl, he'll kill a brick, you know. So he accepted it, because he accepted their will, something they wanted to do. 'Go ahead, girls, and God bless you.'" He takes a drag off his cigarette.

"Later on they were living in San Francisco. I was living in Los Angeles, and they came to my house before they left for Jonestown. This was the first time I heard any kind of negative vibes. It seemed to be some kind of trouble in the brew, but that's why Reverend Jones was looking to leave the country. So they came to my house, and they explained to me that they was going, that Reverend Jones had found this property in Guyana, and that they were going to go with him.

"Marthea was saying, 'If I write to you, you'll have to read between the lines,' because there was a possibility that their mail would be looked at by the FBI, or the CIA, or somebody. She let me know that something was awry, afoot, you know. But they were genuinely happy. They were going to Paradise, baby, you know what I mean? This is going to be it."

Shirley had a son named Romaldo, and Marthea had a son named Anthony. When they were kids, Margo would hang out with them.

"They were there, too," Rod explains. "Romaldo played drums, and he was good, too, he could *play*. At nine years old he was hittin' 'em, you know. And Anthony, Anthony would always try to keep up with Romaldo," he laughs. "They were the same age, they was like brothers, you know."

He pauses, lets his thoughts wander along a few moments.

"My sisters wrote to me from Jonestown and told me how nice things were: how the plants and the vegetables were big, everything just seems to grow so well there and how harmonious it was. They sent me some newspaper clippings saying that it was like the Garden of Eden over there: different types of people, and all ages, and schoolteachers, and lawyers, and doctors, and all kinds of professional people over there. It was like a glimpse of how our society could really be. I was really happy about it, you know, and I was making preparations to go to see them."

≈ ≈ ≈

In the archive at the California Historical Society there is a transcript of an audiotape recording of Rod's sister Marthea making a statement against the U.S. government. These were standard speeches once the people got to Jonestown: reviling the government, swearing allegiance to Jones and to each other, promising never to go back to the States, and vowing to commit revolutionary suicide if necessary. As coined by Black Panther Party cofounder Huey P. Newton in the 1960s, the term *revolutionary suicide* reflected his belief that the system has only one response to revolutionary struggle, and that is to crush it and everyone involved. It was one of several phrases of revolutionary rhetoric that Jones adopted—and adapted—for his own use.

Marthea's statement read:

My name is Marthea Hicks and I refuse to live in a world full of confusion. I refuse to see my child in a school filled with police and reading books he will never understand and things that will never do him any good. I refuse to watch children take pills everyday at twelve o'clock noon just to settle them down. I refuse to smell the stench of goddamned ghetto. I refuse to live in this type of society one more day. When I came to Peoples Temple, I found the right way. And the damned society won't let us do what we want to do. And they have followed us all the way over here to Guyana to destroy our lives. So tonight we say—and I say—just damn the whole thing and I will just commit suicide tonight—revolutionary suicide.

Margo tells Rod about the statement, how it ended with the words "revolutionary suicide." Rod pauses for a long time.

"When I heard about all of this trauma that had went down," he sighs, "it was really unbelievable. I just could not believe that my sisters could do something like that—kill themselves, you know—because of the way we were raised. I just couldn't believe that could happen. It was a very strange time, because there were so many things that we didn't know, so much spooky stuff going on.

"And when the deal went down, they sent a body here, with my sister Marthea's identification. I went down to view the body. They sent the body in a bag. We had it sent to Swanson's Funeral Home, who was a close friend of my father. So I went down, put on these clothes and stuff, this mask and everything, you know, and opened up that bag. My sister had such a beautiful smile and perfect teeth, and so I knew immediately that it wasn't my sister. They sent a body with Marthea's driver's license, but it was not her. I told my father, I said, 'Pops, whoever this person is, let's just bury them, and just don't say nothing.' I was afraid for my parents, my brothers and sisters, everybody. We were trying to hush and be quiet. They sent the body and we buried it, and that was it. But we never heard anything about Shirley or the boys. They sent one body out of four. Now where's the rest of my family? Could nobody answer for them? It's like part of my family just disappeared to me."

He pauses.

"The last letter that Shirley wrote me, she was getting ready to marry some guy, a brother over there. This guy had a boat. She kept talking about this boat, and her getting married, how nice he was and everything. That gave me some kind of hope, because she said, 'Read between the lines,' and this and that."

"What do you mean 'it gave you hope'?" Margo asks.

"I was starting to investigate and talk to people. Dick Gregory was the first person that I heard saying that there was some kind of devilment going on, even to the point that it could have been a trick to go there, to that place, a setup. You know, it's a possibility that your country—the CIA or the FBI—wants you offed. Look at the brothers in Chicago, the Panthers. We all know now that they were definitely assassinated by the FBI. Them boys was asleep when they came in and killed them."

"You think there was a conspiracy like that in Jonestown?" Margo asks.

"My sisters were dedicated to a living God. It wasn't about just killing yourself for Jim Jones, you know what I mean? To this moment, I don't believe that they—." He pauses.

"The way Dick Gregory explained it, the way they were laid in a circle like that. He said if a person died from cyanide, it's like putting a hot coal down your neck, so how could you lay in a circle like that? Unless they were placed in a circle after death. Dick Gregory had seen film of a person dying of cyanide poison, and it wasn't a peaceful thing. So who placed them like that? Can you tell me that?"

Some of the aerial photos of the bodies in Jonestown picture people facedown, in a circle, some with the arms lying over the body next to them. This image is what Rod is referring to.

"It still puzzles me," he says. "It probably always will. My sisters were trying to find some happiness. That's the only barometer I have to really measure this thing, is the history and the lives of my sisters."

Rod takes another pause, a deep breath. And then he says to Margo, "I'm glad that you on this. That *you,* somebody that's part of the family, 'cause that's truly what myself and a lot of people need, is some kind of closure to this. I calmed down, you know, time had a way of doing that, but to this day, part of me believes that Shirley and the boys are someplace. I don't know if they're dead or alive, honestly. I had looked at maps of the river there, how it goes on toward Brazil. I said, 'They could zip down and go on to Brazil, in the Amazon, they could stay up there forever.' Yeah, it's crazy. Sure is, baby."

"Do you think your sisters were brainwashed?" Margo asks.

"The brain is a very strange thing, boy, somebody gets inside your brain, they got you. What else have you got? They take that, you ain't got nothing else.

"I wrote a song sometime after they died, say,

I could see by the way you're acting
it's time for us to part,
You can keep everything I've given you, including my heart.
Just treat it kindly.

But if it's not asking too much give me back my black mind.
I'm tired of being stomped on, broke, beat up, you can keep that,
I'm tired of that brother any way, keep that.
But listen, just treat it kind.
Just give me back my mind."

Rod laughs loudly—and so does Margo—for a long time. They seem to shed some sorrow together. Rod's voice steadies. He finds his rhythm again.

"But you know, the way I look at it, my sisters did not leave here looking for all that trauma. They were looking for something good, and they just got *waylaid*, man. That brings some peace to my heart. They didn't leave here saying, 'Well, we're going to go over here and be a bunch of crazy people.' 'I'm looking for something good.' Nothing ventured, nothing gained," he sighs.

"I think out of the whole thing, you and the rest of the crew, perhaps can find something here that can help another shipwrecked brother or sister before they do some crazy stuff."

Stigmata

··

OCTOBER 1, 2002
SAN FRANCISCO

MUCH OF THE SUMMER we spend transcribing and editing interviews. In the fall I return to the Bay Area, having arranged to meet with Jack Palladino, a well-known investigator who once worked for the whistle-blower whose story was the basis for the Russell Crowe film *The Insider.* Jack makes a cameo appearance in the movie. He is also a literary agent and counts former President Clinton among his clients.

Jack has interviewed more than ten thousand people during a career spanning three decades. His cases included some of the most famous trials in American history: Sonny Barger of the Hells Angels; Huey P. Newton of the Black Panther Party; and the trial of Larry Layton, Peoples Temple member, for conspiracy to kill a U.S. congressman.

Jack was part of the Larry Layton defense team to investigate what happened. He and his fellow investigators (including Melody Ermachild Chavis) visited Jonestown several years after the murder/suicides to find it exactly the same as it was in 1978, "except the bodies were gone," Jack tells me. He and Melody interviewed hundreds of former Temple members in the aftermath of Jonestown.

When Jack was retained by Layton's court-appointed counsel Tony Tamburello for the Peoples Temple case, it became pretty clear from the initial interviews with survivors that Larry Layton was not "a mover and a shaker" in Peoples Temple. In fact, according to Jack, it turned out Larry was "very much a passive victim of things, a sad sack, a person who became the spark of Jones's contempt." Larry Layton had been married to Jones's primary mistress, Carolyn Moore.

Jack was first drawn to the case not because of Larry Layton but be-cause it was historic, a chance to participate in history. "There's a very large element of voyeurism in being a private detective," Jack admits bluntly. "At its best it's historical voyeurism. Edward R. Murrow would understand."

Second, as he interviewed people and studied the case, Jack began to realize that these Temple members "were not fools," but that in fact "the people who died there, and the people who've been left behind, may rep-resent some of the best and most fundamental impulses in American culture."

And that's what got him hooked. "I wanted to tell that story."

As a seasoned professional investigator, Jack is skeptical that we can wrestle the story of Peoples Temple and Jonestown into two hours of theater. "I understand you got a literary problem, versus my problem as investigator, which is take every thread, tie them together, make this happen, and who cares? Six-month trial? That's okay. We got a captive audience. You gotta come everyday!" he jokes.

"I'm not suggesting mine, necessarily, but you may need a voice: an outside voice like an *Our Town* narrator," Jack proposes, citing the Thornton Wilder play.

Jack shoots his words as if aiming at a target. His mind is faster than any computer. As was the case with Melody, some of the names have faded in his mind, but the stories stored in the database of his memory are as vivid as the day he had heard them. He has a detective's mind, but a philosopher's soul.

I first meet Jack in his office in an old restored Victorian house in the Haight-Ashbury district of San Francisco. There is a dark wooden seriousness and what feels like the formidability of knowledge about the place—hundreds of books and papers line shelf after shelf along the walls—with framed photos of Jack shaking hands with all manner of im-portant people, from politicians to movie stars.

He has all of his interviews from 1979 on audiotape and the tran-scripts typed up on paper, decades of material. The occasion of our meet-ing has prompted him to "modernize" by scanning and downloading all of his *Reports of Investigation* related to Jonestown into his brand new MacBook Pro so that he has easy access to all the material as we speak.

After the two of us talk in his office for about an hour, he unrolls his shirtsleeves, grabs his suit jacket, and we walk to a local pub where we grab a quiet booth. One of the first things I learn: nothing is sacrilegious to Jack. He just lays it all on the table, story after story about Jones—his lovers, his aides, punishment, sex, power—and he doesn't sugarcoat a thing.

This is Jack Palladino:
"I used to imitate Jim Jones really well. I had all of the tapes, and what I used to do is, I would put the tapes in my 240Z—that's a 240Z, best car, never a moment's struggle—put the tapes in that Datsun and blowing out the speakers, Jim Jones going at full blast, and I'm going right along with him, so that I could actually *do* the speeches, and I had all the intonations and everything down," he boasts. "Well, in my business, you'll learn. It's a defense. I have survived all of the people who ever worked for me. And the reason is that I have a kind of coroner's or gallows' humor. You can't keep doing it otherwise. So, I would imitate Jim Jones, and I got to be pretty good, and then at some point I got tired of it. But still it was a kind of an amusement," he adds with pride.

I ask Jack to tell me what he remembers from his visit to Jonestown.
"You arrive at this place," Jack replies, "and it is a place of death. You get to this Kaituma airport, which is just a field. It's perfectly okay, but it's nothing more than a field. You've got to land on it with your little plane. When you land, your contacts there are waiting for you, with the same goddamn tractor that pulled the people of Jonestown. It's now become part of the village, I gather. So we're all getting hauled in exactly the same way as the congressman and all the people.

"But you really need a tractor because nothing else would cut it," he continues. "You realize, that kind of clay-mud on the road, the tires of the tractor get covered with it. And when you walk in it, it gets in your feet and they weight about four pounds. You can't get it off, you can't slog through it—you could, but every step would be agony as you go—and as we're going in, whatever the distance is, I don't know, a mile, two, three miles, we realize, not only where we are, but how hard it was to get in and out of there. Already we're quieting down—all of us—who've been chattering and doing one thing and another, me in particular with my imitations of Jones, because I was beginning to be reminded of what this was."

He takes a rare pause.
"It's an oppressive, hot, humid, fetid place, this place that Jim of

course described as paradise, swept by tropical breezes and always temperate. We come into this camp, and except for the fact that the grass was a little taller, it was just as it was in November 1978."

He pauses again. "This event, you had to go way past your intellect," he says soberly. "You had to really understand the loss that people went through. I was a young investigator at the time. I thought I could understand this. I thought I could control it, learn every story, tie it all together, but it floored me. Here we are, in 1981, we're coming into the remains of Jonestown, and there's the sense of the ghosts, really. And I don't mean in some science-fiction spiritual sense. I mean just a *real loss*. A realization that dreams and lives were lost here—and incredibly so. I see the sign tilted, with the slight misquote from Santayana, 'Those who do not remember the past are condemned to repeat it,'" he sighs.

"Melody told me about the trip. She told me nothing was changed," I say.

He nods. "I have pictures. It was just . . ." He struggles to describe the experience. "Fundamentalist Christians have a concept that's captured in a series of books called *Left Behind*. I represent the author, best-selling books of all time, fifty million copies. What they're about is the assumption into heaven of the true believers. All those who doubt or are sinners are left behind, and what the world would be like for them, okay?" He pauses. "When you walk into Jonestown, it's like: left behind. It's as though somehow, in some religious vaporization, everything disappeared. It's just as it was, except the bodies are gone. But you can see them. You can see.

"It really just hits you that it is a place of death. That it is sacred and profane at the same moment, and that really horrible things happened here. Despite my harsh work, I sometimes can be moved pretty strongly, but the sense of loss, the sense of betrayal that people were so lied to, and the work that was put into it. They attempted to actually make something out of this deceit that they were fed, and you could just see it. The buildings that had been put up, the attempt to clear land, the attempt to actually grow something in this hostile environment. It was all still there. I was stunned into a kind of silence. I retreated into some of the things that I do. I took photographs. That was my job. I walked through things so that I would remember from what people had told me, how that all matched together. We grew increasingly silent, and then finally we all gathered together to go.

"On the flight back to Georgetown, I think we all had this feeling of being lost in the clouds. We're flying back and there's no horizon— we really are lost in the clouds—and the pilot hasn't really said it, but we're thinking, 'There are mountains around here. We are in the middle of some clouds in a small mono-engine plane, and he doesn't know where he is. We've done this trek, we've gone to this place, and now we're all going to die in the course of it.' The surreal and depressing qualities that had already taken over had now been further heightened. The pilot does finally get below the clouds. He finds the river, which takes you into Georgetown, and he's okay."

Jack opens up his new computer. "I met many of these people in 1981," he explains. "Their fundamental belief system had been so shattered that it could never be put back together. I mean, they could have something that got them through the day, but the horizons are very difficult."

Jack searches through his files on the laptop. "What I started to say is that the business of an investigator at the kind of level of what I do, these kind of cases burn people out. It's really a career-ending kind of thing. People don't realize it for a year or two after it, but it's a career-ender. It just leaves you racked."

He looks up from his computer screen.

"Two interesting things happened. When Melody Ermachild went home at night, she would have to talk to her family about what she was doing, the things people were telling her. She was trying to get support, trying to make them understand who these people were, what was going on. At some point, the family said, 'You can't tell us any more. We can't take it. You cannot sit here at dinner and tell us these stories. We cannot listen to them.' So she began to see a therapist once a week so she'd have someone other than me who she could share it with, somebody who could listen to these stories and give her a way to handle the suffering she was seeing—and in many ways, because she's a good investigator, internalizing—and not inflict it on her family anymore.

"The second thing that happened is I had a very good secretary, one of several working in my office. When she resigned, she left a letter that I've never forgotten. It said, 'I love working here, I'm very fond of you and your partner, Sandra, but I can no longer stand to have these stories of misery and death pass through my machine every day.' That was her note. And she left in '82, right in the middle of this."

Jack raises his eyebrows, looks at me from across the table to make sure I understand the significance of these stories, then offers some advice.

"For me as an investigator, how I deal with this stuff, is I actually find the goodness in people. It's a really odd thing to say, but the main thing I've learned in my work is about the fragility of people. I'm not a very fragile person, so it was very hard for me as a young guy to understand that it's more amazing how most people get through life than that they fail. I didn't understand that for a long time.

"The second thing is the extent to which people really reach out and step forward, if you give them a chance, if you give them an opportunity to be their best selves, they repeatedly do. If you just look at the events, it'll burn you out. If you look at the people you contact, it will keep you going."

Jack's words strike a chord.

"The final thing is," Jack continues, "as you get older—and I'm now thirty years in this business—you end up going places you would never have gone, talking to people you were sure you didn't want to meet, and it's great!" His smile is large and sincere. "It actually opens you up and it keeps doing it all the time. It's the great part of the work. It keeps you from being ossified. It forces you to do this. This kind of event is a life-changing experience for an investigator. For some people, it really scarred them. But I'm saying to you, that you meet incredibly decent people and you hear wonderful stories."

He returns to his laptop. "There were very few people who survived that day in Jonestown," he remarks. "One of them had a wonderful name, and I'm gonna see if I can pull it back," he pauses as he scrolls through files. "We interviewed her in Los Angeles. She's an elderly black woman in her eighties, probably looked in her nineties, with that kind of leathery skin.

"Hyacinth," he recalls, "it was Hyacinth. They had the old people in Jonestown stacked up like cordwood basically. They would collect all their Social Security checks, and Jones would use it for his own purposes. They were terribly malnourished—except for Jones, who of course had a freezer run by propane that had meat in it—but the rest of the people were just warehoused basically. Hyacinth was in Jonestown in a bunk bed when she hears the announcement over the PA system to report to the pavilion. She gets very frightened. She's been trained, you know, White Nights and the GDF, the Guyanese Defense Force, is going to attack and all that, so she hides under the bunk bed. And she falls asleep. So whoever came in to poison people in her cottage—they poisoned a batch of people, especially some of the older folks, in their bunks—they see her lying there and she looks dead. They just didn't bother to poison her, because they thought that she'd already been done. Didn't squirt her with anything or inject anything.

"So she wakes up in the middle of the night, walks out into the middle of Jonestown, and everybody's dead. She's convinced she's the only survivor. She is the only survivor who lived through the whole thing and walked out the next day alive. There are people who escaped, we have several of them, but she's the only one that was right there and walked out. Her story is a great little vignette of what she saw, what she believed. It thrust you right into the mind of elderly, highly religious, and unfortunately very controlled people. Hyacinth is a wonderful story."

I had talked to a lot of folks by the time I meet Jack. What I really wanted to know—have him confirm or deny—pertains to the question of the good in Peoples Temple. "How could it have been as good as they describe and as tragic as it ended at the same time?" I ask him.

He tells me that of the ten thousand–plus people he has interviewed in his life, he always asks the same question at the end of the interview: "When's the last time you were really happy?"

The answers vary, but in the case of Peoples Temple, Jack explains, "Jones gave people joy, and you can't put a price tag on that. That's why they stayed. Because no matter how bad it got, they were still holding out that they could find that joy, they could find that ecstasy, they could have that memory of that period of time and that spark, that ecstasy, that joy back. That's why they stayed, and that's why they held to the end.

"We're not talking about getting a gold watch at your retirement," he adds, "or getting really drunk at the office party. We're talking about real joy and ecstasy. When you're disenfranchised, either for political reasons or because you're a victim of racism, you felt better than you ever did in your life in Peoples Temple. I think that that is something that we're getting at, it's something more about the human condition—about the need—that question. When's the last time you were really happy?"

Jack goes on to describe a scene from one of his interviews: "Jim Jones would go and sit next to people on the bus who were beaten down and tired, and he would give them that something that would carry them through, a word of encouragement, a hug that would energize them, anything to carry them through to the next moment of exhaustion."

But he also has another story that he wants to pass along, as a counterpoint to the previous one. For this one, he looks to his laptop: "She was a Temple staff member as well as Jim Jones's barber," he reads from his notes, "and therefore privy to many of his secrets. Jones once told her the purpose of the fake healings and miracles was to instill fear in people. He stressed in particular that if they thought he could control the flow of his own blood, they would believe he could do anything."

Jack looks up to see if I am following, then continues to read: "Jones would be up there in the robes and the whole works, and he would say, 'You have to give. *Father* can't survive if you don't do this. Father needs you.' And then he would squeeze his arms and blood would pour out of his palms. The Stigmata of Christ," Jack gasps in recollection. "Blood would pour out of his palms. People would go into ecstasy. They'd go into fits. They would give anything up. We talked to the woman who rigged the ox blood under the robes under his armpits, ran a catheter under his skin, so that the little tube came out at his palms. She tells the story after the Temple. Isn't that a story? Oh, that's a story. That's a visual, too," he adds. "I don't know if you're gonna get an actor who wants to have this rigged, but it's important to understand. You had a need. He had a power."

Jack continues to scan through his files. "The Katsaris family— this could be one of your through-lines."

Steven and Anthony Katsaris are not on our interview list because they denied our requests. Jack doesn't care. He wants to tell me about them anyway, as if to say, "Don't take no for an answer, kid."

"They are fascinating for a variety of reasons," he explains. "First is that the father, Steven, is uniquely qualified to have handled what happened to his daughter, Maria. One of the things he said to us was, 'I never understood how out of control events were for me. I thought, given my training in working with disturbed children, I would be able to handle whatever was happening to my daughter. But every step of the way,

Jones was ahead of me. Every step of the way, and I never knew it until it was too late.' I'm thinking, this guy's a trained psychologist, he'd been a Greek Orthodox minister, and he runs a school for disturbed kids, and he couldn't save his own daughter.

"Second, his daughter Maria was smart and articulate. She and her brother Anthony are only a couple of years apart and terribly close, according to every account. Their father was convinced that Anthony could save Maria. And of course what we now know is that she ordered Anthony's death. She actually ordered his death. Not just rejected him, not just sent him off, ordered his death, okay?"

"That day in Jonestown after their meeting in front of the press?" I ask.

"After the meeting, when Anthony tries to give her a cross and he touches her, she yells for a guard. Yeah, it's lovely," he adds with bitter sarcasm.

"Third," he continues, "Maria herself. She's an entry into one of the real themes that people don't understand about this case. I'm sure *you* do, but what people don't understand is the empowerment of women. The secret handshake was sex, but what he did was he elevated to the second tier—right underneath him—young women to have all the control, to have power that they would never have seen otherwise. They were empowered by him, empowered by God, empowered by sex, empowered by thrills, empowered by ideology, whatever it is. Empowered. And they took it on. If there ever was an example when power corrupts absolutely, this was it. We don't think of young women leading the death march, brutalizing others under their control, but they did. They did it with an incredible sense of control and power. They did it with love in their hearts."

He pauses. There is real disgust in his voice as he continues. "Jones is such a hypocrite. There's an incredible tape. A woman who had been put in one of their punishment boxes in Jonestown, a coffin-size kind of thing—call it a roomy coffin—dug into the ground with a sliding lid. On the tape, Jones learns that some of the children have been making noise and throwing dirt clods on this thing. He goes out, to address the issue of excessive punishment because the kids have been throwing these clods at the box. In this incredibly unctuous voice, you hear him address the woman in the box. Then you hear the box—you can actually hear the wood as they're sliding the lid open—and Jones says, 'They really shouldn't have done that. I've talked to the children, and they're not gonna do this anymore. Father loves you.' Rrrrrrrrrr," Jack re-creates the sound of the lid sliding back over. "You realize this woman is in a box, in the ground, it's a hundred degrees. 'Father loves you'? So you think about crossing Jones, you hear that box slide back and forth."

"How long did people stay in the box?" I ask, dismayed.

"Days, couple, three days," Jack says matter-of-factly.

"How do you explain some people in Jonestown not knowing about the box?" I ask him.

"They know about the box," he counters.

"Everybody knows about the box?"

"They have to know about the box," he insists.

"There are some people who say there were no boxes in Jonestown" I argue.

Jack tries to explain. "We have tapes that Jones made. They're having a meeting. Jones is reprimanding somebody for lack of belief or something else, and the crowd beats the person. You can hear them being beaten. You can hear them yelling and striking. The box wasn't a secret. Nothing was a secret.

"One of the things you have to realize here is: this is a man who pees on stage into a cup held by Larry Layton during sermons. This is a man who openly and flagrantly takes other people's wives and has sex with them. This is a man who has anal intercourse with men so that he can control them.

"It's not like it's a big secret!" His voice rises as he schools me. "'Oh my God, if they ever find out, Jones will lose his power.' No! It's part of the power! He's above the rules. He's the rule maker! It really is the kind of Right of Kings concept, and people accepted it. Jones was a Godhead!"

"Even the older black women who were there?" I continue to challenge.

"You're right," he concedes. "I have no idea how they comprehended this. That would seem to be very hard to place with their conservative ideas. Jones didn't hide this. Now, when he was in California, he did," he clarifies.

"But you're saying not down in Jonestown. He couldn't hide it there."

"Right," Jack replies. "For one thing, you couldn't go anywhere in Jonestown. Jones had essentially marooned everybody as though they were on some tropical island. He had your passport, he had all your money, had total control. You're hundreds of miles from anyplace. The loyalty of the people in Port Kaituma is open to question. They regard all these Americans in Jonestown as bizarre.

"He even swayed Ryan to his side, at least for a while. Congressman Ryan's view as he was leaving for the airstrip was that Jones was a success! He got a thousand people here and, what, two and a half percent want to leave? Two dozen out of a thousand? This is nothing.

"What Ryan didn't understand is what a house of cards it really was. Because to Jones it doesn't mean two and a half percent, it's the loss of complete control. It was as if your arm said, 'I'm departing from you.' It's your arm! Your arm can't leave! People who want to take your arm are your enemy."

Jack pauses. Talking about Ryan segues into his last question for me. "Have you ever listened to the last-hour tape?" he asks.

"I've only read a transcript. I haven't listened to it," I explain.

The last-hour tape, or "death tape," is an audio recording of the mass murder/suicide in Jonestown. Peoples Temple recorded everything: services, White Nights, band sessions, oral histories of their members. And they recorded the events of November 18, 1978.

"I have the last-hour tape," Jack says quietly. "You can hear the children crying. You can hear the mothers wailing as they realize their children are actually dying. It's not just a little cup. They had hypodermic needles, and they squirted the poison into the mouths of the little babies. Once they began to kill, what the others saw as the future of Jonestown—of the movement—was lost. The others in a sense lost hope."

"Who did the squirting, Jack?" I ask.

"They did it themselves," he replies somberly. "Jones was incredible. He had a demagogue's incredible instinct for how to make things work and happen. Even the deaths in Jonestown."

There isn't really much more to say after that. The last words I have recorded on tape—the final thing Jack left me with before he said good-bye—is a last sardonic imitation of Jones, "*Father* loves you," before the tape clicks off at the end.

The Dream

....

THE CALIFORNIA HISTORICAL SOCIETY (CHS) is a library and museum in downtown San Francisco that houses the Peoples Temple collection. The museum and reading room are on the ground floor and in the basement are scores of collections, from the San Francisco earthquake to the Beat poets of the '50s and Haight-Ashbury and the Summer of Love in the '60s. All that remains of Peoples Temple is kept there, too.

Denice Stephenson was in the process of cataloging and archiving many boxes of material that had been donated to the California Historical Society but had not yet been processed. She is our gatekeeper to this collection and has also agreed to be our project's official archivist. Her connection to the material and to our project is not accidental. Denice is married to David Dower, the artistic director who commissioned the play, and both David and Denice are longtime friends of Becky Moore and Mac McGehee.

I remember my first visit to the archive very well. I sign in, get a visitor's pass, put my belongings in a locker, and proceed to the main library room. Denice is there to greet me with a few gray archive boxes on a book truck—some highlights she thinks I should see. The archive boxes are beautiful, made from thick, acid-free cardboard to better preserve the documents inside.

As she sorts through all of this material, she identifies documents, letters, and photos and put them aside for us to see—whatever she thinks will be relevant to our interviews. As we meet more and more survivors, she will pull photos of them and their families, and other found text.

We will develop the play not only from the words of the interviewees, but also from the history we find in the archive. In this way, the play will become a conversation between the living survivors and the people who died in Jonestown.

The Peoples Temple collection is stored in the vault below the CHS library reading room. Requests are made on slips of paper, which the librarian/archivist takes downstairs to the vault, a warehouse-type room designed for maximum preservation of historical documents, regulated for temperature and light.

The material is retrieved from the vault and brought back up to the reading room, where guests—who must wear white gloves—can view it under the watchful eye of professional librarians to make sure no damage comes to what remains of history. We become familiar faces in the archive as we make our way through more than a hundred archive boxes in the collection, which are wheeled up on book trucks, three to five at a time.

Guests to the archive are not typically permitted downstairs, but after our repeated trips, the archive director agrees to allow us the privilege to go down to the vault to see it for ourselves.

The day comes that we visit the basement archive. Greg, Margo, and Steve are all there with me, a rare occasion. The whole team is there, in fact: Denice and David, and the head librarian of the collection, Mary Morganti, who leads the small group.

We take the elevator into the basement. The vault itself is lined with a series of fourteen-foot shelves in long rows packed tightly together row upon row. On the outside edge is a circular crank that creates an opening in between each long shelf, an aisle to pass through to retrieve the material. The cranks are intimidating devices that manually move the shelves along a track.

As Mary turns the crank and the shelves part, their movement is quite dramatic, as if the Red Sea is parting just for you. Light sensors are triggered and the newly formed corridor lights up. For the first time we see the true volume of material—hundreds of boxes on Peoples Temple alone—on both sides of the aisle.

"That's it," Mary says. "Have at it," she jokes.

My collaborators start walking down the long aisles pulling down random boxes. One discovers Jim Jones's robe, another a brooch given to Marceline Jones as a gift from Jim. They find the *He's Able* album and then a map of Jonestown. There is a thrill in seeing some pieces, like a bulletproof vest that Jim Jones wore in San Francisco during his more paranoid days. I wonder about our growing collection of cassette tapes, if they will one day end up here, too, as part of the collection.

As we investigate the archive, taking objects out of boxes and, with Denice as our guide, discovering their history, it is a powerful experience, and one that I realize could become part of the play. The action of taking an object out of a box could be a way to tell a piece of the story. And the archive could be the theatrical container for all of the stories.

As I watch my collaborators handle the materials in the collection with such reverence, I am suddenly struck by the questions: *What happened to this movement? What happened to the dream?*

PART III

TO WHOM MUCH IS GIVEN

Sixty-seven Cents

A FEW DAYS after Jack Palladino fills my head with stories from Jonestown, I meet Tim Carter for the first time. I fly to Portland, Oregon, from San Francisco and make the drive south on 1-5 to the tiny liberal haven of Eugene. Tim Carter, like a few of our interviewees, is on Jonestown speaker's bureau of the Jonestown Institute.

Tim has talked a lot about Jonestown over the years. He is among the handful of people who were in Jonestown on November 18 and who lived to tell the world what they had seen. Tim has told his story many times, but never to a playwright. I find his e-mail on the Jonestown Institute Web site.

He responds right away and agrees to the interview.

I pass Tim's house, make a U-turn, and park my car along a lonely side street in his rural neighborhood. I pull off onto some dirt and rocks that serve as a shoulder. The houses in the neighborhood are small, ranch-style houses, some faded in color.

Tim Carter was born in Berkeley, California, to a middle-class Irish Catholic family and spent his formative years growing up in Burlingame on the San Francisco peninsula. His father was a white-collar worker who came from blue-collar roots, a coal mining family in Punxsutawney, Pennsylvania. Tim's mother, who converted from Judaism to Catholicism when she married his father, died when Tim was fifteen from complications due to a rheumatic heart. By default Tim became the emotional head of the household to his younger sister, Terry, and even younger brother, Michael. Yet he knew not long after his mother died that he was going to have to "get away." His father's alcoholism was out of control, and the abuse they experienced was "everyday, constant. There's a lot of reasons why abuse happens, but it doesn't make it any easier to experience," Tim says openly.

Tim is very welcoming when I arrive, and we have an easy rapport. Of all our interviews so far, Tim seems the most open and eager to talk. He often talks while smoking, exhaling smoke through his words. He offers me coffee and over the course of the weekend we drink pot after pot. I spend two twelve-hour days with Tim going over the details of his life before and after Peoples Temple.

This is Tim Carter:

"Growing up, I never actually knew any black people, and I was scared to death of any gay man. In other words, I was an idiot." It's a blunt admission. "And to prove it, I joined the Marine Corps. I didn't go to college. I enlisted! It was 1966. It took me about five minutes into boot camp before I thought, 'Oh my God, I've made the biggest mistake of my life.' Once you're in the Marine Corps, you don't get out. You either get out and run and worry about going to jail for the rest of your life, or you go through it. I didn't have any political consciousness at the time. I really didn't. We were fighting a war, but I hadn't stopped to question: Is the war right? Is the war wrong? I just wanted to do my time and get out.

"When I got to Vietnam," he says soberly, "I volunteered to go out to the bush—four days before Tet happened. Tet was a massive North Vietnamese Army and Vietcong military offensive in February of 1968. I didn't volunteer any more after that. On the first day of Tet, I watched this guy running across the rice paddy trying to evade the machine gun fire from our perimeter, and I watched the guy get shot and go down. It hit me, 'That was a human being. This was a human being you just watched die.' Everything changed in Tet."

He pauses.

"When I started seeing the death, and when my life started being threatened, I thought, 'Why are we even fighting this?' These people have been here for centuries, fighting for centuries. What are we here for? Here I am with a gun in my hand, with people trying to kill me and I'm supposed to kill them. I don't want to kill anybody and I don't want to be killed. We'd see bodies of Vietcong and North Vietnamese soldiers brought into the compound, they'd have personal effects on top of the bodies. One of the bodies had a picture of a family: a wife and kids. Did they want to be out here killing me? Given a choice, they'd probably rather be home with their wife and kids. It's not real complicated. It cuts across all cultures. I went through a complete political metamorphosis and realized that my country had lied to me, my government had lied to me. Vietnamese people would say, 'There was no war until you got here.' I got filled with a real rage inside because my brothers were dying—for nothing. I mean, literally nothing. Their lives were being thrown away."

≈ ≈ ≈

In August 1968 Tim had an experience that he describes as a "spiritual epiphany," in addition to the political transformation that was already taking place inside him. This spiritual experience occurred about six miles north of Da Nang in Vietnam, and according to Tim, what happened that day has guided every step of his life since.

"I don't have any answers for you," Tim tries to explain. "I have only what I've experienced. But it's real, it's not imagined."

His voice is serious and solemn.

"I was sitting on this hill," Tim continues, "Hill 244 in Da Nang. I was reading a book called *The Harrad Experiment,* written by a guy named Robert Rimmer. It was about this group of college kids that decided to live communally and also sleep together—one on one. It wasn't an orgy kind of thing. But the whole premise of the book was, what is love? What does love really mean? So I was thinking about the nature of love, what it actually meant to love, and all of a sudden I ceased to be. I became light. I became everything in the universe, and everything in the universe became me. *I ceased to be.* There was no me, it just was." He pauses. "Complete being is the only way I can think to describe it. And the feelings of love were so complete and so strong as if you took the purest emotion of love that every human being on the planet has ever experienced— whether it be for a pet, a son, a daughter, or a spouse—the purest form of love, and put it all together into one giant feeling—one giant thing. It was overwhelming. It was light and it was warmth. I have no idea if it was a second or six seconds or ten seconds. I don't have any idea."

Tim finally takes a breath.

"At first I thought I was dead. But when I had a consciousness again, I thought, 'Oh my God, I'm gonna die,' because I was just given this wonderful gift where I know that everything in the universe is love—the entire history of the world—and the good guys win. It's all light. There isn't anything in the universe outside of light. Here I am in Vietnam, which is kind of the antithesis of light. I thought, 'Why else would I be given this gift unless I am going to die?'"

He registers a tiny smile.

"I didn't know what it was. I just knew that I experienced something beyond words. When I came down off the hill, I talked to my bunkmate, Art Lazerini. I told him what had happened. I asked, 'Do you think I'm nuts?' He goes, 'Yeah.'

"But I knew that my life had changed from that point in time on. Along with what I'd learned about politics, I knew that I was *in* this world but not really *of* this world. From that day—from that moment on—I made it my quest to try and learn about what it was that I experienced."

That spiritual quest would eventually lead him to Peoples Temple four years later in 1972.

"When I was in Vietnam," Tim explains, "Martin Luther King Jr. was shot, Bobby Kennedy was shot, and there were the Chicago riots at the Democratic Convention. To me, the whole world had gone insane. I had no idea that there was a kind of spiritual awakening and awareness—an explosion—that had taken place back in the States. I didn't find that out until I got home."

Tim was in San Francisco in 1970 when Kent State happened, an antiwar protest during which National Guardsmen fired into a crowd of students on the Kent State campus, a number of whom were just walking to class. Four students were killed and nine wounded.

"I was so angry I was crying," Tim recalls. "It was those same people that sent me off to war, that nightmare—that ugly—where young men were being blown to bits internally and physically, and what did they get? They got, what, a flag and a casket? So some rich motherfucker can get even richer?" he rails. "I went out and bought a hunting knife. I went down to San Francisco City Hall. I wanted the revolution to come down right then. All of a sudden, this little voice inside me said, 'And accomplish what?' I knew I wanted to change the world. But I knew I had to find a spiritual solution." His voice is as passionate as his words.

When I ask him how he joined the Temple, he refers me to an article he had read in the *San Francisco Examiner.*

"It was around September of '72," Tim smiles. "And that's when those articles by Les Kinsolving showed up."

We later found the article from September 17 at the California Historical Society. Here is an excerpt:

"The Prophet Who Raises the Dead" by Rev. Lester Kinsolving
Redwood Valley—A man they call The Prophet is attracting extraordinary crowds from extraordinary distances to his Peoples Temple Christian (Disciples) Church in this Mendocino County Hamlet. The followers say he can raise the dead. They come from all over the West—from as far away as San Francisco, Seattle and Los Angeles—to the Temple, 7 miles north of Ukiah.

It was the first of the series of articles by Reverend Kinsolving. It was intended to dissuade people from going to the Redwood Valley church, but for Tim it had the opposite effect.

Following his experience on the Da Nang hill in Vietnam, he was interested in the metaphysical, the spiritual. He had jumped with both feet into the cultural revolution that was happening in the Bay Area, particularly the music scene at the Fillmore. He read books—*Siddhartha, Autobiography of a Yogi,* among them—and studied Eastern religions. He was on a quest for something, he did not know exactly what, perhaps for a place to take all that he had experienced in his life and find a spiritual home. He had heard about Jim Jones but did not know where to find him, until he read Kinsolving's piece.

"And that's when I went to Redwood Valley, trying to get into a meeting, and they said, 'No, we don't have meetings open to the public here. You'll have to come to San Francisco.'"

But Tim persisted in his efforts to attend a service. "So early January of '73, my sister Terry and I went to a meeting in San Francisco," Tim recounts. "Now, I didn't realize that I was being interviewed, because Temple folks were really skilled at that. We went and sat down in the meeting. Jones came out and started talking, and what he was saying was like the perfect synthesis of everything that I believed in spiritually and politically."

≈ ≈ ≈

This is an excerpt from a sermon by Jim Jones from around the time of Tim's first visit:

> America's got a false sense of security. She's too fat, too content, she's too materialistic, and the bombs never hit her shores. That's why we push our "big guns" all over the country and all over the world. The commander of your United States Marines said that there's nothing but dirty, dollar-grubbing capitalistic fingers in Vietnam. We were never there to bring freedom. We were never there to protect those people from communism. He said, "I've been a baron, a robber on three continents for U.S. Steel, Standard Oil." Walter Cronkite showed you, just the day before yesterday, the entire terror of what we're doing. Showed a school, showed an orphanage, showed a hospital that had been bombed to powder. [Voice rises in ministerial cadence.] And if you don't give of yourself, and discipline yourself, you're a murderer, you're a traitor, you're worse than all the killers that are making the napalm, because you know better.

≈ ≈ ≈

Tim's first time inside Peoples Temple was profound on another level as well. "So the meeting goes on," he describes, "and you might know, they always passed the donation plate two or three times a meeting. They were passing the plate, and I gave my last sixty-seven cents. And I leaned over and I told my sister Terry, 'Well, that's my last sixty-seven cents, so I hope you got money for cigarettes.' And we're sitting there up in the balcony, and Jones points up and he says, 'And you up there that just gave your last sixty-seven cents. You know that gift means far more than these people who give $10 who can afford to give $100.'

"And I thought, 'Wow.' I mean, to me that stuff was very real. A lot of people say, 'Well, psychic phenomenon is bullshit.' Well, it's not bullshit. At least in my world it's not bullshit. Now, what I didn't know was that there was somebody sitting immediately behind me, listening to every word I was saying and relaying that up to Jones. I learned that after Jonestown. They overheard me say that and they wrote it down and they sent it up to Jim on a 3×5 card."

Even so, for Tim, the impression had been made. This man Jim Jones was "real." And Tim knew that day that he wanted to join, to make the commitment. "I was a street person, all right," he explains. "I was a Vietnam vet, and I was a hippie who came in off the streets. And I'll only speak for myself. As soon as I walked into the Temple, I was home. I knew those people. I had known those people all my life," he says emphatically.

"When I came back from Vietnam, I was radicalized, completely and totally," Tim continues. "Peoples Temple made perfect sense to me. The fact that we were socialist wasn't hidden. There were all sorts of movements going on politically then. The youth movement, the Black Panthers, the American Indian movement, they were calling for revolution: 'Tear the motherfucker down. And tear it down now!'" Tim chants as if still at a protest. "You could see it happening in the country. It was real. It was tangible. Peoples Temple was part of that. I was part of that movement as a member of Peoples Temple. We would have politicians come like Supervisor Harvey Milk—openly gay at a time when no one was—who was a friend. I'm proud to have called him a friend."

Tim wipes his eyes after many hours of talking.

"I think the powers-that-be—the two percent that control the ninety percent of the wealth in this country and growing—said, 'Not in our lifetimes.' Look what happened to Harvey Milk: assassinated. Look what happened to the Black Panthers: shot in their rooms while they slept."

Tim pauses again.

"This is not a free country," he says with bitterness and resignation. "It never has been a free country. There's just an illusion that we live in a free country. If you challenge the establishment, they're going to bring you down any way they can. By any means necessary. They have no compunction whether they kill two people or ten people or a thousand people. It makes no difference to them. And Peoples Temple openly challenged the system."

≈ ≈ ≈

I want to talk to Tim about the last two days in Jonestown, his eyewitness account of what he had seen and experienced that day in November 1978, the day his world died. But he makes it clear that if we are going to do this, we have to do it right. We have to go in steps.

He has gathered all the evidence before him, all the magazines and newspaper articles that he wants me to see, all the proof that he and the Temple have been wronged, have been mischaracterized and subjected to character assassination in the press.

"Fat Americans consume two-thirds of the world's resources and leave the rest of the world to live in poverty, but if I die for an ideal I'm a cultist!" Tim exclaims as he shows me the 1978 headlines one by one. You could feel that he was tired. Tired of a life of violence that included his mother dying, Vietnam, and then Jonestown. Tim got out of Jonestown. And yet, by his own admission, part of him died there, too.

When he came back to the States, he was vilified in the press, labeled as one of "Jones's lieutenants," a fact that stings him to this day. He found out about his wife's funeral, not from her family but from a reporter at the *Los Angeles Times* who called to ask him for a quote. When Tim showed up to the funeral, her parents saw him but did not even acknowledge him, much less invite him to come sit with the family. Tim stood alone to the side. The same *Times* reporter covered the story by writing, "Tim Carter was in attendance, wearing a cheap suit."

The media was suspicious of Tim after Jonestown, but to me he was wrapped up in that guilt of walking away—walking out of the jungle—wrapped so tightly that he could barely breathe. He is still searching for a meaning in the deaths at Jonestown, still searching for a way for those lives to matter. There is no rational explanation for why he lived and they died. Something in him said, "Live," even as the people were dying. I feel an immediate connection with Tim. I want to make their lives matter, too, if only to relieve some of his survivor's guilt.

≈ ≈ ≈

"There are a lot of us who are having a really hard time," he explains. "Anybody who talks to you who doesn't talk about the pain, or you can't feel that pain, then they're lying to you, Leigh, they're lying to you. I don't care if you left the Temple or didn't leave the Temple. The real legacy of Peoples Temple is pain. That's the real legacy."

Nefarious

BACK IN SAN FRANCISCO, Margo had been working hard for months to pin down Jim Jones Jr. for an interview. She finally does. Jim wants to meet us on Geary Street in the Fillmore, a predominantly black neighborhood in San Francisco where the Peoples Temple church once stood, until it was destroyed in the 1989 Loma Prieta earthquake.

In contrast to his brother, Stephan Jones, who leads with his intellect, Jim Jones Jr. leads with his charm. Stephan is Jim and Marceline's only biological son, and "Jimmy," as he was—and sometimes still is—called, was one of the several whom the couple adopted. Jim Jr. was the first African American child to be adopted by a white couple in the state of Indiana, rounding out Jim and Marceline's "rainbow family."

At his suggestion, we meet Jim at a little donut shop. He wants to invoke the old days, "give some context," and show us around.

When Jim Jr. introduces himself to the three of us—both Margo and Steve Wangh are with me—he does so with a firm handshake and a quick, "Jim Jones. Good to meetcha. Let's go inside."

He holds the door to the donut shop open for us.

The place is distinctly San Francisco with a no-frills vibe—linoleum floors, handwritten signs, coffee in Styrofoam cups, and a donut case with crullers near the cash register—but it's the characters in there who make the place. It's a hang-out-and-gather type of spot as much as anything else. The most important thing that happens here is not the coffee but the *connection*.

A formidable presence at 6'4" tall, Jim is all business in a stylish suit and tie. He is in fact a salesman, and he's on a break from work, which explains his speedy pace. He is working hard to make us feel comfortable. He wants to be our guide.

"My company I work with calls me 'Mr. San Francisco,' which is a unique name for me, seeing my background, but this is *my* town," he tells us.

Yet there's a downside to this, too. "I work in San Francisco. I can drive anywhere in this city and have a memory of Jonestown or Peoples Temple."

One of Jim's sons is a local basketball star. Rob is a high-scoring dynamic player and gets a lot of press coverage for his athletic prowess; he has a presence of his own that he has worked hard to develop. Nevertheless, the headlines accompanying many of the stories about the young basketball star read, "Grandson of Jim Jones," and always refer to "the cult leader" or "cult mastermind."

After years of living with this, Jim seems to take it all in stride, even joking about his famous father and the fact that he shares his name. One day, he explains, he decided to print *Jim Jones* on his office nameplate at work rather than *James Jones*. It was a huge decision for him and a more direct invocation of his father and his history. "So now I'm Jim Jones. Deal with it."

This is Jim Jones Jr.:

"Let me just kinda go chronologically over my life, okay? I'm a Negro child in the state of Indiana in an orphanage. Ten weeks old. I get adopted by Jim and Marceline Jones and have a very affluent life. I mean, growing up in the Jones family, man, a silver spoon was put in your mouth, in my perception. I mean, we traveled to Brazil, Argentina, Hawaii as a preschooler. I saw the world. Well, I'll tell you right now. Normal case and tenses, I would have been in a foster home or a group home, probably got into a life that wasn't healthy or beneficial. And Jim Jones brought me into this life and gave me that silver spoon and gave me an education.

"The children of Jim and Marceline are different from each other. You probably noticed that already," he says with a laugh. "There has always been a piece of competition between my brother Stephan and me," Jim admits. "I don't know why. Stephan had his blood, but I had his name.

"But if you take all the living children of Jim Jones," he continues, "you'll get Jim Jones. Very charismatic, charming. I got that thing going on." He laughs again. "The martyrism, the 'I gotta give my life for my fellow man thing,' that's my brother Stephan. All right. Then you have the intellectual, that's my sister Suzanne. Then you got the 'I gotta make money,' that's my brother Tim. So we got homemade, and we have all the takeouts. Dad went to the 'hood and got me, and he wanted some Korean food and got Suzanne and Lew, and he wanted some Midwest food and got Tim, you know. We were all takeouts. Steve was homemade," Jim says finishing off his theory. "That's not a bad analogy, is it? It's a friendly analogy, okay."

When we ask him what it was like growing up in an interracial family in Ukiah, California, a conservative place, he is again full of theories and stories. He breaks down the Ukiah days for us with "the reality story."

"I was about nine years old, in the third grade," he recalls, "and I went in the bathroom, and, I hate to say it, at nine years old I could spell every four-letter word," he laughs. "And I see this word on the bathroom wall. I start saying it. 'Nigger.' No one in the bathroom says anything. I get on the bus and I'm singing it. Everybody in the whole bus is singing with me. To the Mickey Mouse tune, 'N-I-G-G-E-R, nigger.' Mr. Pruitt, the bus driver, says, 'Mr. Jones, should you be saying that word?' I say, 'It ain't four letters.' I walk in the house, 'N-I-G-G-E-R, nig—.' *Bam.* Jim hits me. 'What did you say?' I jump up. 'Nigger.' *Bam.* 'What did you say?' 'Nigger.' *Bam.* Fourth time, I'm a little slow, but I finally get it. I'm standing up slower. 'What did you say?' 'A word I saw on the bathroom wall.' He says, 'Do you know what that word means?' 'No.'

"He puts on his jacket, we go up to the school, he makes me show it to him. We go down to the principal's office. He reads him the Riot Act. I have no idea why he's mad. He then takes me home. He then explains to me what *nigger* means. He said, '*Nigger* is a word that they use against Negro people, black people, derogatory, to put them down, it means black heart, and that was used in slavery.' 'Slavery? What was that?' I'm serious. He goes, 'Well, you're a Negro.' 'I'm *what*?'" Jim Jr. shouts. "And thus, Jim Jones brought me into this life and gave me an education."

≈ ≈ ≈

Jim has something else on his mind. He tells us that he thinks it's "in vogue" to talk about the Temple as being a bad place. He tells it to other survivors straight. "You were having a good time in there," he reminds them when they talk only about the bad. He does not want us to think about him as a victim.

"There's nothing that can minimize the pain and the loss that have happened to myself and others," he explains, "but I honestly believe that my father felt he was still doing the right thing. And, for the things he did wrong, I forgive him. For the things he did right, I appreciate him."

Jim also explains that he does not have a very high threshold of tolerance for survivors who continually rehash the pain and the trauma of Jonestown. He feels very strongly it is time for them to "move on."

"They want to go to a dark place, fine," he says, " but let's not blame Jim Jones on how your life is today. That's just like blaming your mom for not going to your soccer game and that's why you're a heroin addict. 'My life is so bad because I came out of Peoples Temple.' I'm sorry. Let's put it out there. I look at it as my life is so good because I survived it."

We bring up some of the people we've met who are really struggling, like Juanita Bogue, but Jim shrugs. "You have to make a choice," he replies. "You want to look over your shoulder, or do you want to turn your cap forward? I'm sorry, I don't mean not to have sympathy or empathy, but the reality is, I lost my wife, my childhood sweetheart, my unborn child, my mother, my father. I didn't have anybody. I didn't have a child to love and devote to. I had nothing. It would have been easier for me to die back in Jonestown than to live. I had no reason to live, okay?

"But let's turn it around. Let's look at what Peoples Temple did for you prior to Jonestown. You chose to leave. Are we having a little bit of guilt that you ran out in the middle of the night? I get very passionate about that because I just feel that staying in 'I want to blame Jim Jones. I want to blame Jonestown' when you know the fact that you're alive today gives you an obligation to wake up every morning and to *engage*. You survived. How many people didn't survive? You have an obligation to not sit there and wallow in self-pity."

He doesn't want to dwell too much on this point. Instead, he stands up and says, "It's time to walk around."

≈ ≈ ≈

We drop our coffee cups in the trash and head out of the donut shop. Out on Geary Street, Jimmy sets the scene for us. There's a post office where the Temple once stood, but Jim gives us more. "Look up here," he points. "Imagine. Imagine, if you will, twelve, thirteen buses, the big Greyhound buses, all double-parked. Peoples Temple would be from that post office sign over here. That was another auditorium over there. Between that hall and the post office you had a club called the Thirty-Eight Club. That was another hall. It was part of the Chitlin' Circuit.

"You heard of the Chitlin' Circuit before?" he asks and smiles when we shake our heads.

"The Chitlin' Circuit was where some of the African American— well, back then they were Negro stars—performed before they made the big time. Before Lou Rawls got big, he performed here. Before the Four Tops were on *top*," he laughs, "they performed here. The Temptations were always tempting, but you get the idea. What my buddies and I used to do on these long services, in the wee hours of the night, we used to climb up on the roof of the Temple, jump over the alley, and look down through the glass skylight. And we watched the Chi-Lites, Compunction, the Four Tops, Lou Rawls. We would sit down and look into the skylight and watch these groups perform. Those are some memories."

He walks us a little ways farther down the street. "This was all Temple," he describes, "all the way, the Meese Theater was here, but all this was the Temple. The back lot was where all the buses parked at night." He turns to face the opposite direction. "Across the street is Hamilton Gym. That's where we grew up playing ball. I haven't walked into that place for over twenty-five years. The other day, I'm walking into it with my boys, they're having a running pickup game, and I'm like, 'Oh my God,' you talk about déjà vu. It hasn't changed," he laughs.

Next on our agenda is a surprise introduction. Jim walks a little bit farther down the street and around the corner to a barbershop—an old-style place with barber chairs and mirrors and black combs in glass containers filled with blue-tinted water—and introduces us to Reggie Pettus. Reggie is his barber from back when he was a boy, back when he was still called Jimmy.

Reggie waves and smiles as if he is expecting us. A much smaller man than Jim, Reggie wears an old-fashioned white barber shirt and black pants. It's like time has stood still in this place. Jim encourages Reggie to tell us about the old neighborhood.

"Back in the day it was beautiful," Reggie describes. "We had Afro-

American hotels, we had beauty shops, barbershops, restaurants, clothing stores, shoe stores, night clubs. It was superb," he adds almost breathlessly. "A nice neighborhood to live in at that time. Then the redevelopment came in. They tore everything down. Promised to rebuild it, but they never did. We've been around for the whole duration. Went through the whole thing. We saw the changes. As far as my barbershop goes, my uncle started it up in 1952. We were down on Ellis Street, and they moved here in 1968. Right now we're working on fourth generation. We used to have a shoeshine parlor. They called it Red's Shoeshine Parlor."

The barbershop's history includes a connection to Peoples Temple, and to Jim himself.

"One time, they were cutting my hair, and I said, 'Reggie, do you know, outside my family, you're one of the few people alive who have known me since I was eight years old?' You know, that's true."

"That's true," Reggie says, nodding his head.

"I wanted to come here," Jim remembers, "because if I didn't, there was a white woman in Redwood Valley who would cut my hair, and she wasn't *doin'* it." They both laugh. "So after all this happened, this was like my one connection back. You know it's funny, because I never would walk around the corner, though. Never would."

The two men recall that the barbershop and the Temple had another neighbor—the Black Muslims—and Jim is reminded of another story.

"In terms of the Muslim thing," Jim recounts, "I'm around fifteen and a half years old. We're living in the city, and I go through this whole thing about my Africanism, my blackness. I want to go join the Nation of Islam. Now, we're having some joint meetings. I want to become a fruit of Islam. Not fruit of the loom, fruit of Islam. Okay?" He and Reggie crack up. "I think we just had a convention with them down in LA. So I got my hair cut short. I'm getting me a part. I'm getting a little red tie thing. It was cool with Dad, you know, so I joined. I was down there going through the indoctrination. Louis Farrakhan was the new leader of the Nation, and the big thing was: white people are devils. White people can join the community, but they were still devils. I'm like, "Shit, my brothers picked on me, you know, fuckers, you know, goddammit, hell, yeah, they're devils, you know, fuck them." He laughs again. "Then they were like, 'Well, you live in a Caucasian home, but you cannot accept gifts from them.' All of a sudden I'm like, 'Whoa, whoa, whoa, I got a question on this. I can't accept gifts from them, right? I can't be owing them, that's what it is?' I said, 'Let me ask a question. If my grandmother's gonna give me a Ford Cortino in October, is that cool?' 'No, you can't accept it.' I was *out* of there," Jim laughs. "That's about as black as I got."

Everything is a joke with Jim, but Steve keeps him focused on the question of his politics by asking him about now. What would he say now about his blackness?

"Well, now, I've become so politically correct, I'm by myself," Jim jokes. Steve asks him to elaborate. "I don't know that much about you," he says, "but let me use me as an example. I used to be in a group of African Americans. But now, I'm an African American who has a degree, so that puts me in a smaller group. I'm an African American who has a degree who is a Republican and a Catholic. Smaller group. African American who's a Republican, Catholic, degree, who's married to a Caucasian. Smaller group. An African American works in the pharmaceutical industry. Smaller group. So by the time I'm ending my story, I'm by myself. I'm by myself. So, how can I reach out to another person and organize together to change something? I'm all by myself.

"That's our society," he adds. "That has nothing to do with politics. That's just how our society is. In the Temple it was just the opposite. Everyone was equal. Everyone was part of the same group, the same whole."

Jim thinks for a moment. "Let me get serious with you here," and he is. "In retrospect, see, I was a true believer. I truly believed, and I still do, that you can change the world. You can take passion, effort, and desire and carve out a better place. If I didn't believe that, why get up in the morning? What's different now from then is that I know it has to start from me. What Jim Jones—my father—did is that he tried to create it, tried to put it on people. It doesn't work that way. Because you know people still wanted the KFC next door, you know what I mean? They believed, but they weren't willing to give up all the things that meant believing, you know, that day-to-day housekeeping of believing. Thus, that dream became a nightmare. My father didn't want to lose their faith, support, commitment, and total devotion. So then he had to use coercion." Jim pauses.

"I remember one incident in Jonestown where I faked two different assassination attempts on my father to get people to believe. People would say, 'My God, why'd you do that?' When you believe, 'the end justifies the means,' that's from Malcolm X. But the next line of that is what my father never taught me: 'The ends justify the means,' Malcolm said, 'but if the means are nefarious, thus will be the ends.' I didn't get that. I didn't get that.

"I saw it all." He claps his hands once for emphasis. "But the end justified the means. People needed to have a reason to believe. They got distracted. They fell out of faith. I rationalized it from my father telling me, 'People are not believing, Jim, we need to create a crisis.' These are his words, 'We need to create crisis to bring people together.' Now these are mine: Look at 9/11. You ever seen this nation so tight?" he asks.

"Look at it this way. I didn't struggle in Jonestown. I had it good. I had $5.7 million in my name after Jonestown. I signed it away because it was blood money. I don't know if I would've done that at forty-three years old and struggling with my career!" He laughs. "But at eighteen I was a revolutionary! I believed! Man, I should have kept a million back." Everyone laughs. "I was a socialist then. Now I'm a staunch Republican who loves Arnold Schwarzenegger! What can I tell ya?" Jim shakes his head and smiles. "Just put your cap forward and keep moving on."

We Were Rising

NOVEMBER 21, 2002
OAKLAND, CALIFORNIA

A MONTH LATER our team reconvenes in the Bay Area for another round of interviews. We attend the twenty-fourth anniversary at Evergreen Cemetery on November 18. This is the second year of our project. The feeling at the cemetery is distinctly different. We are able to reconnect with many of our interviewees. We feel less like outsiders, more like we belong.

Then Greg and I fly north to Portland to meet with Jean and Tim Clancey, two former Temple members now living a quiet rural life in Eugene, not too far from Tim Carter, who provides the introduction.

We arrive at their home, a gray-blue house with red shutters. There is a barn on the side of the house with a small corral for their horse. Their yard runs several acres, filled with wildflowers. Jean and Tim live a quiet life with regards to their Jonestown story, too. They haven't spoken to the media—or anyone—since the immediate aftermath. They were in their early twenties when Jonestown happened, and both have silver hair now.

Jean answers the door with a warm smile. Her husband, Tim, enters the living room a few moments later, smiling too, and introduces himself. They were not in Jonestown on November 18. They survived because they were in the Temple in San Francisco. They married five months after Jonestown and have built a full life together. Many interviewees recalled an instant connection with Peoples Temple or Jim Jones, a feeling of coming home. This was not the case with Jean. Her conversion she calls a gradual one. She is fiercely intelligent with a quiet, reflective intensity. Tim is reserved yet open, and deeply reflective, too.

159

This is Jean and Tim Clancey:

"I was very offended by Jim at first, very offended," Jean explains. "I didn't like the sunglasses. I didn't like his talk. I was offended. So why did I stay? I stayed. I got gradually re-formed or reshaped into this. Also there were some very heavy pulls. When I walked into the Temple in Redwood Valley and there's Debbie Touchette singing—I think she was still Debbie Ijames at the time—I mean, just beautiful. Such a sense of good committed people really trying to establish an alternative way of being together—economically, socially—it really did have a strong pull. It was not an easy integration on my part, but I felt like I was supposed to be there. This is my job. This is my duty."

Jean was a high school teacher for a short time on an Indian reservation in Sonoma County, California. She remembers doing odd jobs after that one, part time, in several different schools, and generally feeling directionless.

Following the death of her grandmother, she spent a summer with her grandfather and his family in Bloomington, Indiana. There she recalls having "many long and heartfelt discussions" with her mother's cousin, Barton Hunter.

Barton Hunter was the chairman of the Disciples of Christ who had ordained Jim Jones as a minister when Jim was thirty-three years old. Barton was very active in the Fellowship of Reconciliation, an interfaith peace organization in the United States. He had been involved in the Paris Peace Talks and the Freedom Rides. In contrast to Jean's conservative-leaning family, speaking with Barton was like a breath of fresh air. She felt she "could talk to him very freely." She recalls that Barton sensed her "disenchantment." He sent her back to California with the recommendation to visit Jim Jones.

"Which I didn't do," Jean says bluntly, even as her voice remains calm. "I had no intention of going to Redwood Valley or to church or anything like that—and didn't. Then, come January, Barton and Dorothy, his wife, again recommended going to see Jim Jones."

Jean remembers their words: "You haven't got work. You can get a job that matters. A job that would count for something. Get involved and stop spinning your wheels." So she went. Because of her familial ties to Barton Hunter and the Disciples of Christ she was being "heavily courted" by Peoples Temple to join. Sharon Amos and Karen Layton talked to her the day she visited. They later sent letters, "big fat letters," almost daily. "Come, these are the best people in the world. You will matter for something here," the letters read.

Jean is not at all reticent to talk, but she is careful with her words. She is doing her best to help us understand what to her is still infinitely difficult to relay.

"When I first was in Redwood Valley, Jim called me out. He said, 'You say you don't like me because I talk bad about Jesus, but really you don't like me because I'm a socialist.' And he had me. He just had me. His insight wasn't something that you get from an information card. He was observing me. What he was saying is that all that Christianity stuff is passé, the higher good is socialism, and you don't know diddly-squat. If you join us, you will be among the greatest people in the world in a movement that's going to challenge the CIA, racial inequality, economic inequity, everything. What is being supplanted is your theology, your worldview. So when it comes to turning your glance away from the things that are going on, you've already made that compromise. You've already said, 'I don't know anything about socialism. I was born into capitalist sin. I was born into racist sin.' Socialism is your theology, and Jim Jones is the only one who can deliver you, because he's the only one who knows. So women had sex with him. If somebody needed the shit beat of them, people did it. I mean, stuff happened. Abuse happened. In my mind, it happened because we're in this limbo, this purgatory, this hell, and we are given this standard, which those of us who really believed, tried our darndest to uphold. Whether it was celibacy or no alcohol or work—living on two dollars a week—you just couldn't do enough to purge yourself of this unrighteousness you were born into. You were born into money. You were born into the bourgeoisie. I can't speak for black people, but this is what hit me, a middle-class, religious, white kid who was deeply distressed about what was going on in the world. And it goes and it goes and it goes and it goes, and pretty soon you are no longer thinking your own thoughts or being your own person: you are a penitent in this process of becoming the socialist entity."

She pauses, searching her memory for an example. "Before Peoples Temple started going down to San Francisco, they'd bring buses of people to Ukiah up from San Francisco. They would have big dinners in the parking lot between the Temple building and the parsonage—big potlucks—and feed a lot of people. The whole congregation would sit down and have dinner together. All the adjacent property was vineyards. One day during the meal there's screaming and yelling in the parsonage. Somebody came out with a shirt that was bloody. It had bullet holes in it. He said, 'He's been shot. Jim Jones has been shot!' It was really a shock. We all gathered in the Temple. People were weeping. We really thought it was real." Her eyes gaze downward. "I have to say now—I would say— that scene was fabricated. But we were told then that he had healed himself. He came out and was healed. You're just caught up in this great sense of . . ." She struggles to find the word.

"Psychodrama," Tim suggests. He has been quiet but is listening intently.

"It was a psychodrama," Jean agrees. "You feel like you're part of something bigger than yourself, something important. There was a tremendous sense of belonging."

Tim Clancey first heard of Jim Jones from Tim Carter. "We were off on a trip with some friends to Colorado and ran into somebody who'd heard of Jim Jones," he explains. "Tim Carter was really the driving force there. He was really on a spiritual quest. Tim went up to San Francisco to check this out, and you know his story," he nods. "I was involved with a woman, Mary Lou, and Mary Lou and Tim's sister Terry were very close friends, and Tim talked the rest of us into going. To me, it was kind of a bizarre experience. It was kind of surreal, from the moment when we got in there and the greeter crew surrounded us and tried to figure out who we were and what we were up to," Tim describes.

Greg prompts Tim to talk further about the greeter crew.

"I grew up in a church. My father was a minister. I'd had a background in churches, but I never encountered anything like this: to be grilled before we went into the church itself surrounded by greeters to figure out who we were. The greeter crew was anywhere from three to five Temple members—usually an interracial group, of varying ages quite often—who were assigned to figure out who was coming into the church and whether they were evildoers or what not. I was a little taken aback. But in those days, I was pretty easygoing and took it in stride. They finally let us into the service," Tim recounts. "We were all sitting in the upper balcony, and Jim Jones directed some comments our way. Caught our attention."

"The sixty-seven cents in the donation plate," I say.

"That's right," Tim confirms. "At the time Tim Carter believed Jones had read his mind."

"It's suspension of disbelief," Jean adds. "It's very powerful. It makes you feel very important in a very strange way. It does. It makes you feel chosen, recognized, important."

"But like Jean said," he continues, "once inside the church it was an amazing experience to have that kind of camaraderie with black and white, old and young, all these people together here in a warm and caring environment. That was the thing that really drew me to the church."

Jean also spent time as a greeter. "I was on the door. I was on the committee that screened. I hated doing it. First it was Sharon Amos, then Terri Buford, they were in charge, but they got taken into the inner circle. I will be forever thankful that I did not—ever—get taken into the inner circle. I think I had a couple opportunities and politely declined. But you'd make little notes and you'd run them backstage, and then he would call people out. It was patently clear that he was calling people out with the information that was given from the cards. After a while I figured that one out. Although I also always held out that that was done because he would have reached the point of exhaustion had he had to use his psychic powers for everyone, so there were undoubtedly several that were genuine healings or genuine callings out, and we just sort of padded the rest. You can tell yourself anything."

Jean looks down. "I let in a doozy one time into the San Francisco Temple," she confides. "She was an older black woman, very religious, all dressed in white. I don't know what their religious name would be, but they were all in white, head to toe, shoes, hats, everything in white. They thought that they were washed in the blood of Christ or something. And I let her in. She sat in the front row, and she stood up and she challenged Jim. This might have been her golden opportunity. She challenged him right there in the meeting. He was furious. She was quickly escorted out. And I'm sitting up front in the choir, and Maria Katsaris came up to me and said, 'When Father calls your name, stand up and fall over dead.'

"So, you know my heart is racing over what's going on. Sure enough,

Jim has this revelation that whoever let this person in—then he called my name. I stood up and he said, 'Look what you've caused.' I didn't want to be on the door in the first place. I didn't want to make those decisions in the second place. I didn't want to be in that position, but you did it, because to not do it was to leave. So, he went, 'Bam!' I fell over. I did a good job. I almost convinced myself that that was happening. I remember being picked up. I think I cut my lip. I was picked up and carried to the back. It was an act of my will. He did not slay me or cause this to happen, but for anybody looking, who would know? At this stage of my life I would look at that and say, 'How could you do something like that?'"

She has a look of distress on her face as she tries to explain. "It's like you have to prove that you're really with us by these little acts of compromise, putting Jim, or putting the Temple, or putting the movement ahead of your own sense of propriety or code of ethics."

There is one more example of these compromises that she wants to tell.

"I was driving Jim Jones's bus one time. There were thirteen Greyhounds, but bus number seven was his. We were driving from Ukiah to San Francisco. I'm driving along this highway, which has since been widened, but for a while it was head-on kind of traffic, lot of curves, around the Russian River. Jones came up behind me and he said, 'Pass that car.' I said, 'It's a blind curve.' He said, 'Pass that car.' So here's my big test, what am I going to do? I've got a bus full of people. And so I passed the car on a blind curve," she admits. "That's how far it could go. I mean, because I believed he was supernatural or something."

"Was psychic," Tim adds.

"I surrendered to that. Paid a high price to surrender to that," Jean whispers.

Her husband nods, then picks up the conversation. "In the early San Francisco days there was a call to come forward and become a member. And once you did that, there became an increasing pressure to join the communal part of the church, to move in with everybody else.

"Mary Lou and I were living in a little cabin in Pescadero, which is on the coast. We would go to services on the weekend up in San Francisco. I was making candles for a living, barely enough to get by—not a major profit-earner there," he laughs, "but it was enough to pay the bills and have a roof over our heads. Gradually, Mary Lou became more enamored of the church and wanted to become a member. Jim's politics were fascinating. He was talking about social injustices and striking a chord that was very sympathetic to me."

Many survivors we spoke to recounted the political power of Peoples Temple, particularly in San Francisco. "The move to San Francisco was done to broaden the base of the church," Tim explains.

"Political base," Jean adds. "Jim's ambitions started with the Housing Authority."

"Jim went in there and started rallying the troops and bringing people into church and talking about political issues and getting people out to vote," Tim says with a hint of pride.

"We could deliver," Jean says with a nod.

·"We could deliver votes," her husband agrees.

≈ ≈ ≈

Tim Carter had also described the Temple's involvement in San Francisco politics. "When Walter Mondale came to San Francisco to campaign, Jim Jones rode with him in the limo from the airport to the rally downtown." And another scene: "When Rosalynn Carter came, they were supposed to have this rally for her, and there were not very many people. So they called up the Temple and said, 'Can you please get some people down here?' We took four buses—two or three hundred people—and packed the place. That rally made national news for the 'warm and enthusiastic reception she received.' That was pretty heady stuff for a kid from Burlingame who had ideas of changing the world."

Grace Stoen Jones had also recounted the Temple's involvement in San Francisco, the campaign to elect George Moscone for mayor: "We put five hundred people on the street within an hour leafleting for Moscone, we had money, we had numbers. And when Moscone won, we were in a Planning Commission meeting, and Jim was livid because he hadn't gotten a call from him with a job. And it was like 2:30 in the morning, he says, 'Get that guy on the phone right now!' I say, 'But it's two—.' 'I don't care if it's 2:30 in the morning, you get that guy on the phone!'"

≈ ≈ ≈

Jean explains that there were at least three thousand members of Peoples Temple by that time, and just as many letters could be produced in a single day and sent wherever needed to influence elections, legislation, whatever was required.

Beyond the local and national Democratic Party, Peoples Temple had connections with some of the more liberal Left and even communist groups in San Francisco.

"We were connected to a group that was bringing in people from Chile," Jean recounts. "Salvador Allende had been elected. He was a socialist, but a freely elected president of Chile, and within a year or two he was overthrown. We were receiving refugees from Chile. They were coming into San Francisco."

"They would come and speak at the church, and we'd host them, we'd help in fund-raising for their cause," her husband adds.

"On this one occasion, there were probably about ten of us, maybe twelve," Jean describes, "sitting downstairs in the San Francisco Temple. There was a side room with couches. We're all sitting around Orlando Letelier, a man who was a very, very close friend and political mate of Allende, and minister of defense at the time of his assassination. He came to the United States to tell people who would hear what had gone on down there. Sitting there in our midst, he said, 'You need to know that it was your Marines, your Green Berets, who were in the Hall of Justice taking over our government.' He told us that the United States government was directly involved, had engineered the overthrow of Allende."

"Historically that has been documented at this point," Tim adds.

"We told him that he was in danger," Jean recalls. "'You can't go around saying this kind of thing. You won't live.' He was actually killed within a relatively short time of that meeting in a car bomb outside the embassy."

"In Washington," Tim clarifies.

"In Washington, D.C. He and his young aide," Jean adds. "That kind of shocking awareness about what was going on had a big impact on us. Dennis Banks, and the American Indian movement, is another example. His wife had been jailed following a shootout with federal officers at the Oregon border. She was imprisoned. Dennis Banks came and made an appeal to us, and we raised the bail on the spot and got his wife out of jail."

"And Angela Davis," Tim chimes in.

"Angela Davis came to speak," Jean nods. "She did. She did. Jane Fonda, too."

"There was a great climate of conspiracy going on at the time," Tim explains. "The whole COINTELPRO program that was going on with the Panther movement."

"Huey Newton's mother actually attended the church," Jean tells us.

"There was quite an awareness of this undercurrent of sabotage and government surreptitious activities," Tim says. "We were just in great distrust of what the government was doing in our names." He pauses. "Very similar to what's going on today. The whole potential for that same kind of behavior is in place again with the Patriot Act."

"Right," Jean nods.

"Jim Jones used that experience—that very real experience—to also insinuate conspiracies against the Temple," Tim explains.

"Right, and against him," Jean adds.

"Everyone's afraid to voice criticism for fear of being called on the carpet," Tim says. "You're working nonstop, just physically at your wits' end. You're doing everything you can for the cause. Work, work, work until you just couldn't anymore because Father never sleeps. It's almost like a one-upmanship: who can work the most hours, for the longest period of time? Who can sleep the least? If your brain is sleep deprived, it just isn't functioning properly. You don't have the benefit of a calm, balanced perspective to allow those questions in your head to have the weight that now they obviously would. We didn't have that perspective at the time."

≈ ≈ ≈

Jean is quiet for a moment. "I have this ongoing series of dreams," she begins. "When I was a little girl, my aunt had an old 16mm movie camera. She had great big lights, and at family events all of us had to gather in a room, and she'd turn on these lights—you were blinded they were so bright. My dream was like that. We're in the living room of a house with white walls, white ceilings, bright-white lights. The place was being lit up beyond brilliant, like stage lights, just intense white light. Then the room flooded with voices, and the voices all rose. It seemed they were up on the ceiling. They were circling around indistinguishable one from the other, just a mingling of voices—hundreds—hundreds of voices just filled the room." She takes a breath. "That's all I remember."

She hesitates for a moment before explaining. "It has occurred to me that the voices need to be heard. Not just the living, but some of the dead." After a long pause, she adds, "Most of the people who died over there were black, 75 percent or more. So if you want to know why we're quiet," she sighs.

Tim gets up from his chair as if on cue. He walks into the kitchen and returns with a manila folder.

"Tim made reference to these," Jean explains. "I think they will shed some light on where we're coming from. There are some documents here. I'm not sure how these actually came into our possession. Either Dick Tropp gave them to me, or someone else sent them back to the U.S. I don't know," she pauses. "I have them, and I'm giving you copies. These are testimonies from people that were collected over there in Jonestown. Large number of them are older black people, and when you read about their lives, then there's really nothing else to say." She looks down. She is emotional at this point.

"We've thought about trying to publish them ourselves," Tim explains, "but we just weren't able to put that together. It's kind of a quagmire of how to negotiate all the complications of it. We wanted you to be able to see, to read them. I think it will give you an understanding of more individual life experiences than you've been able to—."

"And what this promise held for people," Jean breaks in, "and it was a false promise, but—."

"I think you have to take some of it with a grain of salt," Tim adds.

"Dick may have had the notion of making some kind of propaganda piece, but when you read them, they're not propaganda," Jean clarifies.

"Some of them you can see are just true to the bone," Tim nods. "Jones was sincerely moved by the plight of the downtrodden, be it black, white, green, brown, whatever. He was sincerely sympathetic to those who got a raw deal. He wanted to speak up and address that. That was the good side of Jim Jones. It was a tremendously good side because that's what drew so many people to him. The downside obviously is that there was a lot more going on in his head than a lot of us realized. He became a very twisted, complicated figure. How he came to bring it to the end that he did, I—I don't know."

"We'll spend the rest of our lives trying to figure it out," Jean reflects.

≈ ≈ ≈

Dick Tropp is the man who documented and recorded these testimonies. Jean refers to him as "the literary man." He had collected many of these testimonies, which we as shorthand begin to call the "Clancey papers" because they were given to us by Jean and Tim.

"I was just thinking of something that Dick said when he was doing the *Peoples Forum*, the Peoples Temple newspaper," Jean recounts. "We were up all hours with that darn thing, and he said, 'But it's so good to be working for something that you believe is helping people rise to their highest as opposed to exploiting the lowest, or pandering to the lowest common denominator.' I remember that comment he made. We felt that we were rising to our highest and helping others to do the same. We were quite disdainful of all the trappings of society that pander to our lowest instincts." She pauses. "It was attractive to feel that you were that one lit-tle grain of yeast that was going to make the bread rise. You were nobody in yourself, but together you were formidable."

Jean smiles as if she can see her friend just as he was in 1976 when Peoples Temple was thriving in San Francisco. "Dick Tropp was writing articles from his heart. He was writing articles about important things. I don't know if you've looked at any of the *Peoples Forums*. I'm sure there are some around," Jean suggests.

≈ ≈ ≈

We take a break for lunch. Jean has prepared some sandwiches and lemonade. "If you are gonna make this play of any consequence," she asks, "are you personally coming to any awareness of how we as human beings can, with the best of intentions, proceed along such a path and end in total catastrophe? Are you starting to discern elements here, or insights into human nature? I mean, I don't believe the Peoples Temple was that unique."

"I think we have to show the audience that journey—not tell them but show them—from beginning to end," I answer.

After lunch she hands us the manila envelope with the testimonies. We say our good-byes and promise to visit again for a follow-up interview before we finish the play.

Jean leaves us with an image of Dick Tropp: a literary man, studious, hardworking, an intellectual giving everything to the cause. All-nighters spent working, writing. She has kept his memory alive all these years, so much so that we can see him now as well. We can see him, not only through documents, but as a man, alive and yearning. Striving: "You were that one grain of yeast that was going to make the bread rise."

The Basis of a Book

....

CALIFORNIA HISTORICAL SOCIETY
SAN FRANCISCO

WHEN I BEGIN TO DREAM about the play, Dick Tropp becomes an important character. I can see him in my mind's eye in his cubby in San Francisco writing and rewriting articles, sending them to print. Or at a typewriter in his cottage in Jonestown, a simple wooden structure smelling of mildew and damp wood, built by hand by the people he loved.

We deliver the manila envelope with the testimonies to the California Historical Society, and Denice Stephenson catalogs them by last name, first name, ethnicity, age in 1978, and any nickname or alias they might have had.

As I review the testimonies, I again picture Dick Tropp, this time with a '70s style reel-to-reel, his headphones in place, recording the words of the people. We find a letter to Jim Jones in the archive detailing and confirming his project:

> To: Dad
> From: Dick Tropp
> I have begun collecting oral histories of members of our church. These stories will be the basis of a book on the history of Peoples Temple and Jim Jones. Notes for this are piling up.

The testimonies in the envelope are of varying length, some just a paragraph or two, but others up to twelve pages long. We have more than sixty of them. It seems as if many of these testimonies were taken in Jonestown. Often within the transcript Dick would add personal notes and observations. Each testimony begins with a name, date, and place of birth. On first glance, one of these testimonies stands out because of the date: "HENRY MERCER b. 1885."

I was born in Jessup, Georgia, April 3, 1885. I went to school to the 6th grade. I knew that the white kids had something that I just couldn't have. But to go back a bit first. One thing I can tell you, when I got to be a young man, I was working one night at the ice plant and a honkey picked me up in a car and said, "I just got to kill me a nigger tonight." And I was scared to death. He put a pistol to my head and drove all around. And he brought me back and he said, "Well, you're a good nigger, go ahead and go to work. You ain't the one I'm looking for." That was in Georgia. Wayne County.

There was a time, if you was a black man, you couldn't come through there on the trains, and if you did, they'd throw rocks at the train. I was working down at the depot one night, and we had a white fellow kill a black man on the train and nothing was done about it.

I never saw a lynching, but I saw it after it happened. It's an ugly looking thing. What they do, they hang you up on the trunk of a tree and they'd cut your penis off and put it in your mouth. I went away from there. I went straight from Jessup to Philadelphia, and I stayed away 26 years.

I worked on the railroad. We were getting a dollar a day. In 1929 I joined the Unemployment Movement in Philadelphia. Everybody was unemployed and nobody knew what to do. They was giving us soup, watery soup and we had to go to the station house to get it. We were in line and some Communists came along and distributed leaflets and I take one of the leaflets and read it and it said, "meeting tonight" at 612 Brooklyn Street. And we went there. We had a discussion on strategy. We was going to organize the workers, which we did.

The Spring of 1930 it was, in the middle of May, we met there with a hunger march. We carried 150 of us to Harrisburg, Pennsylvania. We had 300,000 people unemployed in Philadelphia and the government was not giving one nickel of relief, not one cent of relief.

The Democratic Convention came off about 1932. Roosevelt came out and he said, "One third of the people are unemployed." Then came WPA. 10,000 people in Philadelphia, it was the biggest project we had. We had some miserable conditions on the WPA job though. We decided to call a strike, and the leaders were singled out as Communists and transferred away to other projects that was much tougher. I was one.

They transferred me to a stone quarry. Around 1939 I got a job at a naval yard but I never did sign the denial that I was a Communist because I was a Communist and I never did sign it.

I was Chairman of the Propaganda Committee, and I had a tough time. If you was a Communist at that time you had a tough time. After that we had Joe McCarthy, in the 1950s.

I had other jobs. I was a Union Steward in the union and we got along pretty good. We had some terrible working conditions. That was around 1968. We was having little skirmishes but no strikes. But it was at that time that we called a strike, and that's when I got it—I got my eyes blinded from tear gas.

When I got out of the hospital, I joined the Senior Citizens' Action Alliance. I worked in that from 1968 to 1973, and we done a lot of good.

In the winter of 1973 I was sitting down on the corner one night, and I had WTC radio station on, and I heard this song and I heard this Peoples Temple Christian Church with Jim Jones as minister. I liked the message. I called the station and asked for the address, and the man said, "The best I can do for you is Redwood Valley." Took a bus to Redwood Valley and I called a taxi. The taxi driver took me around looking for the church. When I got to the Temple, I got up to speak. I said I'd never liked preachers all my life, that I'd been a revolutionary for 40 years and I never did like preachers, because they didn't want to do nothing but eat chicken and buy Cadillacs. The congregation went wild and cheered for a good while, and I went back to sit down. Jim said to me, "You don't know how you thrilled my heart when you talked about the preachers." And I laughed. I seen some things I never seen before. I seen a dog up there with Jim, and a cat came and sat on my lap. I said, "My goodness, there's some love going around here, even the animals are loving you."

I'll never go back to the U.S. again. Jonestown is the onliest place you can relax, it's the onliest place you can be safe, and I love it out here. I wouldn't go back to the States if I had the best room in the best hotel with a silk suit and a pocket full of money.

I never was an Uncle Tom myself and I *hate* that, I hate that, just like I hate a defector, a counter-revolutionary. I feel like going out and chewing them up when they do anything against the working class, against the poor people. Sometimes, I cry about it [his voice breaks], the hurting things, to think about it, 'till Jim Jones came and rescued me [sobbing]. You don't know until you go through it. People say, "I'm a socialist, I'm a socialist." But they don't know.

Dick Tropp had next typed the following note within the text:

(There are things that Mr. Mercer felt were too painful to discuss in his life, things he had witnessed.)

Then Mercer's voice continues:

It takes more than you know to be a socialist [sobbing].

≈ ≈ ≈

Another testimony in the stack represents another generation: "DIANNE 'DEANNA' WILKINSON b. 1950."

Born in 1950 in a place called Cook County, Illinois. I was delivered at a Salvation Army Booth Hospital. I am of mixed race. My mother white and my father black. I was just one more "nobody" born into the dirty filth of a Chicago city street. My life began with both parents alcoholics and out of work. As a small infant, I became the victim of a parental quarrel and somehow, got caught between them arguing. When my father threw hot grease at my mother, it hit me, burning me so badly that I still have the permanent scars of burn damage on my face, neck, mouth and ears. My parents deserted me soon after and the welfare system took over my life.

At the age of one year I had the unhappy pleasure of coming in contact with a woman by the name of Alice Moten . . . better known to me as "the Devil." Life with her in Indianapolis, Indiana was hell. By the time I reached 5, my musical talent was being exploited. Most of my life those years was spent staying up night after night practicing the piano until it was time to go to school the next morning . . . or being beat for *not* practicing. As a result I failed many of my school years, and "served my time" in a special education class for the "retarded," which threw me far behind in school for the rest of my life.

I can't remember how old I was when I attempted to commit suicide. I tried hanging a rope around the water pipe and putting my neck in the noose. I stood on a chair and jumped . . . but, the pipe broke.

I felt my life was destined to become nothing . . . and I was right. I lost my job because of coming to work drunk or high on diet pills and marijuana. I met this one young man I thought was nice and started dating him. I was dumber than cow shit. I fell for any line that was nice and sweet. I started meeting different people . . . the wrong people who I thought were my friends and liked me. We'd get high and sell joints and nickel bags, ride all night long. Until one day I saw a friend stick herself with one of those needles and I saw how she got hooked. I looked up to her. She was 31 and I was 19. I thought maybe if I got an older guy he might be settled and maybe things can change. I went with a man, he was about 40, he had a good paying job as a bricklayer. You know when you're a black man in a poor community a brick laying job is considered good position and money. I found out that he was a half-steppin' pimp who hustled women on the side. He didn't let on to me that he was a pimp and I was too dumb to realize it. He did set me up with a job at Marion County Hospital in Indianapolis and I was doing pretty good until I started drinking and staying out late. One night he wanted me to stay home and I told him to kiss my ass. He beat up until I couldn't see out of one of my eyes. I called in sick the next morning and she says, "Well, Miss Wilkinson, if you can't come in, we can't use you."

I really started letting my whole self fall down after that. I took an overdose of speed and had to be rushed to General Hospital to have my stomach pumped. I was 20 years old. I continued to stay out in the streets getting into more things than I could handle.

During my childhood my stepmother came in contact with Peoples Temple and Jim Jones. I met some of the Temple children who all befriended me, including Jim's children. They were children of every race and they were really nice to me. I thought a lot of Jim because he was living in the middle of a black neighborhood in the heart of the ghetto on 13th and Broadway in Indianapolis. Also, that his adopted black son was named after him, Jimmy Jr. The Jones family had a lot of pets and all of them, especially Jim, were really kind to me. This is the only recollection of any happiness in my entire childhood.

But Jim and his family went away, and during the time I was separated from them, I left home and got really messed up and messed over. When Jim returned, he came to Indiana and held a meeting. I didn't know right away that Jim and his family had since moved to California. Jim didn't even ask me if I had any money. When I told him about what had been happening in my life . . . he asked me to come to California with them. As I sat on the beautiful Greyhound bus Jim had bought for his people, I looked out the window and waved goodbye to Indiana. Goodbye to the pain and misery and knowing I never—ever had to look at that life anymore.

At the end of the document, Dick typed the following note:

AFTERWARD: Although Deanna speaks very modestly of her musical talent, she is recognized by many people as a musical "genius." She is lead singer of the "Jonestown Express Band" and also known as "Lady Soul." She has received standing ovations in the major nightclubs in Georgetown, the capital of Guyana. She is an excellent organist, pianist, and composer of both music and lyrics.

As we go through the stack of testimonies, we notice a repetition in the format. We catch phrases that suggest the questions Dick is asking when conducting these interviews: Who was I before Peoples Temple? What have I seen of racism and injustice? Who am I now? How have I changed since joining the Temple? What do I love about Jonestown?

Toward the end of the stack, there is a self-described "sketch" written by the collector of these stories himself:

I started out in Bedford-Stuyvesant, grandson of Jewish immigrants from Eastern Europe. Studied cello from age 9. Went to University of Rochester, where I majored in English and Comparative Literature. Graduated with highest honors, went to Europe on a travel scholarship. Tried to pursue academic route at Berkeley, 1965–1966 on a Wilson Fellowship. I was supposed to go "to the top" of my field, but somehow I had a profound dissatisfaction with it all. I had been experimenting with psychedelic drugs, had drifted into the "hip" culture of Berkeley, I lived on several communes. I was a participant in civil rights demonstrations and marches, and by the mid-sixties I was attracted by revolutionary ideas.

I met Jim Jones in the spring of 1970.

To be brief, I have found a place to serve, to be, to grow. To learn the riddle of my own insignificance, to help build a future in the shadow of the apocalypse under which I felt I was always living.

And then he adds:

CODA: I look back on the past as if to another world, a dead and dying world. A new center of gravity has been established in my life—and, to my great relief and happiness, it is not *me*.

≈ ≈ ≈

Dick Tropp had a mission: to let all the stories be told. His life was cut short before he finished, as too were the lives of those he had interviewed. We are now holding a large portion of his unfinished project in our hands: a history of a people as told in their own words. By including his work with ours, perhaps both the voices of those who survived and those who perished could together tell the fuller history of Peoples Temple. If it were not for Dick Tropp, most of that history would have been entirely lost.

Beyond Truth

MARCH 12, 2002
OAKLAND, CALIFORNIA

IT WAS EARLY in our process when we first spoke to former Temple member Garry Lambrev. The dramatic story of his departure from the Temple had left a strong impression, but it wasn't until later that we felt the full weight of his words.

Garry's closest friend in the Temple—his "closest person in the world"—was Liz Forman (now Liz Forman Schwartz). She had left the Temple just after the first of August in 1976, and Garry was concerned about her. He described his thoughts at the time:

"When Liz left, I could only think that, without the guiding light, without the reason to hope and believe, and without the community of Peoples Temple, that she would find herself so lost, that she might do what I almost had done when I had last been outside of the Temple, which is take my own life. Jim Jones quietly suggested that I not contact her," he laughs. "Just let her be.

"She didn't dare give her real reasons for leaving," he continues, "for fear of bringing down the wrath of Jim Jones. She just wanted to get out. I didn't know at the time that the reasons she was giving were just cover. I thought about it, and I said, 'You can't just let her go like that. Her life is too important.'

"So finally one night I called. I was the only person who had her phone number. Even Jim did not have that phone number. She was hiding in a mobile home of a friend in Marin County. I started to try and convince her. She cut me off. She said, 'Garry, I don't want to hear any of that stuff. I'm way beyond it.' I said, 'What are you beyond? You can

178

never be beyond truth!' Garry laughs at the memory of his own folly. 'Then you're really lost. You're beyond truth, baby, we have no converse here.' She said, 'No. You've got it all wrong.' I said, 'What do you mean, I've got it all wrong?' She said, 'You don't understand at all what's going on.' That hurt my pride. I said, 'So what do you have to say? I'm not afraid of truth. Try me.'

"So she dropped an emotional atom bomb on me: the severe torture of a good friend of mine in the Temple. This man was an Anglo-Chilean exile who had been a friend of guitarist Victor Hara, a young guy married with a small kid. But he had had an affair with a boy, an African American boy who was ten years old. And as a result, my friend had apparently been tortured—literally—within an inch of his life in the Temple. He had been taken out in front of the assembled council, of which Liz was a member, so that they could view his injuries.

"That story did it for me, even though, as Liz told me that night, there were other stories as well. Not forgetting what my friend had done—or how wrong that was or how that should be dealt with—I just knew that I couldn't be part of an organization whose God ordered something like that. Supervised something like that. I was really aghast.

"I spent my last night in Peoples Temple doing guard duty on the tower adjacent to the wire mesh gate of the Temple compound in San Francisco. And Liz and I were planning to meet at the McDonald's next to Golden Gate Park, at midnight. But prior to that I was still doing guard duty. The person with whom I was doing guard duty that night was Lisa Layton, the mother of the Layton family that plays so prominent a role in the Temple. It was that night she chose to share with me stories of her experience as a Jewish child of Kristallnacht in 1938. At the end of her story, she turned to me and said, 'Be grateful that you are here. You'll never go to a concentration camp.' Lisa went down to Guyana a year or two later. She died of cancer about a month before Jonestown."

He pauses before adding, "That conversation with Lisa Layton was my last participatory experience inside Peoples Temple."

It's No Mystery

MARCH 21, 2003
NEW YORK CITY

LAURA JOHNSTON KOHL suggests that I write to Janet Shular, a woman Laura refers to as "her sister," who now lives with her husband, David, in Ohio. I craft an e-mail to Janet telling her about the struggles we are having finding black survivors, particularly women, who are willing to talk. On the same day I send the e-mail, President George W. Bush announces to the American people on national television that the war in Iraq is about to begin. Days later, Janet's response arrives:

> I wanted to take the opportunity to provide you some initial information and insights as related to the project and what I am willing and able to share about PT. First, I too will be more than a little relieved when the "stunning (fireworks display of) shock and awe"—also known as murder and pillage—are over, *if* that can happen in this millennium.
>
> As you read this, remember: I went to the Temple at age 30. I am about to be 63 in April, on the 10th. I am speaking from the perspective of an adult who voluntarily chose to be *at* and *in* PT, not from the position of a child/victim who had to be there.
>
> My story does not belong only to me. I had a biological family, who loved and valued me, prior to the PT experience, as did my husband. We married nearly 33 years ago (17 May 1971) in a "group marriage formality" at the Redwood Valley PT.
>
> Many people who came to the Temple were not looking for anything. They just stumbled into PT while on their life journey, people thought that by being in PT, they had a better chance at attaining a desired level of peace and joy in their lives.

It's *no* mystery. A great majority of the African American people were poor, and since Jim targeted that economic and social level, they were there in large numbers. Has anyone ever told you that they attended a meeting in Hollywood or Beverly Hills? I think *not*! How could he entice persons of those communities into giving up all of their comforts to gain a "better" life where everyone was "equal"?

For the most part, as I saw and see it, blacks and whites enjoyed living together in ways that transcended the issue of race. For some of the black people, it was a real joy to be in the company of whites and *not* be in fear of being spat upon or called a nigger. Remember: the kind of white people who joined PT were, to an overwhelming degree, kind people who had interest in justice. If not, they got converted.

So, long *before* the curtain went up and came down, the stage was set with a strong cast of have and have not characters. That fulfilled the biblical quote: "To whom much is given, of whom much is required."

What drew me to the Temple is complex. . . . It was the sixties. The sixties were more than "Flower Children," Free Speech, Free Love, and rock bands. The sixties was "The Era of Assassination" combined with war. Both Kennedy brothers had been assassinated; Martin King; Malcolm X. The many years of "Jim Crow" laws were ending in southern states, but there was still racial prejudice and discrimination, both there and in northern states. The Peace Corps was very popular. The Black Panthers organized and served breakfast to poor children, which threatened the establishment. There was Vietnam. There was Alcatraz. In America, there was action and there was (the appearance of) *real movement* toward a better way of life for *all* Americans.

From this "black" perspective, it *was* wonderful to be living in an integrated community because it was billed as being like *no* other place on earth that could equal its commitment to the masses of poor and downtrodden. It was sold as a place where *everyone* was equal and therefore treated equally; where any person, regardless of race or class or gender, was believed to have the power to and the support for confronting and overcoming *any* injustice. Everyone had "Father" who knew *everything* and who would protect *all* of his children, both from and against everyone and everything at *all* times. Omnipotent to the utmost! (Uh oh, tongue in cheek here.)

It's really too simplistic to try to look at it or to put it in terms of "black" or "white" and leaders or followers, because first and foremost, *everyone* was a follower and *everything* must be viewed from that position. PT was not a place where people just "talked the talk." They were expected to and, if it wasn't done on their own free will, they were manipulated into "walking the walk." *Most* families were interracial, by choice or by *any* means necessary.

What do you think that it has meant at any point or time in the history of the world for any person or groups of people to have the minority make determinations and decisions for and about their lives and the lives of their children? It's an answerable question. Look at the history of Native Americans. Look at the descendants of slaves.

First and foremost, PT *was* a society of secrets, secrecy and sabotage. "Loyalty" and "secret missions for Father" covered a multitude of sins, complaints and accomplishments. I often "heard" (a secret released or propaganda at its best) that Jim wanted to keep the white people close to him because he did not trust them and the closer they were, the better he could watch (as in manipulate) them.

Further, *any* suggestion that any group or body did the governing is purely false, mere illusion. What the so-called governing group did do was to provide information and ideas to Jim. Jim *always* did *all* of the *real* governing. He and he *alone* was the *ultimate* authority. He held the only veto. He had the final say. It would seem that what happened in the end would validate that.

You state that the focus of your play is about living and not about dying. Well, I'm sorry, but *every* single aspect of Peoples Temple or/and Jim Jones was about death. The death of self, the death of previous political or/and religious beliefs, the death of the previous style of dressing, the death of the pre-PT diet, the de facto death of the family of origin; the death of ego (everyone's excluding his); the death of desires for tobacco, sex, alcohol, money. It was *all* about dying all along the way, from beginning to end.

Who could have imagined or known the end? Hindsight here is now 20/20, of course, and I now see that it ended just as it started, with the requirement being physical death. Obviously some of us did see it coming.

What I want to convey here is the pure irony that you are having the PT experience simply by dealing with the dichotomies therein. One *major* contradiction:

1. Most people there were the "living dead" until they were on that final tract that led them to becoming the "dead dead."

2. More people, just as a result of meeting Jim and joining PT, had a true rebirth in terms of a greater zest and love for living than you could

possibly imagine. I mean they were energized to serve their fellow man at every level. *Both* of the statements above *are* true.

≈ ≈ ≈

I was floored, yet more convinced than ever that we have to meet Janet and David. I write to Janet, thank her for her honesty, and assure her that our aim is to humanize the people. Even if we should fail, we are going to try. Greg and I are preparing for a trip to Chicago. I close my response by asking if we can meet her on the car ride home from Chicago en route to New York. She and David live in Yellow Springs, Ohio.

She agrees to have coffee with us. A first step.

We are nervous when we arrive, but Janet and David put us at ease right away. On the driveway in front of their house we meet their three-year-old grandson, Jayden, along with their son. There is a dusty camper hitch parked on the side of the driveway that looks like it has done its share of family traveling.

We spend a few hours with Janet and David, and they are convinced after our talk to participate in the project. We discuss a time to fly back for a formal interview. David is undergoing cancer treatment and they are careful not to schedule the interview anywhere near his chemotherapy. He wants to have energy when we meet again. He wants to be able to focus.

≈ ≈ ≈

We stop for coffee at a local place in downtown Yellow Springs, a small, yet bustling college town. As we load up on sugar and caffeine and put gas in the car, Greg reminds me of something that scholar John R. Hall said to us when we interviewed him at the University of California–Davis. John was a kind man, with a square beard, short silver hair, and metal-framed glasses. Hall had given us access to research material and interviews he had done a decade earlier. And as our work goes on, a few things he said have stayed with us.

This is John R. Hall:

"That was a real utopian decade or so in the United States from the '60s through the '70s, and to some extent, you can look at the murders and mass suicide at Jonestown as the end of that utopian movement for everybody—not just for them—but for everybody."

I remember when Hall said this. He also said, "We've really lost any interest in a utopian reconstruction of American society and, you know, many of the problems that were identified in the '60s and '70s are problems that are still with us today. It's not that we've solved those problems. There were many tragedies about Jonestown, but certainly that was one of them."

Hall's words hang between us as we hit I-80 East and head back to New York.

PART IV

THE PROMISED LAND

What a Place for Them

NOVEMBER 18, 2003
OAKLAND, CALIFORNIA

WHEN THE COMMISSION FOR A PLAY about Jonestown first came through in 2001, there was hope that we might complete it in time for the twenty-fifth anniversary in November 2003. It is now two years into our process, and we are not even close to reaching that goal. We are still establishing a basis of trust with the survivor community, still trying to diversify our list of interviewees. So far, our process has been one of listening and gathering, collecting stories and information, and recovering fragments of history from the archive. Our next step is to construct a cohesive narrative from all of these varied parts. The challenge is that there isn't just one protagonist, or even twenty. There are hundreds of protagonists in this story—thousands even—and the most powerful protagonist of all seems to be the movement itself.

Margo is able to attend the twenty-fifth memorial at Evergreen Cemetery in Oakland. We also learn that Nell Smart will be flying in from Indiana to be there. Nell lost her four children in Jonestown as well as her mother, Kay Nelson, and her uncle, Jim McElvane. Two of her four children are buried with the unidentified and unclaimed bodies at Evergreen, and Nell is considering scattering some ashes of her two children—the ones whose bodies were returned to her after Jonestown— there at the gravesite.

Margo catches up with Nell after the service. Nell had only a few minutes, and it's chilly outside, so the two women sit in Margo's silver Nissan on the hill at Evergreen and talk. There is a large gathering for survivors following the service, and Nell is eager to join her friends there, some of whom she has not seen in many years. Margo knows she only has a few minutes to make an impression.

I know Nell only through the audiotape that Margo recorded in the car that day. We never used a video camera on the project. Audiotape is simpler and less invasive, yet Nell's hesitancy on the tape—her discomfort—is unmistakable.

"I am the African American on the project," Margo explains. "So my mission is to make sure that the story is balanced. People talk for different reasons, but so far we have a lot of white voices."

Nell laughs and says, "I just kind of feel this could be lengthy, you know."

Margo laughs too, and the tension between them eases. "I understand that, but let's start a dialogue—."

"We can finish over the phone?" Nell asks.

"Yeah, we can finish it over the phone," Margo answers.

≈ ≈ ≈

Three months later, I am back in the Bay Area for more interviews. Margo and I make a date to talk with Nell by phone. She has decided to go public with her story, and to participate in the play. We first want to document her reasons for changing her mind.

This is Nell Smart:
"I guess I was kind of quiet for all those years. Then I thought, 'Well, I would like for people to know that Peoples Temple was not a cult.' And me sitting here being quiet is not going to change what people think. It's a stigma, you know. 'Those poor black people were ignorant black people.' That's the way it's been received or it's been presented, that the blacks were either illiterate or not as sophisticated as the white people who joined, so therefore they were duped.

"As far as a *cult,* I hate that term, but I understand. What else are you going to call it when it's something different? It's a different culture so you shorten it to 'cult.' So in that respect it was a cult, it was definitely a different culture."

Nell explains that she was a counselor in the Temple in Los Angeles, a member of the Temple's governing body. For her, Peoples Temple was "not a church, it was a meeting of people." It was the environment, the fellowship, which drew her in. She also tells us that the LA Temple was a huge moneymaker for the church. A lot of the members who lived in Redwood Valley and San Francisco lived in communes and worked inside the church. They didn't have jobs that brought in personal income. This was not the case in LA. Many people had jobs and gave huge tithes to the church. She really wants us to understand this distinction.

Nell remembers quite clearly what Jones said at the first meeting she attended, the words that first day that "hooked her."

"I was pretty dubious about the healings." She lets out a laugh. "Because I was *dubious* about the healings, you know. I had mixed feelings about that when I was in the Pentecostal church, and I had mixed feelings about that in the Temple. But I was in a relationship with a man at the time that was going nowhere. It was not a good relationship, one of those things women find themselves in when they're single moms and they're looking for someone. The man really had no interest in my children. It was not good for me. It was not good for my children. And that morning Jim said, 'Women do not have to take all this *bullshit* from men.' Those were his words! Here was a man standing up there seemingly understanding the things that men put women through. What he said was very few words, but it hit me, because most men were chauvinistic at the time and would never allude to the fact that women were taking things off men.

"Jones was good," she lets out another laugh, "I mean, the man was *good*. I don't know how he did it to this day, but the man had a *way*. It was amazing. And that's what made me think: maybe there's something here."

We naturally ask her about her children, what led them to join, and how she felt about them being in Jonestown.

"We lived in LA," Nell answers. "There was police brutality even back then, drugs were on the rise, and there were gangs. I was a single mom at the time with four kids, trying to go to school in the evening and working full time. My kids wanted to be at the Temple rather than to be hanging out with the gang members, and I thought, 'This is good.' The kids weren't going to mess with drugs either, you know, because Jim Jones was totally against that. No matter what *he* did, the kids didn't mess with drugs. So as far as I was concerned, it was a very positive thing for them.

And my friends would say, 'Well, all your kids want to do is go to church.' And I'd think, 'Well, what a place for them.'"

Nell had taken a job doing disaster relief for the federal government, so she traveled a great deal for her work and attended the Temple less and less often.

"Even after I left the Temple, my kids still found a way to go," Nell recounts. "They believed in it. True believers. And since my mother went, she would always make sure that they got there. So when the kids came to me and said, 'We want to go to Guyana with Grandma Kay'—my oldest daughter, Tinetra, had graduated from high school—there was not much I could do with an eighteen-year-old who decided she wanted to go. I thought, 'Fine, you want to go spend some time in the jungle, you'll be *back*.'" She laughs. "So my oldest daughter went over, and the letters I got from her sounded like she was happy. So when it came time for the younger kids to go—they were fourteen and fifteen—I said, 'I'm going to go over there with you, because I want to see what it's like.' I couldn't put any limits on Al, the oldest, or Tinetra, but the younger two, I said, 'You can go for a year and go to school over there and then come back.'" Nell pauses. "And they were there four months to the day."

We explain to Nell that part of our job as playwrights is to anticipate questions or judgments that the audience might have when coming to see the play. I wonder how she would answer someone who asks, "How could you let your kids go to Jonestown in the first place, never mind without you?"

Nell answers calmly, "When I went to Jonestown, I was amazed at what they had done. It was like, 'Wow,' out of the middle of the jungle they had done this? It was kind of like pioneers, you know. It was not my lifestyle," she adds quickly. "I couldn't see myself not being able to jump in my car and go down to the store, you know. I guess I was just a little too capitalistic for that lifestyle. I'm not the pioneer type. But I felt comfortable leaving the children there."

Nell lost her family—her four children, her mother, and her uncle—all in one day, one moment, one event. As carefully as I can, I ask her how she was able to put her life back together after such a loss.

"Oh, it wasn't easy. It wasn't easy at all," her voice cracks and breaks. "You go through periods of time where you would think, 'I can't take it,' you say, 'I'll just kill myself.' When I look back now it would probably make a good comedy because you're sitting there on the kitchen floor saying, 'What can I take that won't hurt?' Cyanide must hurt, you know it hurts, you know they suffered. And you're here worrying about how much it hurts. I didn't have a gun so I couldn't shoot myself. I wasn't gonna stab myself to death. I did this so often, I was finally like, 'If you're gonna do it, do it, otherwise get on about the business of living. Your kids would expect you to.'" Nell lets out a deep sigh. "Then you drink a lot, you know, you almost become an alcoholic, but you find ways to get through it. You talk to people, you talk to friends. For a long time you only let certain people know that you were involved, only people who could understand it and never condemn. Some are listening because they're curious. Some are listening because they genuinely know that you need to talk. But you didn't care. As long as they listened, you didn't care. The people that I worked with were my support. That helped me get through it."

When we ask Nell about the legacy of Jonestown, she brings out some of the questions that still haunt her.

"I blamed everybody including God. I blamed my uncle, then I blamed the world, I blamed society." She pauses. "In some ways, we as a society do have to take responsibility. Our system of government does not address the issues that are happening with people. It's the system that causes some person like Jim Jones to be able to come in and say, 'Look what you're not getting, look what you should be getting.'

"That hasn't changed much. You've still got a lot of fat white men sitting up there in government. It's not about the people. It's about that almighty dollar. We're in a bad situation now. You've got people who are on the bottom rung, they're never gonna make it. They have to worry about how they're gonna feed their children, how they're gonna heat their homes in the winter. Of course you've got people who *are* making it, who have the money, who have the wealth, but it doesn't trickle down. It only trickles down a couple inches, and that's it. Everybody else gets the crumbs.

"Looking back," she explains, "I don't condone what happened. But there were senior citizens' homes, and a lot of the young people, young couples, donated their time to make sure that the senior citizens were taken care of. It wasn't like the nursing homes that you see today where they're beaten and stuff like that. I went through a period of time where

I hated Jim Jones, after all this happened, but then I had to sit back and think, well, you were in it. Was it all that bad? No, it wasn't *all* that bad. Not from where I was. Nobody was calling it a cult until after November 18, 1978."

She is most haunted to this day by the question of how her children died. Were they injected with the poison? Did they take the drink willingly? There were never identifications of two of her children, much less the exact cause of any of their deaths. This is not an easy subject to approach with Nell, but it is clear from her answer that she has contemplated this question intensely and often.

"I know that my oldest daughter probably took the poison very willingly because Peoples Temple was just something she had found in her life that she truly believed in. Whether the other three did or not, I'm not sure. I'm sure my mother must have really agonized over it, wondering, thinking, 'Nell is going to hate me, because I couldn't protect her children.'

"When I think about that, I cry, because my mother was a very strong woman, and without her I would not be the person I am today. I went through periods where I thought, 'How could she do this?' But I know this woman suffered. I know that she suffered knowing that I was going to blame her, and I did for a moment, but not anymore. She was my strength. And I probably would not have gotten over it had it not been for her teachings." Nell begins to cry. There is a long pause on the tape, one of those silences that as an interviewer you are tempted to break, torn between wanting to ease their discomfort and wanting to hear that which is so difficult for them to say.

"Oh man, I'm sorry," she whispers, "it's a little hard to talk about that. My mother was a matriarch, so I'm sure the three younger ones were crowding around her. I'm sure that they were saying, 'Grandma Kay, do we have to do this? What can we do?' I can see it in my mind's eye. I can almost visualize how it went. My mother didn't know what to do to protect them, and she was worrying about what I was going to say. So that's the one thing whenever I think about it. That's the one thing. I hurt for her. Because I know she hurt for me."

Exodus

CALIFORNIA HISTORICAL SOCIETY
SAN FRANCISCO

OUR PROJECT ARCHIVIST, Denice Stephenson, is laying out the passport photos on the archive tables. The sheer volume of nine hundred photos is a striking thing to see. Denice has photocopied the passport images and put them together in binders. Most members of Peoples Temple had to surrender their passport once they were in Jonestown. Very few people were able to hold on to theirs.

Greg has returned to the Bay Area, and we all gather at CHS to talk through some images and documents that we feel could be important to the play.

We begin the day by flipping through page after page of these passport images, all the faces, young and old, black and white, some smiling, some stone-faced.

As we turn the plastic sheaths that now hold the individual photos, four faces in a row, twenty to a page, Denice points out the ones related to survivors we have met, including Nell Smart's mother, Kay Nelson, and her daughter Tinetra.

Denice has been archiving documents and photographs, but on this particular day the binders she has created with the faces of the people seem more like the work of an artist. They are haunting and beautiful. There are both victims and perpetrators in these binders: people who killed themselves, people who were murdered, and people who murdered, all in the name of "the cause." As we flip through, you can't tell one from the other.

We arrange for part of the day at the archive to be spent with Stephan Jones. He has agreed to talk with us about some photos we have seen and set aside. The individual stories we are collecting have begun to come together to tell the story of Peoples Temple—at least certain parts of it—but these photographs definitely have a role to play in our understanding.

We return from lunch to find Stephan already at work. We join him at a long wooden table with a large spread of pictures in front of us. Stephan, wearing white cotton gloves, holds one of these photos, likely from the summer of 1977, showing what many survivors refer to as the "exodus" to Jonestown.

The photo depicts three older, distinguished-looking African American women, dressed in their Sunday best with long fashionable coats with fur trim, dresses, handbags, and shiny black heels. Following behind them, fourth in line, is an African American girl of about twelve or thirteen, also dressed for the occasion. It is a sunny day, and there is a white commuter plane behind them, with a red accent stripe running along its side. The women are walking in a line heading toward the door of the plane to board.

Jim Jones also appears in the photograph, in his signature sunglasses and a dark polyester suit. He is standing close to the second woman in the line, leaning into her, about to take her hand. Jones looks as if he is about to kiss her on the cheek. There is a man in the background filming with what appears to be a Super 8 home movie camera resting on his right shoulder. The feeling captured in the photo is one of expectancy.

"I wasn't there for this," Stephan says as he looks at the snapshot. "But, yeah, they're all done up so they can make the trip. This is definitely part of the exodus to Jonestown. A lot of folks went on regular commercial airlines, but I do think this plane is going."

I inquire about the presence of his father in the photo. Stephan studies it for another moment before answering. "My bet would be that he's getting on the plane with them on this trip, and he's taking some people with him. Mike Prokes is the one filming, maybe to make a spectacle of this particular trip. I'm just speculating, but that would be my impression."

I then ask about the women dressed so stylishly. "Well, I mean, it's a big trip," Stephan smiles. "They're going to a new world and a better life, paradise, leaving their troubles behind. I can't think of a better occasion to dress up for. They are dressed like they're going to church. Heart-breaking because they didn't know what they were getting into. Sad, too, you know, sad. And sweet."

≈ ≈ ≈

The Jonestown agricultural project was still under construction in 1977 when Phil Tracy and Marshall Kilduff published their article in *New West* magazine. The Jonestown pioneers—as the early settlers were called—had been clearing the land near the Venezuela-Guyana border since 1974, and Jones had used the pulpit to pitch the idea to the group. Freedom Land, he called it, or, more biblically, the Promised Land. It would be their refuge from their own country, hopelessly corrupted by racism, sexism, and capitalism.

Hue Fortson—now Pastor Hue in LA—recalled the first time he heard Jim Jones talk about it. "At that time we were on Geary Street," Hue recounted. "And I remember. He was excited—he was excited—he wanted to share something with us as a congregation. He said that he had been searching for a place: 'We can buy some land in this very remote area where we can build our own town, have our own city, have our own country. We can live in peace where our black and white children could grow together. This is the place, where we're not only going to have our milk and honey, but we can run it just like we want it.'" Hue remembered thinking at the time, "'It sounded good.' Jones decided to call it at first, 'The Promised Land.'"

Peoples Temple was in the process of creating this vision: an interracial, intergenerational community, built from the ground up, where everyone worked, and everyone was equal. In 1977, the Temple had the money, the workforce, the passion, and the will to do it.

≈ ≈ ≈

Stephan picks up another photo from the wooden table at the archive, one of a series of photos from the early days in Jonestown, picturing guys with muscles, wearing tank tops and jeans. Other photos lie scattered across the tabletop. Stephan is captured in one, with long hair and a bandana around his head. There are others, too, of newly cleared land, unfinished buildings, and structural frames reaching into an open sky.

He holds the photo in his hand. Two men steady themselves atop the roof of an unfinished building in Jonestown. It is an iconic photo: two strong men with a bright blue cloudless sky above them, building Jonestown. There is an undeniable feeling of danger and raw excitement: the town was going up.

"I wasn't there at the beginning," Stephan explains as he points to the guys in the photo. "There were probably about twenty to twenty-five guys at first, built up to maybe thirty or thirty-five. I would highly recommend you talk to a guy named Mike Touchette. He's in Florida. If you really want to feel the heart and the vision and hope of some of the people who went down, talk to Mike. He loved what he did down there, and he walked the path that became the road to Jonestown."

A few months later, Greg travels down to Florida to meet with Mike Touchette, and they speak at length about what it was like in the early days of Jonestown, while the agricultural project was still a dream in the mind of these young, devoted, testosterone-driven men.

"I arrived around dusk," Greg wrote in his notes of the meeting. "Mike's house was a boxy suburban home with all the blinds pulled down. The yard was mostly a semicircular driveway. Parked in it was a silver pickup. Mike greeted me at the door apologizing for the lack of furniture—he had just moved. His desk was a refrigerator box, and he gave me a low director's chair to sit in. There was nothing else in the room except for some framed cross-stitching on the wall. Mike had wavy, dirty blond hair and moustache, slightly touched with gray. He wore white sneakers with no socks, white tennis shorts, and a V-neck T-shirt."

I listen to the recording of the interview, transcribing as I do. Mike has a deep voice, which nevertheless has a certain youthfulness, particularly when he talks about his great love: Jonestown.

Greg asks Mike to describe what it was like to build something so massive—out of nothing—in the middle of the jungle.

This is Mike Touchette:

"I knew that I had certain dreams that I wanted to do. Certain things that I wanted to do in my life. I knew if I came down to Jonestown I would be able to do them. I'm a pyromaniac—I love fire—and I knew that I could play with fire all I wanted to in the jungle," he laughs to himself. "The other thing was I wanted to be a heavy equipment operator.

I wanted to be a lumberjack in trees, like they do up in the Northwest. Just the sheer thought, the pure thought of getting away and going down there to something that remote and building a city, something inside of me just clicked. I said, 'When do I go?'"

Greg mentions the phrase that Stephan had used, that Mike had "walked the path that became the road to Jonestown."

"When we started," Mike explains, "we went out with our surveyor. I'll never forget it. They had a little tiny footpath that they were following. There were so many trees. They had maybe three or four Amerindians in front of us, and there was three or four of them behind us. All of them had machetes. And what they did, as we're walking in, they were cutting, making a trail. You'd see a place where they'd taken the bark off as they marked their way so they could find their way out. When you walked through that jungle, you could turn 360 degrees and have no clue where you're at. That's what I saw." He pauses as if to marvel at the thought of it.

"At the end, we had over fifteen hundred acres in cultivation of every type of tree, plant, food, anything that we could eat was growing. We were growing hill rice, banana trees, citrus trees, grapefruit, oranges, tangerines, and then in between we had pineapples, we had watermelons, cassava—two types—sweet and sour. Plain and simple, we built a city out of nowhere. Our goal was to become self-sufficient in every aspect of life, from food to clothing to fuel." His pride is unmistakable on the tape.

Mike's father, Charlie, was also in Jonestown in the early days, though Mike makes a point of saying he is not close to his father and does not want to talk about him.

We later learn that Charlie Touchette was an experienced builder who led the group of young people through the process of constructing Jonestown. Mike's grandparents, Helen and Cleave Swinney, were some of the first followers of Jim Jones. They joined the church in Indiana, and the whole family followed Jones to Redwood Valley in 1965. Mike carries the bloodline of one of the oldest and most significant families in the Temple.

"Loved every minute of it," Mike says exuberantly. "I can remember it like it was yesterday. Jesus."

Mike explains that the first building in Jonestown was built by the

Amerindians and constructed solely of poles carved from fallen trees. Eventually, the guys in Jonestown replaced the original thatched roof with an aluminum roof, adding gutters to catch rainwater for bathing. They hung bunk beds from the rafters and used jelly jars with kerosene and homemade wicks for lighting after dark. They cooked on a makeshift hot plate atop a five-gallon drum.

He describes the monsoon rains, coming in from work soaking wet and putting on the same wet clothes to go back to work the next day. "It was part of our choosing," he emphasizes. "It wasn't we were forced. It was our choosing. We were doing it to build a better society. I think all of us—in the beginning—all of us believed we were building a better society."

≈ ≈ ≈

Stephan Jones ended up in Jonestown because, as he tells us that day in the archive, he was making his way *out* of the Temple. His mother, Marceline, had found him an apartment.

"I remember Dad came to my apartment, and he talked to me." He pauses and then backtracks. "I don't know if you know, people that meet me assume my dad was tall. He wasn't. Our builds were very different. He was like five-nine. I remember this conversation. I remember looking down on him. He looks really small to me when I picture this scene. He's turned on his 'I-can't-lose-you-son' approach. I'm not going for it. 'I'm staying here, Dad,' you know. I really had my walls up. He didn't want to lose his son. But I also think it would reflect really badly if his own kid said, 'I'm outta here.'" Stephan, the man who is now about the age his father was during this conversation, laughs at the image of the two of them quarreling in his apartment.

"He couldn't sway me, so he went to Mom and said, 'I really need Stephan to go with me to Jonestown. Can you talk to him about going?' She said, 'Well, I won't talk to him unless you promise me you won't keep him down there.' You know how ridiculous it is to ask Jim Jones to promise you something? As if that would have any weight. But he promised. My mom believed him. So that got me down there."

However manipulated he felt, once he was there he felt the same spark of adventure that Mike Touchette expressed for Jonestown.

"It really was the best time of my life," he reflects as he looks at another photograph. "That year or so that I spent in Jonestown before the exodus. We worked our butts off, you know, eighteen hours a day a lot of times, and we saw the fruit of our labor. We ate like kings. They were spending money, and we were building. We're in the jungle. I'm seeing my muscles grow. I'm coming into my own, so to speak. When we were off, you know, six hours that it was, it was *our* time. We were watching *Dirty Harry* movies and swinging in the rafters. It was a good time in my life, you know, and I learned to work." Stephan pauses.

"*Dirty Harry*?" he repeats for emphasis. "For God's sake. From what little bit you've heard about the Temple, can you imagine it being sanctioned to watch *Dirty Harry*?" Stephan laughs. "We would have been called on the carpet—dressed down. Can you imagine? And not only were we watching *Dirty Harry* but like I'm watching it with guys who knew every line."

Stephan describes the camaraderie, the playfulness: "In the middle of a workday, a guy might tackle another guy, wrestle for ten minutes, then get back to work, unloading the supplies that came in all night, and then working the next day, framing a building, laying the flooring, carrying the wood out of the jungle.

"I didn't realize what it was like to be in Dad's shadow until I wasn't," Stephan reflects. "What a relief that was. And then when he would come down, to also feel the dread—and I doubt that I was the only one feeling that—the dread of Dad coming, because everything changed when he was there. My father was a narcissistic madman, a sick guy, and everywhere you went it just became about him. When he wasn't there, I really was feeling that sense of community that I never felt in the Temple. I felt it. A common purpose."

Once the jungle was cleared, Jonestown itself went up in five or six months. "We were a bunch of young guys that had created our own community." Stephan says, "It almost felt like overnight."

≈ ≈ ≈

Members like Dick Tropp, the literary man, came to Jonestown when it was more inhabitable, yet still an experiment in many ways. There was an excitement in Peoples Temple as Jonestown grew. This was going to be utopia. Dick began to write about it, perhaps as a part of his project to document the movement:

Notes from the Last Frontier. The community I live in is located on one of the world's last frontiers: the tropical forests near the Venezuela-Guyana border. Here, on several thousand acres of virgin jungle allotted by the Guyana government in 1973, a group of Americans has been building an agricultural project. I arrived here in September, 1977. I came in on a fishing boat owned by the community. We traveled up the Kaituma River, through a landscape that has changed little since the days when Sir Walter Raleigh came through, searching for "El Dorado," the fabled golden city. Dreamlike, timeless. More remarkable than the hundreds of acres of tropical forest that are now producing food; more remarkable than the development of this lovely community out of the virgin jungle, the housing construction, streets, electric lighting, sanitary facilities, fruit trees planted everywhere, is the population of Jonestown. Almost one thousand people here from every race, every background. The oldest, a woman whose parents were slaves in Virginia, arrived here in January. She took the upriver trip in our fishing boat, deep into this beautiful, enchanting place. She will be 108 years old in October. We just cannot get the old folks here to "retire." The place turns them on, makes them forget they're old. 250 senior citizens, mostly black, mostly ghetto dwellers are here finding a place of peace and beauty, a new lease on life. The same goes for the over 200 teenagers and young adults who were unable to find the handle for their lives in the big cities. I cannot see anything in front of me now but to continue with the work that is going on here. I will doubtless return to the States at some time in the future, but now, that is far from my mind. The beauty here; the sense of the unexplored; the challenges of building a new community; all are compelling reasons for me to remain. While it may seem that this jungle is a place of escape, a retreat from the modern world, it is quite the opposite: here all is growth, rebirth, new horizons, becoming, development, a *future*.

≈ ≈ ≈

According to Tim Carter, the agricultural project was supposed to take ten to twelve years to build. In the initial planning, it was proposed that people go to Jonestown in a gradual progression so that the community could assimilate them and grow naturally. "We never thought that more than six hundred people would move to Jonestown, max."

Tim described what happened when the *New West* article hit: "The decision to move to Guyana—en masse—was made by Jones in one night. That's what it honestly felt like to me. Within twenty-four hours of the decision, Karen Layton and I were on our way to New York City. We were given $25,000 cash and told that in two days the first group of people would be arriving at JFK to get on the plane to Georgetown," Tim shook his head in disbelief. "Jonestown went from forty-some people to more than seven hundred in the space of two months. And it wasn't supposed to be like that. But Jim said, 'We gotta get down there right now! We can't survive with this media scrutiny. They won't let us live in peace!' We moved seven hundred people when there were like fifty fucking reporters parked right outside the Temple's gates.

"I remember being at JFK," Tim reflected, "and just being shocked at the people that were sent to Guyana. They had no business being there. And I don't mean that in a judgmental sense, but it was not an easy life. It was just not done carefully. And it was a mistake."

≈ ≈ ≈

There is no way to downplay the sense of disillusionment when Mike Touchette, Stephan Jones, and the guys in Jonestown learned of Jones's plan to send so many people to Guyana so quickly. Mike is still sensitive about it. "When they flooded us with all those people, we *begged* them not to do it. We didn't have the room. We didn't have the facility. And we were told, you know, 'Piss on you, we're coming.' And they did."

Once the influx began, the community changed. The pioneers who built Jonestown felt robbed of their dream. Mike recalls the defiance, the rebellion that followed. They would pack up "a bunch of us guys on bulldozers" and go through some of the fields. "We'd see a ripe pineapple, we'd cut the pineapple, we'd see a watermelon, we'd cut the watermelon. Whatever we saw, we'd take it. We would go into the jungle on these machines. There'd be like eight, ten of us, and we'd all be riding on these machines. All we would do is sit and do absolutely nothing but have a good time for the rest of the day. Just to get away. To stop hearing his voice and keep moving. Because all around this area, there was loudspeakers, and he would put tapes on from his sermons, and it would be just hour after hour after hour."

≈ ≈ ≈

As Stephan continues to pore over Jonestown photos in the CHS archive, he remembers a similar feeling. "When the exodus happened, to us it was this invasion of people. It's like: who did these people think they are coming into *my* town kind of thing? We didn't welcome them well at all. I've since been able to look at what that must have felt like to these people, who thought they were coming to paradise, who were shoved into the hold of the ship to come over this really rough sea to get from Georgetown to Jonestown. When the hold opens up, a bunch of tough-looking young guys full of testosterone are standing there and very few—if any—of them are smiling." He sighs. "Landing in Jonestown, having turned over your passport, surrounded by jungle, 'Ah man, what the hell have I gotten myself into?' It only got worse from there." He picks up another photo.

"When Dad got down there, he just went right back into his fearful miserly ways. We worked only twelve hours a day, instead of eighteen like we did before, but it was really the essence of digging ditches and filling 'em back up. He wasn't spending any money. Work went from a means of production to a means of control. When you got off, your time was his time. It was a stifling, insane environment. It was all there, all over again.

"And yet," he muses as he looks at the photos on the table, "the thing it's important to remember: the elements of the Temple that couldn't be found anywhere else were so attractive, so wonderful, so uplifting, that we'd do whatever we had to, to make that right. We'd tell ourselves whatever story we had to, to make that right. It was our community. I think about Johnny Brown, who was pretty fed up with my dad and the workings of the Temple, but at the same time, that was his family. 'Don't you dare come from the outside and mess with it,' that was his family: 'We got our problems, but we'll fix them.'" Stephan glances down at the table. The photographs before us include several with children, and they all look as if they are incredibly happy in Jonestown. "These little memories," he reflects. "I remember sitting watching the children of Jonestown walk up that main path and seeing every color imaginable in the rainbow, and being touched in a place that's deep and meaningful to me. I know I wasn't the only one. I know there were a lot of people who were held by that. So regardless of what got people there, see, once you're in, it's about way more than loyalty to Jim Jones."

≈ ≈ ≈

As the final audiotape of Greg's interview with Mike Touchette in Florida nears its end, their conversation comes around to forgiveness.

"When Jonestown slowly fell apart," Mike recalls, "we actually had a sawmill that we were in the process of getting up and running to use our own trees for our own wood, instead of having to buy lumber. I went there in '74. I was twenty-one. I'll tell it to you like this: I'd go back down today. That's how much I loved it. I loved living down there. The two times I've gone back since, it's like a part of me stays down there. I'm not whole, because part of me is still down there. Oh, I'd go back tomorrow. I'd have to say to my kids, 'Dad's following his heart.' I want to tell you," he continues after a moment, "what Jones did was wrong, what he did to everybody was wrong, but I can't hate him. I watched my grandmother before she died. She ate herself up over him. I told her 'Grandma, you can't do this.' She goes, 'He destroyed my family.' My dad won't even talk about it. I'm just totally the opposite: 'Hook me up,' I'm going down to Jonestown tomorrow, I'll go down tomorrow. It was something that's the love of my heart for that place." He clears his throat. "Truth is, you can look at it religiously or you can look at it philosophically. It ain't good to carry around hate. It destroys you. It eats your body. It's a fact that it's bad for you, that type of feeling inside." Mike pauses. The tape continues to roll.

"One of the things that I did, I totally changed my mind around 1985. What happened was that my wife Debbie, whom I married in the Temple, Debbie Ijames, left me. And her demand was, 'You want to see me and the kids? You've got to come to church.' So I started going to church. I started feeling good about it, and I started believing. And in 1985, '86, I accepted the Lord in my life as my Lord and Savior. I don't care what anybody says, when I did that, my whole life changed, inside and out—my thought pattern, everything. Up until that point, I could look at you and probably tell you that I hated Jim Jones. But, when that happened to me, the experience that I went through, it just totally changed my whole aspect. I don't hate the man. I've made peace. I made peace with the people that are dead. One thing I'll never do: I'll never lie about Jonestown. I'll never lie about the people, what happened, or anything else."

That's Jonestown

OCTOBER 5, 2002
EUGENE, OREGON

IN MY FIRST INTERVIEW with Tim Carter, he is adamant about showing me a video of Jonestown. "When I tell people the story, it helps me
to show them this," he says, holding up a VHS tape. The tape is a copy of
the NBC raw news footage taken on Congressman Leo J. Ryan's investigative trip into Jonestown.

Tim is right. The tape—and Tim's accompanying narration—are essential to understanding how the last two days unfolded in Jonestown.

Tim does not remember how he acquired the tape, nor does he know
how anyone can get it now. "Apparently, you can no longer get this footage directly from NBC. It's no longer in their archive. If you call them,
they'll tell you it doesn't exist."

"What happened to it?" I ask.

"Who the hell knows, Leigh?"

"How did you get it?"

"I honestly don't remember. I've watched it, I think, four times in
twenty-five years. It's just too hard to watch. But I want you to see it. It's
important to me."

Tim pops the tape into his VCR. The footage has obviously been
dubbed many times over—it is not by any means broadcast quality—and
the clock counter runs at the bottom of the screen. A number of the players we have heard about are there: Congressman Ryan, Grace Stoen, the
Concerned Relatives, and reporters.

I sit on his sofa and Tim stands, for now. He sits and stands by turns, takes smoke breaks, gets us more coffee. He is an animated talker. The tape is three hours but between stopping and starting and the conversations underneath, it takes all weekend for us to view it.

In fact, this will be the longest single interview—twelve hours the first day, twelve the second—for a total of forty recorded hours over the course of this and three subsequent interviews.

He hits "play" on his television's remote control.

The opening footage is shot from the window of a plane. The camera catches the expanse of the sky and the clouds in hazy contrast, the colors slightly tainted green and the image grainy, a by-product of the many dubs and dated technology. The sound on the TV is set pretty low, but I can hear the drone of the prop plane as it makes its way from Georgetown, the capital of Guyana, to the airstrip in Port Kaituma, about six miles outside of Jonestown. It is November 17, 1978.

NBC cameraman Bob Brown tries to keep his camera steady on the jungle below and the clouds floating by the plane's window. But from time to time it inadvertently captures the outline of the tiny window or grazes the shoulder of the person sitting alongside him. Just like everyone else on that plane, Brown anticipates the big event—seeing Jonestown for the first time—a place that has different meanings for everyone on board. Each passenger has a distinct agenda: Anthony Katsaris and other members of Concerned Relatives to check on their family members and hopefully persuade them to come home; the congressman to find answers to questions; the reporters to chronicle it all. The one thing they all share: they hope they will find out if the stories they have heard—the ones about guns and torture and White Nights and suicide drills—are true.

As Pat Ryan had told us, "Dad went down sort of banking on the fact that if he had press with him, they wouldn't dare do anything to him. They wouldn't do anything in front of the press. But the press were really nervous because a lot of them had done investigative stories into what was happening, and I think they felt a little bit more secure knowing that they had a congressman with them. They both were hoping that each would protect the other."

There were not enough seats on this tiny plane for everyone in Leo Ryan's entourage, so Grace Stoen waited behind in Georgetown for any news on the fate of her son, John Victor. "I have always felt badly in that I was a defector," Grace confided. "And you always wonder, do they hate you for having defected? I asked Stephan later, 'Did I do this? Did I cause all of this to happen?' He said, 'You know what, Grace? It was like a tea kettle and it was ready to explode.'"

≈ ≈ ≈

As the prop plane makes its way across the jungle, Tim narrates: "The word *Guyana* means land of a thousand rivers. The country was covered in rivers. Now, between Jonestown and Georgetown, there's two hours of flying in these prop planes. I don't know what speed they fly at, but a triple-canopy rainforest, it's a pretty isolated place. You either get there by flying, or you go by boat up the Kaituma River."

Tim points to the coffee table in front of us. "Remember, when Jonestown started, it was a footpath about as wide as this table. We cleared over a thousand acres. Everything that you see, we cleared, by hand. I mean, look at all that. We were building a city. And I really saw, maybe three generations down, my grandkids playing in Jonestown. I actually visualized that."

Tim pauses, then says, "I mean, if you're going to kill yourself, why are you gonna clear all that land? If everybody wanted to kill themselves, why clear twelve hundred acres?"

"It doesn't make sense," I say.

"No," Tim answers. "It doesn't."

I have never seen anything like this footage. The amount of land cleared to create the agricultural project is epic, and I tell him so.

"Yeah, it was epic," he shouts. "It was amazing. That's why people were so stunned and in awe, because it was physically overwhelming just—"

"That it existed," I finish for him.

"As the plane goes around, you'll see more of the community." He begins pointing out familiar landmarks. "That's the Kaituma River. I used to float up and down on that river in our little boat, and in places the jungle would overhang the river, and I was in the middle of South America in a tropical rainforest with all these exotic birds, and animals, and chirping, and the sky is blue, and Amerindian kids are waving to me with big smiles on their faces, and I thought, 'Man, I am so lucky. Not very many people get to live this.' It was a physically beautiful place."

He pauses the tape. "This is the little town of Port Kaituma. The population, I have no idea, but I'm guessing three hundred, five hundred people, something like that, maybe a little bit more."

He starts the tape back up again. About another minute or so passes.

"They're flying by really slow. It'll come back around. 'Cause they still haven't got to the shot where they show the whole community.

"Come on, come back around," he points and waves and talks to the TV. "There!" He pauses the tape: "There's the community! That's Jonestown."

It is a city carved out of the jungle. Jonestown from the air looks mythical in size and scope. It looks like the beginning of utopia. And many people in Jonestown, besides Tim, saw it that way.

≈ ≈ ≈

This is a letter from Annie Moore to her parents, John and Barbara:

How are you doing in the cold, old, U.S. of A? I enjoyed hearing your voices on the ham radio the other day. I am doing fine as I could be in this beautiful, warm, and temperate climate, and so is Carolyn and Kimo. Along with being the night nursing supervisor I am now in charge of our medical supply house along with one of the other nurses. I guess it is something else back there in California with all the lies in the papers about us. I have seen some of the articles and they are the most atrocious lies I have ever seen. I guess whenever anyone does anything good, there is someone always trying to destroy it. So whatever comes, all the treacherous lies that have been printed and publicized about us don't really bother me because I am having a grand time here. P.S. Be sure to bring enough cool clothes when you come—plus some rainwear—in case it rains. You will have to have boots if it does rain so Mom, don't bring your dress-up shoes only. Dress up night will be later on in the evening. Love, Anna Banana

≈ ≈ ≈

When we sat down with John and Barbara, we talked about their daughters' time in Guyana. Here is some of what they said:

"Our daughters didn't ever tell us they were going to Guyana. They told us after they arrived," Barbara explains.

"All the while," her husband John adds, "my principal concern was, here's our grandson, Kimo. It's hard enough to be a child of a Jim Jones. I'm gonna do anything I can to protect him and safeguard him."

"Many parents were estranged from their children by the time they were in Guyana," Barbara adds. "They wouldn't permit some of the parents to visit their own children. We were permitted to visit."

Their daughter Carolyn, the more political of the two daughters, also wrote to them from Jonestown:

> Dear Mom and Dad,
>
> March would be a good time for you to come visit. Our guest housing will be completed by then. We can make arrangements for flights to the interior. It is a 45-minute flight from the capital city of Guyana and is easily arranged. You know, Mom and Dad, that we are Marxists, and you have to take that into consideration when associating with us. You can see the viciousness of the press. I myself saw the Interpol report, which a high officer in the Guyanese government allowed a number of us to read. They are accusing us of the most absurd things—trafficking in weapons and currencies. We know it's our own defectors who are behind this. Why can't they just let us live in peace?

"I went down to Jonestown with the question," John recounts, "what's happening to their paranoia, what's happening to their adulation of Jim Jones, their sense of conspiracy?"

"I had great misgivings even while I was there," Barbara confides. "I didn't say anything to John about it at the time, but I thought, 'I don't like something about this place.'"

"I remember the conversation around the supper table, the last night we were in Jonestown," John reflects. "The entire conversation dealt with conspiracy. They fed each other's fears. There was no one to question the reality of those fears." He pauses and then explains, "When we came back from Jonestown, I held a press conference. I praised the good work being done down there. I was asked by a reporter, 'Reverend Moore, were the people happy?' And I answered, 'It was so obvious.'" He pauses again. "It was very important to maintain our ties with our daughters. That was the most important thing to us."

Barbara defends their decision to stand by their daughters: "We wanted a relationship with our grandson. We wanted to share in the joy of watching him grow."

In hindsight, John and Barbara acknowledge that they were manipulated by Jim Jones, both in the States and after the migration to Guyana. Peoples Temple used John's position in the Methodist church hierarchy as an endorsement of their community, sometimes without his knowledge, much less his permission.

"Many, many times rather than criticize Jim Jones, or Peoples Temple, we were just silent. But there was a cost to that," John says softly.

He pauses once more.

"When I got home from Guyana, I wrote Carolyn a letter saying: this isn't healthy. Nobody challenges Jim Jones about anything. You just are all yes people, and that's not good."

"Did she respond to that?" Greg asks.

"She didn't respond. That was toward the end. She didn't respond," he tells us sadly.

≈ ≈ ≈

Another aspect of the controversy playing itself out in the press was the custody battle over Grace's son John Victor Stoen, also known as John-John. Among the many clippings we found at the California Historical Society, one by Marshall Kilduff of the *San Francisco Chronicle* is headlined "Temple Leader is Accused in Custody Case." It begins, "The Rev. Jim Jones, leader of the controversial Peoples Temple, has evaded in the United States and Guyana, court orders to return a five-year-old boy to his mother, Grace Stoen, a former Temple member."

When Grace left the Temple in 1976, she assigned custody of her son John Victor to several members of Peoples Temple. Greg and I had seen these legal documents, and we went back to speak with Grace about them.

The question of the paternity of John Victor was the high point in the drama for many survivors. Jones claimed to have fathered the boy, and we had heard from other survivors that this question was one Grace would not answer. We try, but after fumbling with a few indirect questions, her discomfort becomes palpable and overrides our desire for a "gotcha" moment, and neither of us asks her about it directly.

Maybe we should have, but in the end, does this question really matter? She lost her son.

But I do ask her this: "By leaving him behind, did you understand at the time that you had given up your legal rights?"

"I just—I didn't know," Grace replies. "All I knew is that he was being turned against me. He had been taken from me. He had been moved to San Francisco. And I understood that he was being told that someone else was his mother, that Maria was his mother, Maria Katsaris." She pauses. "After I left the Temple, of course I'd always thought about my son, but I really didn't have anybody to talk to about it. I used to babysit for a child psychiatrist, and I called him one day and I said, 'Do you think that I can live my life without my child?' And his question back to me, he says, 'Do you really want your child to be with those people?'

"Jim underestimated me," she adds, placing her hand over her heart. "He underestimated me. He didn't know how much I would fight. I knew I could no longer live without my son and I was willing to give my own life to get him back."

≈ ≈ ≈

We ask Stephan about the controversy, too. He shows us a picture of Grace's son John Victor taken in Jonestown. On the back of the photo in the archive is a little Post-it note in Stephan's handwriting, part of his effort to name as many people, places, and events as he could. This one reads: "The child Jones claimed to have fathered and around whom the greatest conflict and controversy swirled, leading ultimately to deaths in Jonestown." He wants to talk to future generations with these tiny notations. He wants the future to know who these people were.

John Victor is about five or six years old in the picture. He is wearing an orange shirt, his head is slightly tilted, and the expression on his face looks confused. He is surrounded by adults: Jim Jones on one side, Harriet Tropp on the other, and a man in the foreground next to Jones holding a briefcase. All three adults have their eyes intensely focused on the boy. A woman approaches. She is carrying two file folders in her arms. The woman is Carolyn Moore Layton.

We ask Stephan about the paternity question. He speaks slowly and is careful with his words. "I absolutely respect Tim Stoen and Grace's assertion that John is their son. But at the time, he was my little brother, you understand? At the time—and still—he's my little brother."

A memo written by Carolyn Moore Layton in Jonestown highlights the significance of the fight over the child:

To Whom It May Concern: Pragmatically the issue of John Victor Stoen is not an isolated custody case to us. We know that if John Stoen were taken from the collective, it would be number one of a series of similar attempts. It was very much for the good of the collective that we decided as a group to make a stand on the John Stoen issue. We will defend even to the death the John Stoen issue.

"I remember one time in particular," Stephan continues, "Dad was planning this event where I would go on a walk with John Victor, and then I would fake an attack on us, like an attempted kidnapping. And that would really shake people up. They would be led to believe that John Victor was almost stolen. Maria Katsaris was the one who cared for John Victor for the most part when he was in Jonestown. She said, 'You have to talk to Jim about this, we can't do this.' We agreed that would be too hard on John. It never occurred to us to say, 'Are you nuts?!' The rationale behind the idea was: people don't know what the threat is and we've got to be vigilant. They're getting complacent. We're vulnerable. I think the number-one motive was Dad liked drama. He loved it."

An audio recording of Jim Jones from Jonestown captures that drama:

Alert! Alert! Alert! Report to the pavilion! Report to the pavilion! This is a White Night! Report to the pavilion. They started a legal action demanding that I turn over the child, and we refused. I refuse to turn over people. I said, "We will die before we turn over any child." I am trying to build a community of love, but we are forced to defend ourselves because these defectors have said, "Bring them back to America." These people who heard communism taught from my breath and my sweat and my blood are now saying that America is the best place on earth. When America is responsible for all the terror against black people and poor people all around the world. Even if you believe in nothing more than saving your own children, if you're not prepared to die for your children, you will not stand up for your children. You have to make that commitment. Patrick Henry said, "Give me liberty or give me death."

The custody case triggered what came to be known as "The Six-Day Siege," during which the people living in Jonestown defended their community against attack. According to Stephan, this was the event in which his father coined the phrase *White Night*. At first Jones referred to the danger that threatened Jonestown as a "black night" then commented that maybe it was racist to call anything as despairing as this "black." And since it was white people who were responsible for this, the danger should be known as a "White Night." He would eventually make the same change for other words or expressions that he found racist: *blackmail* became *whitemail*; the *black market* became the *white market*.

Stephen describes the Six-Day Siege: the people, armed with machetes, knives, and guns, formed a large human barrier around the perimeter of Jonestown. What so many had thought to be the Promised Land had now become a place of total isolation, where people were wielding knives and guns, and preparing for an imminent attack.

Jim Jones got on the ham radio that first night, and with the radio hooked up to the community speakers, explained to people back in the States that John-John was *his* biological son. From the other end of the patch in San Francisco, Angela Davis, Huey Newton, and attorney Charles Garry addressed the community. Here is some of what Angela Davis said:

> I'd like to say to Reverend Jim Jones and to all my sisters and brothers from Peoples Temple who are now in Guyana there: know that there are people here, not only in the San Francisco Bay Area but also across the country, who are supporting you, who are with you. I know that you're in a difficult situation right now and there is a conspiracy. A very profound conspiracy designed to destroy the contributions, which you have made to the struggle. We will do everything in our power to ensure your safety and your ability to keep on struggling.

≈ ≈ ≈

On November 1, 1978, a little over a year since the Six-Day Siege and in advance of his visit, Congressman Ryan sent a telegram to Jim Jones:

> To the Reverend Jim Jones:
> In recent months my office has been visited by constituents who are relatives of members of your church and who expressed anxiety about mothers and fathers, sons and daughters, brothers and sisters who have elected to assist you in the development of your church in Guyana.
> I have listened to others who have told me that such concerns are exaggerated. They have been supportive of your church and your work. In

an effort to be responsive to these constituents and to learn more about your church and its work, I intend to visit Guyana. I do so as a part of my assigned responsibilities as a Member of the House Committee on International Relations.

While we are in Guyana, I have asked our Ambassador, John Burke, to make arrangements for transportation to visit your church and agricultural station at Jonestown. It goes without saying that I am most interested in a visit to Jonestown, and would appreciate whatever courtesies you can extend to our Congressional delegation. Sincerely yours, Leo J. Ryan, Member of Congress.

≈ ≈ ≈

Grace Stoen visited with Congressman Ryan before the trip to Jonestown.

"We went down to Guyana as an entourage with Congressman Ryan. They flew us to Washington, D.C., so that we could talk to the State Department before the trip. I warned them. I said, 'Do you know that there's a possibility that you could lose your life?' And Ryan goes, 'Why are you saying this stuff?' And I said, 'Because Jim Jones wants to go down in the history books as a great humanitarian leader.' I told Ryan, 'I know Jim Jones. I'm willing to go, but I go with knowledge. You're going to have to kill me now to keep me away from my son.'"

≈ ≈ ≈

Back in Tim Carter's living room, we are making our way through the NBC footage from Ryan's trip to Jonestown. "I've seen the photographs of the aerial view," I say to Tim, "but I haven't seen it on video. It's different."

"It's different because you get an idea of the depth of how big everything is, and the contrast to what's around it." Tim fast-forwards to the next part of the tape that he wants me to see.

The shot shows a group of people milling around on the dirt road at Port Kaituma that serves as the airstrip. "Now, this is Mike Prokes and, I think, Johnny Brown talking with them. First, Ryan's gonna talk to some officials and the official's going, 'Well, you need permission from such and such.'"

Tim explains that on the day of Ryan's arrival, Jones contacted his aides in Georgetown, hoping they could persuade the government of Guyana to protect him from U.S. investigation and stop the visit. So for hours, while Jones made calls and sent telegrams, he kept Ryan and his party waiting on that tiny airstrip before he would allow them to be picked up and driven into Jonestown—a six-mile ride on a dirt road—on a tractor-trailer provided by the community.

The NBC cameraman captures an image of a truck pulling up. Their transportation has arrived.

"That's the same truck and trailer that was used by the guys that were shooting later on," Tim says, "which turns my stomach."

≈ ≈ ≈

Dick Tropp and his sister Harriet were writing memos to "Dad" (their term of affection for Jim Jones) in the days leading up to this event. One of Harriet's memo calls for the "beautification of Jonestown" in preparation for the visit, including painting fences, cleaning up, and planting flowers. Dick's memos advocate for the welfare of the community:

> Dad: I strongly feel that the community needs at least one and probably two days off a week, where they could go to the library, to a movie, spend time with their children. I have picked up the feeling from several people I have talked to. There is a law of diminishing returns.

When we again meet Dick Tropp's friend Jean Clancey, we ask her about the writings we had found and collected in a large binder of resources for the play, including one in which Dick talked about the White Nights:

> To Dad, personal:
> I've written this out of what I feel is a duty and responsibility. I think that other White Nights strengthened this organization. I don't really know if this one did. My apprehension is that among people with a fair degree of savvy and intelligence, there is going to be a feeling from now on that the White Night is really a kind of elaborate and ritual testing. Already the same format has been followed too often—we go through the test, take a "vote," and the right and wrong sides of the vote are pretty much felt by the fact that those voting against immediate "revolutionary suicide" are subject to questioning that contains within it not-so-subtle intimidation.

"There's a quality in some of his writings of desperation," Jean reflects. "Maybe he felt if he could keep writing, that there was still hope. He was writing to stave off what he might have sensed was coming."

And in a final memo, just before Leo Ryan's visit, Dick writes:

To: Dad
From: Dick Tropp
When Congressman Ryan comes, our aim should be to educate him, and show him a side of America he may not know about in his world. So, if possible I would like to present Ryan with texts of many of the oral history stories of our residents so he can read about the lives of people who had to go through a lot of pain in the USA.

In one of the last dated letters from Dick Tropp he requests postage stamps and directs the people back in the States to "sell my cello."

≈ ≈ ≈

On November 9, 1978, just over a week before Congressman Ryan's arrival in Guyana, the residents of Jonestown wrote "A Resolution of the Community" that they wanted delivered to the congressman, and which they had hoped would dissuade him from coming. We saw the original document at the California Historical Society:

Many of us, the undersigned residents of Jonestown, Guyana, have been visited here by friends and relatives. However, we have not invited and do not care to see Congressman Ryan (supporter of military aid to the Pinochet regime of Chile), media representatives, members of a group of so-called "concerned relatives," or any other persons who may in turn travel with, or associate with, any of those persons. Dated: This 9th day of November, 1978, Jonestown Guyana.

Hundreds of signatures fill dozens of pages. Larry Layton's signature was one of them. This petition would surface again at Layton's second trial in the United States. The first ended in a hung jury and mistrial, and this petition was the only new evidence that the government presented to demonstrate his participation in a "conspiracy" to kill Ryan.

≈ ≈ ≈

Tim restarts the tape and we watch the footage of the congressman and his entourage boarding a tractor-trailer at the Port Kaituma airstrip for the six-mile ride into Jonestown. The camera follows much of their journey.

Tim describes the agricultural project as it reveals itself to the visitors' eyes. "Here are our school tents. This is the radio room. And my cottage was the next row up. That's where I lived. And what looks like a field behind it, that was gonna be all cottages. We had posts dug for another fifty cottages that were gonna be built within three months. Isn't that amazing?"

There is incredible pride in his voice. As I see for myself all the jungle cleared, the buildings built, I see what Tim wants me to see: that Jonestown was a massive physical achievement.

"Here's the road going out of Jonestown. And the piggery would be over here," he gestures off the screen. "This group of buildings back here was where the laundry was done, and we had an experimental food kitchen over there. Over here is where we were making our own bricks. We were making our own soap. We had our herbal factory, we had our candle factory, and this group of buildings up in here is where the machine shop was. That's the pavilion right there.

"Oh, that's a perfect shot," Tim exclaims. "This was Jones's house right down here. And that—," he points to the screen, "was what we called a hospital where the beds were. That's the nursery. All the furniture in the nursery we built ourselves. That was part of the fun of it. Pop Jackson lived there."

≈ ≈ ≈

We had already seen a picture of Pop Jackson at the California Historical Society. In the photo the elderly black man is sitting on one of two twin beds in his hut. A nightstand between them is neatly covered with a white tablecloth, a small gold-and-brown alarm clock, and a bottle of hand cream. A framed picture of Jim Jones hangs on the wall above the nightstand. Pop has a big smile on his face. He is wearing a shirt with thin vertical stripes alternating in white, blue, and orange, brown slacks, and colorful suspenders with a brown-and-blue print on them. The print and the stripes seem to go together. Pop looks stylish. His little cabin feels warm and homey.

I tell Tim about the photo when he mentions Pop and my impression that he was happy. "He was," Tim replies. "Pop Jackson and Mom Jackson had their own cottages. Pop Jackson was like 104 years old, going on fifty. Some of the people that were there, Leigh, were so remarkable as human beings. I mean, Pop Jackson was more active than I was.

"We had eliminated illiteracy in Jonestown," Tim explains. "One of the very first things we did with the school was give lessons to any of the seniors who wanted to learn to read or write. What some of these people saw and what they lived through, their stories are just amazing."

Pop Jackson's oral history was among the testimonies collected by Dick Tropp in Jonestown. On the top of the page, in all capital letters, the document reads:

POP JACKSON b. 1874.

I'm settling around here free this morning. Ain't nobody got no pistol on me. Ain't nobody running up behind me, "Pull over there." White man always wanted to know what you doing—where you been last night. "Put your hands on that car," and they go around putting stuff in your pocket. You better take that stuff out of my pocket. Everybody that come up that want to do something for a nigger, they shot him. They shot Martin Luther King for trying to talk for his race. They killed the two Kennedy brothers for trying to talk for the people, shot him right through the head. And you tell me . . . ahh, shit. They say, "This is the white man's world." As long as you work with the white man, you live. If you didn't, they do you just like Martin Luther King, you're shot. I could spend my life telling you because I spent my life back there. And all the dirty things I'm telling you, they happened. Now, when it comes to Jonestown, I'm telling you it's the best place that ever was. I want Jonestown to be cared for because it cared for me. When I came here it was just getting started. I been fooling around the United States for a hundred years and it didn't do a thing for me. The United States is the last place you ought to stop to. You in danger. You should go around that because if you go around, you'll live longer.

≈ ≈ ≈

"These things that look like paths," Tim explains, "those are all boarded walks. Those are all sitting this far off the ground because of the mud," he gestures with his hands to indicate about eighteen inches in height. "They ran all through Jonestown. I don't know how long they were in terms of miles, but it takes a while to build a boarded pathway, this one was like 350 to 400 yards long, and it goes off to where the showers are over here. Most of that was put in the last two and half months of Jonestown. And with all these little fences and stuff," Tim stands up, "it was beginning to look kind of homey.

"I'm gonna go have a cigarette, and I'm gonna leave this on. That was important. This is one of the reasons why I wanted you to see this. We weren't preparing to die. We were preparing to live."

≈ ≈ ≈

Like Tim Carter, Stephan Jones has more images he wants us to see. These photos, taken by Temple lawyer Gene Chaikin, are professional grade. Stephan doesn't have the originals—he has "copies of copies"— but he believes they reflect the spirit of Jonestown.

Stephan speaks admirably of the man who took these photos. "Gene Chaikin was a brilliant man with a lot of ideas about agriculture and real hope for building a community in Jonestown." The lawyer, who had joined Peoples Temple in Ukiah, had been an adviser to his father but had become disillusioned about his antics once in Jonestown. Stephan tells us that Gene didn't know that his wife, Phyllis, had been enlisted to spy on him, so any criticism or even questions about decisions or judgment went straight to Jones himself. Gene was soon stripped of any influence or status in Jonestown, and eventually, according to Stephan, he was periodically drugged.

"Some of the people who were drugged were just given these low doses that kept them . . ." Stephan pauses to search for the word, ". . . ineffective. They were told by the doctors that they were treating them for malaria or some kind of jungle fever."

What the drugs were and how they were given to people, Stephan wasn't sure, but he did tell us that people who disagreed with his father, even the people who tried to reason with him, were put into what they called the Intensive Care Unit (ICU) and drugged.

Talk of the ICU elicited another story. There was a nineteen-year-old woman, Shanda James, who wrote Jim a note calling off her sexual relationship with him. She wanted to be with someone her own age, she said, another nineteen-year-old that she had fallen for in Jonestown. Shanda handed the note to the guys in security. One of them happened to be an ex-boyfriend, so on the way to Jones's cabin, he read the note, then handed it to Jim.

Stephan explains that as the guys walked away from the cabin, Jim came blasting out the door and said, "Oh my God, go get Shanda. I told her we couldn't have sex anymore, she's threatening to commit suicide. I don't know what she's gonna do. Go get her and stop it."

"They knew what the note really said," Stephan explains. "They knew my dad was a fraud. And in that moment, everything changed for these guys in terms of who they were in Jonestown, and who they were to Jim Jones. Changed completely. But they still went and got Shanda. And took her to the ICU. And they came running to me, and I was outraged by that. I go confront Dad. And Dad and I, we're screaming at each other, him calling me a fucking liar and me calling him a fucking liar, and me telling him what he's doing to Shanda and what he's doing to my Mom is wrong. And Shanda was fifty yards away from where we were standing. And I never walked in there and carried her out. I was too busy with pulling the curtain back on Oz." He shakes his head. "I still liked being an enforcer. I was a tough guy. I was the great revolutionary."

He quietly resumes flipping through the photos. He stops at one. "Look at that. Beautiful shot." He vacillates between good stories and evil ones, and seems to hold both in equal parts.

"What Gene did is he went around and he took pictures. This is his legacy. These photos speak of one man's vision for his community. This is what he loved about Jonestown."

As Greg and I are flipping through the black-and-white copies, some other shots—original photographs—appear from within the stack. Stephan takes them from us, studies them a moment, and says, "Now, what's been mixed in here are actually photos from when the congressman came to Jonestown."

He starts going through the stack himself to see what else he can find. He pulls out another photo of the guys playing basketball in Jonestown and smiles.

"Was this a big coup—getting the basketball hoop?" Greg asks.

Stephan hoots, "Big coup?! It was a total act of rebellion!" We all laugh.

"Mike Touchette pulled out the welder and we just welded it out. This was a foundation for an unbuilt building, and the floor was already laid, but Dad didn't want to spend any more money to build a house, so it's like, 'We're making a basketball court.' And we got an afternoon off and didn't tell anybody. We just made the hoop and that pole, went out there, and sunk it."

The "court" Stephan refers to is a rectangle of wooden planks raised two feet above the ground. I thought it looked pretty hazardous for a court—if a guy needed to lunge to keep the ball from going out of bounds, he would go flying off the court and land in the jungle—so I ask Stephan about it. He just laughs. "It was wild. We went flying off that floor more times than you can know."

We saw real joy in his eyes as Stephan talked about that basketball court, about playing ball with the guys. The danger of falling off the court was part of the fun of it, as was the rebelliousness of playing in the first place, as was the sport itself. Stephan, his brother Jimmy, and several others on the team towered above six feet and were extremely gifted athletes, competitive players.

He holds up yet another photo and points to a young African American man. "Now this is Poncho Johnson. Singing with the band. Whitney Houston did a remake recently, 'Greatest Love of All.'"

"The Greatest Love of All" was one of the songs the community sang for Congressman Ryan the night he came to Jonestown. The photo that has fallen from the stack is from that night, November 17, 1978.

Stephan pauses.

"You know, we weren't in Jonestown that night," he continues. "We were in Georgetown scrimmaging the Guyanese national team. We were bucking the system and disobeying orders, this little rebellious group, enjoying playing basketball. We're seventeen, eighteen years old at the time.

"Dad comes on the radio from Jonestown and says, 'We want you guys back.' I say, 'No.' He gave me his line about how I was disobeying a direct order, and I say, 'Thank you for sharing, but we're not coming back.' He got Mom on, and Mom's talking about why she needs us back. I said, 'Mom, you don't have to talk for Dad.' Which just sent him through the roof. I knew it was sending him through the roof. I said, 'We're just gonna stay here.'" He pauses again. "I've since really wrestled with, 'God, did she really want us to go back there?' She knew things were getting ugly. When Mom and I were together, we had the ability to talk Dad down from the edge. And Mom lost that anchor."

And with the most regret we've heard in his voice so far, he says, "I believe I was an anchor to Mom. I know I was."

≈ ≈ ≈

Tim Carter resumes the VHS tape after his smoke. Our conversation does not wind down during smoke breaks, but, rather, it heightens: the "smokes" seem to free his mind to remember. We come back to the tape. Tim presses "play" again. His adrenaline runs high.

"So next thing you're gonna see is us setting up for the assembly for Congressman Ryan and his party. The woman in the white pants is Shirley Hicks. She and her sister Marthea were from Detroit."

I make the connection. Shirley Hicks is the sister of Rod Hicks, Margo's childhood friend from Detroit. Shirley wears a tight-fitting sleeveless polyester jumpsuit with a wraparound neck, exposing her back and shoulders. She taps her foot, raises both arms, and begins to conduct the band. The Jonestown Express has a horn section, drums and percussion, several guitars.

"What's hanging up in the background?" I ask.

"That's the sign that says, 'Those who do not remember the past are condemned to repeat it,'" Tim explains. I had heard about that sign—investigator Jack Palladino remembered it from his visit to Jonestown with its slight misquote from George Santayana. "Those who *cannot* remember the past are condemned to repeat it" is the actual quote.

"Notice the songs that were sung on this night—the words to the songs—they were sung with a lot of meaning," Tim emphasizes. "You'll see what I mean. It's part of what I was experiencing as a Temple member that night."

The footage is taken from inside the pavilion.

"There's gonna be a lot of shots of kids," Tim sighs. "And they're really hard for me to look at. They're hard for most people to look at. But like I said, this is raw footage, and every, every second is precious."

NBC cameraman Bob Brown pans across the stage capturing each individual member of the band. Tim names them in sync with the shots: "There's Brian Bouquet playing the sax. The guy next to Brian, his name in Jonestown was John Harris, but his real name was Peter Holmes. He was an ex-con from San Quentin. He changed his life around in the Temple, too. And right there, this kid—he's from LA—his name was Shawn Baker. I think he was like thirteen. He was a prodigy he was so talented. They were a pretty tight little band."

The camera shifts from the band to the crowd, a sea of children up in front near the stage. The image captures a close-up on the face of one of the kids in the group, an exuberant little boy, about eight years old.

"Now, as far as the media was concerned, this was all orchestrated," Tim gestures. "But you can't orchestrate joy like that." The contempt Tim still holds for the media rings in his voice.

"Who is that little kid with the glasses and the green shirt?" I ask.

"I forget whose son that was." Tim begins to cry. "It just breaks my heart."

One of the first songs the band played was "That's the Way of the World" by Earth, Wind, and Fire. A woman in a full-length dress with a tie-dye print steps up to the microphone.

"That's Deanna Wilkinson," Tim says. "She had it. She was a special, special talent. She was with Jim from the time she was a little girl. You can see her face is really scarred. Her parents threw hot grease on her face when she was six years old."

I remember this detail from Deanna's oral history.

"The songs that were sung this night—the ones that are coming up— were picked very specifically," Tim continues.

The camera pans to the left to catch a young couple dancing nearby. "This was staged. That dancing. I don't even know why they did that 'cause to me it looks stupid. It wasn't necessary 'cause we were good enough. Just who we were, and what we were doing, was good enough."

Bob Brown focuses in on a close-up of Deanna's face and eyes. "When Deanna sang," Tim shouts, "people were into it, man. When she sang, she brought the house down.

"We come together on this special day, to give a message loud and clear," she sings. The sound is muffled, but it's still there.

As the music continues in the background, the camera opens up to a shot of the whole community. "In the red back there is Jim Jones with the shades on, and that's Harriet Tropp. And over here, I'm in back. I'm sitting next to Charles Krause of the *Washington Post*. That's Caroline

Moore Layton. This is Jack Beam over here. He had been with Jim longer than anybody else."

Tim stops the tape, and a new regret clogs his throat. "There's my sister Terry, holding Chae-ok, my nephew. That's a really great shot of Terry. That's one of the reasons this tape is so important. My wife, Gloria, she would have been in that shot, right between us, but she had gotten up to get a bottle for our son Malcolm." Now silent, Tim starts the tape back up again.

Deanna reaches the refrain in the song, "That's the way, of the world," and the drummer picks up the beat. "Plant your flower, and you'll grow a pearl. Child is born, with a heart of gold, way of the world, makes his heart grow cold. . . ."

"Nobody ever got tired of hearing Deanna Wilkinson sing," Tim says.

The camera pans again across the audience. "That's Dick Tropp, the guy in the blue shirt."

The music ends, and Leo Ryan steps up to the microphone. "Now, this is one of the more significant things that happened in the last twenty-four hours of Jonestown," Tim says, more animated. "Ryan's going to talk. 'Thank you, blah, blah, blah,' and you're gonna hear this explosion of noise, and the media everywhere said, 'Well, this was rehearsed.' It absolutely was not rehearsed, because it was a chance for every person to say, 'This is how I feel.' I know what *I* felt. I know what I was experiencing. I saw the looks in people's faces, and they were sending Leo Ryan a message—and even he gets overwhelmed, you'll see, he's kind of like, 'Where's this coming from?' What you hear is not rehearsed. It's the people of Jonestown talking. That's important to me for you to know."

Congressman Ryan addresses the crowd: "I'm very glad to be here. This is a congressional inquiry, and I think that all of you know I am here to find out more about your life here in Jonestown. But I can tell you right now that from the few conversations I've had with a couple of folks here already this evening that whatever the comments are, there are some people here who believe that this is the best thing that's ever happened to them in their whole life."

Applause erupts in the pavilion.

"People knew he was trying to talk. It's like, 'Fuck you, you're gonna hear,'" Tim explodes. "Let me put this in context, because literally twenty-four hours from this point in time right here, there were nine hundred dead bodies on that same spot. It's inconceivable," and his anger gives way to tears.

≈ ≈ ≈

Another person in the crowd that night was Vern Gosney. He had arrived in Jonestown just eight months earlier, on his birthday. In our interview with Vern, he tells us that it didn't take long for him to realize he had made a terrible mistake.

"I wanted to leave as soon as I got there," Vern states. "We were met by Stephan and some other people who unloaded the boat. They were extremely hostile. They were armed. There are no cars. There is no communication with the outside world. The disparity between what Jonestown was touted to be, and what it actually was, was quite shocking.

"The night I arrived, it was a Sunday night, and they were giving out cookies after dinner. You see hundreds of people lined up to get a cookie. It was very surreal. I went back to my cabin and I buried my head in my pillow, and I cried and cried. I was looking to what the future is, and I saw nothing. And there was some kind of knowing in me that I had to get out."

Vern describes what happened next:

"We lived in cabins with about twenty-five people. And another young guy, I trusted him and told him that I was planning on leaving, but he revealed what I had told him to Monica Bagby. So, I was walking down the path one day, and Monica is coming the opposite direction, and she says, 'Let's get the fuck out of here.' And so from that time on, we bolstered each other. We'd say to each other, 'We have the right to leave if we want to.' There was so much confusion in our minds.

"When the congressman came, I wrote a note. 'Help us get out of Jonestown.' Signed, Monica Bagby and Vernon Gosney.' And that night for the assembly, I didn't know who the congressman was. He came with a whole bunch of other people. So, I'm scoping out the place from the back of the auditorium, and there is a newspaper reporter who I think is the congressman—Harris, he's the NBC reporter who was killed, Don Harris—I hand him a note, you know, trying to sneak it. And he drops it." Twenty-five years later, Vern still can't believe it. "Drops the note. And I pick it up and I give it to him, and I say, 'Oh, you dropped something.' And this little kid sees me and says, 'He passed him a note, he passed him a note.' The kid ratted me out, you know. He was like nine years old. So everyone is around me, asking me questions. And the congressman came and he said, 'You're the first one to ask to leave.' And I said, 'You are in great danger. You need to leave right away.' He said, 'Well, we have no transportation.' And he's right. There was no transportation. Jonestown provided the transportation for him to come to investigate. And I repeated, 'You're in danger.' And he said, 'We can't leave until tomorrow, but don't worry. You have the congressional shield of protection around you. Nothing will happen.'"

≈ ≈ ≈

All of this drama with Vern happened off camera. What is captured on camera is a moment after the show, as Bob Brown films Jim Jones and little John-John. Jones is awkwardly squeezing the boy's cheeks, trying to coax a smile. The cameraman closes in on John-John's face. Tim explains to me what is going on.

"Jim is making John show his teeth so people can look at *his* teeth and John's teeth and say, 'We're just alike.' Jones is trying to prove that John-John is his kid."

"That is a beautiful kid," I remark.

"Yes, it is," Tim concurs. "And John was off the charts in terms of intelligence and awareness. He was like five going on fifty in a lot of ways. He was just like Stephan in that way. He was precocious, which is one of the reasons why I know he was Jim's son, just from the genes. He was so much like Stephan. And Stephan was very, very close to John-John. Look at that poor child holding his teeth like that. And you can see Grace in his face, too."

But Grace was not there on this night. She had not accompanied Ryan to Jonestown but, instead, had stayed back in Georgetown.

≈ ≈ ≈

Also absent from the pavilion that night was Stephan Jones, who was in Georgetown playing basketball with the guys.

"I didn't meet Ryan," Stephan explains. "If I had, it would have been like, 'Man, you're fucking this up.' You know toward the end, we were sure it was just a matter of time before Dad killed himself on drugs. I don't know what he was shooting—barbiturates of some kind—and I guess there was speed involved. He was pretty much just animating himself on drugs. To go to sleep he'd take them, to get up he'd take them. I saw Carolyn give him an intravenous injection once, and it had his voice slurred in seconds. He said, 'Oh, don't worry, son, it's vitamin B12.' He was whacked, slurring his speech. He'd get on the PA and just talk forever, these monologues." Stephan shakes his head in disgust. "A very strong memory for me is talking to Mom about Dad's drug use, and she said, 'We've got to isolate him and get him off those drugs.' And I said, 'Mom, you don't tell God he's got a drug problem.'

"But from what I can see, Dad rallied himself around this last event. What are the things that my father hated most?" Stephan asks, ticking them off with his fingers. "U.S. press, U.S. government, and defectors. And they served up a shitload of all of it."

≈ ≈ ≈

Tim's tape has rolled to around to November 18, the day of the tragedy. "This is Saturday around 11:00 in the morning," Tim says. "That's Marceline Jones in the red pants. That's Dick Tropp in the yellow shirt over there to the right. That's Charles Krause of the *Washington Post* that's in front of her. See, we wanted to take the media on our own tour, but the media wanted to do what they wanted to do."

"Is that Marceline's voice I'm hearing off camera?" I ask.

"Yeah, yeah," Tim replies.

It looks as if Marceline Jones is trying to manage the media by taking them on the tour of the community.

"This nursery was Marceline's pet project," Tim tells me.

The cameraman captures the sign "Cuffy Nursery."

"Cuffy was the leader of a slave uprising against the British, so that's who it's named after," Tim explains.

The camera then zooms in on the face of a beautiful black baby girl. "This was the first baby born in Jonestown," Tim smiles. "Before this baby, the women delivered in Georgetown. The first three children of the Temple born in Guyana were Carters," he tells me proudly. "My sister Terry's was the first, my brother Michael's was the second, and mine, Malcolm, was the third. Those are the first three Temple citizens born in Guyana. And this baby, she was the first baby born in Jonestown."

The camera slowly pans down the row of cribs lining both sides of the nursery. "Every piece of furniture in this nursery we built by hand ourselves," Tim says with pride. "All those little toys, too, we carved by hand."

There were a few adults looking after the babies. "We had one day care worker for every three children. Marceline managed the care of children very seriously, and the care of seniors." He begins to cry again. "What difference does it make?" he whispers. "Everybody fucking died."

As the tape rolls, he says, "That's Kaywana." His face lightens. "That's my brother Michael's wife, and that's their daughter, my niece."

"Look how beautiful she is," I say.

"I wish I had some shots of Malcolm like this but—." His voice trails off.

Tim pauses the tape. "Okay. This is the beginning of the end in reality," he says, before resuming the tape.

"That's Edith Parks and that's Jackie Speier, the congressman's aide. And Edith just walked up to Jackie Speier and said, 'I'm being held prisoner and I want to leave.'"

"Jackie Speier doesn't look prepared for the jungle in those heels and that dress," I say.

"She's the congressman's aide. I guess that's how she thought she was supposed to look," Tim replies.

"But just at this moment, Harriet Tropp looked at me—I'll never forget this—she goes, 'I guess we're all gonna die.' I remember looking at her thinking, 'What?!' And the reporters just sensed, the story is on.

"It's about 11 A.M. Jones was still not in the pavilion. He arrived around 12:00 or 12:30, after Edith had said she wanted to leave. Edith's announcement is what brought his drugged ass up from his house."

≈ ≈ ≈

There are several interviews on the tape. One is with top Jones aide Maria Katsaris and her brother Anthony, who had come as part of Ryan's entourage. Anthony struggles to break through the emotional wall his sister has clearly built between them.

"Maria was one of Jones's most trusted aides in the final months," Tim explains. "She was just twenty-five and looked even younger.

"I worked with her in the letters office, too," Tim says, "and she and I got to be really close. She changed so much after she became one of Jim's mistresses that it was hard to remember her as she was before.

"Look at Anthony," Tim continues. "This poor guy, he really was upset. He is just saying, 'I can't believe it, this is not her.'"

Anthony is not able to hide his discomfort and pain from the camera as his sister coldly rejects his overtures. She does not budge. She wants her brother to go home and leave her in peace.

The camera catches Jim Jones in profile, and the lens zooms in. "Look at Jones's lips, his face, look at that. The Parks family is leaving as a group and he's trying to talk Edith Parks and everyone into staying, and he was so fucked up, he was so on drugs, he was just out of his mind high. It's the Temple's moment of crisis, and Jim Jones is stoned out of his mind."

≈ ≈ ≈

Off camera Congressman Ryan and Jackie Speier were talking to defectors, including Monica Bagby and Vern Gosney. They were working with the leadership to get any paperwork in order, and to ensure their safe departure from Jonestown.

"The congressman told me, 'Don't ever let me out of your sight,'" Vern recounts.

"And I'm telling him, 'You have got to get out of here. You are in great danger.' He says, 'You have nothing to worry about. Nothing will happen.'

"I said, 'I need to go get my clothes.' So he walked with me into my cabin to get my clothes.

"When I opened the door, there was twenty-five Temple security guards in the door. There was a ladder that goes up to the loft, and one of the guys was leaning on the ladder and he says, 'Where are you going, Vernon?' I said, 'I'm going to San Francisco.'

"And then Marceline Jones came. She says, 'Oh, things are going to be different. If you need companionship, we're going to fix that up for you, we're going to get you somebody, we're going to have a lot of reforms.' I'm carrying this duffel bag of clothes. The security is walking with me, so Marceline could have more time to talk. And at some point I told her, 'There's nothing you can do and nothing you can say that will change my mind.' I signed a paper stating that I was leaving my son Mark there voluntarily. I still wasn't sure I was doing the right thing."

≈ ≈ ≈

"Now, it's 1:30 in the afternoon," Tim announces. "They were getting ready to leave. But it was just the Parks family, and Vern Gosney and Monica Bagby. It was no shock that Vern wanted to leave Jonestown, he'd been in and out of the Temple. Monica Bagby, that was no surprise either. So, things were okay, I mean, I felt good.

"This is the last interview of the day," Tim continues as NBC news reporter Don Harris interviews Jones. It's the last interview of the day and the only on-camera interview with Jones. "One thing to be explored, and that's this question of—well, for us, the thing of fear," Harris says to Jones. Then he pulls out the note from Gosney. "This is a good example: last night someone came and passed me this note." Harris reads the note, "Help us get out of Jonestown. Signed, Monica Bagby and Vernon Gosney."

"People play games, friend, they lie, they lie," Jones scowls. "What can I do about liars? This is a man who's going to leave his son here." Next to me Tim speaks the words along with Jones: "People play games, they lie, they lie."

"Doesn't it concern you, though?" Harris presses.

"Anybody who wants to can get out of here. They come and go all the time," Jones rebuts.

"Lying sack of shit!" Tim explodes at the TV. "Now, if this was the man that I saw when I got to San Francisco, I would have kept on moving. And I'm sure that 90 percent of the people that were there would have just kept on moving."

≈ ≈ ≈

Tim pauses the tape to explain what happened next. "This is about 1:30 or 2:00 on Saturday afternoon now. They are just about to leave. Literally, all of a sudden, the wind came up, the sky turned black. I felt evil itself blow into Jonestown that day on that storm. It was on the wind. It was in the air. It rained, it turned black, boom, lightning, just tons of rain. Bottom line, they couldn't leave because it made the roads impassable. So they all got off the truck and came back into the pavilion."

Tim explains that it is crucial for another reason, though. "The whole mood of Jonestown changed, and Jones's mood changed, 'cause that's when he discovered that nine people had left that morning."

I remember Juanita talking about that trail. "They actually used it, Tim?" I ask.

"Yes," Tim confirms.

"The storm is significant for another reason," Tim continues, "because it was minutes later that the Bogue family—Edith, Jim, Tina, and Juanita—and Harold Cordell announce they want to go." He points to the TV.

"It was still pouring outside. And we were all trapped in that pavilion," Tim describes. "The whole Bogue family had their big screaming match. The one sister Marilee didn't want to leave with the others. She was staying in Jonestown, no matter what the rest of them did. And she did. They all left and she stayed. Harold Cordell's son Jimmy Joe Cordell screams at his father, 'You're a traitor, you're a traitor.'

"And people are crying, everybody's feelings are hurt," Tim stresses. "When Edith and Jim Bogue left, it just sent shock waves through Jonestown. Edith and Jim were some of the hardest-working people in the Temple. And she even said afterwards, 'I loved Jonestown and I loved the people. I just felt if I didn't leave, I'd never get out alive.' She was smart enough to know that."

Tim pauses the tape and explains: "This is when they realize there's too many people now who want to leave. We were milling around waiting for arrangements to be made for a second plane. Frankly, it's a miracle that they found a second plane and a pilot who was available.

"By now, it's about 3:30 in the afternoon. I personally had warmed to Leo Ryan. I was impressed with the man. He said to me, 'If two hundred people wanted to leave, this place would be a success.' I could tell Ryan was genuine when he said it. He said, 'This place is incredible.' But he also said, 'Jones is the most destructive force here.'"

≈ ≈ ≈

Then there is a final defection. "Now, they're calling Bonnie Simon," Tim explains.

Bonnie Simon's husband, Al, is carrying two children, one child under each arm. "But Bonnie didn't know that her husband's gonna leave and take their kids, and you can see her here in a second." The tape shows Bonnie frantically moving toward them, screaming at the top of her voice, "You bring those kids back here! You bring them back! You don't take my kids! Mother! They're taking my kids! No!" There is terror in her voice and on her face.

Tim pauses the tape. "By this time, the rain's let up. But as the news leaked that people were leaving, people started gravitating up to the pavilion. That group energy, this is really where it begins to build. All of sudden, Congressman Ryan realizes even with the second plane now they don't have enough seats to take everybody out of Jonestown. And so it's decided that everybody would leave except for Leo Ryan and the reporters. You could see the jaws of Jones just begin to clench."

≈ ≈ ≈

"Things were starting to snowball," Vern recounts. "We got into the tractor-trailer, and Larry Layton was there. And everybody was going, 'Watch out for Larry, we think he's a plant. We think he's a false defector.' I was walking past this tent full of people to go to the tractor-trailer, and they said, 'You fucking honkey! I hope they shoot the fucking plane down, you fucking traitor.'"

≈ ≈ ≈

When the tape resumes, there is a lot of chaos on the screen but what is happening off camera—what Tim witnessed—is even more foreboding. "I more than witnessed it. I lived it. Ryan was talking to me, Mark Lane, and Charles Garry when it happened. Don Sly came up, grabbed Ryan around the neck, and said, 'All right, motherfucker, you're gonna die.' He put the knife up there, and we all jumped on him and got the knife away. Then Jones asked Ryan, 'Does this change everything?' And Ryan said, 'It doesn't change everything. But it changes things.'"

Tim explains that Ryan was concerned that there were still others who wanted to leave Jonestown—but for his own safety, and the safety of those in his party, he has agreed to leave.

Vern describes that as the tractor-trailer was pulling away from Jonestown, he yelled to Ryan, "You are leaving people here who do not want to stay!"

But it was time to go. The congressional party—including now up to sixteen defectors and the newsmen and relatives—set off for the airstrip in the Temple truck. The cameraman begins filming again on the airstrip as Don Harris conducts an exit interview with Leo Ryan. The congressman looks disoriented from the knife attack, and Harris presses him for a quote about the dramatic turn of events that led to their quick exit from Jonestown.

Ryan tries to maintain his equanimity, but between being clearly shaken and the poor quality of the audio, his words are somewhat disjointed: "The attitude of many of those who are [inaudible], and this is before any kind of violence occurred, the attitude of many—." Then more assertively he emphasizes, "Can I just add that there are an awful lot of good people there, that are there, I think on a—on a positive and—uh, supportive and an idealistic basis, uh, trying to do something that is different and important to them."

A few moments later, the camera focuses in on the approach of the tractor-trailer. It stops. Several men jump off. The image is out of focus, but you can see shots being fired in the distance. NBC cameraman Bob Brown drops the camera. He's been shot. The end of the tape is the most haunting. The image goes horizontal, then seconds later the screen goes to white "fuzz," and then to black.

Congressman Leo Ryan was killed instantly, as were journalists Bob Brown, Greg Robinson, and Don Harris, and defector Patty Parks. Jackie Speier, Anthony Katsaris, and Vern Gosney were severely injured. Several more sustained less severe wounds and were left for dead as the truck sped away back to Jonestown.

≈ ≈ ≈

There were two planes at the airstrip: a twin-engine Otter and a Cessna. Vern Gosney was waiting to board one of the planes when the tractor-trailer full of young men from Jonestown with guns pulled onto the airstrip.

"We went to Port Kaituma where the planes were waiting, and we offloaded," Vern tells us. "They were separating the people into who was going to go on the big plane and who was gonna go on the little plane. So the plane starts to taxi, and we're going down the runway, and we're just about to take off and the tractor-trailer with these guys with guns crosses in front of us. I'm looking out the window, and I'm saying,

'They're killing everybody, they're killing everybody!' I turn around and that's when Larry Layton shoots me once here and once here," he gestures. "Shoots Monica in the back twice, and Dale's saying, 'Vern, help me get the gun, help me get the gun.' So we wrestle the gun from Larry. I push the seat up where the pilot was and I go outside. I got shot again in the leg. I started to run, the adrenaline is—you're just in another world, in another state of consciousness. There is no pain. There is no nothing. So I'm running, and I fall. I fall into this giant clump of bushes that totally hides me. I remember lying on the ground, and I'm going, 'Oh, I'm dying.' And I lost consciousness."

This is the same scene Juanita Bogue had described to us. The one that left her so traumatized that she did not even realize that she was five months pregnant when she returned home to the States. I remember her words, "They left us all for dead."

≈ ≈ ≈

Tim and I sit in silence in his living room for a while, the two of us staring at the white fuzz on the TV screen. I feel numb and worry about how Tim is doing. But then he continues. "I was in Jonestown when that truck came back from the airstrip," Tim explains. "There was all this screaming. As they pulled up and jumped off, I saw that certain look that you get when you're in combat, and I knew these guys had been in combat. I mean, it's adrenaline, but it's not like any other look. I heard one of the guys say, 'We got the congressman, we got them all.' I literally did not believe them. It was easier to think that Jones would try to kill everybody in Jonestown before he would try to kill a congressman."

There is a long pause—a lot of silence between us. The tape automatically begins to rewind in the VHS player.

"It was about 4:30 in the afternoon," Tim explains. "A simple announcement rang out over the PA system telling everyone to 'Report to the pavilion, please report to the pavilion.'"

He pauses.

"I was asked this just a couple of weeks ago: did you know there was poison there? And the answer is no. Why was there so much poison there? I don't know."

We sit in silence for another minute. "I'm gonna bet all those people are a lot more real to you as people than they were twenty hours ago. I hope that doesn't sound presumptuous, because I don't mean it in a presumptuous way." The VHS tape auto-ejects from the player, and he turns off the TV. I can see the label of the tape with Tim's handwriting: "Last two days."

≈ ≈ ≈

This tape changes everything. The images of hope, of happiness, of accomplishment that Tim pointed out on the tape with such pride descend into incredible darkness as innocent people are murdered on the airstrip. I have not until now grasped the true joy of Jonestown: people smiling, working together, both black and white, young and old, the sheer magnitude of what they built. These images would appear to belie the stories of punishment, late-night paranoid diatribes, and pledges to die for the cause, until you watch the end of the tape. Studying this story, it is hard to hold all of this as being born of the same mind, the same body—the intentions of the same group of people.

Perfect Religion

....

SURVIVOR EUGENE SMITH has never talked publicly about his history in Peoples Temple. After hearing about the vast collection at the California Historical Society, he begins to come regularly to look at photographs. He spends hours at CHS studying his personal history, looking for clues to his past. Denice Stephenson helps him track down photos of his family lost in Jonestown—his mother, Mattie, his wife, Ollie, his baby son, his two adopted children—and he in turn helps her identify the people in the photos. He had forgotten a lot of the names and faces, but the work helps him to retrieve them. Together, they match a number of names to the legions of anonymous passport photos.

She tells him about our project, and our difficulty in gathering black voices for the play. At Denice's encouragement, Eugene agrees to talk to us about what it has been like to hide his life for more than twenty-five years.

≈ ≈ ≈

Margo and I arrive at an old blue Victorian house in Oakland and walk around to the carriage house in back where Eugene lives. He has the stereo on, and we can hear the sound of jazz as we approach the door. We knock a few times before he hears us. Eugene is shy when he opens the door, but warm and easygoing.

He gestures toward the back of the apartment, to the kitchen area. There are three stools set up, two on one side for us, one for him on the other, and the counter in between.

"I guess you haven't had many black men or African Americans in

235

general to talk to," Eugene says as he pours each of us a glass of water and we settle in.

"It started off really tough," Margo acknowledges. "But we're getting there."

"So you have some questions?" Eugene asks hesitantly.

But first there is something he wants us to know.

This is Eugene Smith:

"I was telling Denice that I didn't mind having an interview with you two, but it can't be with a man. I have real problems with Caucasian men. Don't get me wrong, I'm in an environment where I work with engineers everyday, so naturally there are white men, and I can work with them. But in my personal life, you can't be my friend, I'm sorry. It's one of those fallacies of that whole incident, one of the shortcomings, one of my weaknesses, one of the things I just can't seem to shake. I'm really distrusting in that sense. I've just dealt with it the best I can."

Eugene takes a sip of water. He looks down into the glass.

"My memory is clear on a lot of things, I don't know why that is, because when I came back, I tried to forget a hell of a lot. I forgot faces. I forgot faces and names. Situations, though, they're just as strong, they're right there." He snaps his fingers.

"You don't know anything about my story, do you?" he asks with a smile.

"Just a few things Denice mentioned to us. Mostly, how hard it's been for you," I say.

He nods his head.

"Maybe let's start with how I first heard about Peoples Temple and when I joined," he suggests.

"That sounds good," Margo replies.

"My mother had always searched for the perfect religion," he smiles again. "She was always searching to be saved, or searching to find something that would fulfill her life, something was missing there, and I don't know what it was. This woman, who was born in Arkansas in 1903, only had a third grade education. She had worked in mills, she had been a domestic worker.

"And she adopted me when she was fifty-three years of age," he sighs. "She made me. When I entered kindergarten, I was already reading. My mom and I started going to the Temple in 1972, '73. I was in the tenth grade. Fresno High. And her idea with Jim Jones was: this will keep my son out of trouble. 'There are things here you can do, Eugene,' she would tell me. 'You can do photography, you can get into construction, you can get into singing, there's no limit.' There's no ceiling on it, is what she saw.

"My mom was almost seventy years old when she said to me, 'I'm moving. And I'm donating the house to the Temple, to Jim Jones.' I was seventeen years old, and I was starting to live faster and faster and faster, I wanted to know about the streets," he laughs. "My mom would say, 'I don't want you out there on the streets. The streets are no place for you, son. The Temple is the best place for you.' So I said, 'Okay, I'll go.' Mom lived in one of the senior citizen housing units in the Temple and she had friends, she had running partners, so to speak," he smiles. "And for the first time, she was really, really happy."

"What was your mother's name," I ask.

"Mattie Gibson," Eugene replies.

≈ ≈ ≈

His mother's oral history was also among the ones that Dick Tropp collected in Jonestown. It was one of the shorter testimonies in the stack, just three paragraphs, but we remembered the name and looked it up:

MATTIE GIBSON b. 1905 Blevins, Arkansas (175m. south of Little Rock).

When I was a child I had very little schooling. No shoes, no proper food or clothing. I never went past the third grade. We lived in a country area and sharecropped. We didn't really have anything of our own. I worked in the fields. My mother did domestic work for 50 cents a day.

During the Depression I worked for 75 cents a day. My mother was a very "smart and shifty" woman. She had to be. I remember how we had to carry wood to keep the school warm. I remember a boy who was a friend of my brother. They said he was looking in a window. They took him out and castrated him. The people were afraid to talk. The doctor didn't do anything about it. There was no hospital. He died.

My father had his horse taken from him that he had worked and saved for because my sister rode it to town during work time. We had to work extra hard to get money for the barest essentials. They only gave Dad $50 to get his crop started. I had to walk five miles each way to school. I had to wade through icy water—there was no way around. In school I remember brutal beatings. There were lynchings. I have blocked it out.

$$\approx \approx \approx$$

Eugene says his devotion to his mom was the reason he joined. "My mother loved me very much and cared for me, and no matter what, she was gonna be my mother for the rest of my life. So I joined. My first day at the Temple, they told me I'd be on the work crew. I noticed that the hardest workers in the Temple caught the less hell, so I just busted my ass every single day, evening, night.

"Jack Beam took notice of me. Jack was good people. He was real insightful in that 'country-folk' kind of way. For me coming into the Temple, I had no male examples. These men in the Temple became mentors to me. Jim Randolph, he was a music aficionado, loved jazz. Loved really quality systems. 'Cool, the guy's really cool.' In my regular day life, I wouldn't have run into him. Mike Prokes, kind of nerdy, but cool. Tim Clancey, he did the publishing, just a really gentle man, and sometimes it's hard to equate that in modern society. Not a gentleman, but a gentle man. He taught me offset printing and pushed me into photography. And then Don Jackson, he enjoyed photography, said, 'Yeah, c'mon, I'll show you how to work a camera.'

"People were free with their knowledge. If you wanted to go into mechanics and get greasy, go down to the garage. The mechanics were an off bunch. They would make their coffee and they'd stir it with a wrench. That was their thing, 'C'mon in, get some of this good coffee.'"

He shakes his head with a sweet smile on his face that is becoming familiar.

"Not only are you somebody, but somebody cares enough for you to help you get an education, give you clothing, pay your tuition, put you in college. And all you have to do is just be there. That's where a lot of people were at. They saw the breakfast program, they saw the community gardens, they saw the kids make these emotional U-turns from being a complete introvert, attention deficit child to being somebody who can not only speak to adults and look you in your eye, but they actually laugh and play. And to see these kids turn around—that drew people."

He looks up at us, puts his hands around his water glass.

"So what happens is you find that Jim Jones is on the periphery," he explains. "You're there because of these people. My influence came from the people. Jones was a threat. If you messed up, you're gonna be in front of him. But Jones became background for me."

Eugene lost his wife, Ollie, and his biological son in Jonestown as well as two kids he helped parent in the Temple. He remembers very clearly the spark of his relationship with Ollie.

"When we would come back home on those buses from LA," he tells us, "all the teenagers would sit on the floor or get up on the luggage racks 'cause it was so crowded on those buses. And one time Tinetra was up there, and Ollie was up there, too."

"Tinetra? The daughter of Nell Smart?" Margo asks.

"Yeah, that's right," Eugene answers. "She and Ollie were friends. And Ollie said, 'Hey, Eugene, if you want to, come up here.' So I'm talking to her," he blushes, "and then I'm seeing her on a regular basis on Wednesday nights for the members-only meeting, for the youth meetings. Soon we were to the point that we were holding hands. Then we hugged and kissed. It was a very innocent relationship. I was eighteen years old and Ollie was sixteen. Ollie's mother disapproved. Those two years to her Mom was a lifetime. When her mom found out that Ollie had been seeing me, she beat her with a telephone cord. Ollie ran away and she came to the Temple. I remember holding Ollie's hand, and she's crying and I'm crying and I said, 'Something has to be done.' One of the Temple counselors, Anita Ijames, was there, and she goes up and talks to the rest of the elite counsel, and she came back and said, 'If you want to, you two could leave tonight and go get married. But you can't pull the Temple into it. We'll provide all the funds necessary to get you where you need to go, but you can't say the Temple told you that you could do this.'"

They decided to do it. The arrangements were made. "I remember Anita Ijames coming to us and saying, 'Here's what you're gonna do. You're gonna get on a Greyhound bus in Oakland, you're gonna travel across country to Little Rock, Arkansas, and you're gonna get married, because you can marry at sixteen in Arkansas.'"

He pauses for a few seconds.

"I remember getting on that bus at 2:00 in the morning, and I remember that being the longest journey in my life. We were leaving everything that we knew, and we couldn't come back unless we were married.

"We were like, 'Wow, we're gonna be husband and wife. We're gonna be in the revolution. We're gonna raise our kids.' Ollie got pregnant roughly a year later. Now all of a sudden you have a life, and it's correct."

He pauses again.

"I remember one time Ollie and I were sitting out front of the Temple in San Francisco, and we're talking and I'm saying, 'I'm really tired of this. I want to do something else. I want to have money in my pocket.' She says, 'But here, everything's taken care of.' I go, 'I know everything's taken care of. But it bothers me that I have to go to the needs committee—they would have a committee to decide who gets what—and say, 'This week I need boots, I need a couple pair of tube socks and a pair of khakis.' Or, 'I need a suit jacket, and I can't borrow one because I'm a 42 short. I want money in my pocket.' I was just getting really riled up until she said, 'Well, Eugene, you know it could be worse. It could be a whole lot different. I wouldn't be here. And you wouldn't be here either.'

"She was right. So, whenever I wanted to leave the Temple, Ollie wouldn't let me leave. And when she wanted to leave, I wouldn't let her leave either. We had to pay back our debt. Jones said there was no debt. But we knew there was."

Eugene explains that he and his mother, Mattie Gibson, joined the Temple in 1973. This was the year that Peoples Temple leased the land from the Guyanese government to begin developing the agricultural project at Jonestown. The Temple in San Francisco was thriving. They had a printing press, a newspaper, and many political friends. They had their critics, too, and by 1976, more and more of their members were moving to Jonestown.

As he recounts the months leading up to his departure to Guyana, he highlights an important change that he observed.

"People had always gotten punished for things," he reflects, "but the discipline was beginning to go what I considered overboard. Before it might have been little physical punches or whatnot, but now people were being bloodied and it was escalating. I'm not scared, but I'm getting really, really cautious. Ollie's roughly three months pregnant, and I'm thinking, 'Okay, what am I gonna do?' All of sudden, they say, 'Okay, Ollie, time for you to go to Jonestown.' I'm saying, 'Hold it, no, no, no,'" he stresses. "One of the counselors tells me, 'Well, Eugene, you have to be strong. You don't want your child born over here in a capitalistic society, do you? Where they won't get a fair shake?' And I'm thinking, 'Well, no, I don't. But I don't want Ollie over there in the jungle without me.' But see, they knew how to control me. If you have Ollie, you're controlling me. I don't care if it's fire right there, if Ollie's on the other side, I'll go through fire. That's just the way it was. I was her protector."

He drinks the last of his water and returns to the tap for another glass. He struggles to piece together the details and the timing of the last chapter of his time in Peoples Temple. He traces the months back in his head from the birth of his son in Jonestown.

"Ollie was sent down first. She was in Jonestown and I was back in the States. I'm talking to Ollie, you know, via shortwave radio, and I want to see her so bad. I had to wait until the powers that be said it was time for me to go. Eventually, it was time, and I was in one of the groups that drove the buses all the way across country and left from Florida to go to Guyana. I brought this duffel bag of cassettes. I knew I wasn't coming back to the States, so I taped classical, jazz, rhythm and blues, pop, any kind of music I could think of, I recorded everything. So I had hundreds, hundreds of tapes. And in a way, they were my story."

You can see the heaviness beginning to weigh down on him.

"The day I arrived in Jonestown it was raining. It was monsoon season, and it was just raining its ass off. Ollie was nine months pregnant, about to have our baby. I can't wait to get there. We come to the main gate, we're going down the main road, and I could hear the people a good mile away, I can hear them singing, right? And I'm getting amped, I was like, 'Oh man, this is going to be so cool!' As we come around the curve, I can see the pavilion thirty or forty yards off. I see Ollie, and I run up to her and I'm saying, 'Oh, you're so big, you're beautiful, you know.' I'm looking around, trying to take everything in. I see my mother. She's lost a lot of weight but she looks really good. Jones is up there in his seat. I'm listening, and the music gets lower and lower, and the beat slows down until it's almost quiet. And the next thing I hear, 'We heard that there was an agent coming in here with one of you. One of you is transmitting a message to the CIA, so therefore we're confiscating all of your tapes.' My heart dropped. 'Not my tapes! Forget the CIA! Get my music!'" He laughs.

"But Jones wouldn't stop. He was saying, 'We have no question now that our ex-members are being funded and are CIA-connected.' My heart just dropped. What is this? I'm holding on to Ollie really tight, and Jones says, 'The enemy is out there. They're out there. Just outside your eyesight. They want to take our children. They want to torture our children. They want to take our seniors. They're there to take us down. They're doing it because we slapped America in the face and we said, We're gonna create another America the way it should be.' You're two hundred miles into the dark jungle. My mind is just spinning, going, 'I'm so glad I'm here with Ollie.' But at the same time, it's like, 'We gotta get out of here.'"

Eugene sighs.

"Then the White Nights happened," he continues, "you were faced with suicide, you know, drinking the potion. And you can sit here and say, 'I'd never do it, no fucking way, or I would stop somebody from doing it, I would stop everybody from doing it, or I'd go through the crowd and spill it over!' But when you're there, you might have those thoughts, but you don't act on them." He struggles to explain.

"It was strange, during the White Nights, the children always—." He quite suddenly begins to cry. "The children were always so brave. Sometimes people would cry, but the kids, the kids were always so brave, and you think to yourself, you owe them. I can never forget the children because they were so beyond their years in terms of their thought process, and their perception of the world. At four o'clock in the afternoon, they'd be out there in Jonestown in the fields playing kickball, and then nine o'clock that night they were willing to give their life up. They should want to keep it, they should want to live forever, but they didn't. These kids, they were little men and women, and they made you be brave. You didn't have a choice. You had to stand up and be representing the cause, be about the cause, because these kids were willing to give it all up. And here you are, you're nineteen, twenty, you haven't lived a full life either, but you've lived three times as long as they have, and they wanted to put their lives on the line. Then you had seniors that you had to hold them back, 'I'm ready to fight, I'm ready to die,' they'd be saying."

Eugene breaks down, unable to speak this time.

After a few seconds, he composes himself. "I mean, everybody had a different experience. There is no story or no one person who can cover it all."

≈ ≈ ≈

The day the congressman came to Jonestown, Eugene was in the capital. There were many Temple members who worked in Georgetown. They rotated in and out, taking turns managing the business affairs of the agricultural project. The Temple had rented a house called Lamaha Gardens in Georgetown where they all stayed. We asked Eugene to tell us how he got there.

"Everything was going fine for Ollie and me in Jonestown," Eugene explains. "I was enjoying being a father, and there were other new fathers around, and mothers. It was just like another generation coming about," he smiles. "All of a sudden, one of the counselors comes up to me and says, 'Eugene, Father needs you to go into Georgetown.' We always had someone on the docks to bring our things through customs. I said, 'I'm not interested. I just had a child, I got my wife here, I'm happy.' They said, 'We're not really asking. You need to go to Georgetown. You'll be back soon, and Ollie will be fine.'

"So I kissed Ollie good-bye and I went. And that's how I survived. I was in Georgetown on the last day."

Trapped

"DEATH IS REAL and it comes without warning. This body will be a corpse," Greg tells me over salted peanuts and melting ice on our last flight to Oregon. Greg is becoming a serious Buddhist practitioner now, and part of his practice entails studying death in a more intimate way. He has recently taken his Bodhisattva vow, which is a deepening of compassion. The vow means that he is now committed to reincarnating again and again until every sentient being is relieved of their suffering.

He is sharing his Buddhist wisdom with me, what he is learning about death, the terms of death, the fact of death—his, ours, and everyone else's—just before our initial descent, which is unnerving as the plane swoops and drops into its approach to the Portland airport. "And if you don't work with your mind, well, it's going to be bad at the hour of death. You're going to suffer."

I look out the window just as I had on the forty previous flights that we have taken together to do our work over the past six years, first in creating *The Laramie Project* with our other colleagues, and now with the story of Jonestown and Peoples Temple. Greg leans into me, holding the remains of the watered-down ice in his cup, to look out the window, too. He takes the last sip of melted ice, crunching the remaining bits. The plane lands, and we gather up our things like seasoned travelers and head to the rental car shuttle. I drive the first leg while Greg navigates.

Interstate 5 is a straight shot south from Portland. This is my third trip. I took the first one alone. The second time and now the third, we are taking together. We have an important reason for coming back: to interview Tim Carter again in the hope that he will tell us about what he witnessed in Jonestown on November 18, 1978.

When I sat with Tim and we watched the NBC footage of the last two days, our conversation stopped with the last call to the pavilion. Each time we have talked since, he stopped short of recounting the last hours—what he lived through, what he saw. He gave us the broad strokes but never the full details of what happened to him on the last day. We knew in order to finish the play we would need those details in Tim's own words.

On the quiet ride, I wonder if Greg still believes in God. I turn in my seat to ask him, but he is asleep. I want him to see the sunset. I have the thought that the sky might look just as beautiful at the moment of death, or maybe at the end of the world. I have another thought that maybe this *is* the end of the world, on an ordinary day and in an ordinary place like this, the two of us driving into the eternal horizon in a white Enterprise rental car. That would be fitting, I think. It seems half our lives have been spent traveling together, talking to people. And I think about God. *Where is God in this story?* Maybe God is in the exchange—in the empathy and compassion—in the meetings between strangers, in the interviews we are collecting. *But is it helping anyone to remember?*

We arrive at Tim's new place in the early evening. He has just moved into a two-bedroom apartment in a well-kept apartment complex in a different part of town that feels less rural, more developed.

Tim and I sit on some folding chairs on the stained-wood balcony off the kitchen. The balcony overlooks the parking lot, but it is a chance to sit outside, where we can look at the surrounding trees, and where Tim can smoke. He points out his blue minivan in the parking lot that is in need of repairs he cannot afford. A cat cries at the screen door of the balcony to come outside, but just as quickly as she joins us on the balcony, she cries to go back in.

Greg hangs out inside with Tim's two sons and his daughter, along with his stepdaughter. Tim has been with his partner, Vicki, for eight years. Greg tells them animated stories and has the whole group laughing. Outside, Tim smokes and talks, and I listen. We refer to each other as friend, but it is a connection that is different from any personal friendship

I have ever had. Tim also refers to me as his sister and himself as my brother. Greg is his brother, too. Tim trusts our intentions with the play, as indeed he trusted us from the beginning.

The next evening, Tim takes us to his favorite place for Italian food, a local spot with red-and-white checkered tablecloths and signature wine bottles encased in wicker weaving on every table. We have had little social time together, and we are finally sharing a meal.

After dinner, we return to the apartment, and Tim suggests that we all watch *Mission Impossible* on television. With the proposition of a movie, my heart sinks. *Yes, that's right,* I think, *mission impossible.* It will be too late to talk to Tim now. We have one more interview tomorrow with Jean and Tim Clancey, and then we fly home.

The hours fade one into the next. Maybe Tim senses that we have given up, that we are all getting tired. Maybe he senses that this is the "do-or-die" moment, I don't know. But he quite abruptly announces— almost commands—us to go to the back bedroom of the house. He tells us to bring our tape recorder. Greg and I gather our things and follow his lead.

Down the hall is a small bedroom with two twin beds on either side of the room, and a wooden desk just to the side of one of the beds. I sit on the office chair at the desk, while Tim brings in a hard-back chair from the kitchen for himself. Greg sits on the floor, his back leaning up against one of the twin beds. Tim has lit candles, one senses, for their energetic value, maybe for spiritual protection.

"A lot of my desire to talk about Jonestown," Tim begins, "most of it, actually, comes from a commitment, a promise I made to myself that day when those people were dying, that I would not let them die in vain. As grandiose as that sounds, it's what I told myself: 'I won't let you die in vain.' Because basically that's what happened. They died in vain! More than nine hundred people died for nothing. Everything that we did— they died for nothing. What did their deaths end up accomplishing? A definition for the word *cult*. That's what we've been reduced to. And I said, 'I will not let people forget.'

"That's why talking to you guys is important to me, " he confides. "I know all about survivor's guilt from Vietnam. Frankly, it was a lot easier for those who died. It would have been a lot easier to die than it was to live."

He pauses.

"I want to tell you this story. I want you to have it in my own words.

"Where did we leave off?" he asks. "I think we got as far as Dick Tropp. I was walking down the path. Do you remember?"

≈ ≈ ≈

I did remember. On Saturday, November 18, as Tim approached the pavilion, just at the point where the wooded path met the back of the pavilion, he heard Dick Tropp's voice.

Tim picks up the thread: "When they called for the meeting in the pavilion, I got up to where two paths met in the back of the pavilion. Dick Tropp was there. He was going, 'There has to be a way. There has to be a way. This doesn't make any sense. We've come too far.' His sister Harriet is going, 'Oh Dick, you're just afraid to die.' I stopped because I wanted to hear what the hell was going on. I was panicking inside. The pavilion was filled with people, and the armed guards were surrounding it. As I arrived at the entrance of the pavilion, Maria Katsaris came walking by and goes, 'Come here, I think I may have something for you to do.' Was that fate? I have no idea what it was, but it's what happened. 'Wait for me in the radio room.' As we were walking in, my brother Mike was coming out of the radio room. She goes, 'Come here, you, too. I have a mission for both of you.' We sit down on the cot, and she goes, 'Mike Prokes has been given an assignment to take some money to the Soviet Embassy in Georgetown, but we have three suitcases, and he can't do it by himself. Would you be willing to help him?' As this is going on, I heard Christine Miller talking. I didn't know what the exact words were until later."

≈ ≈ ≈

Christine Miller is an African American woman—a hero to many survivors—who stood up to Jim Jones in the last hours. There is a tape—commonly referred to as the last-hour tape, sometimes the "death tape"—an audio recording of the events on November 18, 1978. The following is an excerpt from that recording:

JIM JONES: Now what's going to happen here in a matter of a few minutes is that one of those people on that plane is gonna shoot the pilot.

I know that. I didn't plan it, but I know it's going to happen. They're gonna shoot that pilot, and down comes that plane into the jungle. And we had better not have any of our children left when it's over, because they'll parachute in here on us. I'm going to be just as plain as I know how to tell you. I've never lied to you. [More emphatic.] I never have lied to you. So my opinion is that we be kind to children and be kind to seniors and take the potion like they used to take in ancient Greece, and step over quietly, because we are not committing suicide. It's a revolutionary act. We can't go back. They won't leave us alone. They're now going back to tell more lies, which means more congressmen. And there's no way, no way we can survive. Hmm? Yes, Christine.

CHRISTINE MILLER: Is it too late for Russia?

JIM JONES: Here's why it's too late for Russia. They killed. They started to kill. That's why it makes it too late for Russia.

CHRISTINE MILLER: I don't think nothing is impossible if you believe it.

JIM JONES: There is no—Christine, it's just not—it's just not worth living like this. Not worth living like this.

CHRISTINE MILLER: I think that there were too few who left for twelve hundred people to give them their lives for those people that left.

JIM JONES: Do you know how many left?

CHRISTINE MILLER: [Casual.] Oh, twenty-odd. That's—that's a small—. [Jones speaks over her.]

JIM JONES: Twenty-odd, twenty-odd.

CHRISTINE MILLER: Compared to what's here.

JIM JONES: Twenty-odd.

CHRISTINE MILLER: I was speaking about a plane for us to go to Russia.

JIM JONES: How—. [Sighs.]

[The crowd stirs.]

JIM JONES: —you think Russia's gonna want us with all this stigma? [Pause.] We had—we—we had some value, but now we don't have any value.

CHRISTINE MILLER: Well, I don't see it like that. I mean, I feel like that— as long as there's life, there's hope. That's my faith.

JIM JONES: Well—someday everybody dies. Some place that hope runs out, because everybody dies. And I'd like to choose my own kind of death for a change. I'm tired of being tormented to hell, that's what I'm tired of. [Pause.] Tired of it.

≈ ≈ ≈

The mood in Tim's bedroom is quiet. He is exhausted, and I want to tell him we can stop now—he doesn't have to relive those last hours. But he seems determined to tell us the story, to give us what we came here to find.

"So we changed clothes," Tim continues. "We got over to West House, and there were three big suitcases stuffed with money and gold. The mission was for us to take the money to the Russian embassy. And I was told: 'Go up to the pavilion and see if Jim wants us to have a ride out to the front gate.' I started walking up to the back of the pavilion, and I got up to where the swings were, and I saw bodies. Children's bodies. I didn't count, but I would say, it was at the very beginning, because there were maybe nine or ten dead bodies on the ground, and I heard the screaming. And like a good little automaton that I was, I proceeded directly up to the back of the stage. I heard Marceline Jones screaming, 'You've gotta stop!' I could hear that, but it was like waves on the periphery of my consciousness. And I turned to my right, and at that exact second they were squirting poison into my baby son Malcolm's mouth. And my wife Gloria was—had tears streaming down her cheeks." Tim's voice begins to shake. "I've never been so fucking angry. Why did you let him do that? And I felt so fucking guilty. You fucking abandoned her, you didn't give her any choice, you put her here, she had no choice. And the pain on her face—Jesus, so much pain.

"I fell down on my knees, and I grabbed Gloria and I said, 'I love you so much, I love you so much, I love you so much,' and I could feel her dying in my arms. 'And Malcolm'—and I can't know if she heard me. Oh God, I hope she did."

He sweeps away the tears from his eyes with both hands.

"That was Jonestown. That was the great revolutionary—that was the mass suicide that took place. That's why I want to just take anybody who says that it was suicide and just choke their fucking throat. Because the look on Gloria's face was: trapped. That was the look on her face: trapped."

His heart is breaking in front of us, even as he regains momentary control of his voice. "I started walking back to West House, and I was sobbing, 'They murdered my son, they murdered my son, they murdered my son.' That's all I could say. I was out of my mind, and I thought, 'Just die right now.' I did not want to live. I did not give a fuck about anything or anybody, including myself. I just kept on putting one foot in front of the other. All I was seeing was revulsion and shock and anger and sadness. I don't know what words to use, because the feelings were so extreme. They were beyond anything I've ever felt before or since in my life."

He suddenly begins to cry again. "It hurts as much now as it did then. A lot of good people were murdered that day. I don't need any fucking rationalization and academicians. I don't give a fuck what anybody fucking says—they can interpret and rationalize and study all they want. I was there. I know what I felt, and I am telling you that what happened there that day was fucking cold-blooded murder to 98 percent to 99 percent of the people that were there. That had nothing to do with following Jim Jones to death. It had nothing to do with what was right. It had to be flat-out fucking murder. The figure that sticks in my mind is twenty. Take a vote: twenty people walk away, nine hundred of us die."

He pauses.

"Why didn't I just knock the vat of poison over?" Tim asks. "I've been asked that. Why didn't anybody just knock the vat of poison over? It had never even crossed my mind. It never once crossed my mind."

After a pause, he continues:

"Jones didn't want us to get a ride out to the front gate. So we walked out of Jonestown into the jungle, me and my brother Mike and Mike Prokes with the suitcases. It was so damn wet from all of the rain. Cyanide has a smell to it. You know, it smells like almonds. And I can still hear and I can still smell. You cannot create a nightmare more graphic or horrible than what was going on in Jonestown. If it was a revolutionary suicide, we were a pretty disciplined group of people: people would have been lining up, throwing it back, and lying down to die. None of that happened. None of that happened. It was flat-fucking murder, that's all it was. There was no choice in Jonestown that day. It's not like there were two lines: one for everybody who wanted to die that day and one for those who didn't. There was no choice."

≈ ≈ ≈

Our project archivist, Denice Stephenson, later discovers a letter written in Jonestown on the last day. She compares the handwriting and attributes the letter to Dick Tropp. This is an except from that letter:

To Whomever Finds This Note:

Collect all the tapes, all the writing, all the history. The story of this movement, this action, must be examined over and over. It must be understood in all of its incredible dimensions. Let all the story of this Peoples Temple be told. Let all the books be opened. We know there is no way that we can avoid misinterpretation. This is the last day of our lives. We were at a cross purpose with history. But we are calm in this hour of our collective leave taking. As I write these words, people are silently amassed, taking a quick potion, inducing sleep, relief. We are a long and suffering people. I wish I had time to put it all together—the meaning of a people—a struggle, to find the symbolic and eternal in this moment— I wish that I had done it. I did not do it. I failed. A tiny kitten sits next to me. A dog barks. The birds gather on the telephone wires. Darkness settles over Jonestown on its last day on earth.

Second Chance

After saying good-bye to Tim Carter, the next day we visit with Jean and Tim Clancey. We tell them about the night before, how hard it was to witness Tim's pain and to feel like we caused him more suffering in the retelling of it.

Holding her eyeglasses in one hand, Jean nods her head. She neither agrees nor disagrees with us; she is simply listening. "Those last hours are very painful for anyone who survived," she says. Her voice is steady and calm.

"The last day we were at the short wave radio at headquarters in San Francisco. We knew the congressman was there in Guyana. We could not get through. Somebody cut the radio and we couldn't get through. We were frantic. Then somebody patched through somehow, and the message came across, something to the effect of, 'We've gone to see Mrs. Blackberry. You go, too.' There was a code—we had sheets and sheets and sheets of codes—and I remember suddenly the crushing awareness that this was taking place. We all had pledged that if anything happened, we would take our own lives. It was just each of us alone with our decision, alone with our pledge, our loyalty—to the group, to each other. I remember being in this upstairs room and on the radio Edvard Grieg, from the *Peer Gynt* suite, I think it's called 'The Death of Ase.' It's a very slow, passionate dirge, and I lay down on the ground on the carpet. I just remember lying there, unable to get up to do anything."

Jean recalls a thought she had in that very moment—just a flash across her consciousness—of Tim Clancey, the man she would eventually marry.

"The will to live and survive is so strong. It's so strong," she whispers. "We helped each other. We helped each other survive."

Tim Clancey remembers being in the publications room and lying on the floor and crying. "Just not knowing what to do, whether I should kill myself, which is what we all pledged to do."

As Jean tells it, there came a turning point for her and for many of the survivors left behind in San Francisco. "Young Stephan Jones had the courage to call, he called San Francisco repeatedly from Georgetown, from Guyana, repeatedly, like every half-hour, he was saying, 'Don't do anything. Don't do anything. You haven't done anything?' What a load he absorbed. What a huge, huge thing he assumed. And I credit Stephan with my life because he gave permission to say, 'That no longer applies. Don't listen to that now. You're free from that now.' Stephan said this, and what he was saying was life. And what his father was saying was death. It was transformational. That was the first glimmer of relief, of being free again. Not free of grief certainly, or of confusion and fear, but free. We're alive, we have a second chance."

Jean pauses, then considers. "I'm not sure. Had that voice not come through giving us permission to not kill ourselves. I don't know. It was a terrible, terrible conflict." Another pause, another reflection. "How could my life have been given over so wholly to something, that I would have just followed suit had that voice not come through?"

Tim looks at Jean as if to quiet her agitation, her question. "There were suicides afterward, some within months, some many years later."

Mike Prokes, who left Jonestown with the suitcases bound for the Russian embassy, was one of them, about four months after Jonestown.

Jean and Tim moved into a house together in San Francisco, and in May 1979, five months after Jonestown, they were married. They drove north from San Francisco, looking for a new beginning, stopping in Eugene, Oregon, on one of their trips. Tim was able to find a job, so they found a nice place to live, a house with an acre of land in the backyard, and they stayed.

"We had nice little babies," Jean says as she smiles.

Tim repeats the phrase affectionately, "Had nice little babies."

"It was the passage from death to life," Jean adds.

Yet as Jean reflects on the beauty of her own children, the family she and Tim have created, a particular sting comes to mind. She says loving them makes it even more difficult for her to understand what happened in Jonestown, how they could have started the murder/suicides by killing children.

Her husband interrupts her: "We don't need to go there," he says firmly. Then he says, "We have three beautiful children you haven't met," as if marking the distance between the tragedy and their current lives.

Jean picks up the thought. "Because they're getting smart. They're all in college."

After a long pause, Tim makes his way back around to the subject of Jonestown. "I think, had I been there I would have. I'm pretty sure—." He can't finish the sentence. "I remember one of those Planning Commission meetings, running through the ritual, everyone taking a cup of what was supposed to be poison, and I drank it, sat there waiting for the end to come. Turned out to be a farce, but I fully believed I was heading out to the next pasture. Had I been in that situation in Jonestown . . ." Tim trails off again.

Jean looks at him and then at us and says, "The ultimate perversion of what's the noblest in us, isn't it?"

And then she tells us about another dream, one she had after our first visit.

"Jones was brought in in handcuffs into a room of all of us, dead, alive, all of us, just an empty room, kind of like a police station booking room. And I looked at him and screamed and screamed at him—still—all these years later—." Jean cries as she continues. "What did you do to those people? Those mothers? What did you do to them? What did you do?"

She does not fight back her tears, nor does she indulge them. "It's taken me twenty-five years to just scream at him."

"I don't have any loyalty to him," she continues. "I know who he was. And I don't know how he screwed up so bad, but I am grateful to be alive. I am grateful to have a second chance. I'm grateful for the love that has found me in this second half of my life."

A short time after, we listen to "The Death of Ase" from the *Peer Gynt* suite, the dirge that was playing in the background as Jean and Tim chose life instead of death. This detail almost feels like the poetic touch of a fiction writer, but it happened.

≈ ≈ ≈

Another story of survival from that day was Vern Gosney's. After being wounded (twice on the airplane, once on the airstrip itself) and left for nineteen hours in the jungle, Vern woke up. It was twilight—not quite pitch-dark—and Vern could hear people walking through the bushes. "That's when the pain started," he tells us. "I was no longer in that adrenaline state. I didn't care if they were the assassins or not." Vern called for help. "Help me, help me," he screamed. A group of Guyanese men discovered him on the ground. They leaned over him. They were visibly drunk. One looked down and in a whispered voice said, "Tell me the secret, why they want to kill you? What's the secret? Tell us the secret." Vern in desperation cried out, "Man, there's no fucking secret—no secret—just help me."

Vern continues: "We stayed there all night, and in the morning the Guyanese army came. And the doctor came, gave me two aspirin. They started airlifting people out. They airlifted people out according to their importance. Jackie Speier, the congressman's aide, first, reporters, and I was the last one they took. I had on a pair of brand new tennis shoes, and as the soldiers were carrying me to the plane, they stole the tennis shoes off my feet."

He shakes his head in disbelief.

"I was airlifted by the medical people to a U.S. military hospital in Puerto Rico. When I got there, they asked for a phone number. I gave them my father's phone number, which is the only number I could remember. And then they told him, 'Your son doesn't have much chance to live.' It had been nineteen hours in the jungle. The diaphragm was torn. I had a hole in my stomach. I was shot through the liver. The spleen was gone. So they took out the spleen, sewed up the stomach, and I guess they cut off part of the liver.

"When I got out of intensive care, I was in a room, and they had Marines at the door guarding us, and the psychiatrist came, and he showed me a newspaper clipping of Jonestown. He said, 'Do you know what your son was wearing?' I just described what he was wearing that day so they could try to identify his body."

Vern pauses for a long time.

"I was still in shock, but I think at that moment I had a total break-down mentally. My mother came to be with me," his voice lightens. "And when I came back to the United States, both my parents supported me. Nobody ever said, 'You stupid shit. Why did you go to Jonestown?' They were there for me. It was a great shock, but it was wonderful. That was the beginning of the healing for me and my family."

"Why didn't you take your son with you out of Jonestown?" I ask.

"I didn't know if I was doing the right thing. My mind was so be-fuddled. I was very numb. I had tremendous guilt over leaving my son there and bringing myself out. Going back to get my clothes, and leav-ing my son."

≈ ≈ ≈

In listening to the survivors describe the events that unfolded those last two days in Jonestown, I am struck: horror, guilt, chaos, and death are the origin of the catchphrase "They drank the Kool-Aid." I can't imagine what it is like for Tim Carter and others to hear that phrase freely used in the media or on television or in films. Knowing what I know now, I cringe whenever I hear it. I wonder if the people who use that phrase even know where it comes from. I have a secret wish that everyone in the world could see the pain on Tim's face, in Vern's eyes, or Jean's heart. I wish future generations could see it, too. I believe that if people knew of the human suffering behind that phrase—if they really understood— they would never use that phrase again.

THOSE WHO GOT AWAY

The Known Dead

JONESTOWN, GUYANA

THE ENTIRE WORLD would learn about what happened on Saturday, November 18, on the nightly news. For anyone who was alive in 1978 and saw those first images coming from Guyana, it is a moment that they will never forget.

Initial news reports were of a shooting at the remote South American airstrip, which resulted in the death of a U.S. congressman. Following confirmation of Leo Ryan's assassination came the rumors—then the reports, then the images—of what was termed a "mass suicide" in Jonestown. Aerial photos showed the bodies—mostly of Americans—lying facedown in an area surrounding several open-air structures.

At first the media reported only four hundred bodies in Jonestown. There were known to be more than nine hundred people living in the agricultural project. The question on everyone's mind was: Where were all those other people? There was hope among survivors, hope among relatives that many had been saved by escaping into the jungle. It took several days for American and Guyanese authorities to realize the initial body count was wrong. Bodies were stacked on bodies. The adult corpses covered the bodies of the children. By the following Friday the full scope of the tragedy was known.

The U.S. State Department and the Pentagon were as stunned as the public. There was no precedent for such a disaster, and no protocol for handling it. Initially, the U.S. government proposed to bury the Jonestown dead in a mass grave on site—thousands of miles from American soil, far away from relatives, from their questions, their grief—but the

Guyanese government immediately rejected that idea and insisted that the bodies be repatriated.

For the families who had loved ones in Jonestown, including the family of Congressman Ryan, the only source of information that first week was the media.

≈ ≈ ≈

More than eighty Americans survived that day in Guyana, most by being in the capital city of Georgetown, but about thirty others left Jonestown either before or while the murder/suicides were taking place. Sixteen defectors left with the congressman. Tim Carter and his brother, Mike Carter, and Mike Prokes were sent on a Temple mission to carry suitcases full of money to the Russian embassy in Georgetown. They eventually abandoned the suitcases in the jungle and were met by officers of the Guyanese Defense Force. Grover Davis, Stanley Clayton, and Odell Rhodes, acting independently of each other, hid and escaped in the final hours. Nine members of Peoples Temple, having planned in advance of the congressman's visit and cut a trail through the jungle, had escaped that morning and met up with two other men. These eleven ended up in Matthews Ridge, about twenty-eight miles from Jonestown. Seven other people were on Temple assignments, either on Temple boats or, in the case of Joyce Parks, in Venezuela, when the deaths occurred. And, as Jack Palladino had told us, there was also a single survivor found in Jonestown.

Along with everyone else, Hyacinth Thrash heard the announcement to report to the pavilion, but she decided not to go. Her sister, Zipporah "Zippy" Edwards, told Hyacinth that Jim would be upset if she did not come. Zippy reported to the pavilion and died with the others. Hyacinth stayed in her cabin. She hid in a corner of the room under a bed sheet and eventually fell asleep.

Hyacinth and Zippy had joined Peoples Temple in 1957 in Indianapolis. Zippy had seen Jim on TV and came running into the room shouting, "I found my church. I found my church!" In 1964, Hyacinth felt a lump in her breast—"hard like a tabletop"—and soon the doctor confirmed, "Hyacinth, you've got cancer." Jim Jones and the members of the church "laid on hands" at a Sunday service, which Hyacinth believed cured her of the disease. "The tumor was gone," Hyacinth wrote in the memoir she published about twenty years after the tragedy at Jonestown.

The sisters traveled with Jim from Indiana to Ukiah, California, and then to San Francisco, eventually following him all the way to Guyana. We found a letter to "Dad" written by Zipporah Edwards in Jonestown:

Dear Dad,

I was outside the other night and I looked up at the stars, I never saw such a beautiful sight in my life. They all twinkling as though they were saying to me, "Welcome, I am glad you are free from that capitalist society." It is so lovely here in this country. I look back on my life and just think I never dreamed that I would ever be doing the thing I am doing now, working to help liberate all the oppressed people of the world. And I thank you for all these years I have known you, because I know that it was not by chance that I turned on my TV that Sunday morning and you were there. I never will forget the feeling that came over me when I heard you speak. I knew at once that I had found what I had been looking for and I made my pledge that as long as I lived I never would leave. I have always wished I could have walked with the Christ, but you proved to be much greater than the one I thought about. And I thank you for allowing me the privilege of walking with you. —Zipporah Edwards

Hyacinth was more skeptical about who Jim had become. She had watched him go from a preacher in the Pentecostal tradition to throwing the Bible away. She had also been told just before leaving for Guyana that Jim faked cancer healings, using chicken livers to make people in the congregation think he was removing tumors from the bodies of the sick. She was disgusted by this rumor, yet still believed her cancer healing was real. To her, Jim—at least back in the early days—had been "a Godly man." Hyacinth described what happened on November 19 in her memoir written after Jonestown:

The night before they found me, it rained. The rain running off my face tasted bitter to me, so I just wiped the rain away from my mouth with my hand. But maybe it was my thoughts that were bitter to me. On Sunday morning, November 19, 1978 I woke up and looked around. When I got outside, it was like a ghost town. I didn't see or hear anybody. I went over to another senior citizen building. I looked down the row of beds and all the people were either sitting up or laying in bed. They were all covered with sheets. I said, "Oh, my God, they came and killed them all!" I thought maybe I was dead too. I pinched myself. Was I alive? I heard a voice, just as plain, like a radio playing behind you in the distance, saying, "Fear not; I am with you." I believe it was the Spirit of the Lord. I looked around, dropped my hands, and the fear left me.

Thinking about Zip still worries me, sometimes I felt she was in the bed beside me. She did call to me just as clear, "Hyacinth, Hyacinth." I dream about her often like we were still together talking and doing things. I miss her so much. I prayed a thousand times that God would forgive me for going in with Jim. How could a man kill babies and seniors? But Jim caught it in the end. You can run away from God only so long. God wins in the end. I haven't given up hope. I still think I'm gonna get my healing.

Hyacinth was found by the Guyanese Defense Force ("Were they surprised to see me!") and escorted by military officers to Georgetown, where she was reunited with other Temple members. According to Hyacinth, Odell Rhodes, a Vietnam veteran who had joined the Temple in Detroit when the bus ministry came through town, wept as he told her how people looked after they died, how babies were dying in his arms. Odell overheard the doctor Larry Schacht asking for a stethoscope. With his adrenaline running high, his instincts took over, and Odell walked out of the pavilion. Were he to be stopped by security, he had an excuse: he was going to retrieve the stethoscope for Doctor Schacht. No one stopped him. He hid until it was quiet, then fled into the jungle.

Hearing Odell's accounts of what happened in Jonestown devastated Hyacinth. She wrote in her memoir: "I remember those babies marching past our place with little paper hats on, wearing sandals, sun suits and matching shorts and tops. It's enough to make you scream your lungs out, thinking of those babies dead."

Hyacinth received a settlement from Peoples Temple assets in 1983. She was conflicted over whether or not to accept it, but it was enough for burial money, and she did not want to burden her relatives with funeral costs after she was gone. Besides, by her accounting Hyacinth and Zippy had contributed more than $150,000 to the Temple—including two homes, bank accounts, insurance policies, pensions, Social Security checks, and tithes—during the twenty-one years they had been in the church.

≈ ≈ ≈

Hundreds of members of Peoples Temple residing in California also survived that day in November: about one hundred and fifty active members in San Francisco, eighty in Los Angeles, and twenty in Redwood Valley. The lives of thousands of relatives across the nation were forever changed, as well as the lives of countless former Temple members who still had deep emotional ties to the Jonestown dead.

Without exception, all of our interviewees remembered precisely where they were when they received the news:

Shanette Oliver was watching TV with her mother in Los Angeles when the news about Jonestown broke into regular programming. She remembered her mother's first words, "Oh my God, not us."

Phil Tracy, the reporter who wrote the controversial article in *New West* magazine, recalled, with deep regret, "When the news started coming through on that Saturday night, I felt like the world's worst failure. I had tried to do something to help these people, and they all wound up dying."

Nell Smart recounted, "First you hear that two hundred were dead, and you think, 'Oh God, I have six people over there. You're not going to take them all.' And then four hundred were dead, and then the numbers just kept climbing, and it was like, 'I guess you are going to take them all.'"

Rebecca Moore had told us, "The news came out just bit by bit, you know. First there were only four hundred bodies. Well, there were nine hundred people there, so where are they all? My parents did not accept the idea—or the possibility—that my sisters were dead. But they were the fanatics. I said, 'I don't think they're alive.'"

And Grace Stoen Jones, who was awaiting word about the fate of her son John Victor back in Georgetown: "I just remember hearing the words, 'Congressman Ryan's been shot and is possibly dead and other people have been shot.' And then more and more news came out—the numbers—and eventually we found out that everyone had died. I never

got the body of my son John because I didn't have sufficient medical records, so John is in the mass grave at Evergreen in Oakland with the others."

Liz Forman Schwartz received a call. "Liz, have you listened to the
news?" a friend urgently asked. Liz told us that she did not have the words
to express her response. "You're just so stunned, you're so shocked," she
said.

The FBI had contacted her, presenting her with a list of the known
dead. "I'm trying to hold my composure, and I'm reading down the list:
Bob is dead, Jim is dead, Diane is dead, her children are dead, Maria is
dead, Joel is dead, Claire's children are dead. It's so much more than I can
possibly ever tell you."

My Children Are There

FEBRUARY 9, 2004
LOS ANGELES

SURVIVOR CLAIRE JANARO lives in the Los Angeles area. When Liz Forman Schwartz said, "Claire's children are dead," she was referring to Claire Janaro.

Many of our interviewees remained close to Claire and hoped that she could tell her story. We try to meet with her several times, but she is still emotionally fragile when it comes to Jonestown. She is willing to participate but isn't sure if she can handle the conversation.

It is three years into our process when Claire calls to tell Greg that she wants to meet. We finally sit down with her in her condo in LA.

One remarkable thing about Claire's story is that she had just arrived in Georgetown, Guyana, on the evening of November 18, 1978. She had stayed behind in Redwood Valley, in order to close out the last and largest of the Temple's health care facilities before leaving for Jonestown herself. She was looking forward to being reunited with her husband, Richard, and her two children, Daren and Mauri, who were already there.

When no one arrived to greet her at the airport in Georgetown that Saturday, she knew something was wrong. When she was finally able to make a phone call, she called the house in Georgetown and was told, "Go back. Don't come in. Something terrible has happened." Claire told them, "I came all this way. My husband's there. My two children are there. I am not going back."

She was then advised to find a cab and go to the Pegasus Hotel. As one of the last Temple members living in Redwood Valley, she had very little knowledge about Congressman Ryan's visit or the events that followed.

265

≈ ≈ ≈

According to Claire, before joining Peoples Temple she and Richard were "sitting here being middle-class citizens, very, very ultraliberal," when her high school friend Liz Forman (now Liz Forman Schwartz) told her about Jim Jones. "This is it, Claire, this is it. He believes in everything we believe in and he's wonderful and he's a healer." Claire and Richard lived in Sherman Oaks in Southern California. She was pregnant with her son Daren, and Mauri was in kindergarten. Richard had always wanted to live in the Bay Area, as he had family there, but it was Claire "who made us go."

This is Claire Janaro:

"I was totally converted the moment I walked into Peoples Temple. The kids—the integrated children—the singing, the dancing, the talk of socialism, and a life away up in the hills in Ukiah and Redwood Valley where we were safe from nuclear attack. I was overwhelmed. Jim Jones seemed to love kids. He seemed to have a good time laughing. He had this crazy, wild laugh that was funny as hell, a squeaky high-pitched laugh, and he would do his little dance onstage to the band. Oh, the music turned me on. I was turned on to gospel music. And when we'd go to the big meetings, I would always wind up in the balcony. I'd be jumping and clapping, and Jim would remark, 'There's Claire, she hasn't got any rhythm, but she sure has enthusiasm,'" she laughs softly. "I loved it. I loved the music. I loved everything about it. And I didn't care. I got high. I mean, it was a real high for me. I can't explain it any other way."

The Janaro family moved up north in the summer of 1971, the year before the Temple bought a new licensed care facility, their biggest one yet, a forty-acre ranch that would take fourteen developmentally disabled men. Jones needed someone with a college degree and managerial experience to run it. Claire volunteered. "I always wanted to live on a ranch!" she tells us.

Peoples Temple had several licensed care facilities operating in northern California. They provided the workforce—so they were inexpensive to run—and the state provided the clients. This was an income-producing stream for Peoples Temple for many years.

Claire did the buying and the cooking. Richard took care of the business aspect. According to several Temple members who lived on the ranch, the property was idyllic with apple orchards, organic vegetable gardens, and open pastures. It had a vineyard, and Temple workers processed the grapes. Countless dogs and cats found a home there. They had cows, goats, and chickens. "I'd never milked a cow, but I learned pretty fast," Claire jokes.

There were plenty of people who wanted to live and work on the ranch, and many of the younger generation thrived in the natural, outdoor environment. Three houses and several trailers on the property accommodated everyone who wanted to be there. The Temple also sent people with addiction problems to the ranch—their own version of detox and rehab. A few of the teenage boys who worked on the ranch still refer to Claire as their "mom." Those who survived—Danny Curtin and Mike Carter among them—stay in touch with her and she with them.

People in the surrounding community would come to see the operation, and Jim Jones would often bring visitors through to show the place off. For him, for Claire and Richard, and for the people who lived and worked there, it was a utopia in the middle of northern California.

One of the hardest parts for Claire to talk about—besides the deaths of her children—is the good she felt in Peoples Temple, the sense of purpose and the love. "We were going to convert the world to brotherhood. And that was it. That was the dream. That's why it's been so hard for me to talk or speak about Peoples Temple, because the good intentions ended in such a horrific way. That's why I don't like to talk. I don't like to talk, and I never could. How could I tell a fantasyland story with that ending?"

≈ ≈ ≈

Claire had only ten dollars in cash when she arrived in Georgetown on November 18. But she had two bottles of liquor, which she was able to barter for a cab ride to the Pegasus Hotel. The cab driver did not know all the details, but he knew enough to tell her that there had been some murders: that a U.S. congressman had been killed.

Claire's children had gone to Jonestown in 1977—Daren in May, Mauri in August—after most of the "valley kids" who worked on the ranch were moved to San Francisco. She had been anxious to get her kids out of the city. After Richard left for Guyana in September, Claire was left alone with the ranch. She couldn't wait to be reunited with her family.

When she finally arrived at the Pegasus Hotel, she made contact with Richard. He was alive! He was calling in from Trinidad; he had been on a Temple boat with three other members procuring supplies. He told Claire to get out of the country as soon as she could. "I'm not leaving until we find out about the kids," she said. To which Richard replied, "Claire, you have to assume they're all dead."

≈ ≈ ≈

The shortwave radio was lit up with activity on November 18 in Georgetown, specifically in the radio room at Lamaha Gardens, the house that Peoples Temple rented for its members who worked in the capital.

On November 19, survivor Laura Johnston (now Laura Johnston Kohl) sat at her typewriter compiling the first list of the known dead, piecing together the names from the information that she had from her work as an emissary for Temple members coming into the country. She began her the list with the records of people who had medical coverage.

Along with fifty other Temple members Laura had been escorted to the living room of Lamaha Gardens on the night of November 18 and placed under house arrest. The Guyanese Defense Force (GDF) compiled its own list of names—of everyone in the house—and began interrogating them one by one.

According to Laura, the people in that room had no idea what had happened in Jonestown, much less why they were being detained, until "the Guyanese Defense Force brought out the body bags from the back of the house," Laura recounted as she starts to weep. "And we realized it was Sharon and her family. Sharon Amos and her kids," she repeats through her tears. "Still to this day I cannot figure out how somebody could kill her own kids. The kids that we had known—we all knew them for life. They were all family. Even if Sharon had decided to do something like that herself, I couldn't figure out why she would take her kids with her. It's one thing for an adult to make a choice. Like I made a choice. My choice was to do this—to be in an integrated community, it's my choice in my life, and my choice to live or die with it—that's what free will is all about. I just can't believe that she would kill her kids."

Sharon Amos had been the only member of Peoples Temple outside of Jonestown who acted upon the directive to kill. After receiving the coded message from Jonestown, she escorted four children, three of whom were her own, to an upstairs bathroom. No one knows the sequence of events, but in the end Sharon Amos's three children were dead and Sharon herself was dead. Their throats were all cut. The fourth child sustained minor cuts.

≈ ≈ ≈

Eugene Smith had been in Georgetown a few months. He had been told that his wife Ollie would visit soon and bring their infant son, Martin. "The days are ticking by," Eugene recalls. "I'm getting more and more anxious to see her. I was just passing the time until I could see her."

On November 18, Eugene was in a Georgetown movie theater watching *Tora, Tora, Tora* along with Stephan Jones, Mike Touchette, and the guys from the basketball team. None of them especially wanted to see this new American release, but it had been so long since any of them had seen a movie, it didn't matter what was playing.

Eugene recounts: "The usher comes up and says, 'Something's happened at Lamaha Gardens, you need to get home quick.' So we all leap up, run out of the theater, jump in the Volkswagen van, and we fly across town."

When they arrived at Lamaha Gardens, Eugene searched for his best friend. He heard a voice coming from the yard calling his name, "Eugene, Eugene, Eugene." His friend was hiding in the elephant grass, which lined the fence surrounding the house. When he approached, his friend said, "They're killing everybody upstairs."

"What?!" Eugene replied.

"They're killing the *children* upstairs," his friend answered.

Eugene describes what happened next: "I ran inside and upstairs, and I started walking down the hall, and somebody grabs my arm and says, 'Don't go back there.' I say, 'What do you mean?' 'Don't go back there, Eugene.'

"But I had to go. So I step into the master bedroom. I remember looking down. I couldn't see bodies. I just saw blood coming out of the bathroom. I step back. I can't move. I'm trying to run, but I can't move. It seems like ten or fifteen minutes, but I was only there maybe a few seconds. I ran back downstairs, and I remember thinking, 'If you run, you're gonna get blamed for this.'"

Two of the children who died that day in the bathroom—Martin and Christa—were part of Eugene's adopted Jonestown family, kids he helped to raise.

Eugene made his way to the radio room. He tried to contact Jonestown on the shortwave radio, but there was no answer. He tried an international line to call San Francisco. No answer. He thought to himself, Are they killing everybody? Is everybody dying? He finally reached a man on a ham radio in Cincinnati and asked him to call the Temple in San Francisco. The man called and got through. San Francisco reported, "We're not killing anybody here."

Less than an hour later, the Guyanese Defense Force burst through the front door at Lamaha Gardens. Everyone was placed under house arrest.

≈ ≈ ≈

When Eugene heard about the airstrip shootings, he made the assumption that the U.S. military was responsible. Jim Jones had said so many times during his White Night rants: "They will parachute in on us. They will shoot us all." Still entrenched in the milieu of fear and paranoia Jones had created in Jonestown, Eugene thought to himself: "Who do we fucking trust? We're being held by the Guyanese Defense Force. We've got the U.S. army shooting us. What do we do?"

At one point, as Eugene was falling asleep, a GDF officer cocked his gun, pointed it at him, and said, "You want to kill yourself, fine, you can kill each other, but you killed Guyanese citizens there in Jonestown, and you're not gonna leave here alive." The Guyana citizens that the guard was referring to were local children, mostly ones adopted by Jonestown adults, and a couple of students at the Jonestown school. Eugene protested: "I didn't kill nobody, man. I might have lost somebody myself." As the police continued their interrogations, Laura Johnston continued to type. The first list of people known to be in Jonestown on November 18 became known as "The Johnston list."

There was a media blackout at Lamaha Gardens. The only way for Temple members to get any information was to call their relatives back in the States. As the U.S. Army recovered more and more bodies, Laura's list of names, however incomplete, became vital to family members who wanted to know the fate of loved ones in Jonestown.

On the sixth day of house arrest, the survivors learned the worst: there were no survivors in Jonestown.

"I just dropped to the floor," Eugene recalls. "I almost fainted. I think I did faint. I just began to sob. My wife and my baby boy were dead. I wanted to blame someone. Stephan Jones came to mind. But I had to get beyond that."

The next hours and days were even harder.

"We're all crying, and we're all drinking heavily at this point. I'm drinking fifths of alcohol, and I'm not getting drunk. Can't sleep, I got nightmares. We're running out of food. They're confiscating our currency."

The guards finally escorted some of the Temple members to downtown Georgetown to shop for food. As they passed by in their truck, Guyanese citizens shouted, "It's them! They're the ones! Yankees, Yankees, go home!" Eugene remembers. "It was humiliating. I never felt so embarrassed to be American."

≈ ≈ ≈

Chuck Beikman was in the bathroom at Lamaha Gardens when Sharon Amos killed her children. Several former Temple members we spoke to described Chuck as "a simple man." Chuck was illiterate, couldn't read or write, and was "not a violent man."

According to Stephan Jones, he did not know what had happened in that bathroom with Sharon and her kids, but he believed Chuck Beikman who said that he had not participated in their deaths. Stephan describes feeling an allegiance to Chuck—to all of the people of Jonestown—in those first days: "I never swore an oath, but I felt like I had a responsibility for him."

Stephan does not remember ever talking to Chuck or even seeing him that day, but he knew that he would do anything to protect the man. "Sharon Amos had dragged him into that room," Stephan explains, "so absolutely Chuck has responsibility. But Chuck ain't going down for Sharon Amos, as far as I'm concerned. Or Jim Jones, or the Temple at large. What Sharon had done is grabbed every kid in the house because she was going to save them from a life in fascism. Those kids were killed by a culture. Not by their mother, or by Chuck."

The police, however, were putting pressure on Chuck to confess: they told him if he didn't, Stephan Jones would go down for the crime. Stephan found out much later that a hysterical Sharon Amos screamed at Chuck, "What are you doing? Do something—kill her!" According to

Stephan, Chuck took Stephanie, one of the children in the bathroom, and he cut her lightly on her neck, to make it appear as if he had cut her throat. Stephan said, "That was Chuck's way of saving Stephanie's life."

Eventually, Chuck caved under police interrogation and agreed to give a statement. Stephan was then called in. Since Chuck could not read or write, the police wanted Stephan to write down the statement: "I didn't kill anybody. I was there. I didn't know what was going on." After the statement was taken, Stephan was allowed to leave, but Chuck was taken into custody and charged with murder. By his admission, he was in the room when Sharon Amos and her children died.

Weeks later—after the bodies had been removed from Jonestown, after most of the survivors had been allowed to return to the United States—Stephan was called as a prosecution witness in an early hearing on Chuck's case. Soon after he was sworn in, the prosecutor asked Stephan, "Did Chuck Beikman give his statement under duress? Was he under duress?" Stephan knew he was expected to answer, "No," but instead he answered, "Yes." Everyone in the courtroom, including the defense, was stunned. Chuck's lawyer Rex McKay, a huge man with a baritone voice, was so shocked by Stephan's reversal he let out a laugh that filled the courtroom.

The prosecutor immediately called for a recess.

When the hearing resumed, the prosecutor tried to undermine Stephan's new statement by implying his own involvement in what happened in the house. According to Stephan, this line of questioning angered him immensely. Confident of his innocence, and knowing that there were by that time more than sixty sworn affidavits to account for his whereabouts—that he was nowhere near the house when these murders took place—Stephan sarcastically answered, "Yeah, I did it. And I'm trying to put it off on Chuck."

Again people in the courtroom reacted with shock, even laughter, as they understood the intent of his sarcasm. But the judge interjected, "I want to be sure about this, Mr. Jones. Did you say . . . ?" as he repeated what Stephan had said. Stephan responded, "Yeah, I said that."

The prosecution then closed with, "I have no more questions."

The judge made his ruling soon afterwards: "By my estimation, by the testimony that's been offered here, it's clear to me that Mr. Beikman's statement was given under duress. I will not allow it into evidence." The statement was thrown out. The case against Beikman had crumbled.

The lead investigator on the case was Inspector Lam. At first Lam just shook his head when Stephan began lying on the stand. Stephan could see from the look on Lam's face that he "understood what I was doing. He knew I was fighting for my brother." After adjournment, however, Lam came to Stephan and said, "I wish you hadn't done that," then read him his rights. Stephan was arrested and charged with murder—his sarcastic remark in the courtroom was taken as a confession to the crimes.

Eventually, the process started all over again. Charges were refiled against Chuck—even as they remained in place against Stephan—and the two men went to prison to await trial.

Stephan spent three months in Guyanese prison. "I had all these doubts about who I was as a human being, and how I'd failed the people, failed myself, and failed my loved ones," he says of that period. "And one of the gifts, one of the many gifts of prison, is that I got to see who I really was and how I showed up in that situation. It began with Chuck and how I showed up for Chuck. In a time of crisis, you know, it was something I held on to."

Stephan was eventually cleared. But Charles Beikman pleaded guilty to the lesser charge of attempted murder. A Guyanese High Court judge sentenced Charles Beikman to five years hard labor. Stephan told us that Chuck eventually got out of prison and returned to Indiana, where he had joined the Temple almost thirty years before.

≈ ≈ ≈

Most of the remaining Temple members were held at Lamaha Gardens by the Guyanese Defense Force for three weeks before being allowed to return to the United States, although a few—mostly the survivors who had been in Jonestown that day—were held back to testify at an official Guyanese inquest in mid-December. The Concerned Relatives were flown home first. The rest were stripped of their passports and Social Security cards; they would get them back only after reimbursing the U.S. government for their return trip back home.

≈ ≈ ≈

Tim Carter was one of the survivors who was held back to testify in Guyana. He wrote about those days in a memoir he had begun to write, *Last Call to the Pavilion*. He sent me the unfinished manuscript with his accounts of those first difficult days.

On Monday morning, November 20, Guyana's Assistant Police Commissioner, Skip Roberts, was planning to fly by helicopter to Jonestown to begin the process of determining what happened. He asked Tim Carter to help identify bodies, but when Tim asked if he had any choice, Roberts said, "No." Along with several other Temple members who had escaped Jonestown two days before, Tim returned to a devastating scene of carnage.

"I had seen dead bodies in Vietnam," Tim wrote. "Nothing could have prepared me for this."

Due to the jungle heat, the bodies in Jonestown were bloated and in an advanced state of decomposition. Tim wrote of one body: "Huge abscess on his left temple, face crushed in from rain and decomposition." Tim made one of the identifications that day because he remembered what clothes the person had been wearing on Saturday. Then there was the body of one teenage girl who had these words scrawled on her arm: "Why couldn't you leave us alone?"

Among other demons plaguing him that day, Tim was overwhelmed with persistent thoughts of killing himself. At one point he saw two GDF soldiers in the school tent, one reading letters written to "Dad"—laughing and mocking the words—the other listening to music on a boom box and dancing. Tim confessed to wanting to die "right then, right there." Just at that moment, a third GDF officer walked up behind the man who was dancing and kicked him powerfully between the legs. "What are you?" he admonished. "Animals?! Get out of here!" The GDF officer then approached Tim and said, "I am so sorry. Please forgive them." Tim described that this single act of civility gave him the strength to live one more day.

Tim was allowed to return to his cottage to gather whatever personal belongings he could find. They didn't amount to much: two shirts, two pairs of pants, some socks, and underwear. There was also one picture. It was a photo of him and his wife Gloria taken when she was six months pregnant. He instantly recognized the irony of the location where the picture had been taken: at the dedication ceremony for a new suicide prevention railing on the Golden Gate Bridge. Jim Jones had been asked to give the invocation at the ceremony.

By the end of the day Tim had worked with his brother Mike and Mike Prokes among others to identify and tag more than two hundred bodies. Police Commissioner Skip Roberts then learned that the U.S. Army would not accept any of the positive IDs made by Temple members. When he broke the news to the guys, Tim recoiled with disgust. "The entire day's work was a waste."

≈ ≈ ≈

Tim is one of the most vocal survivors to claim that what happened in Jonestown was murder, not suicide. When I asked him what evidence he had of murder, this was his answer:

"All I can tell you is what I felt, what I saw, what I heard. There was nothing voluntary about what happened for the vast, vast, vast majority of people who were there. Nobody ever talks about the 160 or 170 bodies that had huge abscesses from injections all over them: on their faces, on their arms, their necks, their legs. Didn't make any difference that they'd been murdered. Nobody talks about that!"

Tim's brother Mike survived that day in Jonestown, but his sister Terry, who Tim went to his first Temple meeting with, did not. Tim lost his wife, Gloria, and his son, Malcolm. Mike Carter lost his wife, Jocelyn, and his daughter, Kaywana. Both Carter brothers lost Terry's husband, Lew Jones, one of Jones's adopted children, and their nephew, Chae-ok.

"I loved our family," Tim reflects. "Gloria was Chicano, Jocelyn was African American, and Lew was Korean, so we had a little United Nations. We were the mutts of the world, and everybody knows a mutt's smarter than a pure breed anyway."

On one of my last visits to Eugene, Oregon, Tim shows me a picture of his family, one he discovered after Jonestown. "This was taken Christmas of '77 in Jonestown. This is Terry and Chae-ok, Gloria and Kaywana, and myself and Malcolm. It's the only picture I have of all three of our kids together."

≈ ≈ ≈

Tim Carter and Stephan Jones were two of several survivors who were interviewed multiple times. When we talked to them about the aftermath of Jonestown, we could almost feel the presence of their loved ones in their absence. The parts of the story that remain unresolved repeatedly rose to the surface. Each time we met with Stephan, there was a particular sadness when he spoke about his mother. His regret about not returning to Jonestown on November 17 remains a painful subject. On one of our interviews, we talked about his mother, and what he knew about what happened to her on the last day.

"By most accounts," Stephan explains, "and even if you listen to the tape of the last hour, you hear my Father saying, 'Mother, mother, mother, mother, mother, don't do this.' The only person he called 'mother' was my mom, okay? There were a couple of survivors who told me that my mom fought—struggled—fought against what was happening until the last baby died.

"I don't know what you've been able to grasp, but most people loved my mother. The final night, Mom is fighting—she's fighting—the babies are dying first and that's what she was living for at that point. She was living for these kids, and they're dying. She's fighting it. The story goes that Dad calls in security and they're restraining Mom. And this kid, Poncho Johnson, dives in and throws them all off of her and protects her because you don't handle Mom—you don't handle Mother—that way. So he's in direct opposition to my father's order. My father calls him out, 'What the hell do you think you're doing?' dresses him down. He turns square to my father, stands at attention. My father says, 'You, you take the poison now.' Without even skipping a beat, Poncho walks up and takes that poison."

Stephan loses his words. He stumbles, trying to explain in a rational way, the totally irrational. "So—it's way more complex than—there's no—I can't—I can't—." He swallows hard.

He tries again: "I don't know if you guys know this, but by all accounts all the poison was in one vat. It was simple. The simple act of walking up and kicking that barrel over would have saved hundreds of lives."

The single vat Stephan mentioned was an oblong metal washtub filled with a concoction of potassium cyanide, sedatives, and grape Flavor Aid added to mask the taste.

Stephan pauses for a long time. "I can't get inside people's heads, so I'll never know how many people voluntarily lined up and took the poison. I personally believe it was very few, but even the ones who did, I think it had more to do with loyalty to the people than it did to Jim Jones. And it had to do with despair, defeat, and fear."

Stephan gets emotional here. "The truth of the matter is that while I miss my mother, I have been so angry at my father—the last seven years of his life, I contemplated his death on a daily basis—yet where I am now is that I hope he finds peace. If he were here in this room with me right now, I would hug him and tell him how much I love his heart. Dad would never turn a hug down from me, even at his sickest times. Reconciliation is our own, you know, and can take place without the other person there."

Conspiracist

ONE OF THE LAST INTERVIEWS we conduct in the Bay Area is with Reverend Arnold Townsend, a community activist and organizer. Many of the people who died in Jonestown—particularly within the African American community—hailed from a neighborhood in San Francisco called the Fillmore. Reverend Townsend is familiar with the history of the Fillmore. He said at one time it was "the heart and soul of the progressive Left in America."

Coincidentally, it is the week that gay couples are getting married at San Francisco's City Hall when Margo and I arrange to meet Reverend Townsend. Mayor Gavin Newsom had recently announced that he would allow gay couples to marry. As we make our way to Reverend Townsend's place, we pass City Hall, where just the week before hundreds of gay couples lined up around the block to tie the knot and make history. The event made the local and national news.

Reverend Townsend is an African American preacher, an activist, and a lifelong San Francisco resident. As he opens the door to his walk-up apartment and welcomes us inside, he comments on the events at City Hall: "You wouldn't see this anyplace else in the world," he says with pride.

I glance at a framed picture on the wall in his living room. Reverend Townsend posing with President Bill Clinton. The two men are warmly shaking hands.

"That's me and my friend Bill Clinton," he jokes.

"That's a great photo," I say.

Reverend Townsend has heard about our project and wants us to understand what the deaths in Jonestown meant to this community.

This is Reverend Arnold Townsend:

"When Jonestown happened, here in the Fillmore people came and just gathered at the Temple gate and just stood there. There was nowhere to go. Nowhere to talk. I saw a buddy of mine, Shelby. He's in the joint now; he lost his whole family. And what do you do? Who do you talk to? What do you say in a situation like that?"

He pauses.

"Now I'm not the world's greatest conspiracist," Townsend adds, "but I do know that the things leading up to Jonestown, and then Jonestown as a final straw, in black politics in general, in San Francisco more specifically, created a sense of desperation, a sense of *What's the use?*—a sense of hopelessness that we haven't come out of yet. The African American community knows that those people were in Jonestown because they wanted to see change, real change. The way they got into Jim Jones is because they didn't like shit the way it was. They didn't like the status quo of America. They wanted better for their children. They wanted a change!" He claps his hands for dramatic effect.

"We've spoken to some Fillmore residents," Margo explains. "They all say the same thing."

Reverend Townsend shakes his head.

"What it brought us to now is still trying to recover in an organized, political way—that's the word I'm looking for—*political* organization is not happening in the black community anymore. I mean, you take out almost nine hundred people who would be of the mentoring age now had they lived. They would be the teaching age now. Gone. So I'm not a conspiracist, but, man, Jonestown ripped out the heart of the most progressive community in America.

"Jonestown destroyed this community. It almost doesn't matter whether anybody intended it or not. What happened couldn't have served the reactionary forces in this country and in this state any better than if it was planned."

≈ ≈ ≈

Peoples Temple Christian Church was located on Geary Street in the heart of the Fillmore district of San Francisco. Jean and Tim Clancey had described to us what it was like there in the days immediately following Jonestown. Jean recounts: "I was still in the mind-set that I believed Jim was infallible."

Reporters camped out on the front porch and behind the Temple. The police came through the building looking for dead bodies. There were none, but the search made its point: Temple members were not to be trusted. Everyone was suspect.

The people in leadership positions in San Francisco—including Jean—were still defending Peoples Temple to the media, still clinging to the ideals of the group. Tim Clancey remembers it, too: "There were families, relatives of families trying to get in to the Temple to find out what was going on. We didn't know what was going on. Nobody knew what was going on. We were trying to deal as best we could. People were calling the Temple and demanding to know, 'Where is my family?' It was painful. It was chaos."

"I remember some of our own members, wandering the stairwells and halls, not eating, not sleeping. Some had lost everything—everyone—in Jonestown," Jean says softly. "We'd stand out on the balcony, and people walking by would scream up at us, 'Baby killer, baby killer.'"

≈ ≈ ≈

On November 27, 1978, just nine days after the deaths occurred in Jonestown, Supervisor Harvey Milk, the first openly gay city council member, and George Moscone, the mayor of San Francisco, were murdered in cold blood at City Hall by Dan White, a city council member who had recently resigned. Milk and Moscone had both attended services at Peoples Temple and been celebrated by Jim Jones for their political ideals. Jones had been appointed to the San Francisco Housing Authority on Moscone's watch, and as Jean recalls, "Moscone was a friend."

Dianne Feinstein, who was President of the Board of Supervisors in San Francisco at the time, was appointed mayor. With a city still reeling from the deaths of her colleagues, she also had to deal with Peoples Temple. Within days of becoming mayor, she set up a breakfast in a private room at a restaurant on the waterfront and invited the surviving Temple members to meet with her. She also invited Cecil Williams, the pastor of Glide Memorial Church, among others. She offered counseling at the city's expense to anyone who wanted it and employed psychologist Chris Hatcher to help the community transition back into society.

≈ ≈ ≈

Jean Clancey was at that meeting. "I have to say," she reflects, "Dianne Feinstein, whatever she inherited, she was not ashamed to be public and to open herself to us, and she didn't have anything to gain.

"I still believed in Jim Jones," Jean continues, "and we had a press conference with the media. It was the media of the entire world. There were hundreds of reporters there. There must have been about ten or fifteen of us sitting at a table up in front, and they were just firing away with these questions. We were still in shock, and the questions were wanting the most gruesome details," she sighs. "I went on railing about the United States living off the wealth of Third World countries, that our society is built on the exploitation of the labor mills and—everything—it was quite the party line then, and nobody was interested in that. They wanted the gory details. It was just horrendous. Trying to be a spokesman for something, and we were still reeling personally. It was bad on every hand.

"There was only one person in that room who seemed to care about what we were all about. She may have been affiliated with *Pacific News*. I remember she came up to me afterwards and asked me about our politics. She was the only one."

Jean brings the conversation back around to Feinstein.

"So the people who offered genuine help, you knew it. You knew who was genuine and who wasn't. Something about being at that level of existence—that depth of despair—you knew, you sensed sincerity. And people called whom you would not have expected to call. Some were church leaders. Some were even conservative church leaders who were sincerely concerned about us.

"Then there were people who you would think you could turn to and you could not. It was the most amazing experience, to see people who felt they had something to protect or hide or needed to distance themselves, who had once been your friends. Then people who had a lot to lose—like Dianne Feinstein—stepping forward and saying, 'What can we do for you?' The most amazing thing," Jean reflects.

Defending the ideals of Peoples Temple proved to be futile, and as the days and weeks progressed the internal structure of the Temple began to disintegrate. Jean tells us with enormous sadness that the reality in the end among the survivors in San Francisco was "recrimination, suspicion, and fear." As a person in leadership, she ended up with a cashier's check for $300,000—all the money in the one bank account that she had access to—and agonized over what to do with it. In the end, she put a call out to all surviving members and gave every penny away. But this revelation about the money was the first time that other survivors learned that Jean was a signatory on a Temple bank account, and some resented her for it. What was most heartbreaking to Jean was that the alliances formed among the survivors after Jonestown often fell along racial lines—black versus white. "We didn't have to leave the Temple," she says sadly. "The Temple left us. And in the end, we had to say, I had to say: we were wrong."

≈ ≈ ≈

When Vern Gosney came back to San Francisco after his long physical recuperation, he took up the city's offer of free counseling.

"It was difficult for me to deal with the guilt when I came back," he says. "Going back to get my clothes and leaving my son. I drank over it, I used drugs over it. I tried to block it out as much as I could. You can't. It's not something you can block out.

"It was a very long process," he confides. "When I came back to San Francisco, I started using again. I had all these drugs that the doctors gave me. They thought that people from Jonestown were dangerous. They weren't sure what we might do. Maybe just go kill everybody. So they were very free with the drugs. I drank and used even more heavily for years, until I reached a point of hitting another bottom."

He sighs.

"I finally got clean and sober. And when my consciousness started to clear, everything came back. Everything. The city provided therapy for us at Hunter's Point. That was not a good neighborhood. Every time I went to get therapy I was risking my life to get this therapy," he laughs. "There was one time these guys were chasing me down the street—I had this big fake fro and these giant earrings—I just barely made it to the door." He laughs again.

After a long pause, Vern says, "All my son ever knew was living in a cult, living in Jonestown and in Peoples Temple. That's all he knew. And in order for me to heal, and really live without drugs, I had to deal with that. I had to take responsibility for that."

He then brings the conversation back around to the question I had asked earlier about Jonestown. How some people say it was the best place they had ever been.

"It's interesting, that perspective," Vern reflects. "I guess you can rewrite history, or rewrite your memories and call it *perspective*. Whatever it is you need to believe in order to survive.

"I've heard people say that Jonestown was a lovely place," Vern goes on. "And maybe from what I've heard it was, early on. But from my experience, I don't know what Jonestown they are referring to."

Target Practice

SEPTEMBER 7, 2004
OAKLAND, CALIFORNIA

EUGENE SMITH describes coming back to the States after Jonestown as the hardest part of his journey in Peoples Temple. This is quite a statement given that he had lost his wife, his newborn son, his mother, and two adopted kids he helped to raise.

He left Georgetown, Guyana, on December 29, 1978, on a flight with other Temple members to John F. Kennedy airport. They were accompanied by sky marshals.

"When we left Guyana it was 90 degrees," he describes, "100 percent humidity. I'm at JFK in New York City with a safari jacket, and it's 23 degrees and I am freezing, and I said, 'Can I get into my luggage?' 'No, no you can't.' They took us first and interrogated us.

"They ask us, 'Do you know Jimmy Jones Jr.?'

"'Yeah.'

"'You know what cottage he lived in?'

"'No.'

"'Well, we know that you lived in cottage 17.'

"'I might have lived in cottage 17. So what?'

"'Well, cottage 19 was right across from you, where Jimmy Jones Jr. lived.'

"'So what?'

"Then the line of questioning got more aggressive: 'Were you there?'

"'Obviously I wasn't there, I was in Georgetown.' I said, 'Well, look, before this goes any further, I want an attorney.'"

≈ ≈ ≈

Even though coming back to the United States was so hard on Eugene, there was no place else for him to go.

Eugene's mother, Mattie, was gone, and he had no immediate family. All he had was a fifty-dollar bill in the bottom of his Converse sneaker "that had been washed a million times." He did not have a driver's license, or any other identification.

"When we arrived at JFK, people were beating on the walls and screaming at us," Eugene describes. "I made it a point right there. I'm never going to talk about this."

When the survivors arrived at JFK, the media was there, too. "Cameras going off just like crazy." *Newsweek* had found one of Eugene's letters to "Dad" and published it. He says he remembered the letter well. "You had to say how good it was in Jonestown, how bad it was in the U.S. And Jones had this big thing, 'I am the only man. There's no other man here.' Pushing the men to admit, 'You're a homosexual,' or some shit like that. 'All men are homosexuals.' But that was like a badge of strength to admit that and walk on."

After he was interrogated at JFK, he was handed a summons to appear in front of the grand jury in California three months later. He went to a hotel and pulled out the fifty-dollar bill. "C'mon," he said to fellow survivor Herbert Newell, "I'll treat breakfast. I need change anyway." The two men had breakfast and then got ready to board another plane from New York City to their final destination.

Except Eugene didn't go back to San Francisco. Instead, he flew to LA and just "jumped ship. I ran. I ran." It only took the FBI a few months to catch up with him. They came to his place of employment and said, "We're looking for Eugene Smith." When he came to work the next day, his bosses and coworkers said, "Eugene, the FBI was here. What the hell is going on?" He covered, "I don't know, man, maybe it's a cousin of mine or something."

After the FBI caught up with him, he asked, "Why did you go by my job?" They answered, "We wanted to get your attention."

Among other things, the FBI requested a handwriting sample in case in the future any politicians were ever threatened. Eugene complied. A few weeks later, he quit his job and moved to Fresno, where his mother's best friend lived.

"She said, 'Here's the keys, your car is parked out there. Here's a gun to protect yourself.' So I'd wake her kids up every morning, I'd fix breakfast, get them off to the school bus, and then I'd go outside in the backyard and target-practice all morning long. Just shoot that gun at a target all morning. That was just my way of dealing with it. Because the whole time I was in Peoples Temple, I had no way to protect me or mine."

In the 1990s, when Eugene applied for a new passport to travel to Europe, he had to pay the government back the $320 it cost them to fly him from New York to Los Angeles.

"Some years," Eugene explains, "it's more difficult than others, especially during the holidays. My mom's birthday is Christmas Eve. So from November 18 all the way to New Year's it's like, 'This is shit.' Some years I've gone past November 18 and didn't think about it till January, and it's like, 'Yes! Finally I did it! I went through a whole season and didn't think about it!'"

He acknowledges that relationships have been challenging, too, both romance and friendship. It was "forever" before he was able to get into any kind of romantic relationship. Now, if he gets involved, sometime during "the initial phase" he has to say, "There is something I have to tell you." The woman's reaction to the news is an indicator of whether or not the relationship will move forward.

Eugene knew that he needed to talk to someone when he returned to the States. But when he went to a professional therapist, the first question he was asked was, "Are you willing to admit that you were brainwashed?" To which he replied, "No. I'm not willing to admit that. I might have been fooled. I might have been tricked. I might have been hoodwinked. But brainwashed? I'm asking for help, and I know I need it. Obviously, I have enough clarity in my mind and my way of thinking to know that."

Later, survivors were asked to provide proof of their eligibility for a financial settlement from the disbursement of the Peoples Temple assets. Eugene called it "blood money" and said, "If you don't give it to me, I'm not gonna ask for it. I worked my ass off for years for this organization." He had to take a stand for himself. It was wrong, he thought, to have "to beg for it."

≈ ≈ ≈

In the first months and years back in the States, most survivors were on their own.

When Claire Janaro finally returned home from Guyana, she simply could not get it through her head that her kids were gone. Her husband, Richard, had wired her money in Guyana so she could fly to Trinidad to meet him. "Then the hard part came," Claire says. "Richard was broken, and I was broken, and he didn't want to come back to the States." It was Claire who determined that they "had to go back."

When the survivors returned to the United States from Guyana, the FBI detained and strip-searched them on the plane.

"I flew home with Helen Swinney and Richard. We had nine, ten hours of total interrogation. We did not know why. They wouldn't let Helen stay with us. She had lost so much family. She was one of the oldest families in the Temple, had been with Jim since Indiana. Why didn't they let her stay with us? It was horrendous why they separated her off. They didn't offer us anything to eat, or even coffee. But they were sure we were plotting to overthrow the United States. And they wanted us to name people. Incriminate. I never knew the internal workings of the Temple. I was on the Planning Commission, and I knew a lot and I saw a lot. But as far as money, as far as planning the big things that went on, how Peoples Temple actually operated, neither Richard nor I knew anything."

She pauses.

"It was a very, very hard time," Claire continues. "It was hard nails. Richard literally brought me through it. I couldn't have done it without Richard, I could not have. I got into therapy, and the therapist wanted me to go back to school and get my degree. I only needed a year, maybe a year and a half at most to finish college. I got a student loan and went back, and I pushed myself through the first semester, and I got all As. When I was taking sociology, Peoples Temple was one of the things they wanted us to study. I white-knuckled it through those classes, but when I got into the next semester, I dropped out. I couldn't handle it anymore. I couldn't handle being around the kids that would have been my kids' age.

"We had no medical insurance. The therapy was given to me free, courtesy of my sister-in-law, who was a clinical psychologist. My therapist was the man she trained under, and he was doing it gratis for her. And he was wonderful, but he just tried to pacify me—'It wasn't my fault. Get lemons, you make lemonade'—it wasn't any kind of in-depth therapy. But he held my hand at least."

Claire's eyes are teary. She gets up to get a box of tissues off the side table in her living room.

"Still, I was becoming desperate, so he got me to an MD and got me on antidepressants, which calmed me and enabled me to cope. That was my deepest time. And I just tried getting off of them a few years ago, and I got them down pretty low—too low—and I had a relapse. Never to the point that I wanted to kill myself again, but, you know, that's how bad it gets when you feel like you've murdered your children." She begins to cry. "You've murdered the rest of your family, you're left alive, and everybody's gone. And underneath, I always felt it was my fault because I was the one who talked Richard into it. I pushed him. It never leaves you. You try to make it equal out, but you can't. You always think there's something you could have done."

Claire's husband, Richard, died of Alzheimer's in early 2003.

On our visit with Claire in Los Angeles, Greg notices a picture of a young girl and boy in the jungle. She asks him to bring it to her, and she holds it tenderly. "That was sent to me just before November 1978. That was Mauri. She was in charge of the animals."

She has more photographs to show us. "I have not been able to destroy these. I mean, to me, it goes part and parcel with it. Some people took everything and destroyed it." She singles out a familiar photo of the extended Peoples Temple rainbow family. It is a photo of Jim Jones surrounded by children of all ages and races.

"Jim called and said, 'Bring all the kids who are on the ranch, we're taking a picture,' and so I gathered some from the neighborhood. I watched them taking this picture.

"I have another picture of Daren with a parrot. He was in charge of the birds. Daren was fourteen and a half there. He went to Jonestown on his thirteenth birthday."

"And the two of them were close?" I ask. "They seem close in this picture."

"They were very close," Claire whispers. "They loved each other. They were very good children. They didn't get into trouble, and they were very bright. Both of them were in the accelerated classes."

She pauses here before explaining.

"I just went blindly, taking them out of an education: 'The jungle will solve all the problems in the world, and we'll be safe.' Dumb. I don't know what else to say. I have no excuses other than I just let it pass over me."

Undetermined

MARCH 10, 2002
SAN DIEGO, CALIFORNIA

REBECCA MOORE described how her family, along with other surviving families, was left to piece together what little history could tell them about what happened to their loved ones in Jonestown on the last day, a process that took several years and many sources: news accounts, Freedom of Information Act documents, personal interviews, even a trip to Guyana she and her husband, Mac McGehee, took in 1979. In spite of all of this, Becky Moore's conclusion remains true: "This story will always be a mixture of fact and hypotheses."

At the California Historical Society, our project archivist, Denice Stephenson, shows us a four-page typewritten memo written by Becky's sister Carolyn Moore Layton. The memo is addressed simply to "Jim":

PART ·V. A FINAL STAND

If there were a good way to insure the deaths of everyone I would consider it about the best alternative. I think we concluded before that (1) there is no good, sure way to do this, (2) a number of people would rather sell out and denounce us than die, (3) some young people who would not mind dying for some tangible ideal cannot reconcile themselves to planning their demise.

I am 33 and have had plenty of convincing experiences to frighten me about what can happen in unplanned crises where you cannot insure your ultimate fate and especially the fate of those you love around you.

You have always seemed sure that we could do away with ourselves and the babies, yet, each time Marceline gets totally freaked out at this and I have not seen you yet consider it without letting her know.

What I am trying to say is if we make a stand or decide to die how are we going to do it?

How would you convince Stephan, or would you?

Do you give everyone pills?

Perhaps planning is the answer to all this. Maybe there is a practical way all this can be arranged.

I wish I knew because there are things I would and should burn and things which should be kept if we do choose death. I would like to have everything all organized before I die including what I would like people to come along and find about you and the organization after we are gone. I wish the book were done too.

In an unaddressed letter written by the Temple doctor, Larry Schacht, he weighs the pros and cons of using cyanide as the form of death:

Cyanide is one of the most rapidly acting poisons. I had some misgivings about its effectiveness but from further research I have gained more confidence in it, at least theoretically. I would like to give about two grams to a large pig to see how effective our batch is to be sure we don't get stuck with a disaster like would occur if we used thousands of pills to sedate the people and then the cyanide was not good enough to do the job. I also want to order antidotes just in case we may need to reverse the poisoning process on people.

≈ ≈ ≈

In December 1978, more than nine hundred bodies were airlifted from Jonestown, Guyana, and flown three thousand miles to Dover Air Force Base, Delaware.

Only seven of these bodies were autopsied: William Richard Castillo, Laurence Eugene Schacht (the doctor), Violatt Esther Dillard, Carolyn Moore Layton (Becky's older sister), Maria Katsaris, Ann Elizabeth Moore (Becky's younger sister), and James Warren Jones.

We study the autopsy reports. With slight variations in syntax all of the autopsies conclude: "Owing to the lack of reliable and specific information about intent and the possibility of coercion by others, the manner of death in our opinion, remains undetermined."

One of those bodies, labeled by the U.S. government as "A001" and transported by the U.S. Air Force from Jonestown to Dover, was that of Ann Elizabeth Moore:

Date of Death: 18 November 1978
Date of Autopsy: 15 December 1978
From the Examination of Clothing and Personal Effects:
Clothing: Shirt with key ring and keys, tan pants with a key chain and keys, pocket knife with folding blade present in pants, white panties, white socks, blue tennis shoes with "Annie Moore" on them.
From the Summary: The postmortem findings in this case offer two causes of death. The first is a lethal level of cyanide (in muscle), the second is a mutilating gunshot wound of the head with presumed extensive cerebral damage. The use of multiple modalities for effecting suicide is not uncommon. Notwithstanding this, the absence of witnesses, and the bizarre circumstances surrounding this death make it impossible to choose between the two alternatives with any degree of confidence. Thus, both are listed as causes of death. Similarly, the circumstances and the presence of two lethal injuries obscure the manner of death. Had there only been cyanide present, the presence of a note indicating intent at the scene (as reported in the media) would have allowed a strong presumption of suicide. However, since it cannot be determined if the gunshot wound was self-inflicted or not, and if not, whether it was inflicted before or after death by another person, the possibility of homicide cannot be entirely eliminated. Hence, the manner of death must be left undetermined.

Another of the bodies autopsied was that of James Warren Jones:

From the Examination of Clothing and Personal Effects: The body is clothed in a red shirt with the label "Fruit of [the] Loom, Extra Large," tan trousers labeled, "Sears Perma-press," 36×30, no belt, brief type underwear with the label "3H Fruit of [the] Loom" and the name "Steve" initialed into the waist band, black socks and black lace shoes with the label "84550, Comb, 305z."
From the Summary: The manner of death is consistent with suicide because of the finding of a hard contact gunshot wound of the head. The possibility of homicide cannot be entirely ruled out because of the lack of specific and reliable information.

It was no accident that these two were among the seven who were autopsied, since they were the only two people in Jonestown with gunshot wounds. The autopsies were inconclusive: the wounds were consistent with suicide, but murder could not be ruled out.

≈ ≈ ≈

Annie Moore had also written a letter on the last day, in a notebook with the words "Guyana Exercise Book" printed on the cover. The notebook was discovered near her body after Jonestown. Here is some of what Annie Moore wrote that day:

> November 18, 1978. I am 24 years of age right now and don't expect to live through the end of this book. I am at a point right now so embittered against the world that I don't know why I am writing this. Someone who finds it will believe I am crazy or believe in the barbed wire that does NOT exist in Jonestown. . . . When I write this, I can expect some mentally deranged fascist person to find it and decide it should be thrown in the trash before anyone gets a chance to hear the truth, which is what I am now writing about. . . .

The note was written in blue ink, except for the last line, which appears in black ink: "We died because you would not let us live in peace."

≈ ≈ ≈

When we sat down with John and Barbara Moore, we spoke with them about the process of piecing together their daughters' histories in the aftermath of Jonestown and in the decades since. Here is some of what they said:

"When people say, 'How many children do you have?'" Barbara explains, "Well, 'I have three, but two of them died.' I don't say they died in Jonestown. I just say, 'They were in an accident,' or something. Unless I know the person well enough to know they can understand and take this kind of a—news."

John is emotional yet maintains his composure: "I wondered from the first what role Annie had the last day. She was the nurse and was in charge of the drugs and that sort of thing. What role she had actually in administering those drugs, I don't know. I just don't know," he says softly. "I still don't know the answer to that question."

He pauses. His voice begins to crack. "Anyway, we *have* to know that Carolyn gave the drugs to her son—our grandson Kimo—and that's hard to deal with. We didn't know about Jim Jones's sex life until it was all over. We thought that he and Carolyn were—." He struggles to find words to describe the relationship. "That she was kind of his mistress, I suppose his principal mistress, but anyway she was . . ."

"One of the harem," Barbara finishes bluntly.

John nods. "Apparently, at the end, Carolyn was the one who was the most influential, other than Jim Jones. So those are the hardest parts about it. And . . . just thinking of that last day how all those people dealt with that and faced that. It felt from early on that probably the sense of loyalty to their peers had as much to do with it as anything Jim Jones got started. They chose to be a part of the group and they lived with the group and they died with the group."

As our interview comes to a close John asserts what is most important to him for us to know. His language is steady, and he is careful in his use of words.

"Barbara disagrees with me, and she gets upset when I say it, but long ago I understood. I haven't felt guilty, but I felt I share in the responsibility. I am the father of two children and a grandson who died there, and our lives are still interwoven, and whatever their lives are, I'm some part of that. It didn't happen because of me—there are hundreds of actors in that tragedy and that drama—but I was one of them."

Barbara takes his hand and adds: "Well, the other hard thing was the publicity, the *National Enquirer* and other papers. I remember going to the drugstore, and here was a picture on the *National Enquirer,* big picture of all these bodies, facedown—it was one of the famous pictures—and I felt like running down the street and screaming, 'You don't understand! It isn't the way you think it is!' And so there were those feelings at times."

"It was the first few days," John says, "when Barbara, she spontaneously said, 'Jim Jones murdered our children. I will not let him destroy—'" John breaks down for a long moment before he finishes. "'—me. I will not let him destroy me.'"

He wipes away a tear, and then the preacher in him finds his way back to the conversation.

"In my experience," he continues, his voice full again, "two Scripture passages came to mind. One: love never ends. And the other, a passage which is usually said, 'Everything works out for the best.' But there's one translation that says that 'in everything God is working to bring about that which is good.' So I said, 'Well, you have a choice to make. How are you going to respond? What will you do?' It's not just: why did this happen? I think that's a question people ask. But what will you do about what has happened? What will you do *out* of what's happened? So I said, I would like to work with God to bring whatever good I can out of this. And that's what Barbara and I, and our daughter Becky and her husband Mac, have done. That tragedy is still there, but new life and new hope—the resurrection—can arise.

"We decided from day one that we would be public. Affirming our children and the young people who died, their humanness. We decided that we would take our stand. That decision was the single decision that marked us as different from most of the people who were touched by Peoples Temple. We could affirm the humanness, and we did that. All along the way."

Something to Gain

SEPTEMBER 5, 2003
EUGENE, OREGON

ON OUR LAST TRIP to Eugene, Tim Carter has an idea. He knows that I am a sports fan, so he suggests that we go for a walk together. He wants to show Greg and me the memorial to the Oregon long distance running hero Steve Prefontaine. There is a memorial on the rural winding road where the twenty-four-year-old "Pre" died in a car accident. Jean and Tim Clancey live nearby, so we all plan to go.

We walk together, stopping briefly in front of the bronze memorial. We stand around for a few minutes in silence. Then we begin the return trip back to Tim and Jean's for lunch. Greg walks ahead with Tim Carter and Tim Clancey, and I can see his hands gesticulating as he tells animated stories. Jean and I are walking more slowly, and after some distance opens between us and them, she quietly asks me, "What do you hope to accomplish with all this? Is there anything here to offer that hasn't already been said?"

We walk in silence for what feels like a very long time, and then I answer in the most honest way that I can: "I am not really sure. I hope that the audience is able to appreciate the humanity of the people involved in this story. That's all."

With a twinge of skepticism in her voice, Jean replies, "Well, good luck with that. Undoing what people think of us is not an easy task."

Again we walk in silence, before I speak. "There is one thing I want to ask you about."

"Go ahead," Jean says.

"We've seen letters," I say. "All in the same format—talking about violent revolution and threatening violent acts against the government. And we've heard tape recordings of people proclaiming, 'I am a violent revolutionary.'"

"Yes," Jean answers plainly. "I think I was gonna blow up the Senate. I don't even know where the Senate building is, but I was gonna blow up the Senate," she shakes her head. "I never even went to Washington, D.C." She sighs. "There were meetings after Jonestown with the Secret Service in the Attorney General's office. We were quizzed on those letters. We had to account for those statements."

"They're quite shocking," I say.

"Right, and Jim would read those and giggle and laugh. We would collect them. You'd see him reading them and just giggling."

"One of the most disturbing things of all that I've heard," I continue, "and we've heard a lot—about punishments, deprivation boxes in Jonestown, drugging people in ICU to keep them quiet. But of all of it, the most disturbing is a transcript of a tape where the kids are doing a kind of one-upmanship of each other referring to their relatives who had left the Temple."

"Oh?" Jean says.

"And they're saying what they would do to them because they left the Temple. How they would torture them because they were disloyal. Young kids saying, 'I'll mutilate them' or 'I'll kill them,' and all the while Jones laughing in the background," I explain.

"Yeah, that insidious laugh."

"It's disturbing," I say.

"It is," Jean confirms. "It is."

And then I confide, "The hard part for me as a playwright is that I want to vindicate everybody—"

Jean interrupts, "Oh," as if surprised.

"To make a play where people are vindicated."

Jean finishes my thought, "Where the people are good."

"Yes," I say, "where the people are good."

"And Jones is evil."

"Yes."

"That the people are good and innocent and misled and duped by an evil force," she says.

"Well, it's not that simple, but yes," I confess.

This is the most maternal Jean has been up to this point, and the most prescriptive, and I let her continue without interruption.

"But, Leigh, it's the human condition," she begins. "We asked Jim Jones to be something. We played into it. We asked him for something a person cannot be. And we can say we were disillusioned, but what is more useful is to recognize that human capacity to not take responsibility for our own thoughts and actions. It serves a need for us. Anyone who signed on had something to gain.

"If it was relief from your own personal confusion, Jim gave simple answers. If it was your ennui, he gave a reason and a purpose to engage and exist. If you were in a ghetto and you were scared to death your kids were gonna go to jail, this man will give my kids a job and an education. Everybody had something to gain, and everybody put these demands on him."

She pauses.

"I'm not vindicating him," she clarifies forcefully. "He invited it. He was playing God. He really was playing God. He was the mutineer, and we joined the mutiny. Once when we had to give testimonies, I remember standing up and saying, 'I have found the way, now I can believe.' Something grandiose. 'Justice in the universe.' It's naïveté, but it's such a symbiotic thing, he has a megalomaniac need to be that for people, and we fed it, we fed that. We confirmed his power.

"But ultimately from an adult perspective it comes down to living the way you want to be. In the here and now, with who you are, with the people that you're with, with the integrity that you can have, with the impact that you can have right here and to be accountable for what you do. Even on the smallest level.

"But, no, we wanted to change the world. And we are accountable for what we did, whether in the context of Peoples Temple or the Vietnam War or whatever it was. We are accountable for our own actions. I did these things. I am accountable. Even though, in that moment, in that time, there was a reason, an excuse, for what I did."

She turns to me and says, "You have to answer to yourself, don't you? You have to answer to your conscience. If your play has any value, what people will take away from it is, *Where could I have gone?* Not just a sentimental 'Oh my God, look what the world lost, all these wonderful people.' But, 'It could have been me, too.'"

≈ ≈ ≈

When we arrive back at the Clancey property, everything seems peaceful, from the profusion of wild flowers to Jean's horse standing patiently in the barn.

"Do you miss it?" Greg asks.

"Peoples Temple?" Jean replies.

"The community," Greg clarifies.

"I miss some of the people," Jean answers. "I do not miss being on the door. I do not miss the presence of Jim Jones. I still in my dreams wrangle with trying to separate and I want out! I want no part of him. Or his legacy here," she says bitterly. "I don't have any answers, but I miss a lot of people. I would love to be able to sit down to talk. But then, you see," she continues, "there are some people in the Temple who are alive who we shared greatly with and we don't—we don't go back. So maybe it's a sentimental notion. We stay away from all the memorials. We've stayed away. We've gotten letters and invitations. Maybe that will happen someday. But do I miss the Temple? No."

Jean reflects, "If Jones had just believed, if he had just believed in his people enough, if he just believed in the goodness of these people and just let them be, if he could just have exited himself and let this go. But of course, he's God, he created it, it's his. He has the right to take it with him when he goes."

One of her last descriptions is an image from another dream she had about the people who died. "In my own mind, they're at rest," she says. "They're beautiful, dressed in white. They're across the river in a beautiful green meadow, just beautiful black faces. Awesome. In my own mind, they are at peace."

Legacy

....

MARGO HANDS ME A CASSETTE TAPE at the Starbucks on West Grand Avenue in Oakland. She has just interviewed Donneter Lane, an African American civic and community leader and head of the Council of San Francisco Churches in 1978, whose leadership was instrumental in getting the unclaimed bodies buried at Evergreen Cemetery in Oakland.

I take the tape home and transcribe it. Ms. Lane speaks slowly, a slight shake in her voice, reflective of her age, but her words are stoic and strong.

This is Donneter Lane:

"The San Francisco Council of Churches got involved right away, and we organized the Guyana Emergency Relief Committee. We filed the brief to bring the bodies back home. The military mortuary is in Dover, Delaware, so that's where the bodies had to go first. Nobody knew what was going to happen, how it was gonna happen, but we knew we had to bring the bodies back home. There was a political war going on in the city. Mayor Moscone and Supervisor Harvey Milk got killed. There was so much chaos.

"Nobody wanted those bodies. The cemeteries here didn't want them. We went to everyone. I got calls and letters. People said, 'They made a choice to go there, and they were responsible for the death of a congressman and the death of the people.' Evergreen Cemetery was the only one that said, 'Yes.' They had a plot. There was room for four hundred bodies. It was way up there, way up there on a hill.

"Evergreen received all kinds of threats. Local people were angry. It

300

was a matter of making plans to prepare the bodies, put them in a casket, and seal the caskets. That's how they got to Dover from Guyana, and that's how they left Dover to come here. We had to get a trucking company that could bring so many bodies at a time.

"We tried to get in touch with families to be sure that it was okay for the bodies to be released to us. There were no tombstones. People didn't want to believe they had families there, so they didn't come to put tombstones. Other people were afraid.

"We went up that hill there for the service. The only people who were there were members of the relief committee and a few family members. It was a painful job for us, very painful. But we finished it."

≈ ≈ ≈

The site of the mass grave was marked with a small stone erected at that first memorial service by the Guyana Emergency Relief Committee. It read: "In memory of the victims of the Jonestown tragedy, November 18, 1978."

≈ ≈ ≈

The Peoples Temple assets were frozen in 1979 and placed under the supervision of the San Francisco Superior Court. By the time the court-appointed receiver settled the claims brought against the Peoples Temple estate four years later, more than $1.8 billion in claims had been filed. The receiver had recovered—and disbursed—$13 million. Most of those who filed claims—for wrongful death, for property turned over to Peoples Temple—received pennies on the dollar, if they were honored at all. And the records of Peoples Temple's existence—approximately a hundred boxes—were sent to the California Historical Society.

≈ ≈ ≈

Reggie Pettus, the local barber we met with Jim Jones Jr. in the Fillmore, told us what became of the Temple building on Geary Street in San Francisco: "After Peoples Temple left, these Koreans came in and bought the church. And in '89, the big earthquake just wiped it out. That's what happened to the church. It just wiped it out. To me, it was an omen. You weren't supposed to be there, you killed all those people, so it just wiped out his church. That was the only building in this whole area that was destroyed. The earthquake came through here, and it knocked out the ceiling and it knocked out the windows. But we're still here. It was crazy. It's a post office now.

"But see, what we couldn't understand about Jones is how a white guy could mesmerize all these black people to go over there and then turn around and tell them to kill themselves? He just wiped out the whole community, just about wiped it out."

Stephan Jones told us about breaking into the Temple after that earthquake, before the building was demolished. He knew it wasn't safe, but he went in anyway. "I was across the street at a bar, and I got a little drunk and said, 'I'm going over.' You know it was boarded up, stuff was falling down, and a Korean Christian church had taken it over, so a big cross—a big crucifix up on the wall—Christ looking down on me. I was climbing around, and I knew I wasn't supposed to be in there. Nobody's around, but I've got that same kind of feeling of shame that I always had when I was walking around the Temple. I remember this ever-present sense of shame that I wasn't doing what I was supposed to be doing, just fearing that I'm going to be in trouble in a minute. I had that same feeling walking through this completely abandoned place."

He explained what happened next.

"There was a phone. I picked up the phone—it still had a dial tone—and I called my brother. I said, 'You'll never believe where I am.'

"And he said, 'Where?'

"I said, 'I'm in the Temple.'

"'What are you doing there?'

"I said something like, 'I don't know, man, I'm just lovin' you right now.'

"He went, 'Okay. I love you, too. Don't do anything stupid.'"

≈ ≈ ≈

Jim Jones Jr. reflected on what it was like for him in San Francisco in the aftermath of Jonestown.

"I was working for a courier company from two 'til ten o'clock, an eight-hour shift. I would go around to all the Wells Fargos, go in and pick up a bag of checks, and take them to the Wells Fargo Bank right across from the Oakland Coliseum. I was there for two or three months, you know, and I was good. I was eighteen years old, I had a driver's license. This is 1979.

"And I remember my boss made some kind of joke or something about Jonestown. 'That's not funny,' I said. He went, 'Well, why?' I said, 'Because a lot of people died.' He goes, 'Oh, those people were brainwashed.' I said, 'But still, they're dead. And anyway, that was my father.' He goes, 'You serious?' 'Yeah.' He said, 'Where are your keys?' I said, 'In the car.' He goes, 'Get your shit out of the car, you're fired.' Just like that. I remember walking up Seventh Street down by Market, I walked all the way up to the top of Market, all the way up the hill. I'm thinking to myself, 'My father always said, if we came back here, we would be lepertized.' To an eighteen-year-old mind, when I told people who I was, I was lepertized."

≈ ≈ ≈

Tony Tamburello was the court-appointed defense attorney for the Larry Layton case and subsequent trials who worked with Jack Palladino and Melody Ermachild Chavis. When we spoke to him in 2002, on the twenty-fourth anniversary of Jonestown, Tamburello prophesied how history might remember Peoples Temple and Jonestown, and what their legacy might be. His statement haunted me as we approached the end of our work:

"There were a lot of people who thought that Jones didn't die in Jonestown and would surface someplace else," he explained. "In the tape of the last hour, the thing that really bothered me the most is toward the end where Jones says, 'What a legacy.' It really offended me to no end. He thought this was his legacy. To be so warped to say that—that he believed that it was a legacy—but it's turning out to be true. People will always remember him. He doesn't have fifteen minutes of fame: he succeeded. It's twenty-four years later, and they still remember him. They call it Jonestown. You know, it's stupid to call it Jonestown—you know what I mean?—everything's affiliated with him. He was a murderer, he was an abuser—and 'What a legacy,' you know. That's his legacy. Nobody remembers hardly any of the people who were there. History will not even remember what it was all about, other than that Jones killed nine hundred people or more. So I guess he was right."

Nell Smart's reflections were different: "Jim Jones left a horrible legacy," she told us, "but he also left a group of people that proved his point that black and white can live together.

"And I guess the time that I really feel whole," she continued, "is when I'm with people from the Temple. It was just a very small part of my life that I was with them, but it made an impact, and I always hate leaving. It really is like leaving family."

When we finally sat down with Janet Shular and her husband, David, she concurred: "Sometimes I think, this world is crazy, we have forgotten our humanity. In the end, everyone in Peoples Temple suffered terrible, painful losses, but from the many loving bonds that we were able to cultivate and sustain—under the most difficult of circumstances—I still find a motivation to just keep keeping on."

Neva Sly confided: "Those of us that escaped, the defectors, weren't sure how the others were going to feel, you know? And they weren't sure how we were going to feel toward them. Until we saw them, and it was like none of it really mattered, we were still family. It's a different kind of family. It's not like people that you're going to stay in touch with all the time. But it's a knowing that you were all of one cause at one time, and therefore family. If any of the kids called me and needed help, I'd be there. I think most of us would. Because we grew up together, I guess. No matter what age, we grew up together. If you've gone through Jim Jones, you've grown up with something strange. And there's nobody else that can understand what we've been through except us. There's no way of explaining our emotion. We still have emotional ties, we still remember the kids. It's not so much the fact they're gone—it's the beautiful memories, too."

I Won't Say Anniversary

....

NOVEMBER 18, 2004
OAKLAND, CALIFORNIA

I WALK UP the now-familiar hill at Evergreen Cemetery. Another year has passed, another anniversary, this one three years after our journey began. I notice Stephan Jones sitting cross-legged on the edge of the grass, separate from the main event. We share a smile, a wave.

I watch as others arrive and greet Stephan, some shaking his hand, some embracing him.

An image comes to mind of the young Danny Curtin, coming back for the twentieth anniversary after not seeing or talking to anyone in the Temple for that length of time, making his way up that hill, unsure of himself, not knowing who or what he would find there, and then the light and the trees and the silence giving way to an embrace, a recognition and reunion. Many survivors had similar experiences on their first trip to Evergreen Cemetery; for many of them, the twentieth was also the first anniversary that they were able to attend.

"I showed up late," Danny tells us. "I walk up that hill, and I'm quiet as hell, I don't even want to be there. It's just the struggle of going through all the memories. I go up there and people started crying and coming back to me and hugging me. It just brought back the day."

Danny is in his middle forties when we meet him, but he has retained his boyish looks. He has reddish-brown hair and wears jeans and a polo shirt. He had grown up in the Temple, a boy who worked on the ranch in Redwood Valley and who played the drums in church. We interview him while sitting at a courtyard picnic table in downtown San Francisco near a construction site where he worked.

There are men in thick cargo pants with their hard hats on the table, eating sandwiches in the afternoon sun. Danny remains uncertain about talking to us. He keeps mostly to himself and keeps his history hidden to protect his children. He still fears for their safety even after all these years. "You never know," he says, "you never know." Danny left the Temple before the exodus to Jonestown. He had become disillusioned with Jim Jones when a good friend of his in the Temple died of a heart attack while they were working together. Young Danny went to "Father" to ask him why he had not saved his friend from dying. Jim Jones answered, "Do you think I can save every motherfucker in here?"

And yet when he lets himself give in, Danny's heart is still full of love for Peoples Temple. Danny describes himself in the Temple as a drummer, "little drummer boy," though he struggles to describe the good.

"I saw a woman get up on the anniversary. She started to cry, a white woman crying in front of all these black people, saying how it was still the most wonderful time in her life. When she sat down, she was corrected by a black woman who said, 'Well, it might have been wonderful for you, but how many of us lost our whole families?' I saw both sides. Yeah, I felt her pain, you're damn right. Some white woman saying, 'Well, it was the best thing I ever had.' It was to her, because she'll never feel that again. Never.

"Look, the best thing any of us can do now is go to work together, but 'You go back to Oakland, I'll go back to Marin,' we all go back to our own, and I'll see you tomorrow. See you tomorrow."

Danny explains that what he is referring to is the racial divide between the predominantly black neighborhoods of Oakland and the white enclaves of Marin.

"Nah, in Peoples Temple," he continues, "you live with these people, you work with them. It becomes you. You become them. It's that personal. It's that personal. So, yes, it was wonderful, and it was also as tragic as it was wonderful. How about that one?"

I think, too, of Nell Smart. On that same anniversary, she brought her children's ashes with her, those whose bodies had been identified. "I don't like the word *anniversary*," she explained, "I won't say *anniversary*. The first *memorial* service that I went to, the twentieth, I just couldn't seem to find an opportune time to put their ashes in the ground there. Then I thought, 'Well, I'll keep them,' because I knew that I'd go back.

And when I heard we were having a private ceremony for survivors only on the twenty-fifth memorial, I thought 'Good.' I wanted to put their ashes there with those that had not been identified. Just to be sure that they would be together in death, you know, even as they were in life. I wrote each of them a letter, and we burned the letters, and we buried them. It was healing for me, it really was. My oldest was Tinetra, oldest son was Al, my next son was Scotty—he was the middle—and my youngest daughter was Teri. And my mother was Kay Nelson."

Still struggling to find closure, Nell was not able to put the children's ashes there on the twenty-fifth anniversary either.

≈ ≈ ≈

Andy Warhol once said something to the effect that death is the most embarrassing thing that can happen to a person. You spend your whole life trying to take care of things so that you won't bother anybody, and then people are left with having to deal with your remains, planning your funeral, cleaning up your life. In the case of Peoples Temple, death took place on the world stage. For many survivors and their loved ones and families, this made it difficult to grieve, to collectively process, or to understand.

"They wouldn't even let us bury the dead," Tim Carter said to me, speaking through sobs mixed with bitterness and rage. He had shown me his copy of *Newsweek* magazine published right after Jonestown. The cover photograph depicted scores of bodies and the vat of poison. "This is what we are to most people, and that's a reality. This is what Jonestown and Peoples Temple are to the vast majority of people. We're the cult of death. Period. Cult. Death. That's all that people need to know."

≈ ≈ ≈

Some time had passed since our interviews, but Tim and I keep in touch. I tell him that in discussing this story with a friend, my friend commented that their actions were unforgivable. "I've heard people say that," he tells me, "we aren't deserving of forgiveness. And there's a part of me that doesn't know if we actually are. I think we're certainly worthy of consideration in terms of lessons that can be learned. And I'm sorry that I helped perpetuate the lie. His lie," he qualifies. "What I believed in wasn't a lie, and the people weren't a lie, but Jim Jones was certainly a lie." He pauses. "I know that I did the best I could. I survived. I wasn't supposed to die that day. I was supposed to live. And I have to believe that someday the lives of the people who died in Jonestown will mean something."

≈ ≈ ≈

Eugene Smith had never before talked publicly about his history in Peoples Temple. He described what it was like for him to hide much of his life for all these years:

"I had to create a history for myself, a life. Good example, where I work now, I've been there twelve years. I don't really care about my name coming out—I almost want it to—because people in day-to-day life don't realize how hurtful they really are. I work with this guy, and he always says, 'Well, you're single, you can do whatever you want, you don't have to worry about your babies,' and it's like, 'You don't know me. You don't know nothing about me.' And the women at work are always telling me, 'You need to have children, you need to get married. Why aren't you married? You have so much to offer.' You can't tell people in the work environment, 'My wife died in Jonestown. So did my children.' How do they respond to that? I just want people to understand that you can't judge people by what they look like to you or who you think they are."

Eugene thought about what he wanted to say next. He searched to find peaceful words for a not-so-peaceful thought.

"I've tried to not be a mad black man, because an angry black man in this society is a targeted black man. You make yourself a target by being so angry. And anger a lot of times is a shortcoming for things that you just haven't taken time to work with. Sometimes you're angry because you don't have the skills or the wherewithal to deal with it." He paused. "And so now I'm forty-seven years old, and it's amazing because this life is all new to me. This wasn't an option: living to be a middle-aged man. I haven't been to jail, I haven't been arrested," he laughed.

"Coming back to the U.S. after Jonestown, I'd never had a bank account. I never had a job where I received a check. I didn't understand business. Day-to-day things I missed out on. Now I make plans for retirement, I got a retirement plan going on. I guess it says a lot to how my mother raised me."

Then one of his final thoughts:

"Truthfully, I don't think we'll ever be seen as survivors. I think we'll always be seen as *those who got away.* I think we're going to be hated in a certain segment of society. We will always be seen as freaks. I don't think society ever understood what it was about. It wasn't just Jim Jones: it was my daughter, Christa; my son, Martin; it was my wife, Ollie; it was my mother, Mattie. It was thousands of stories and thousands of scenarios that happened along the same timeline. And now we're to this point: *let's bring it all out.*

"I remember seeing Mervyn Dymally at meetings. He was lieutenant governor then and he's in the state legislature now. I remember Willie Brown at meetings. He's mayor of San Francisco now. I remember Jane Fonda at meetings, and Jimmy Carter's wife, Rosalynn Carter, and the black actress Esther Rolle at meetings. A lot of people that had that involvement are just like, 'Hush. Hush,'" he whispered.

"My whole thing behind talking to you is this. I feel it's necessary to hear a black man's story—." He stopped to correct himself: "Not a black man's story, but a black man's *insight* to what went on with him. 'Cause I don't represent all the black men there, and I don't represent the black race that was there. I represent Eugene. Eugene and Ollie and Martin and Christa and Mattie, that's all I can represent. And I've been hiding my life for twenty-five years. And I'm so tired of hiding my life."

A Bittersweet Gift

APRIL 2004
BERKELEY, CALIFORNIA

IN OUR LAST INTERVIEW with Stephan Jones—the last of ten interviews over the course of two years—he reflects:

"Your memory is a bittersweet gift. Because what comes back to you, when you're in that kind of grief, is all those things you took for granted about them. Those are the things that jump out at you, out on the street: the smells and the subtle mannerisms, and the carriage and style and dress and the quality of voice and laugh that you hear everywhere. They're everywhere. And those are the things you take for granted when people are alive.

"I remember sitting all by myself in a room staring at the wall, and I would hear my mother's voice like she was in the room. My memory of her was so acute that I would still hear her voice in my head like I would when she was alive. It was so sharp. I'd just hear a certain lilt to a voice or a smell—and I can't describe the smell—but I know I smelled my mother's breath everywhere.

"The bittersweet gift of grief is that all those things you took for granted, all those things you didn't even know you loved about them are brought back. I am so glad to have a chance to do things differently now. I forget on a daily basis what a blessing that is. And that is the work of life, to remember that."

≈ ≈ ≈

One of the most poignant photographs Stephan ever showed us was a picture of a large group of people dancing in the basement of the Temple in San Francisco, a large open room with brick walls and a linoleum floor. The mood is clearly playful. People are laughing, clapping their hands, kicking up their feet. There are mostly young people in the photo, in caps and printed shirts with elaborate patterns, bellbottom slacks, and wide belts with buckles. The group has arranged itself into lines of seven or eight. I imagine they're doing the Hustle, or a popular dance from that era. Others are gathered in the doorway of the room. In the photo's background, a large group of older folks are watching the young ones dance. A woman in a wheelchair with a knitted afghan covering her legs smiles broadly, perhaps remembering her own youth and her own dancing.

Stephan smiled at the photo when he showed it to us. "I have a lot of hope for creation, for humankind, I really do," he said.

I noticed the yellow note attached to the back of the photo, Stephan's way of documenting with a simple Post-it on which he could jot down notes of faces and names. He would revisit the photos again and again, filling in the blanks as his memory was jarred in the hope that he would eventually remember everyone. The Post-it label reads:

"Dancing downstairs @ the SF Temple. '75–'76. Curly haired boy in foreground w/eyes closed, clapping hands is Danny Beck. Boy directly behind him is Clarence Klingman (Cole). Woman behind him, smiling and singing, is Laura Johnston. Cut in half on left front is Ricky Johnson. Woman in background, framed in doorway with black shirt and white buttons, singing and kicking left leg forward is Deanna Wilkinson, lead singer for Temple band and choir. All those identified went to Jonestown."

Of all those named in the photo, only Laura Johnston (now Laura Johnston Kohl) survived.

And while Stephan eventually abandoned his mission to identify all the faces in the tens of thousands of photos in the archive—recognizing the sheer impossibility of the task he had taken on for himself—that very work continues each year, around the memorial event in Oakland. The California Historical Society opens its doors at special hours, and the survivors gather to look at photographs, share memories and recollections, piece together their own history, and continue to remember the people who died. Their collective memory is stronger than any one individual mind, and the pain is always lessened in the solace of the company of those who understand. Their sorrow inevitably gives way to joy on these occasions—and laughter. Happiness, too, is a part of their story, however difficult it is for some of them to claim it.

≈ ≈ ≈

Thirty years after Jonestown, during the earlier stage of my writing this book, Fielding "Mac" McGehee finally completed what he considered his most important work: all of the 918 people who died in Guyana on November 18, 1978, have been accounted for and named.

A few years later, Mac joined with Jim Jones Jr. and former Temple member John Cobb in organizing an effort to create a long-overdue Jonestown memorial with each name engraved onto four simple granite panels and installed at Evergreen Cemetery at the mass grave of unidentified and unclaimed bodies. Nine years after my initial encounter with Reverend Jynona Norwood at Evergreen Cemetery, Norwood was no further along in her efforts to complete her memorial, and so the committee sprang into being to fill that vacuum and to actually build one. The committee raised the money for the granite panels in three weeks and eventually received contributions from 120 people. All are publicly named.

This memorial was consecrated in a simple Service of Dedication on May 29, 2011. About twenty people—former Temple members, Jonestown survivors, defectors and apostates, relatives and friends—spoke during the ninety-minute service. The Guyanese ambassador to the United States attended and addressed the people who came for the dedication. The Reverend John Moore, whose wife Barbara died in his arms in 2004 after sixty years of marriage, gave the benediction.

Six months later, at the annual memorial service on November 18, 2011, surrounded by members of both families—her biological and Temple families—Nell Smart buried the remains of her two identified children with her two in the mass grave at Evergreen.

The Jonestown Web site continues to grow, with hundreds of remembrances of those who died, reflections of those who survived, and scores of primary source documents. The seventy tapes Mac McGehee had transcribed in 2001 have grown to nearly three hundred, a number that's enhanced by the assistance Mac receives from Temple survivors and other "vortexers" in the actual transcription process. Survivor and interview subject Laura Johnston Kohl has written a book about her experiences.

Rebecca Moore has two more Jonestown books. Denice Stephenson published a book of primary source documents. Other survivors, including some we did not have a chance to interview, have written or are in the stages of writing their own memoirs or autobiographies.

Many survivors have launched grown children into the world. Many, including Tim Carter, are grandparents now. Tim's grandson was named Malcolm James after the son he lost in Jonestown.

≈ ≈ ≈

Before the play's premiere, Eugene Smith predicted that it would be a "two-edged sword." As happens with this story, once he began to describe the "edges," more came to mind, and it became a six-edged sword before he was through: "I think some people are going to come to the play because they want to see what it's about, just out of curiosity. Other people are going to come to have something to criticize. Other people are going to come because it's closure. For other people, it's going to open up a whole new set of problems and things they hadn't even thought about and now they have to deal with. For others, it's going to be a true heartbreak because their particular story is *not* going to be told. Other people are going to see it as, 'Just leave it alone, just fucking leave it alone. It's done. Leave it alone.'"

After

MAY 2005
BERKELEY, CALIFORNIA

WHEN OUR PLAY *The People's Temple* finally opens in Berkeley, California, the survivors and their families are in the audience. They come from as far away as Indiana to see what we have done with their stories.

The play begins with a song. The actor portraying Stephan Jones walks onto the stage and pulls an archive box from a shelf. The box contains a choir robe. As Stephan holds up the robe, a woman appears as if conjured by both the robe and his willingness to remember, and she performs a cappella "He's Able," a gospel song featured on the Peoples Temple album of the same name:

> As pilgrims here, we sometimes journey.
> We often know not which way to turn.
> But there is one, who knows the road,
> Who'll help us carry, who'll help us carry, our heavy load. . . .

The rest of the ensemble joins her on stage, clapping out the beat as the tempo kicks up for the refrain:

> Don't you know God is Able?
> He's Able.
> He's Able.
> God is Able.
> To carry you through. . . .

Our play was developed collaboratively over several years, through a series of workshops with actors, designers, dramaturges, and our project

314

archivist, all exploring the poetry of movement, lighting, sets, sound, and costumes. This model puts the theatrical elements on an even playing field with the text in a laboratory setting: everything is put under a theatrical microscope, everything is examined and mined for its narrative and poetic potential. This process began while we were still interviewing and continued for another year after most of the interviews had been conducted.

We had collected hundreds of hours of interviews and organized binders full of media clippings and other documents, anything that mentioned the interviewees we had met or the people they lost in Jonestown. The volume of research we used to write the play was massive, amounting to thousands and thousands of pages. In the play we used about 10 percent of what we collected.

The entire collaborative team, including the actors, studied Peoples Temple history exhaustively, combing over photographs, documents, and interviews. After delving into this history even a little, the emotional stakes of the story became evident to everyone. We all felt a responsibility to get this story as "right" as we possibly could.

≈ ≈ ≈

After a performance of *The People's Temple* at Berkeley Repertory Theatre, a man walks to the front of the stage. He stands at the lip of the proscenium. The actors and I have just finished a "talk back" with the audience—answering questions about the play and our process—and everyone is filing out of the theater. The man gestures urgently for me, so I go to him. The seating sections are several feet below the stage, so I kneel down to bring my face to his level. We shake hands and he introduces himself as Anthony Katsaris, the brother of Maria Katsaris, who died in Jonestown. Anthony went to Jonestown with Congressman Ryan as a member of the Concerned Relatives and was seriously wounded on the airstrip in the attack on Ryan's entourage. There is NBC footage of Anthony and his sister on the last day in Jonestown, as he tries to convince her to come back home. She rejects his overtures with a lethal coldness. Investigator Jack Palladino had told us that Maria had ordered the murder of her brother Anthony that day in Jonestown.

The story of the Katsaris family was one that Jack encouraged us to find, but the family was not willing to talk during our interview process.

Standing before me now at the Berkeley Rep, Anthony is visibly shaken. His wife begins talking at the same time he does. It is hard to catch their words, but I distinctly hear Anthony's wife say, "Our daughters don't even know they had an aunt. He needs to talk about this."

Anthony was the first person I interviewed in our postproduction process. Then Mike Klingman, Stanley Clayton, Debby Layton, and Jim Cobb felt either compelled to be included or safe enough to talk after seeing the play, maybe in part due to the overwhelmingly positive reception it received. Mike Klingman and I sat at a Starbucks in Berkeley as he told me the emotional story about how Jim Jones had saved his daughter's life. A true and unmistakable miracle, he called it. Stanley Clayton, who had seen a poster advertising the play on the street, wandered into the lobby of the theater, just wanting to talk. Debby Layton had a change of heart and wanted her story to be included with the others.

The Berkeley audience seemed to receive the survivors with a new generosity, not as "other" but as a part of themselves. And this recognition within the Peoples Temple community seems to have marked a turning point in the healing process for many survivors. Eugene Smith's comment—"We will never be seen as survivors. We will only be seen as the ones who got away"—may in the end be softening. The theater had served a role in the life of this community to help them wrestle with— even reconcile—parts of their own history.

Just as important were the reactions from those we had interviewed whose stories had been told onstage. After seeing the play, reporter Phil Tracy sent us an e-mail message: "Thank you to all for an incredible effort to make, despite all odds, art out of what was, without the slightest doubt, the saddest moment of my life."

Juanita Bogue's second-oldest son commented, "I think I understood my mother for the first time in my life."

Janet Shular's husband, David, succumbed to cancer before the play opened in Berkeley, but she was there on opening night. Other survivors—the members of her extended Peoples Temple family—were there to comfort her.

The play opened to critical acclaim. The reviewer for the *San Francisco Chronicle* wrote:

The unique power of theater to explore compelling stories as a communal experience is profoundly and movingly at work in *The People's Temple*. . . . The voices fill the theater with hope, regret, faith, skepticism, joy, anger, suspicion, panic and immeasurable sorrow. . . . [*The People's*] *Temple* is gripping drama and a forcefully honest re-examination of our own history. . . . That it's taken so much longer to put together than the docudrama about the murder of Matthew Shepard—or the ones about the murders of Mayor George Moscone and Supervisor Harvey Milk that occurred soon after Jonestown (Emily Mann's *Execution of Justice* at the Rep in '85)—is a testament to the horrendous scope of the Jonestown tragedy. The delay in no way detracts from the play's immediacy.

≈ ≈ ≈

There are more stories of Peoples Temple in the world than were captured in our play or in this book—hundreds, thousands more stories. This event ripples out in unquantifiable ways. There is no single project or entity—not even the archive in San Francisco—that can hold all the stories of Jonestown and Peoples Temple.

Dick Tropp's directive to "collect all the tapes, all the writing, all the history" will only happen in time, through generations of study and writing by historians, scholars, artists, and—most importantly—the survivors themselves.

It was impossible for us to keep interviewing, though we could have. We could have spent our whole artistic lives investigating Peoples Temple and Jonestown and never fully finished the job.

The Reverend John Moore summed it up eloquently when he described the survivor stories: "Some people have gone on with their lives. As always happens with tragedies, they destroy some people and other people go on. The wounds are always there, but they grow, that tragedy in your life becomes integrated into your life." He then added, "Any utopian illusions I had were shattered. A utopian community killed our children. But how do you temper that so as not to give up on that idealism, not to give up on the dream? Surviving is about living in the present with that hope."

≈ ≈ ≈

When the play was in development, my collaborator Steve Wangh created a document he called "What Needs to Be Told?" The document contained a missive. Following the heading was a list of all the dramatic plot points in the history of Peoples Temple and Jonestown. There were hundreds upon hundreds, and somehow we thought we could cover them all. After every developmental reading or workshop, we would refer to this document and maybe check one or two things off the list, each time feeling more and more defeated. *This story is impossible to tell.*

Eventually, in order to finish the play, we had to change the question. The question could not be "What needs to be told?" However ethically bound we felt to history, the questions had to multiply and become "What do we as artists want to share? What do we have to contribute to the conversation and canon of Jonestown?"

Our responsibility as artists is not to tell the entire history of an event, but to tell the things that move and inspire us, the stories that are the most dramatically compelling. We have multiple responsibilities: to history, to our interviewees, and to our craft as storytellers. The entirety of the work, both the collecting of the research and the art making, is part of the artistic process. The work of art is the marriage of content and form.

My colleagues and I were then—and still are—committed to a model of theater making that allows space and time for the material to teach us what it wants to be, to discover through experimentation what theatrical form is best suited to the material. We place ourselves in a dialectical relationship with the text and all the elements of the stage. Yet, in the case of Peoples Temple, we eventually had to create some parameters. We had two hours and a willing audience who would show up to see a story whose ending they already knew: almost everyone was going to die. We knew—from our own experience—that coming to the theater to see a play about Jonestown was an act of bravery. We had to proceed carefully, mindfully. We had to take care of both the survivors and the audience. In the end our ethics of representation became simple: we had to let the voices of the survivors speak for themselves; we had to trust that the relevance of their story was there.

As a playwright, I was challenged by the idea of wrestling this expansive history into a two-hour stage event, and as a theater director, by the question of how to dramatize these events on stage. My creative life was consumed by these artistic questions for five years, and my head and heart were full of stories.

It is impossible to ever "finish" with this story. What I heard on my very first day on the project, testimony spoken at the first memorial I attended, turned out to be true: *this story never leaves you.*

≈ ≈ ≈

We titled our play *The People's Temple* to distinguish it from the Peoples Temple (always spelled without the apostrophe), signifying a broader theme rather than a history of Peoples Temple.

The set for the play was composed of a series of shelves containing hundreds of archive boxes inspired by the shelves at the California Historical Society in San Francisco. Over the course of the play, the actors transformed the archive boxes by attaching passport photos of the people who died in Jonestown (which were blown up to be visible from the audience): one photo per box, so that by the end of the play most of the boxes were adorned with the faces of the people. After each performance, many audience members were drawn toward the front of the house, making their way onto the stage to walk among the shelves, to reflect and view the photos. The set, beautifully designed by Sarah Lambert, had become an accidental, yet powerful, public art installation. This action of viewing the passport photos had even more potency when the audience included survivors. People wanted to see the faces close up. As artists, we were very moved when Becky Moore pointed out, "You let us see their faces, not the bodies lying facedown in the jungle. Their faces were upright."

One of the key components to performing theater based on history or interviews is the empathy that the actor cultivates for the characters they are portraying. The actors spent time with interviewees. They spent time in the California Historical Society archive studying photographs, listening to stories, understanding as best they could the complicated history of Peoples Temple. Margo Hall portrayed both Marthea and Shirley Hicks in the Berkeley production. Our costume designer Gabriel Berry replicated the sexy white jumpsuit from November 17, and Margo stole the show in it. Even though Shirley and Marthea died in Jonestown, Margo knew them more intimately by virtue of the time she had spent with Rod Hicks, their brother in Detroit, who left Margo with this dictate: "Perhaps you can find something here that can help another shipwrecked brother or sister before they do some crazy stuff."

Greg Pierotti was naturally drawn to the story of Dick Tropp—a prolific writer, even up to the end—and portrayed him in the play. In one of the play's most powerful moments, Greg, dressed in a simple blue cardigan sweater and wearing Tropp-style horn-rimmed glasses, reads the final words of the letter that Dick wrote on Jonestown's last day: "A tiny kitten sits next to me. A dog barks. The birds gather on the telephone wires. Darkness settles over Jonestown on its last day on earth." Greg then removes the sweater and glasses, places the two objects in an archive box, and restores the box to the shelves where it belonged—the history of the movement collected in these boxes—as one of the last theatrical gestures of the play.

≈ ≈ ≈

Our play ends as it begins, in song. The ensemble enters and approaches the actor playing Stephan Jones, who is sitting at an archive table, poring over photos. The company joins Stephan. He looks up from his work. His isolation dissolves. As the lights fade to black, they lift their voices in song:

Walk a mile in my shoes
Walk a mile in my shoes
And before you refuse, criticize and accuse,
Walk a mile in my shoes.

≈ ≈ ≈

Our collective memory is fading—perhaps intentionally, given how painful the story is. The stories of the people who survived (both who they were before this catastrophic event and how they have lived since) teach us that there is much more to the story of Peoples Temple than what its popular canon holds. My hope is that the stories of the survivors will shape the legacy and history of Peoples Temple and Jonestown for future generations. In my experience, the people with whom my collaborators and I spent time (sometimes many hours, sometimes days) were not mindless victims with Jim Jones as mastermind and perpetrator. They did in fact have agency. While some still blame Jones for the events that ruined their lives, the majority of the survivors we spoke with had spent the past twenty-five years recognizing, understanding, and articulating their complicity in the events that took place in Jonestown. They have faced and come to terms with their choices and decisions. The process of surviving seems to me one of reclaiming their agency, not of denying it.

In the end, all we can do is count our play—and now this book—as our attempt to complicate the stories about Peoples Temple and Jonestown.

The 918 Deaths of November 18, 1978

Stephen Michael Addison ▪ Ida Marie Albudy ▪ Lillian Boyd Alexander
Linda Sharon Amos ▪ Martin Laurence Amos ▪ Wayborn Christa Amos
Jerome Dwayne Anderson ▪ Marcus Anthony Anderson
Marice St. Martin Anderson ▪ Orelia Anderson ▪ Samuel Moses Anderson
Shantrell Akpon Anderson ▪ Tommy Lee Anderson ▪ Luberta "Birdie" Arnold
Linda Theresa Arterberry ▪ Ricardo David Arterberry
Traytease Lanette Arterberry ▪ Lydia Atkins ▪ Ruth Atkins
Viola Elaine Backmon ▪ Monique Bacon ▪ Geraldine Harriet Bailey
Mary Jane Bailey ▪ James Samuel Baisy Jr. ▪ Jon Deshi Baisy ▪ Kecia Baisy
Shirley Mae Wilson Baisy ▪ Siburi Jamal Baisy ▪ Trinidette Cornner Baisy
Wanda Wilson Baisy ▪ Eric Tyrone Baker ▪ Jair Alexander Baker
Shawn Valgen Baker ▪ Tarik Earl Baker ▪ Mary B. Baldwin
Rory LaVate Bargeman ▪ Terence Vair Bargeman ▪ Becky Ann Barrett
Ben Franklyn Barrett ▪ Cathy Ann Stahl Barrett ▪ Jack Darlington Barron
Christine Ella Mae Bates ▪ Geneva Mattie Beal ▪ Eleanor Marie Beam
Jack Lovell Beam ▪ Rheaviana Wilson Beam ▪ Daniel James Beck
Rebecca May Beikman ▪ Ronald La Mont Beikman ▪ Alfred Bell
Beatrice Claudine Bell ▪ Carlos Lee Bell Jr. ▪ Elsie Ingraham Bell
Ethel Mathilda Belle ▪ Lena Mae Mary Camp Benton ▪ Yolanda Patrice Berkley
Daniel Bernard Berry ▪ Ronnie Dewayne Berryman ▪ Julia Birkley
Mary Love Black ▪ Odell Blackwell ▪ Ernestine Hines Blair ▪ Norya Blair
Marilee Faith Bogue ▪ Selika Glordine Bordenave ▪ Claudia Jo Norris Bouquet
Pierre Brian Bouquet ▪ Corlis Denise Conley Boutte ▪ Mark Anthony Boutte
Donald Robert Bower ▪ Kenneth Bernard Bowie ▪ Anthony Bowman
Delores Bowman ▪ Edna May Bowman ▪ Regina Michelle Bowser

Georgianne Patricia Brady ▪ Michaeleen Patricia Brady
Michelle Margaret Brady ▪ Avis Jocelyn Garcia Breidenbach
Lois "Rocky" Fontaine Breidenbach ▪ Melanie Lee Breidenbach
Wesley Karl Breidenbach ▪ Dorothy Ann Brewer ▪ Kimberly Louise Brewster
Miller Bridgewater ▪ Juanita Jean Bright ▪ Lawrence George "Babo" Bright III
Ruby Jean Bright ▪ Amanda Denise Brown ▪ Jerross Keith Brown
Joyce Marie Polk Brown ▪ Luella Holmes Brown ▪ Robert O. Brown
Ruletta Brown ▪ Yolanda Delaine Brown ▪ Lucioes Bryant ▪ Princeola Bryant
Christopher Calvin Buckley ▪ Dorothy Helen Buckley
Frances Elizabeth Buckley ▪ Loreatha Buckley
Minnie Luna Mae Murral Buckley ▪ Odesta (Odessa) Buckley
Rosie Lee Burgines ▪ William Paul Sean "Billy" Bush ▪ Ruthie Mae Quinn Cain
Beyonka Rena Cameron ▪ Ronald Ray Campbell Jr. ▪ Mary Francis Canada
Thelma Doris Mattie Ross Cannon ▪ Vities Rochele "Vita" Cannon
Jeffrey James Carey ▪ Karen Yvette Carr ▪ D'Artangan Angelino Carroll
Dante Augustine Carroll III ▪ Randall Earl Carroll ▪ Rondell Jerome Carroll
Ruby Jewell Carroll ▪ Wrangell Dwayne Smith Carroll
Gloria Maria Rodriguez Carter ▪ Jocelyn Brown Carter ▪ Kaywana Mae Carter
Malcolm J. Carter ▪ Maurice Chaunte Carter ▪ Patricia Ann "Patty" Cartmell
Patricia Pauline "Trisha" Cartmell ▪ Tyrone James Cartmell
Walter Clayton Cartmell ▪ Sophia Lauren Casanova ▪ Mary Frances Castillo
William Richard Castillo ▪ Georgia Mae Catney ▪ Stephanie Katrina Chacon
David Lee Chaikin ▪ Eugene Bernard Chaikin ▪ Gail Stephanie Chaikin
Phyllis Alexander Chaikin ▪ Jossie Evelyn Chambliss ▪ Loretta Diane Chavis
Robert Louis Christian ▪ Robert Louis Christian II ▪ Tina Rayette Christian
Vernetta Carolyn Christian ▪ Mary Louise "Marylou" Meyer Clancey
Joicy Ellis Clark ▪ Leola Laverne Clarke ▪ Nancy Clay ▪ Ida Mae Pleasant Clipps
Brenda Carole Cobb ▪ Joel Raymond Cobb ▪ Sharon Rose Swaney Cobb
Arlander Cole ▪ Arvella Cole ▪ Mary Coleman ▪ Ruth Virginia Coleman
Susie Lee Collins ▪ Inez Stricklin Conedy ▪ Angela Maria Connesero
Bertha Pearl Cook ▪ Mary Ella Cook ▪ Barbara Jeanne Cordell
Candace Kay Cordell ▪ Chris Mark Cordell ▪ Cindy Lyn Cordell
Edith Excell Cordell ▪ James Joseph Cordell ▪ Julie Rene Cordell
Loretta Mae Coomer Cordell ▪ Mabel Joy Cordell ▪ Natasha LaNa Cordell
Richard William Cordell Jr. ▪ Rita Diane Cordell ▪ Teresa Laverne Cordell
Carrie Lee Corey ▪ Ricky Anthony Corey ▪ Mary Maide Cottingham
Lucy Crenshaw ▪ Millie Stearn Cunningham ▪ Betty Leon Daniel
Steve Nathaniel Daniel III ▪ Michael Daniels ▪ Najahjuanda Jherenelle Darnes

Newhuanda Rhenelle Darnes • Ollie B. (Elondwaynion Jhontera) Darnes II
Searcy Llewellyn (Braunshaunski) Darnes • Velma Lee (Najuandrienne) Darnes
Hazel Frances Dashiell • Barbara Marie Davis • Brian Andrew Davis
Celeste Marie Vento Davis • Cynthia Marie Davis • Deron Kentae Davis
Frances Bernadette Davis • Gerina Maxine Davis • Isabel Davis
Isabell Minnie Davis • Johannah Danielle Davis • Lexie Smith Davis
Margarita Virginia Romano Davis • Robert Edwin Davis • Beatrice Dawkins
Derek Dawson • Burger Lee Dean • Edith Fredonia Delaney
Tammi Sherrel Delihaussaye • Eddie Lee Dennis • Ellihue Dennis
Gabriel Dennis • Orde Dennis • Ronnie Dennis • Lovie Hattie Ann De Pina
Acquinetta Evon "Anita" Robertson Devers • Darrell Audwin Devers
Roseana Eartia Dickerson • Bessie Lee Dickson • Violatt Esther Dillard
Katherine Martha Domineck • Farene Douglas • Joyce Lalar Douglas
Nena Belle Downs • Exia Marie Lawrence Duckett
Jeanette Blugina Harrell Duckett (Dee Dee Lawrence)
Ronald Charles Duckett (Nicky Lawrence) • Corrie Duncan
Ebony Patrice Duncan • Sonje Regina Duncan • Verdella Duncan
Ellen Louise "Penny" Kerns Dupont • Florine Dyson • Irene Eddins
Irene Edwards • Issac Edwards Jr. • James Edwards
Shirley Ann Newell Edwards • Zipporah Edwards • Erin Jahna Eichler
Evelyn Marie Eichler • Laetitia Marie Eichler (Tish LeRoy)
Ever Rejoicing (Amanda Ella Poindexter) • Tinetra LaDese Fain
Amanda Fair • Sylvester Clarence Fair • Barbara Louise Farrell
Marshall Farris • Michael Donnell Felton • Donald James Fields
Lori Beth Fields • Mark Evan Fields • Shirlee Ann Fields
Felawnta Tyece Finley • Lucretia Yvette Finley • Casey Nakyia Finney
Betty Jean Bender Fitch • Dawnyelle Fitch • Donald Kirk Fitch
Maureen Cynthia Talley Fitch • Michelle Renee Wagner Fitch
Raymond Xavier Fitch • Thomas Ray Fitch • Rebecca Ann Flowers
Toi Fonzelle • Anthony Lamar Ford • Edward Lee Ford • Fannie Ford
Mary Lee Ford • Viola Belle Duncan Forks • Hue Ishi Fortson Jr.
Rhonda Denise Fortson • Beulah Foster • Betty Jewel Fountain
Frankie Jay Fountain • Jewel Lynn "Tiny" Fountain
Christopher Darnnell Franklin • Laketta Lashun Franklin
Robert Eddie Lee Franklin Jr. • Constance Janet Frohm • Shiron Fulton
Kimberly Anne Fye • Bof William Gallie • Cleveland Desmond Garcia
Mary Helen Garcia • Susan Garcia • Tanya Rena Cox Garcia
Tiffany La Trice Garcia • John Lawrence Gardener • Danielle Gardfrey

Dominique Gardfrey • Kenneth Darren "Dude" Gardfrey
Shonda Marie Gaylor • Herman W. Gee • David George • Gabrielle George
Philip George • Eugenia Gernandt • Mattie Gibson • Jason Gieg
Renee Elaine Gieg • Robert Wendell Gieg • Stanley Brian Gieg • Betty Jean Gill
Irma Lee Gill • James Gill • Viola May Godshalk • Henry Lee Logan Gomez
Wanda Denise Gomez • Claude Goodspeed • Lue Dimple Goodspeed
David Lee Goodwin • Mark Hartley Gosney • Willie James Grady
Willie Lee Graham • Juanita Green • Anitra Rochelle Greene
Amondo Griffith • Camella Griffith • Emmett Alexander Griffith Jr.
Mae Kathryn Griffith • Marrian Louise Griffith • Mary Magdaline Griffith
Frankie Lee Grigsby • Ronald Windus Grimm • Susan L. Grimm
Tina Lynn Grimm • Pauline Groot • Clark Andrew Smith Grubbs
Gerald Richard Grubbs (Ken Norton) • Kelly Franklin Smith Grubbs
Kevan Deane Smith Grubbs • Lemuel Thomas Grubbs II • Sylvia Elaine Grubbs
Patricia Lee Grunnet • Mercedese Mavis Clare Guidry • Jann Elizabeth Gurvich
Brian Guy • Keith LeJon Guy • Kimberley Denee Guy • Ottie Mese Guy
Sharitta Renae Guy • Thurman Guy III • Rochelle Dawana Halkman
Carl Gloster Hall • Heloise Janice Hall • Eddie James Hallmon
Francine Renita Mason Hallmon • Tiquan Ramon Hallmon
Hassan Ali Hannley • Karen Marie Harms • Artee Harper • Ollie B. Harrington
Annie Mae Harris • Don Harris • Dorothy (Shajhuanna) Lesheene Harris
Josephine Harris • Liane Harris • Magnolia Costella Harris • Nevada Harris
Willie Maude (Constance Nicole) Harris • Eyvonne Paris Hayden
Florence Edith Heath • Michael DeAngelo Heath • Heavenly Love (Helen Ford)
Joseph Leo Helle III (Joe Beam) • Beatrice Mattie Henderson
Charles Douglas "Chuckie" Henderson • Charles Garry Henderson
Kenya Lakiah Henderson • Patricia Ann Bowman Henderson
Nena Davidson Herring • Anthony Allan Hicks • Marthea Ann Hicks
Romaldo Benjamin Hicks • Shirley Pat Hicks • Emma Mae Hill Osialee Hilton
Bernell Maurice Tardy Hines • Mable Ellen Walker Hines • Rosa Mae Hines
Tanai Claudine-LeDese Holliday • Peter Holmes Jr. (John Harris)
Hazel Lark Horne • Judy Lynn Houston • Patricia Dian Houston
Phyllis Dian Tuttle Houston • Doris Helen Howard • Barbara Faye Hoyer
Judith Kay Stahl Ijames • Maya Lisa Ijames • Alice Lorraine Inghram
Ava Jillon Inghram • Beatrice Alberta Jackson • Beatrice Mazell Burl Jackson
Darrell Dwayne Martin Jackson • David Betts "Pop" Jackson
Donald Francis Jackson • Eileen Renee Jackson • Gladys Margarette Jackson
Jonathan Jackson • Kathryn Denise Graumann Jackson • Leticia Lyn Jackson

Lourece Jackson • Luvenia "Mom" Jackson • Paulette Karen Kelley Jackson
Ralph Edwin Jackson • Richard Stuart Jackson • Rosa Lee Jackson
Thelma Jackson • Lavana James • Margaret James • Ronald De Val James
Toni Denise James • Daren Richard Janaro • Mauri Kay Janaro
Eartis Jeffery • Margrette Jeffery • Berda "Birdie" Truss Johnson
Bessie Marie Jance Johnson • Bette Jean Guy Byrd Johnson
Carma Lisa Johnson • Clara LaNue Johnson • Denise Johnson
Derek Damone Johnson • DeShon Johnson • Earl Luches Joseph Johnson
Garnett Blake Johnson • Garry Dartez "Poncho" Johnson
Gerald Duane Johnson • Gleniel Johnson • Gwendolyn Joyce Johnson
Helen Johnson • Irra Jean Johnson • James Douglas Johnson
Janice Arlene Johnson • Jessie Ann Johnson • Joe Johnson Jr.
Koya Tynisa Johnson • Mahaley Johnson • Maisha Danika Johnson
Mary Allie Johnson • Mary E. Johnson • Naomi Esther Johnson
Patsy Ruth Johnson • Richard Lee "Ricky" Johnson • Robert Johnson
Robert Keith Johnson • Ruby Lee Johnson • Saleata Lateais Johnson
Samuel Lee Johnson • Thomas William Johnson
Verna Lisa (Shawntiki) Johnson • Willa JoAnn Johnson
Adline "Addie" B. Jones • Agnes Pauline Jones • Annette Teresa Jones
Ava Phenice Cobb Brown Jones • Brenda Yvonne Brown Jones
Chaeoke Warren Jones • Earnest Jones • Eliza Jones • Forrest Ray Jones
James Arthur "Jimbo" Bishop Jones • James Warren Jones • Jessie Weana Jones
John Moss Brown Jones • Kwame Rhu Amarka Jones • Larry Darnell Jones
Lerna Veshaun Jones • Lew Eric Jones • Marceline Mae Baldwin Jones
Marchelle Jacole Jones • Mary Theresa "Terry" Carter Jones
Michael Ray Jones • Monyelle Maylene Jones • Nancy Mae Jones
Sandra Yvette Cobb Jones • Stephanie Lynn Bishop Jones
Timothy "Night" Borl Jones • Valerie Yvette Jones • Vellersteane Jones
William Dillon Dean Jones • Yvette Louise Muldrow Jones • Dessie Jones Jordan
Fannie Alberta Jordan • Lula Elizabeth Jordan • Emma Jane Jurado
Maria S. Katsaris • Rosa Lorenda Mae Keaton • Tommie Sheppard Keaton Sr.
Elaine Roslyn "Pat" Keeler • Darell Eugene Keller
Anita Christine Ijames Kelley • Viola B. Kelley • Barbara Alberta Kemp
Mellonie Denise Kemp • Rochelle Annette Kemp • Elfreida Kendall
Emma Addie Kennedy • Carol Ann Kerns
Corrine Mae "Rennie" Jackson Kice • Robert Edward Kice
Thomas David Kice Sr. • Thomas David Kice II • Charlotte King • Leola King
Teresa Lynn King • Wanda Bonita King • Carolyn Ann Thomas Kirkendall

Sharon Jean Kislingbury ▪ April Heather Klingman
Clarence Elmer Cole Klingman ▪ Martha Ellen Cole Klingman
Matthew Todd Cole Klingman ▪ William Arnold Cole Klingman
Demosthenis "Dan" Kutulas ▪ Edith Kutulas ▪ Donna Louise Briggs Lacy
Georgia Lee Lacy ▪ Tony Oscar Linton Lacy ▪ Pearl Land ▪ Lossie Mae Lang
Carrie Ola Langston ▪ Marianita Langston ▪ Zuretti Jenicer Langston
Jameel Regina Lawrence ▪ Nawab Lawrence ▪ Carolyn Louise Moore Layton
Karen Lea Tow Layton ▪ Daisy Lee ▪ Karen Marie Lendo
Adrienne Rochan Lewis ▪ Alecha Julianne Lewis ▪ Barry Eugene Lewis
Casandra Florene Lewis ▪ Dana Michelle Lewis ▪ Doris Jane Lewis
Freddie Lee Lewis Jr. ▪ Karen Louise Scott Lewis ▪ Lisa Michelle Lewis
Lue Ester Lewis ▪ Beverly Marie Geraldine Livingston
Jerry Dwight Livingston ▪ Gordon Evrette Lockett ▪ Carolyn Sue Looman
Vincent Lopez Jr. ▪ Love Life Lowe (Georgia Belle Owens)
Love Madgeleane Joy (Olar Watts) ▪ Ruth Whiteside Lowery
Lovie Jean Morton Lucas ▪ Christine Renee Lucientes ▪ Diane Lundquist
Dov Mario Lundquist ▪ Minnie Magaline Lyles
Dorothy "Dee Dee" Williams Macon ▪ Rori Lynette Bell Madden
Lillian Malloy ▪ Willie Lovell Malone ▪ Alfred Shellie March II
Alfreda Suzette March ▪ Anita Elaine March ▪ Earnestine Thomas March
Charles Marshall ▪ Danny Leon Marshall ▪ Diana LaVerne Marshall
Shaunte Marshall ▪ Vicky Lynn Dover Marshall ▪ Irene Mason
Mary Mayshack ▪ Cheryle Darnell McCall ▪ Donald Wayne McCall
Estelle Dunn McCall ▪ Eileen Kelly McCann ▪ Maria Louise McCann
Michael Angelo McCann ▪ Allie McClain ▪ Carol Ann Cordell McCoy
Leanndra Renae McCoy ▪ Lowell Francis McCoy II ▪ Marcenda Dyann McCoy
Patty Ann McCoy ▪ James Nelson McElvane ▪ Alluvine McGowan
Annie Jane McGowan ▪ Joyce Faye McIntyre ▪ Clara L. McKenzie
Levatus V. McKinnis ▪ Diana McKnight ▪ Earl McKnight
Ray Anthony McKnight ▪ Raymond Anthony McKnight
Rose Marie VeZain McKnight ▪ Deirdre Renee McMurry
Sebastian R. C. McMurry ▪ Takiyah Chane McMurry
Theodore Devanulis McMurry ▪ Jessie Belle McNeal ▪ Henry Mercer
Mildred Ada Carroll Mercer ▪ Virginia Middleton ▪ Christine Miller
Lucy Jane Miller ▪ Cassandra Yvette Minor ▪ Cuyana Lynette Minor
Annie Lee Mitchell ▪ Beverly Ann Mitchell ▪ Beverly Darlene Mitchell
Callie Mae Mitchell ▪ Lawanda Jean Mitchell ▪ Lee Charles "L.C." Mitchell
Shirley Ann Mitchell ▪ Tony Lovell Mitchell ▪ Ann Elizabeth Moore

Betty Karen Moore • Clarence Edward Moore Jr. • Edward Moore
Leola Kennedy Morehead • Marcus Emile Morgan • Oliver Morgan Jr.
Pearley Morris • Erris Andrew Morrison • Lugenia Morrison
Yvonne Morrison • Mary Nathaniel Morton • Eura Lee Moses
Danny McCarter Moten • Glen Moton • Michael Javornia Moton
Pamela Gail Bradshaw Moton • Russell DeAndrea Moton • Viola Mae Moton
Esther Lillian Mueller • Mary E. Murphy • Detra Renee Murray
Jane Ellen Mutschmann • Gertrude Nailor • Cardell Neal
Enola Marthenya "Kay" Nelson • Allen Newell • Christopher Newell
Hazle Maria Newell • Jennifer Newell • Karl Newell
Darlene Rudeltha Newman • Lonnie Alexander Newman
Luigi Lemoyne Newman • Benjamin Keith Newsome • Ida May Nichols
Fairy Lee Norwood • Susan Jane Jerram Noxon
Winnieann Zelline O'Bryant • Bruce Howard Oliver
Shanda Michelle James Oliver • William Sheldon Oliver • Jane Elizabeth Owens
Michkell "Mickey" Carroll Owens • Rhonda Rochelle Page
Beatrice Lucy Parker • Bethany Shawnee Parker • Gloria Victoria Parker
J. Warren Parks • Patricia Louise Chaffin Parks • Lore Bee Parris
Thomas Joseph Partak • Antonio Jamal Patterson
Carrol Anthony "Pat" Patterson • Robert Paul Jr. • Lucille Estelle Payney
Irvin Ray Perkins Jr. • Lenora Martin Perkins • Maud Ester Perkins
Richardell Evelyn Perkins • Leon Perry • Rosa Lee Peterson
George Edward Phillips III • Glenda Bell Polite • Donna Louise Ponts
Lois Agnes Ponts • Oreen Armstrong Poplin • Marlon Deitrick Porter
Bessie Mae Proby • Jim Jon "Kimo" Prokes • Eva Hazel Pugh
James Robert Pugh • Denise Elaine Hunter Purifoy
Kathy Jean Richardson Purifoy • Cynthia Pursley • Estella Mae Railback
Darlene Elizabeth Ramey • Robert Louis Rankin • Kenneth Bernard Reed
Willie Bell Reed • Bertha Jones Reese • L. Bee Reeves • Asha Tabia Rhea
Jerome Othello Rhea Jr. • Patricia Ann Holley Rhea • Isaac Jerome Rhodes
Marquess Dwight Rhodes Jr. • Odenia Adams Roberson
Gladys Ammie Roberts • Benjamin O'Neal Robinson • Greg Robinson
Leeosie Robinson • Orlando Demetric Robinson • Shirley Ann Robinson
Anthony Eugene Rochelle • Jackie Rochelle • Kim Dwight Rochelle
Tommie Charlene Rochelle • Mary Flavia Rodgers • Mary Johnson Rodgers
Ophelia Rodgers • Edith Frances Roller • Dorothy Jean Rollins
Marguerite Yvette Romano (Bippy Davis) • Renee Sylvia Davis Romano
Gloria Yvonne Primes Rosa • Kamari Rosa • Santiago Alberto Rosa

Therman Raylee Rosa • Kay Rosas • Elsie Zilpha Ross • Annie Joyce Rozynko
Christian Leo Rozynko • Michael Thomas Rozynko • Lula M. Ruben
Elizabeth Ruggiero • Roseann Ruggiero • Julie (Judy) Ann Runnels
Leo Joseph Ryan • Linda Colisa Sadler • David Anthony "Ant" Sanders
Dorothy Jean Sanders • Douglas Sanders • Flora Bell Sanders
Alida Rosa Santiago • Laurence Eugene Schacht • Angelique Marie Scheid
Donald Eugene Scheid Jr. • Deborah Faye Jensen Schroeder
Tad Schroeder • Pauline Scott • Marvin Wesley Sellers • Rose O. Sharon
Mary Louise Shavers • Rose Janette Shelton • Aisha Kizuwanda Simon
Alvin Harold Simon Sr. • Alvin Harold Simon Jr. • Anthony Joseph Simon
Barbara Ann Simon • Bonnie Jean Simon • Crystal Michelle Simon
Jerome Mark Simon • Jose Simon • Marcia Ann Simon • Melanie Wanda Simon
Pauline Louise Simon • Summer Renae Simon • Zateese Lena Simon
Dorothy Georgina Clark Daniels Simpson • Jewell James Simpson
Nancy Virginia Sines • Ronald Bruce Sines • Donald Edward (Ujara) Sly
Mark Andrew Sly • Alfred Laufton Smart Jr. • Scott Cameron Smart
Teri Lynn Smart • Barbara Ann Grissette Smith • Bertha Charles Smith
Christa Lynn Smith • David Elbert Vester Smith
Edrena Demetria "Dee Dee" Smith • Gladys Smith • James Alfred Smith
Jeffrey Dale Smith • Jerry Gilbert Smith (MN Gilbert) • Karl Wayne Smith
Kelin Kirtas Smith • Kivin Earl "Freeze Dry" Smith • Martin Luther Smith
Michael Vail Smith • Ollie Marie Wideman Smith • Shirley Faye Smith
Stephanie Marie Smith • Vernon Smith • Winnie Fred Smith
Youlanda Grissette Smith • Clevyee Louise Sneed • Eloise Sneed
Novella Novice Sneed • Willie Delois Sneed • Helen Snell
Dorothy Pearl (Shawanna) Soloman • Dorrus Henry Soloman
Scyria Lesheena "Tiny" Soloman • Delicia Jeanette Souder
Martha Mae Souder • Wanda Kay Souder • Alfred Richmond Stahl Sr.
Bonnie Lynn Stahl • Carol Ann Stahl • Lula Mae Stalling
Donna Elizabeth Stanfield • YoVonne Renee Stanley • Abraham Lincoln Staten
Ameal Staten • Frances Lee Stevenson • Aurora May Stewart
Terry Frederick Stewart Jr. • John Victor Stoen • Sharon Lee "Tobi" Stone
Tobiana Johanna Dilorenzo Stone • Tracy Lamont Stone • Adeleine Mae Strider
Nathaniel Brown Swaney • Stephanie Kay Swaney • Cleave Lonzo Swinney
Daren Eugene Werner Swinney • Timothy Maurice Swinney
Wanda Shirley Werner Swinney • Christine Shannon Bowers Talley
Ronald Wayne Talley • Vera Marie Talley • Armella Tardy • Elliot Wade Tardy
Lillian Marie Taylor • Lucille Beatrice Taylor

Virginia Vera "Mom" Dean Taylor • Alma Coley Coachman Thomas
Bernice Thomas • Ernest Thomas • Evelyn Thomas • Gabriel Thomas
Lavonne Shannel Thomas • Scott Thomas Jr. • Willieater Thomas
Etta Thompson • Vennie Thompson • Camille Tiffany Tom
Albert Ardell Touchette • Carol Joyce Swinney Touchette
Michelle Elaine Touchette • Essie Mae Towns • Harriet Sarah Tropp
Richard David Tropp • Cornelius Lee Truss Jr. • Dana Danielle Truss
Alfred Walter Tschetter • Betty Jean Tschetter (Kim Yoon Ai)
Mary Alice Stahl Tschetter • Alleane Tucker • Janet Marie Tupper
Larry Howard Tupper • Mary Elizabeth Tupper • Rita Jeanette Tupper
Ruth Ann Tupper • Bruce Edward Turner • James Elmor Turner Jr.
Ju'Quice Shawntreaa Turner • Martha Elizabeth Turner • Roosevelt W. Turner
Syola Williams Turner • Gary Lee Tyler • Lillie Mae Victor
James Edward Ford Wade Jr. • Roberta Lee Wade
Terence O'Keith "Keith" Wade • Inez Jeanette Wagner • Mark Stacey Wagner
Barbara Jean Walker • Derek Deon Walker • Gloria Dawn Walker
Jerrica Raquel Walker • Mary Nellie Walker • Tony Gerard Walker
Brenda Anne Warren • Gloria Faye Warren • Janice Marie Warren
Annie Bell Washington • Grover Washington • Huldah Eddie Washington
Earlene Kidd Watkins • Gregory Lewis Watkins • William Allan Watkins
Neal Shaun Welcome • Bessie Mae Wesley • Darius Daniel Wheeler
Jeff L. Wheeler • Marlene Diane Talley Wheeler • Lisa Ann Whitmire
Cheryl Gail Gray Wilhite • Janilah Cherie "Nini" Wilhite
Kennard Joseph Wilhite • Kennard Joseph (LaShea) Wilhite Jr.
Deanna Kay "Diane" Wilkinson • Charles Wesley Williams
Lisa Renee Williams • Louise Teska Lee Griffin Williams • Theo Williams Jr.
Mary Pearl Willis • Janice Louise Wilsey • Ezekiel Wilson
Jerry Lee Wilson Jr. • Jewell Lee Pitts Wilson • Joseph Lafayette Wilson
Erma Miriam Fisher Winfrey • Alizzia Yevette Winston
Curtis Laurine Winters • Dorothy Lee Brady Worley
Mary Beth Jansma Wotherspoon • Mary Margaret Wotherspoon
Peter Andrew Wotherspoon • Arlisa Lavette "Lisa" Wright
Keith Arnold Wright • Leomy Wright • Stanley Glenn Wright
Elois Christine Cobb Young • Ramona "Mona" Lamothe Young

Acknowledgments

....

RESPECT AND DEEP GRATITUDE must first be given to the survivors and to all the interviewees who so generously shared their stories, as well as their personal photographs, letters, documents, and memories with us. There are many survivors who encouraged us, who helped us connect to others in their community, some who agreed to be interviewed and some who did not, some who are represented here and others who are not—but each had a role to play in our process. Thanks must also be extended to the University of Minnesota Press, especially Pieter Martin, who had incredible patience with a playwright turned nonfiction writer, Louisa Castner, and to all the editors, readers, and the advisory board of the press, particularly John R. Hall.

In addition to the survivors, crucial contributors to this volume include my colleagues who conducted the interviews with me as we painstakingly created the stage play, *The People's Temple*: my main collaborator, Greg Pierotti; Margo Hall; and Stephen Wangh. My collaborators were generous enough to allow me to write about our collective artistic experience and process. I thank them each for the privilege of their collaboration and their trust.

I also thank: David Dower for his vision as commissioner of the play, for his effort in raising the money for the play's development and production, as well as funding the organization of the Peoples Temple collection at the California Historical Society; Denice Stephenson, who served as our project archivist, for her contribution to our play (without her efforts, artists, historians, survivors, and now the public would not have access to the vast Peoples Temple collection); Tony Taccone, artistic director, and Susan Medak, managing director, at Berkeley Repertory Theatre, and the entire theater staff, who courageously brought the play to the Bay Area community; and Mary Morganti at the California Historical Society, who generously supported our research every step of the way.

Additional thanks to Rebecca Moore and Fielding "Mac" McGehee and the Jonestown Institute for support and permission to publish the list of the 918 dead; to Marian Towne for permission to quote an excerpt of Hyacinth Thrash's memoir, *The Onliest One Alive*; to Jo Holcomb for her careful reading and editing of this manuscript in its earlier stages; to Ellen Reeves for her editing eye, questions, and advice; to Mac McGehee and Sarah Lambert for their extensive hands-on editing and support of this manuscript throughout its development process (I could not have done this without your eyes, your support, your rewrites, and your creative collaboration and contributions); to Amitabh Jordan, for ongoing professional support and emotional encouragement; to Penney Leyshon, for facilitating healing throughout this process; to my parents and family, who have always supported all of my artistic endeavors; to Kelli Simpkins and the entire acting ensemble and design team for their contributions to *The People's Temple*; to my sister, poet and novelist Melissa Fondakowski, whose brilliant editing hand guided me through the first stages of this manuscript and whose encouragement convinced me to write it; to Tim Carter and Stephan Jones, who believed that I could write this volume and that it might mean something to those who survived. And finally, to Reeva Wortel, whose love, support, and collaboration always guide me toward deeper meaning in my work, and who reminds me every single day how precious this human life really is. Thank you.

Index

African Americans. *See* black community; black Peoples Temple members; black politics
agricultural project, Jonestown, 195–201, 203, 206, 216, 240
airlifting: of bodies from Jonestown, 291; of survivors of the Port Kaituma shooting, 255
Allende, Salvador: overthrow of, 166
Alternative Considerations of Jonestown (Web site), 23
American Indian movement, 166
Amos, Sharon, 161, 163; directive to kill followed by, 268–69, 271–72
amphetamines: Jones's use of, 113
archives. *See* California Historical Society, Peoples Temple archives
autopsy reports, 291–93

Bachers, Marianne, 80
Bagby, Monica, xiii, 17, 74; attempt to leave with Ryan, 224, 228, 229; shooting of, 233
Baker, Shawn, 222
Baldwin, Marceline. *See* Jones, Marceline
Banks, Dennis, 166

Barnes, Bill, 112, 113
Bates, Christine Ella Mae, 73
Beam, Jack, xiii, 223, 238; on community in California, 14; on early days of church in Indiana, 14–15
Beck, Danny, 311
Beck, Don, 70
Beikman, Chuck, 271–73; trial of, 272–73
Berkeley Repertory Theatre, xviii, xix, 315–16, 319
Berrigan, Daniel and Philip, 52
Berry, Gabriel, 319
Bible: Jones's hatred of the, 20, 67, 261
black community: and aftermath of Jonestown, 235–36, 279, 282, 301-2; outreach to, 72–73, 181; stigma within, related to Jonestown, 29–30, 188
Black Muslims, 156–57
Black Panthers, 124, 149, 167, 181
black Peoples Temple members: and aftermath of Jonestown, 279, 282; deaths in Jonestown, 168; elderly, 5, 9–10, 132–33, 173, 200, 216–17, 237–38, 261–62; position in the church, 69, 181, 189; representation

of, 29–30, 188, 309; survivors' reticence to being interviewed, 29–30,
58, 180, 188, 235–36; testimony
from, 172–75

black politics, 66, 279

Bogue, Chad, 81–82, 84, 95–99; learning
about Jonestown, 81–82, 97; murder
trial, 81, 97, 98

Bogue, Edith, 230

Bogue, Jim, 95, 230

Bogue, Juanita, 80, 81, 86–99, 100, 154,
316; Chavis on, 84–85, 86; desire to
leave Jonestown, 89–90, 230; escape
from Jonestown, 92–95; interview
with, 88–99; life after Jonestown,
95–99; memories of growing up in
Temple, 88; memories of Jonestown, 89–96, 99; sons of, 81–82,
84, 87, 95–96, 97–99; on tragedy at
airstrip, 233

Bogue, Marilee, 93, 230

Bogue, Thomas (Tommy), 89, 104

Bogue, Tina, 230

Bouquet, Brian, 221

Bradley, Tom, 68

brainwashing, 4, 5, 19, 25, 54, 93, 94–95,
96, 110, 125, 167, 286, 302, 303

Briggs, Donna, 101, 104

Briggs, Michael, 81, 83, 101–4

Brooke, Edward (senator), 71

Brown, Bob, xii; killing of, 232; shooting
NBC raw news footage of Ryan's
investigative trip to Jonestown, 205,
221, 222, 225

Brown, Jerry (governor), 68

Brown, Johnny, 202, 213

Brown, Willie, 68, 309

Buford, Terri, 163

Burke, John, 213

bus crusades, 63–64, 71–73; Gulfport,
Mississippi, incident, 72–73

Cain, Tracy, 81

California foster care system: Jones's use
of, 109, 114

California Historical Society, Peoples
Temple archives, xix, xx, 71, 123,
138–40, 171, 301; articles found in,
140; bus flyers, 71–72; developing
The People's Temple from interviews
and, 139, 140; Moores' donations
to, 24, 53–54, 290–91; passport
photos, 193–96; photo collections,
55–56; statements of revolutionary
suicide, 123–24; survivors visiting,
235–36, 311–12; testimonies collected
by Tropp, 171–77, 237–38; visiting
basement archive, 139–40

cancer healings, 54, 102, 260–61

Carroll, Jon, 112

Carter, Gloria, 223, 249, 274–75

Carter, Jocelyn, 275

Carter, Kaywana, 227, 275

Carter, Malcolm, 223, 226, 249, 275

Carter, Michael, 226, 267; family lost by,
275; mission to Russian embassy in
Georgetown, 247, 250, 260

Carter, Rosalynn, 165, 309

Carter, Tim, 143–50, 159, 245–50,
296, 313; on agricultural project
in Jonestown, 200–201, 206, 216;
background of, 143–44; on Jonestown tragedy as murder versus
suicide, 275; Tim Clancey and,
162–63; family lost in Jonestown,
249, 275; family of, 245; funeral of
wife, 150; interview with, 144–50,
247–50; joining the Temple, 147–49;
on last day in Jonestown, 247–50;
on media's misrepresentation of
Peoples Temple, 307; memoir of
days held in Guyana to testify,
274–75; mission to Russian embassy

in Georgetown, 247, 250, 260; political beliefs of, 149; political transformation during Vietnam War, 144–45; reason for talking about experiences, 246–47; showing video of Ryan's investigative trip to Jonestown, 204–7, 213–18, 221–32, 234; spiritual epiphany and quest, 145–47, 162; on surviving, 307–8; survivor's guilt, 150

Cartmell, Patty, 33, 36

Castillo, William Richard, 291

Catholic Worker movement, 52

Central Intelligence Agency (CIA): Hughes-Ryan Amendment requiring congressional oversight of, 40, 45; paranoia about, 241–42; suspicion of, 122, 124

Chaikin, Gene, 218, 219

Chaikin, Phyllis, 218

Chavis, Melody Ermachild, 80–87, 127, 303; on Juanita Bogue, 84–85, 86; on Briggs, 101; collection of clothing buttons, 100; as death penalty investigator, 80–81; interviews with survivors in 1979 and 1985, 82–83; interview with, 81–85; theory of roots of violence, 81–82

Chicago riots at Democratic Convention (1968), 146

children of Jonestown, xix, 202, 262; births in Jonestown, 226; at concert/assembly for Ryan, 222; foster children, 101–4, 105, 109, 114; killing of, 137, 249, 254, 276; White Nights and, 242

Chile: refugees from, 166

choir, Peoples Temple, 19, 39, 66, 311; album, 19, 70, 314; children's, 19, 70

CIA. See Central Intelligence Agency

clairvoyance, 69, 148, 163

Clancey, Jean, 159–70, 214, 296–99; on aftermath of Jonestown, 280, 281–82; on choosing life on day of mass murder/suicide in Jonestown, 252–55; on Dianne Feinstein, 281; dreams of, 167–68, 299; as driver of Jones's bus, 164; as greeter, 163–64; interview with, 160–70; introduction to Jones and Peoples Temple, 160–62; on personal responsibility, 298; on letters about revolutionary violence, 297; marriage of, 253; on personal responsibility, 298

Clancey, Tim, 159–70, 296; on aftermath of Jonestown, 280; choosing life on day of mass murder/suicide in Jonestown, 252–55; Eugene Smith on, 238; interview with, 160–70; on introduction to Jones and Peoples Temple, 162–63; on joining San Francisco church, 164–65; marriage of, 253; on political power of Temple, 165, 166–67; on socialism, 161; on violent revolution, 296–97

Clarke, Richard, 92

Clayton, Stanley, 260, 316

Cobb, Jim, 316

Cobb, John, 312

collectivism, 108–9

communes in San Francisco in 1970s, 107–9; day care program, 108; food-buying program, 108

Communists in 1930s, 172–73

Concerned Relatives, xii, 18, 43, 205, 273, 315

conspiracy, climate of, 167

Corcoran State Prison, 101–2

Cordell, Edith, 78, 230

Cordell, Harold, 230

Cordell, Jimmy Joe, 230

Cronkite, Walter, 148

cross-country bus crusades, 63–64, 71–73
Cuffy Nursery, 226–27
cult: Peoples Temple as or as not, 5, 25, 188, 307
Curtin, Danny, 267, 305–6
cyanide: death by, 125, 191, 276; Schacht on pros and cons of, 291; smell of, 250; vat of Flavor Aid poisoned with, 250, 276, 307

Davis, Angela, 66, 167, 212
Davis, Grover, 260
Day, Dorothy, 52
day care: in Jonestown, 227; of San Francisco communes in 1970s, 108
death penalty: children of Jonestown families facing, 81–82
deaths on November 18, 1978, in Jonestown, 29, 65, 70, 73, 101, 125, 137, 190–91, 192; airlifting of bodies from Jonestown, 291; autopsy reports, 291–93; of black members, 168; bodies with gunshot wounds, 292–93; burial of the dead, 3, 24–25, 300–301; final list of, 323–31; identification of bodies, 23–24, 124, 274–75, 312; impact on Fillmore neighborhood in San Francisco, 279; list of known dead, 264, 268, 270. See also Evergreen Cemetery (Oakland, California)
"death tape," 137, 247–48, 276
defection, final, 227–32
Democratic Convention: of 1932, 172; of 1968, riots at, 146
Dillard, Violatt Esther, 291
Disciples of Christ, 13, 160
discipline/punishment, 161, 240; in Jonestown, 89, 90, 91, 99, 135–36; punishment boxes, 89, 135–36
Dower, David, xviii, 58, 138, 139

Drath, Bill, 32–33
"Drink the Kool-Aid": as catchphrase, xviii, 22, 27–28; inaccuracy of, xix, 84, 99, 250, 256, 275
drugs and drug abuse, 64, 77, 83, 113; in aftermath of Jonestown, 282; drugging of members critical of Jones, 218–19; Gosney's drug addiction, 77–78, 79; Jones's use of drugs, 64, 83, 113, 225–26; Peoples Temple treatment programs, 77, 267
Dymally, Mervyn, 68, 309

Edwards, Zipporah "Zippy," 260, 261
elderly, the: impact of Jones on black, 9–10, 173; in Jonestown, 26, 132–33, 173, 200, 216–17, 227, 237–38, 242, 261–62; living on Social Security, 109, 132–33
Esquire magazine, 109–10
Evergreen Cemetery (Oakland, California): annual Jonestown memorial services at, 3–7, 25, 159, 187, 305–7; mass grave of unidentified bodies of Jonestown at, 3, 25, 300–301; Service of Dedication for Jonestown memorial at, 312
Execution of Justice (Mann), 317
"exodus" to Jonestown, 194–202; agricultural project and, 195–201; New West article on Peoples Temple and, 195, 200–201

faith healings, 14, 15, 34, 54, 75, 102, 118, 120, 162, 189, 260–61
Family Good News, The (newsletter), 73
Farr, Bill, 68
Farrakhan, Louis, 156
FBI, 264, 285, 287; Peoples Temple documents collected by, 22–23
Feinstein, Dianne, 280–81

Fellowship of Reconciliation, 160

financial settlements, 262–63, 286, 301

Flavor Aid, 83–84, 99–100; vat of poisoned, 250, 276, 307

Folsom Prison: Congressman Ryan's experience in, 42

Fonda, Jane, 167, 309

Food Conspiracy, 108

Forman, Liz. *See* Schwartz, Liz Forman

Fortson, Hue, 64–70, 195; appointment to Planning Commission, 69; church of, 64–65; fears of, 67; impact of Peoples Temple on, 65, 69–70; interview with, 65–70; joining Peoples Temple, 67; sermon described by, 66–67, 71

foster children in Peoples Temple, 101–4, 105, 109, 114; Jones's use of State of California's foster care system, 109, 114

Freedom of Information requests for information, 22–23, 26

Fresno Four case, 68

Garry, Charles, 212, 231

Gavin, Steve, 119, 120

gay members, 74. *See also* Gosney, Vernon; Lambrev, Garry

Georgetown, Guyana: calls from, xv, 220, 253, 268; Lamaha Gardens in, 243, 268–72, 273; survivors in, xv, 220, 225, 243, 260, 262, 263, 265, 267–73; Temple offices in, 28, 243

Gibson, Mattie, 236–38, 240; testimony of, 237–38

Glide Memorial Church (San Francisco), 24, 49, 281

Gosney, Mark, 76, 78

Gosney, Vernon, xiv, 17, 74–79; on aftermath of Jonestown, 282–83; arrival in Jonestown, 224; background of,

75–77; at concert/assembly for Ryan, 224–25; on departure and final tragedy, 228–29, 231–33; interview with, 75–79, 224–25, 228–29, 232–33; joining Peoples Temple, 76; on Stephan Jones, 74–75; leaving son behind, 229, 256, 282; note passed to Harris asking for help, xiii, 74, 75, 224; shooting of, xv, 232, 233; survival of, 255–56; wife Cheryl, 75, 76–77

government: climate of conspiracy, 166–67; investigation of Jonestown tragedy, 40, 264, 285, 287; Jones's paranoia about, 40, 241–42; members' statements against, 123–24. *See also* Central Intelligence Agency; FBI; U.S. Army; U.S. State Department

"Greatest Love of All, The" (song), xii–xiii, 220

Greenpeace: Leo Ryan as environmentalist with, 42

greeter crews, 162–64

Gregory, Dick, 124, 125

Gulfport, Mississippi, incident, 72–73

Guyana Emergency Relief Committee, 300, 301

Guyanese Defense Force (GDF), 260, 262, 268, 270, 273

Hall, John R.: interview with, 183–84

Hall, Margo, xix, 3, 7, 29, 74, 101, 151, 187, 279; interview with Rod Hicks, 121–26; interview with Jim Jones Jr., 151–58; interview with Donneter Lane, 300–1; interview with Nell Smart, 188–92; interview with Eugene Smith, 235, 236; roles in *The People's Temple*, 319–20

Hansberry, Lorraine, 52

Hara, Victor, 179

Harris, Don, xiii, 74, 224; exit interview with Leo Ryan, 232; Gosney's note passed to, xiii, 74, 75, 224; interview with Jim Jones, xiv, 229; killing of, 232

Harris, John (Peter Holmes), 222

Hatcher, Chris, 281

healings, faith, 14, 15, 34, 75, 118, 120, 162, 189; cancer, 54, 102, 260–61; purpose of, 134

Henry, Patrick, 211

Hicks, Marthea, 7, 121, 122–23, 221, 319–20; statement against U.S. government, 123–24

Hicks, Rod, 221, 320; beginnings of doubts about Peoples Temple, 124–25; interview with, 121–26

Hicks, Shirley, 7, 121, 122–23, 124, 125, 221, 319–20

Holmes, Peter (John Harris), 222

Houston, Bob, 42

Houston, Sam, 42–43

Hughes-Ryan Amendment (1974), 40, 45

Hunter, Barton, 160

Ijames, Anita, 239

illiteracy program in Jonestown, 217

Indianapolis, Indiana: Jones's church in, 13, 14, 33, 109, 175, 260–61

"Inside Peoples Temple" (Tracy and Kilduff), 105, 111

integration of church: Jones and, 13, 14–15, 52, 66, 266, 306; Peoples Temple as functional multiracial society, 38, 39, 65–66, 163, 181–82

Intensive Care Unit (ICU): drugging of critical members in, 218–19

interviews: with Juanita Bogue, 88–99; with Michael Briggs, by letter, 102–4; with Tim Carter, 144–50, 247–50; with Tim Carter, narration of NBC raw news footage of Ryan's investigative trip to Jonestown, 204–7, 213–18, 221–32, 234; with Chavis, 81–85; with the Clanceys, 160–70; with Danny Curtin, 305–6; with Mervyn Dymally, 68; with Hue Fortson, 65–70; with Vern Gosney, 75–79, 224–25, 228–29, 232–33; with John Hall, 183–84; with Rod Hicks, 121–26; with Janaro Claire, 266–68; with Grace Stoen Jones, 18–21; with Jim Jones Jr., 152–58; with Stephan Jones, 8–13, 14, 55–59, 310–12; with Laura Johnston Kohl, 28–29; with Garry Lambrev, 32–38; with Donneter Lane, 300–301; list of, xxi–xxii; with Becky Moore, 24–27; with John and Barbara Moore, 48–54, 293–95; with Palladino, 129–37; with Pat Ryan, 43–46; with Liz Forman Schwartz, 39; with Nell Smart, 188–92; with Eugene Smith, 236–43; with Julie Smith, 118–20; with Mike Touchette, 196–98, 201, 203; with Rev. Townsend, 279; with Phil Tracy, 107–16

Jackson, Don, 238

Jackson, Fred, 4

Jackson, Pop, 216–17; testimony of, 217

James, Shanda, 218–19

Janaro, Claire, 265–68; family lost in Jonestown, 265; interview with, 266–68; joining Peoples Temple, 266; return home to United States after Jonestown, 287–89

Janaro, Daren, 265, 266, 267, 288–89

Janaro, Mauri, 265, 266, 267, 288–89

Janaro, Richard, 265, 266, 267–68, 287, 288

Jewish members. *See* Amos, Sharon; Schwartz, Liz Forman

Johnson, Poncho, 220, 276

Johnson, Ricky, 311

Johnston, Laura. *See* Kohl, Laura Johnston

Jones, Chae-ok, 223, 226, 275

Jones, Grace Stoen (Grace Stoen), 6, 17–21, 43, 165; absence from concert/assembly for Ryan, 225; custody battle over John Victor, 209–12; on hearing news of tragedy, 263–64; on hierarchy of church, 20; interview with, 18–21; investigative trip with Ryan, 205–6, 209–10, 213, 225; on involvement with Peoples Temple, 18, 19–20; leaving Temple (1976), 209.

Jones, Jim, Jr., xii, 151–58, 284, 312; adoption of, 152; on aftermath of Jonestown, 302–3; on being a true believer, 157–58; childhood of, 152–53; competition between brother Stephan and, 152; description of Temple's neighborhood in San Francisco, 155–56; on his blackness, 157; interview with, 152–58; on joining Nation of Islam, 156–57; living with father's name, 152; on survivors, 154

Jones, Jim (James) Warren, 291; acceptance by members as God, 35–36, 52–53, 67; as addictive personality, 9; appointment to San Francisco Housing Authority, 68, 111, 165, 280; approach to new people, 34–35; approach to politics, 68–69, 72; attempts to persuade defectors from leaving with Ryan, 228; attempt to stop Ryan's visit, 213–14; autopsy report, 292; bodyguards, 110, 111, 112; Briggs's memories of, 102, 103; children of, xii, 22, 151–58, 276 (*see also* Jones, Jim, Jr.; Jones, Lew; Jones, Stephan); clairvoyance, 3×5 cards used for, 69, 148, 163; Jean Clancey on, 160, 161, 298; coining of White Night, 211–12; at concert/assembly for Ryan, 222; control of life in Jonestown, 89–91, 94–95; control of the press, 116–17, 119–20; control/power over members, 67–68, 89–91, 94–95, 135–37, 163–64, 167, 182, 202, 241–42; custody battle over John Victor Stoen, 209–12; on "death tape" with Christine Miller, 247–48; decision to die, xix; decision to move en masse to Jonestown, 200–201; disillusionment caused by, 306; downside of, 168–69; drug use of, 64, 83, 113, 225–26; empowerment of women by, 135; exposure as fraud, 219; faked assassination attempts on, 157–58, 162; fear of, 103; final interview with, 229; founding of Peoples Temple, 13; as God, 298, 299; good side of, 168; hatred of the Bible, 20, 67, 261; healings, 14, 15, 34, 54, 75, 102, 118, 120, 134, 162, 189, 260–61; image of, 66, 67; image of, in bus flyers, 71–72; integration efforts, 13, 14–15, 52, 66, 266, 306; interview with Harris, xiv, 229; interview with Julie Smith, 119–20; Janaro on, 266; Stephan Jones on, 9–13, 56–57, 276–77; joy/ecstasy imparted to members by, 133–34; legacy of, 303–4; manipulation of John and Barbara Moore, 209; marriage, 13; mistresses of, 47, 51–52, 127, 294 (*see also* Katsaris, Maria; Layton, Carolyn Moore);

New West magazine exposé of, 105, 111, 113–16, 195, 200–201; ordination as Disciples of Christ minister, 13; paranoia of, 40, 51–52, 119, 140, 241–42, 270; on political power of Temple, 166–67; as psychopath, Singer on, 5; reasons for going to Jonestown, 91; response to challenges/criticism, 163–64, 218–19; revolutionary rhetoric adapted by, 123; Ryan's telegram to, 212–13; sermons of, 15, 20, 23, 35, 66–67, 70–71, 88, 136, 148, 201; sexual partners and sex abuse, 83, 101, 104, 113, 136, 161, 218–19, 228, 294; social justice involvement, 52; sources of income for, 109, 113, 114; successful collectivism of, 108–9; symbiotic relationship of Temple members with, Jean Clancey on, 298; as teacher, 37–38, 88; theological logic of, 52–53; tirades against United States prior to Ryan's visit, xi–xii; use of climate of conspiracy, 167; vision of "Promised Land," 195; way of talking, 66–67; wife of (*see* Jones, Marceline); "Year of Ascendancy" (1976) for, 117

Jones, Lew (adopted child), 153, 275

Jones, Marceline (wife), xii, 13, 14, 57, 70, 151; attempts to stop Vern Gosney from defecting, 228–29; influence on Stephan going to Jonestown, 198; in last hours of Jonestown, 249; Stephan's accounts of, 9, 220–21, 276–77; tour of Jonestown given to media, 226–27

Jones, Stephan (biological son), xii, 51, 151, 153, 269; absence from Jonestown on night of concert/assembly for Ryan, xv,

220–21, 225–26; accounts of mother (Marceline), 9, 220–21, 276–77; on aftermath of Jonestown, 271–73, 276–77; on basketball court at Jonestown, 219–20; on bittersweet gift of grief, 310; breaking into San Francisco Temple after earthquake, 302; building Jonestown, 198–99; calls to San Francisco on last day of Jonestown, 253; description of, 9; directive of, 13; discussion of passport photos, 194–96, 201–2; on documenting photos, 56, 311–12; early childhood, 57–58; on "exodus" to Jonestown, 201–2; on father in final hours of Jonestown, 276–77; on father's personality and impact, 9–13; Gosney on, 74–75; in Guyanese prison, 273; interviews with, 8–13, 14, 55–59, 310–12; John-John Stoen and, 210–11, 225; on Jones's drug use, 225–26; at memorial service at Evergreen Cemetery, 6, 305; memories of ICU at Jonestown, 218–19; photos shown by, 55–56, 218–21, 310–12; portrayal in *The People's Temple*, 314, 320; protection of Beikman, 271–73; relationship with father, 9–12, 56–57, 198, 199, 219, 220–21; Pat Ryan on, 45–46; on Six-Day Siege, 211–12; on trip from Indiana to California, 14

Jones, Suzanne (adopted child), 153

Jones, Terry Carter, 147, 148, 162, 223, 226, 275

Jones, Tim (adopted child), xii, 153

Jonestown: accomplishments in, 190, 200; agricultural project, construction of, 195–201, 203, 206, 216, 240; allegations about conditions of, xi; average day in, 90; boarded walks through, 217–18; books on, 312–13; coded message to members outside, 70, 252, 268; deaths (*see* deaths on November 18, 1978, in Jonestown); decision to move en masse to, 105, 115, 200–201; discipline in, 89, 90, 91, 99, 135–36; elderly members in, 26, 132–33, 173, 200, 216–17, 227, 237–38, 242, 261–62; "exodus" to, 194–202; first baby born in, 226; government investigation into what happened at, 40, 264, 285, 287; illiteracy program in, 217; joy of, 133–34, 220, 222, 234; legacy of, 81–82, 84, 191–92, 320–21; mass murder/suicide in, xvii, xix, 26, 249–50, 252–55; mass murder/suicide in, as end of utopian movement, 184; mass murder/suicide in, "death tape" of, 137, 247–48, 276; members wanting to leave, xiii–xiv, 74, 75–80, 89–90, 92; NBC raw news footage of investigative trip to, 204–7, 213–18, 221–32, 234; need for money in, 90; news reports of tragedy, 259–60; Palladino's visit to, with Chavis, Tamburello et al., 129–31; pioneers, 195, 196–98, 201; Planning Commission, 20, 69, 254; planning of mass death at, 25–26; public response to, 24–25; practice rituals in, 25–26, 94, 137, 242, 251; testimonies taken in, 168, 169, 171–77, 217, 237–38; Tropp's description of building of, 199–200; vision of community, xi, xviii, 195, 198, 202; White Nights in, xi, 70, 115, 133, 137, 205, 211–12, 214, 242, 270. *See also* survivors

Jonestown Express Band, 176; concert for Ryan, xi, xii–xiii, 221–22

Jonestown Institute, 23, 27; Jonestown speaker's bureau of, 27, 143; Web site, 35, 312

Jonestown memorial at Evergreen Cemetery, 312

jonestown report, the, 23

Jonestown Vortex, 24

joy/ecstasy in Peoples Temple, 133–34, 181, 220, 222, 234

Katsaris, Anthony, xv, 135, 205, 227, 228; at performance of *The People's Temple,* 315–16; shooting of, 232

Katsaris, Maria, 134, 135, 163, 227–28, 247, 291; John Victor Stoen and, 210, 211; rejection of brother Anthony, 228, 315

Katsaris, Steven, 134–35

Kennedy, John F., 181

Kennedy, Robert, 146, 181

Kent State, 146

Kilduff, Marshall, 112, 117, 195, 209; *New West* magazine exposé, 105, 111, 113–16

Kimo (Prokes; son of Carolyn Moore Layton), 47, 294

King, Martin Luther, Jr.: assassination of, 50, 146, 181, 217; expansion of Temple after assassination, 36–37

Kinsolving, Lester, 117, 147

Klingman, Clarence Cole, 311

Klingman, Mike, 316

Kohl, Laura Johnston, 5–6, 27–29, 90, 180, 268, 311; book on experiences by, 312–13; on Anderson Cooper's news show, 27–28; interview with, 28–29; list of known dead, 268, 270; on outreach to black community, 72; reason for joining Temple, 28

Krause, Charles, 222, 226

Ku Klux Klan, 110

Lacy, Georgia, 102, 104
Lacy, Phillip, 104
Lam, Inspector, 273
Lamaha Gardens, Georgetown, 243;
     survivors in, 268–72, 273
Lambert, Sarah, 319
Lambrev, Garry, 31–40, 45, 178–79; on
     acceptance of Jim Jones as God,
     35–36; background of, 31; descrip-
     tion of Jim Jones, 34–35, 37–38, 40;
     interview with, 32–38; on loss of
     dignity, 36
Lane, Donneter: interview with,
     300–301
Lane, Mark, 231
Laramie Project, The (play and HBO
     film), xviii, 8, 31
Laurel Street Tabernacle, 14–15
Layton, Carolyn Moore, 22, 25, 26,
     47, 127, 222–23, 291; childhood of,
     49–50; joining Peoples Temple,
     50–51; Kimo (son), 47, 294; letter
     to parents, 208; marriage of, 49,
     50; memo on custody battle over
     John Victor Stoen, 210–11; memo to
     Jones on final stand and deciding to
     die, 290–91; as mistress to Jones, 47,
     51–52, 294
Layton, Debby, 16–17, 43, 115, 316
Layton, Karen, 161, 201
Layton, Larry, 17, 136; legal defense
     team for, 80, 82, 127–28, 303 (*see
     also* Chavis, Melody Ermachild;
     Palladino, Jack; Tamburello,
     Tony); marriage and divorce from
     Carolyn, 50–51; as passive victim,
     127; shooting of Vern Gosney, 233;
     signature on "Resolution of Com-
     munity," 215; trial and conviction
     of, 17, 23, 215; Vern Gosney on, 17,
     231

Layton, Lisa, 17, 179
Left Behind (series of books), 130
Letelier, Orlando, 166
Lewis, Chris, 103
Lewis, Fred, 4
Linton, Tony, 101, 104
Loma Prieta earthquake (1989):
     destruction of Peoples Temple
     church in, 151, 301–2
Los Angeles Temple, 63–64, 188–90; as
     moneymaker for church, 189

Macedonia Baptist Church (San Fran-
     cisco), 37
Malcolm X, 158, 181
Mann, Emily, 317
mass murder/suicide, xvii, 26, 249–50,
     252–55; "death tape" of, 137, 247–48,
     276; as end of utopian movement,
     184; practice drills for, 25–26, 94,
     137, 242, 251. *See also* White Nights;
     pledges to die
McCarthy, Joe, 173
McElvane, Jim, 187
McGehee, Fielding "Mac," 22–27, 138,
     290; identification of Jonestown
     dead, 23–24, 312; transcriptions of
     Peoples Temple recordings made
     by, 23, 35, 312
McKay, Rex, 272
media/press: deaths in Jonestown, 232;
     Harris's interview with Jones, xiv,
     229; at JFK airport upon return
     of survivors, 285; Jones's control
     of, 116–17, 119–20; Jones's hatred
     of, 226; Kinsolving's articles about
     the Temple, 117, 147; labeling of
     Carter after Jonestown by, 150;
     news reports of tragedy, 259–60;
     New West magazine exposé of
     Peoples Temple, 105, 111, 113–16,

195, 200–201; press conference after Jonestown in San Francisco, 281; press members accompanying Ryan, 43, 205; Smith's interview with Jones, 119; tour of Jonestown community, xiii–xiv, 226–27; Tracy's interview with Jones, 110. *See also specific newspapers*

Mendelsohn, Robert, 119

Mercer, Henry: testimony of, 172–74

methamphetamine use, 83

Methodist Hospital (Indianapolis): integration of, 13

Milk, Harvey, 149; murder of, 280, 300

Miller, Christine, 247–48

Mondale, Walter, 165

Moore, Ann (Annie) Elizabeth, 22, 25, 26, 47, 48, 291, 293–94; autopsy report, 292; childhood of, 49–50; joining Peoples Temple, 50, 51, 53–54; letters of, 53–54, 207, 293

Moore, Carolyn. *See* Layton, Carolyn Moore

Moore, John and Barbara, 24, 26–27, 47–54, 115–16, 207–9, 317; affirmation of humanness of Jonestown victims, 295; death of Barbara, 312; description of survivor stories, 317; donations to California Historical Society, 24, 53–54, 290–91; interview with, 48–54, 293–95; letters from Annie and Carolyn, 207, 208; press conference, 208; process of piecing together their daughters' histories, 293–95; at Service of Dedication, 312; visit to Jonestown, 208

Moore, Rebecca (Becky), 22–27, 47, 48, 138, 290; books by, 22, 313; childhood of, 49–50; on hearing news of tragedy, 26; interview with, 24–27; after seeing *The People's Temple*, 319

Morganti, Mary, 139

Murrow, Edward R., 128

Moscone, George (mayor), 44, 68, 111, 165; murder of, 280, 300

Moten, Alice, 174

Mount Zion Baptist Church, 102

National Catholic Reporter, 107

National Enquirer, 294

Nation of Islam, 156–57

NBC Nightly News (TV), 43

NBC raw news footage of investigative trip to Jonestown, 204–7, 213–18, 221–32, 234; attempt to leave Jonestown, 228–32; concert/assembly for Ryan, 221–24; exit interview with Ryan, 232; final defections, 230–31; flight into Guyana, 205–7; Harris's interview with Jones, 229; journey by tractor-trailer to Jonestown, 215–16

Nelson, Kay, 187, 190, 192, 193, 307

Newell, Herbert, 285

Newsom, Gavin, 278

Newsweek magazine, 285, 307

Newton, Huey P., 66, 123, 127, 167, 212

New West magazine: break-in at, 112–13; exposé of Peoples Temple, 105, 111, 113–16; exposé of Peoples Temple, exodus to Jonestown and, 195, 200–201

9/11: Jim Jones Jr. on, 158

Norwood, Reverend Jynona, 4, 5, 6–7, 312

137, 247–48, 276

November 18, 1978, tragedy: attempts of members to leave Jonestown, xiii–xv, 228–32; discovery of both murder and suicide on, xix; killings at Port Kaituma airfield, xiv–xv, xvii, 17, 43–44, 93, 232, 259; mass suicide reported, xvii. *See also* deaths on November 18, 1978, in Jonestown; mass murder/suicide

Oliver, Shanette, 263

Palladino, Jack, 80, 82, 127–37, 221, 260, 303, 315; on burnout from investigation, 131–32; cases of, 127; on defections, 137; interviews with survivors, 127, 128, 132–36; on empowerment of women, 135; interview with, 129–37; on Jones's faking of the Stigmata of Christ, 134; on joy/ecstasy felt by Temple members, 133–34; on punishment in Jonestown, 135–36; visit to Jonestown, 129–31; on work as investigator, 132
paranoia, 40, 51–52, 119, 140, 241–42, 270
Parks, Dale, 17
Parks, Edith, xiii–xiv; announcement of desire to leave Jonestown, 227, 228
Parks, Jerry, 92
Parks, Joyce, 260
Parks, Patty, xiv, 93, 232
passport photos, 193–96
Peace Corps, 181
Peer Gynt suite, "Death of Ase" (Grieg), 252, 254–55
Pentagon, 259
Peoples Forum (newspaper), 169
Peoples Temple: accomplishments of, 53, 238, 266–67; archival material on (*see* California Historical Society, Peoples Temple archives); Barnes's column on, 112, 113; choirs, 19, 39, 66, 70, 311, 314; choir albums produced by, 19, 70, 140, 314; cities targeted by, 72; cross-country crusades, 63–64, 71–73; as cult, 5, 25, 188, 307; discipline of members, 78, 161, 240; disintegration of, 282; diversity of members of, xix; drug treatment program in, 77, 267; drug users in, 77; expansion in Ukiah after King's assassination, 36–37; expansion to Los Angeles, 63–64, 188–90; family unit broken down in, 88; financial settlement after Jonestown, 262–63, 286, 301; founding of, 13; freezing of assets, 301; as functional multiracial society, 38, 39, 65–66, 163, 181–82; government investigation into Jonestown, 40, 264, 285, 287; greeter crews, 162–64; hierarchy of, 20; history of, xviii; impact of first experience of, 147–49; income sources for, 189, 266; integration in, 52, 66, 266, 306; involvement in social issues, 52; legacy of, 150, 303–4, 320–21; licensed care facilities of, 266–67; money given away in aftermath of Jonestown, 282; move to California and building of church, 13–14; *New West* magazine exposé of, 105, 111, 113–16; offices in Georgetown, 28, 243; outreach to black community, 72–73, 181; Planning Commission, 20, 69, 254; plan to move to Soviet Union, 40, 248; plays produced in San Francisco, 52–53; political power of, 165–67; predominantly black membership, 29, 168; reasons for joining, 169, 173, 175, 176, 180–83, 189, 266; recordings made by, 14, 19, 23; secrecy in, 182; senior citizen housing units, 237; services, 103; Sunday meetings, 35; torture and, 179, 297; vision for Jonestown,

xi, xviii, 195, 198, 202. *See also* Jonestown; San Francisco Temple; survivors

People's Temple, The (Fondakowski, Pierotti, Wangh, and Hall), xix–xx, 313, 314–21; actors, 319–20; development process, 314–15, 318; ending of, 320; hopes for, 320–21; opening of, 314; postproduction interviews, 316; reactions of survivors to, 315–16; research used to write, 315; reviews of, 316–17; set for, 319; title, choice of, 319

Pettus, Reggie, 155–56, 301–2

Phillips, Joe, 33–34

Pierotti, Greg, xix, 8, 193, 203; on Buddhist view of death, 244; explanation of project, 16; interview with Mike Touchette, 196–98, 201, 203; role in *The People's Temple*, 320

Planning Commission, Peoples Temple, 20, 69, 254

pledges to die, 27, 70, 123, 234, 252–53, 263, 268–69

politics: Jones's appointment to San Francisco Housing Authority, 68, 111, 165, 280; Jones's approach to, 68–69, 72; political power of San Francisco Temple, 165–67

Port Kaituma airstrip: shooting at, xiv–xv, xvii, 17, 43–44, 93, 232, 259

press, the. *See* media/press

prisons: children of Jonestown in, 81–82, 101–4; Jones sermon on, 71

Prokes, Mike, 213, 238; eventual suicide of, 253; mission to Russian embassy in Georgetown, 247, 250, 260

Promised Land: Jones's vision of, 37, 195. *See also* Jonestown

"Prophet Who Raises the Dead, The" (Kinsolving), 147

psychodrama, 162, 211

racism: of Bible, Jones on, 20; freedom from, at Peoples Temple, 76, 91, 133, 195; incidents of, 9–10, 33, 50, 72–73, 153, 172, 181, 217; Jones's changes to racist words and expressions, 212; at Laurel Street Tabernacle, 14; lynchings, 172, 238

Raisin in the Sun, A (Hansberry), 52

Randolph, Jim, 238

Redwood Valley church, 37, 147; attraction to, 76, 173, 180–81, 266–67; expansion from, 63; facilities, 13–14, 52, 266–67; growing up in, 88–89, 305; impact of first experiencing, 39, 53, 160–62; inviting San Franciscans to, 37; Kinsolving's articles on, 147; meetings in, 103; services, 103; survivors in, 263

Reiterman, Tim, 6

"Resolution of Community, A" (residents of Jonestown), 215

revolutionary suicide, 123–24, 214, 248

revolutionary violence, 297

Rhodes, Odell, 260, 262

Roberts, Skip, 274, 275

Robinson, Greg, 232

Rolle, Esther, 309

Russia: plan to go to, 40, 248

Ryan, Leo J. (congressman), xi, 84, 137; addressing crowd in Jonestown, xiii, 223; attempt to leave Jonestown with defectors, 228–32; background of, 41–42; concert/assembly for, xi, xii–xiii, 220, 221–24; disbelief about danger, 93, 94, 213, 225, 228; final assessment of Jonestown, 230; funeral of, 44; hearing on death of, 44–45; Hughes-Ryan Amendment sponsored by, 40, 45; killing of, xiv–xv, 17, 43–44, 93, 232, 259; knife attack on, 231, 232; NBC raw news footage of investigative trip to Jonestown, 204–7, 213–18, 221–32, 234; note passed to Harris for, xiii, 74, 75, 224; plan to kill, 82, 93; reason for investigation of Peoples Temple and Jonestown, xi, 42–43; "Resolution of Community" against visit of, 215; storm preventing initial attempt to leave, 229–30; telegram to Jones, 212–13; trip to Jonestown, 41, 43, 205–7; Tropp's plans for visit of, 215; week as prisoner in Folsom Prison, 42

Ryan, Patricia, 6, 40, 41–46, 205; interview with, 43–46

San Francisco: buses to, 164; communes in 1970s in, 107–9; expansion of Peoples Temple to, 165; Fillmore neighborhood, 278, 279; Food Conspiracy program in, 108; Fresno Four case in, 68; Jones's appointment to Housing Authority in, 68, 111, 165, 280; Peoples Temple outreach to people of, 36–37; politics, 68, 119–20, 165, 279, 309; refugees from Chile in, 166

San Francisco Chronicle, 37, 111, 117, 118–20; article on custody battle over John Victor Stoen, 209; review of The People's Temple, 316–17

San Francisco Council of Churches, 25, 300

San Francisco Examiner: Barnes's column on Peoples Temple, 112; Kinsolving articles in, 117, 147

San Francisco Temple, 70, 240; in aftermath of Jonestown, 280–82; choir, recording of, 70; coded message from Jonestown on day of mass murder/suicide, 70, 252, 268; destruction by earthquake (1989), 151, 301–2; photo of dance at, 311; political involvement of, 165–67; survivors left behind in, 252–55, 263, 270, 280–82

Santayana, George, 130, 221

Schacht, Laurence (Larry) Eugene, 262; on pros and cons of using cyanide, 291

Schwartz, Liz Forman, 38–39, 178–79, 265, 266; on hearing news of tragedy, 264; interview with, 39.

Seductive Poison (Layton memoir), 16–17

Senior Citizen's Action Alliance, 173

sermons, Jones's, 20, 35, 66–67, 70–71, 88, 148

sex and sex abuse, 83, 101, 104, 113, 136, 161, 218–19, 228, 294

Shepard, Matthew, xviii, 8, 31

Shular, Janet, 180–83, 304, 316

Simon, Bonnie, 230–31

Singer, Margaret, 4–5, 27

Six-Day Siege, 211–12

Sly, Don, 231

Sly, Neva, 70, 304; on bus crusades, 63–64, 72–73

Smart, Al, 307

Smart, Nell, 187–92; children of, 189–90; children of, burying ashes of, 306–7, 312; on hearing news of tragedy, 263; interview with, 188–92; on Jones's legacy, 304

Smart, Scotty, 307

Smart, Teri, 307

Smart, Tinetra, 190, 193, 239, 307

Smith, Eugene, 235–43; arrival in Jonestown, 241–42; family lost in Jonestown, 235, 239; on hiding his

life and history, 308–9; interview
with, 236–43; joining Peoples
Temple, 237, 238, 240; mentors in
Temple, 238; mother of, 236–38,
240; predictions for play *The
People's Temple,* 313; recounting of
deaths at Lamaha Gardens, 269–70;
on return to United States after
Jonestown, 284–86; survival of,
243, 269–71; on White Nights, 242;
wife of, 239–43; work at California
Historical Society, 235
Smith, Julie, 111; interview with, 118–20;
on interview with Jones, 119–20;
intimidation by Temple staff, 118
Smith, Ollie, 239–43
socialism, 266; process of becoming
socialist entity, 161
social justice issues: Temple's involvement in, xi, xii, xix, xviii, 13, 19,
32–33, 36–38, 49, 52, 66, 71, 109,
168, 181
Social Security: Temple members living
on, 109, 132–33
Soviet Union: plan to move Temple to,
40, 248
Speier, Jackie, xiii, xiv–xv, 44, 227, 228,
255; shooting of, 232
Stephenson, Denice: book of primary
source documents, 313; work at
California Historical Society,
138–39, 140, 171, 193, 235, 236, 251,
290
Stoen, Grace. *See* Jones, Grace Stoen
Stoen, John (John-John) Victor, 6,
18, 20, 206; custody battle over,
209–12; paternity of, 18, 21, 209, 225;
Six-Day Siege and, 211–12
Stoen, Tim, 18, 19, 20
suicide: revolutionary, 123–24, 214, 248,
250; practice rituals, 25–26, 94, 137,

242, 251. *See also* mass murder/sui-
cide; pledges to die; White Nights
survivors, xvii–xviii, xix, 26, 260–77;
airlifting of, 255; audience reactions
toward, after seeing *The People's
Temple,* 316; in California, 263, 270;
deprogramming of, 82–83; desire
for history of Peoples Temple to
be told, xviii–xix; different groups
of, 83; in Georgetown, Guyana,
260, 265, 267–73; interrogation of,
284, 285, 287; Jim Jones Jr. on, 154;
means of survival in Guyana, 260,
265–66; Palladino's interviews with,
127, 128, 132–36; reactions to *The
People's Temple,* 315–16; reticence
to talk, 29–30, 58, 180; in San
Francisco, 252–55, 263, 270, 280–82;
visiting California Historical
Society collection, 235–36, 311–12.
See also children of Jonestown;
interviews; *specific survivors*
survivor's guilt, 150, 246, 282
Swinney, Cleave, 197
Swinney, Helen, 197, 287
Sympathetic History of Jonestown, A
(Moore), 22

Tamburello, Tony, 80, 82, 127, 303
teacher: Jones as, 37–38, 88
Tectonic Theater Project, xviii
"Temple Leader Is Accused in Custody
Case" (Kilduff), 209
testimonies documented by Tropp, 168,
169, 171–77, 237–38; Pop Jackson,
217; Henry Mercer, 172–74; Tropp's
sketch, 176; Dianne "Deanna"
Wilkinson, 174–76
Tet offensive (1968), 144
"That's the Way of the World" (song),
222, 223

Thrash, Hyacinth, 132, 260–63; memoir written after Jonestown, 261–62
torture, 179, 297
Touchette, Charlie, 197
Touchette, Debbie Ijames, 160, 203
Touchette, Mike, 219, 269; interview with, 196–98, 201, 203
Townsend, Reverend Arnold, 278–79; interview with, 279
Tracy, Phil, 105–16, 195, 316; on hearing news of tragedy, 263; interview with, 107–16; *New West* magazine exposé of Peoples Temple, 105, 111, 113–16, 195, 200–201; regrets of, 115–16
Tropp, Dick, 170, 226, 317; at concert/assembly for Ryan, 223; documenting building of Jonestown, 199–200; on last day in Jonestown, 247, 251; memos to Jones advocating for community, 214; mission of, 171, 177; on plans for Ryan's visit, 215; portrayal in *The People's Temple*, 320; sketch of self, 176; testimonies documented by, 168, 169, 171–77, 217, 237–38; writings of, 171, 176, 200, 214–15, 251
Tropp, Harriet, 210, 214, 222, 227, 247

Ukiah, California: Peoples Temple move to, 110. *See also* Redwood Valley church

Unemployment Movement in Philadelphia, 172–73
U.S. Army, 270, 275
U.S. State Department, 23, 259
utopian movement in United States, 183–84
Vietnam War: Carter's experiences in, 144–46, 149
violence: Chavis's theory about roots of, 81–82; revolutionary, 297. *See also* deaths on November 18, 1978, in Jonestown; discipline/punishment; mass murder/suicide

Wangh, Stephen, xix, 80, 151, 318; study and editing of Jones's sermons, 35, 70–71
"We Must Never Forget" (song), 4
White Nights, xi, 70, 115, 133, 137, 205, 242, 270; coining of term, 211–12; Dick Tropp on, 214. *See also* pledges to die; suicide
Wilkinson, Dianne "Deanna," 311; singing at concert/assembly for Ryan, 222, 223; testimony of, 174–76
Williams, Cecil, 280–81
Wilson, Joe, 93
Winfrey, Oprah, 97
WPA, 172

Z Space Studio, xviii

Leigh Fondakowski is a professional playwright and has been a member of Tectonic Theater Project since 1995. They were nominated for an Emmy as coscreenwriter of the adaptation of *The Laramie Project* for HBO and were a cowriter of *The Laramie Project: Ten Years Later*. They participated in the NEA/TCG Theatre Residency Program for Playwrights in 2007 and were a MacDowell Colony fellow in 2009.

Their play *The People's Temple* has been performed under their direction at Berkeley Repertory Theatre, American Theater Company, Perseverance Theatre, and the Guthrie Theater. It received the Glickman Award for Best New Play in the Bay Area in 2005.

They also developed the original play *SPILL*, based on interviews with people of the south coast of Louisiana in the aftermath of the Deepwater Horizon/BP oil spill.